D122746

SIMPSON

The publisher gratefully acknowledges the generous contribution to this book provided by the Simpson Humanities Endowment Fund of the University of California Press Foundation.

MARY AUSTIN AND THE AMERICAN WEST

Portrait of Mary Austin by Helen Kohlmeier. Henry Mead Williams Local History Department, Harrison Memorial Library, Carmel, CA.

MARY AUSTIN
AND THE AMERICAN WEST

Susan Goodman
Carl Dawson

UNIVERSITY OF CALIFORNIA PRESS

BERKELEY   LOS ANGELES   LONDON

University of California Press, one of the most distinguished university presses in the United States, enriches
lives around the world by advancing scholarship in the humanities, social sciences, and natural sciences. Its activities
are supported by the UC Press Foundation and by philan-
thropic contributions from individuals and institutions.
For more information, visit www.ucpress.edu.

University of California Press
Berkeley and Los Angeles, California

University of California Press, Ltd.
London, England

Library of Congress Cataloging-in-Publication Data

Goodman, Susan, 1951–
  Mary Austin and the American West / Susan Goodman
and Carl Dawson.
      p. cm.
  Includes bibliographical references and index.
  ISBN 978-0-520-24635-5 (alk. paper)
  1. Austin, Mary Hunter, 1868–1934. 2. Authors, American—20th century—Biography. 3. Women and literature—West (U.S.)—History—20th century. 4. Western
stories—History and criticism. 5. West (U.S.)—In literature. I. Dawson, Carl. II. Title.
  PS3501.U8Z88 1997
  818'.5209--dc22
  [B]
                                   2008027797

Manufactured in the United States of America

17 16 15 14 13 12 11 10 09 08
10 9 8 7 6 5 4 3 2 1

This book is printed on Natures Book, which contains
50% post-consumer waste and meets the minimum re-
quirements of ANSI/NISO Z39.48–1992 (R 1997) (*Perma-
nence of Paper*).

For Rhoda Rudnick, June Hanson,
and Maureen Murphy

CONTENTS

PREFACE

Myths have grown up about me because I have done what I pleased.

MARY AUSTIN

Interview, the Boston Evening Transcript, 1928

MARY AUSTIN (1868–1934) PUBLISHED *The Land of Little Rain* in 1903, at the age of thirty-five. More than a century later, her book still attracts readers because of Austin's originality and prescience, and because she brought to Americans a new perspective on the Western desert, its people, its barren beauty, and its place in a complex and misunderstood region. No one appreciated *The Land of Little Rain* more than Austin's good friend Ansel Adams, who used his own photographs for a later, edited version of the book. "The sharp beauty of *The Land of Little Rain*," Adams wrote, "is finely etched in the distinguished prose of Mary Austin. Many books and articles have probed the factual aspects of this amazing land, but no writing to my knowledge conveys so much of the spirit of earth and sky, of plants and people, of storm and the desolation of majestic wastes, of tender, intimate beauty, as does *The Land of Little Rain*."[1]

For Austin, the American West extended far beyond the scope of her first book to embrace the Southwest, the Northwest, the mountains, the missions, the indigenous peoples, the history of Spanish settlements, even the "Movie West." Though wanting at times to escape her reputation as a Western writer—who, as she liked to say, never wrote "Westerns"—she returned obsessively to Western places, finding her strength and topics in the region that had fired her imagination. The West for Austin, as for many of her countrymen, shaped the ways she thought about America and about herself. In 1893, the year of the World's Columbian Exposition, the young historian, Frederick Jackson Turner, announced the closing of the frontier, and with it the end of an ideological boundary separating civilization from savagery, which had run its westward course. Turner saw the West as part of an evolutionary progression measured by the social and industrial conditions of Europe and the eastern United States. Austin could not have disagreed more. She understood the American West to be a singular region, exempt not from history or mythology but from capitalist assumptions and flawed hypotheses about beginnings and ends. If anything, she intuited that the closing of the Western frontier may well have been its opening, in the sense of a vital subject for writers and painters or a nostalgic public searching for a national myth. Like other dreamers and doers who envisioned the United States as a work in progress, she thought of the region as a great experiment in democracy.

The author of over thirty books of fiction, poetry, and nonfiction, Austin prided herself on a range of talents. "I can function as the homely housewife," she told an unsympathetic friend, adding that she could play chauffeur or speak to any group, whether members of the Women's Club of Silver City or the Fabian Society in London. She could and did "function" in ways her friend had never heard about, and that Austin would not defend. "*This*," she said, "is my life."[2] Was Austin's career, which one reviewer cataloged as poet, naturist, dramatist, social historian, lecturer, reviewer, political strategist, and organizer, less or more than her own assertions? Answers can be found in the range of her thinking, the people she knew (among them Willa Cather, Joseph Conrad, Jack London, Mabel Dodge Luhan, Lou and Herbert Hoover), and the places she lived in and wrote about: London, New York City, the artists' colony at Carmel, and above all the twin poles of her life, California's high desert and New Mexico's Taos and Santa Fe.

There are different Mary Austins, as for her there were different Wests.[3] The memoirs of her friends divided her as she divided the land: she was scrupulously honest or a fraud; a genius or one of the near-great; resentful of or gracious to younger writers. Many read her candor as unbridled egotism, others as genius outstripping Walt Whitman's. Our Mary Austin is a complex and energetic, sometimes exasperating and always challenging woman, who survived the end of her marriage, breast cancer and heart disease, unhappy love affairs, and the institutionalization and death of her mentally disabled daughter to become the voice of the American West. We trace her growing interest in regional and national causes, such as land use and water claims, American Indian rights, and the demands of women for political power. Austin's life reflects the rise and achievements of Western culture in the first third of the twentieth century; its unstated plot is the emergence of California and the Southwest in the national consciousness. We offer this book as an exploration of someone who never stopped exploring, whose personal issues remain public issues vital to the West, and whose life touches American nerves in ways that beg for the telling.

Before turning to Austin's journey, from Carlinville, Illinois, to California's San Joaquin Valley, we pause to thank those who have helped us to find Austin's life richer and more compelling than we could have expected.

Our thanks first to friends and colleagues who have supported our work: Jerome Loving, Robert D. Richardson, Linda Wagner-Martin, Leo Lemay, Don Mell, and Richard Zipser. We are grateful to Deans Bobby Gempesaw and Thomas Apple of the University of Delaware. The university's director of research, Carolyn Thoroughgood; the director of libraries, Susan Brynteson; and the librarians of the Morris Library have all helped us during the writing of this book. Our research assistant, Monica Zaleski, deserves special thanks; her goodwill and tireless research enliven every chapter.

Andrew W. Mellon Fellowships and a General University Research Grant from the University of Delaware made possible our months at the Huntington Library in San Marino, California, and we thank the Huntington staff for their patience and skill. We want particularly to mention Robert C. Ritchie, the W. M. Keck Foundation director of research, and the reader services staff, Christopher Adde, Jill Cogen, Meredith Berbee, Juan Gomez, Kate Henningsten, Mona Noureldin, Catherine Wherey, and Stephen R. Tabor, a bibliophile who discovered two "first" printings of *The Land of Little Rain*.

We are grateful to Austin's first biographers, Augusta Fink and Esther Lanigan; to the pioneering work of scholars who knew Austin personally, including T. M. Pearce, and Carey McWilliams; and to those active today, especially Karen S. Langlois and Melody Graulich. Few people have done more to keep Austin's work alive than Professor Graulich, whose splendid editions have made Austin more available to contemporary readers. Larry Evers, Barney Nelson, Mark T. Hoyer, John Walton, Kevin Starr, and Franklin Walker helped focus our thinking about California and the Southwest, as did Lois Rudnick, whose work on Mabel Dodge Luhan challenged our own. At a later stage, Louis Warren generously supported our book for publication.

We have had the assistance of special collections librarians at the Alderman Library, University of Virginia; the Arizona Historical Society, Tucson; the Bancroft Library, Berkeley; Barnard College Library, New York City; the Bentley Library, University of Michigan; the California State Library; the Center for Southwest Research, University of New Mexico; Cornell University Library; the Herbert Hoover Library, West Branch, Iowa; the John Hay Library, Brown University; the Library of Congress; the Lilly Library, Indiana University; Mills College Library, Oakland; Newberry Library, Chicago; New York Public Library; the Pelletier Library, Allegheny University; the Schlesinger Library, Radcliffe College; the University of Minnesota Library; and the U.S. National Archives and Records Administration. Denise Sallee at the Harrison Memorial Library in Carmel generously obtained a photograph of the painting we use as our frontispiece and led us to Don and Joan Miller, who graciously showed us their, and once Mary Austin's, house. Rose McLendon, also at the Harrison Memorial Library, helped us with permissions and sources, as did Marilyn Kim at the Southwest Museum, now part of Los Angeles's Autry National Center.

At University of California Press, we want to thank Mary Severance for her patient oversight, and Julie Van Pelt, our copy editor. Finally, we owe a great debt to Stan Holwitz. A peerless editor, Stan has shepherded us through two projects with good humor and aplomb.

CHRONOLOGY OF MARY AUSTIN'S
LIFE AND WORK

1868   Mary Hunter, the second of three surviving children, born 9 September in Carlinville, Illinois, to George Hunter (1833–78), an immigrant from Yorkshire, England, and his wife, Susanna Savilla Graham (1842–96).

1878   Death of George Hunter on 29 October. Death of sister Jennie (b. 1870) two months later. Eldest son, James Milo Hunter ("Jim," 1866–1917), becomes titular head of the household. Susanna works to support the family, and Mary cares for her younger brother, George Hunter (1877–1933).

1884   Attends Blackburn College in Carlinville, majoring in science. Transfers to the State Normal School in Bloomington, Illinois, but withdraws for health reasons.

1888   Graduates from Blackburn College. Family joins Jim to homestead in the Tejon district, near Bakersfield, California. Austin meets General Edward Beale, who encourages her to write about the West.

1889   Moves to Rose Station, then to the Mountain View Dairy. Teaches primary school. Becomes aware of water issues in California.

1890   Engaged to Stafford Wallace Austin (1861–1931), a graduate of the University of California, Berkeley.

1891   Marries Wallace Austin on 19 May.

1892   Moves to Bakersfield. Publishes first story, "The Mother of Felipe." Moves to San Francisco, where Wallace works on a never-realized irrigation project. Meets the poet Ina Coolbrith. Birth of only child, Ruth Austin. Settles in Lone Pine, Inyo County. Comes to the realization that her daughter is developmentally disabled. Marriage already faltering.

1893   Continues to fills notebooks with observations about her surroundings. Thinks of the Owens Valley as a place of exile that teaches her failure. Periodically flees to San Francisco and Los Angeles.

1894   Wallace appointed superintendent of Inyo County schools. Austin homesteads on the mesa between Alabama Hills and Mount Opapago. Pursues friendships with shepherds and local characters who figure in her books.

1895   Accepts a teaching position in Bishop, California, to set money aside for Ruth's care.

1896   Death of Susanna Hunter.

1897   Joins Wallace in Lone Pine, where she teaches and works on stories and her first book.

1898   Finishes Wallace's teaching term after he becomes county superintendent of schools. Meets William James in Oakland, California.

1899   Moves to Independence. Wallace accepts a position as registrar of the Desert Land Office. Moves to Los Angeles and teaches at the normal school (later the University of California). Meets Charles Lummis and joins his circle of artist friends, including Charlotte Perkins Gilman and Grace Ellery Channing, as well as the anthropologist Frederick Webb Hodge. Intensifies study of California deserts, Native peoples, and Spanish culture.

1900   Joins Wallace in Independence. *The Atlantic Monthly* publishes "A Shepherd of the Sierras."

1902   Opposes the diversion of the Owens River's water to Los Angeles and becomes spokeswoman for valley residents.

1903   Publishes *The Land of Little Rain;* hailed as an original Western voice.

1904 Visits Carmel and San Francisco and forms friendship with the poet George Sterling. Continues fight for the Owens River's water. Wallace fails to enlist the support of President Theodore Roosevelt. Researches sheepherding for *The Flock*.
The Basket Woman: A Book of Fanciful Tales for Children

1905 Final separation from Wallace. Places Ruth in a sanatorium in Santa Clara.
Isidro

1906 Settles in the artists' colony in Carmel. Meets writers such as Sinclair Lewis, Ambrose Bierce, and Jack and Charmian London. Witnesses and writes about the San Francisco earthquake.
The Flock

1907 Diagnosed with breast cancer and decides to spend her last days in Europe. Secures contract with Harper & Brothers during stay in New York. Sails for Italy.

1908 In Rome meets Prince Cagiati and Cardinal Merry del Val, who introduces her to Mother Veronica of the Blue Nuns. Becomes reacquainted with Grace Ellery Channing and comes to know Edward Gordon Craig and Isadora Duncan. Notices that the symptoms associated with her breast cancer begin to lessen. The cancer disappears.
Santa Lucia

1909 Lives in Paris before going to London. Becomes a regular at the home of Herbert and Lou Hoover and through them meets the women's rights activist Anne Martin. Makes the acquaintance of Henry James, Mrs. Humphrey Ward, William Butler Yeats, and George Bernard Shaw. Visits Joseph Conrad and begins a friendship with H. G. Wells.
Lost Borders

1910 Returns to the United States and relocates in New York City.
Outland published in England under the pseudonym George Stairs.

1911 In February, *The Arrow Maker* debuts at the New Theatre. Falls in love with the journalist Lincoln Steffens.
The Arrow Maker

1912 Forms a lifelong friendship with Mabel Dodge (Luhan) and meets John Reed, Emma Goldman, Elizabeth Gurley Flynn,

Margaret Sanger, Henrietta Rodman, and Hutchins and Neith Hapgood. Works for the women's movement. Lecturing provides a substantial part of her income.

Christ in Italy: Being the Adventures of a Maverick among Masterpieces

A Woman of Genius

1913   Serves as a publicist for the Panama-Pacific International Exposition in San Francisco and attends the premier of her play *Fire* in Carmel.

The Lovely Lady

The Green Bough

1914   Austins officially divorce. Daniel T. MacDougal arranges for the production of Austin's *The Arrow Maker* in Carmel and becomes her closest male friend.

California, The Land of the Sun (published in England)

Love and the Soul Maker

1915   Declines to join Henry Ford's peace initiative in Europe.

The Man Jesus: Being a Brief Account of the Life and Teachings of the Prophet of Nazareth

1916   Plans pageant, staged on the east steps of the Capitol, for the National Woman's Party.

1917   James Hunter dies. Austin becomes embroiled in battle for guardianship of niece Mary. Contributes to *The Sturdy Oak: A Composite Novel of American Politics by Fourteen American Authors;* profits go to the women's suffrage movement. Supported by Herbert Hoover, organizes communal kitchens to help the war effort. Summers at Byrdcliffe, the arts-and-crafts community in Woodstock, New York.

The Ford

1918   Daughter Ruth dies. Austin visits Santa Fe and conducts a survey of the Spanish-speaking population of Taos County. Appointed to the School of American Research in Native American literature.

The Trail Book

The Young Woman Citizen

1919   Starts a theater in Santa Fe. Contracts with the L. J. Albert World Celebrities Lecture Bureau. Explores automatic writing with Dr. Walter Prince.

1920   *No. 26 Jayne Street*

1921   Travels to England. Meets Rebecca West and attends meetings of the Fabian Society. Publishes "Aboriginal Literature," in *Cambridge History of American Literature.*

1922   Honored with a dinner at the National Arts Club in January. Joins forces with Mabel Dodge (Luhan) and John Collier to fight the Bursum Bill.

1923   Takes 2,500-mile trek through the Southwest with Daniel T. MacDougal and Ina and Gerald Cassidy. Meets D. H. and Frieda Lawrence. Health continues to worsen.
       The American Rhythm

1924   Moves permanently to Santa Fe with the encouragement of Mabel Dodge Luhan. Begins close friendship with the artist Frank Applegate and his wife Alta.
       The Land of Journeys' Ending

1925   Builds Casa Querida, her "beloved house" in Santa Fe. Serves on the Council of the Institute of Social and Religious Research for the Survey of Race Relations at Stanford, as well as on the Spanish-speaking Communities for the Carnegie Americanization Study.
       A Small Town Man
       Everyman's Genius

1926   Invited to participate in a symposium on psychical research at Clark University. Lectures at Yale. Willa Cather stays at Casa Querida and works on *Death Comes for the Archbishop.* Austin undergoes abdominal operation.

1927   Represents New Mexico at the Seven States Conference to discuss the proposed Boulder Dam and the allocation of Colorado River water. Works with Frank Applegate to form the Spanish Colonial Arts Society. Meets Ansel Adams, with whom she will collaborate on *Taos Pueblo.* Signs papers donating her brain to Cornell's Brain Collection.
       California: The Lands of the Sun (published in the United States)

1928   *The Children Sing in the Far West*

1929   Begins collaboration with Arthur Leon Campa. Entrusts El
        Santuario de Chimayó to the Archdiocese of Santa Fe. Receives
        degree from Mills College. Invitation from the Mexican
        government to address the Conference on Cultural Relations in
        Mexico City. Election to the Literary Council of the Authors'
        League of America. Returns to Carlinville to research her
        autobiography, *Earth Horizon*. Renews friendship with Robinson
        and Una Jeffers.

1930   *Taos Pueblo*

1931   Devastated by the death of Frank Applegate. Develops
        friendships with Witter Bynner and Carey McWilliams. Turns
        down doctorate from Tufts University.
        Starry Adventure
        Experiences Facing Death

1932   Insults H. G. Wells and Anne Martin in *Earth Horizon: An
        Autobiography.*

1933   George Hunter killed by a deranged patient. Austin accepts an
        honorary doctorate of letters from the University of New Mexico.

1934   Dies 13 August.
        Can Prayer Be Answered?
        One-Smoke Stories

one

DESERT PLACES

1868–1892

They cannot scare me with their empty spaces
. . . I have it in me so much nearer home
To scare myself with my own desert places.

ROBERT FROST,
"Desert Places," 1936

IN 1836, OVER FIFTEEN FEET of snow fell in Carlinville, Illinois. Farmers hauling corn and livestock to the Mississippi River town of Alton frantically reversed their routes, dumping wagonloads of feed and abandoning hogs that, piggybacking against the cold blast, froze in gruesome stacks. Wagons froze, and men with them, trapped in a "polar wave" of blinding speed.[1] Mary Hunter Austin, who wrote about the disaster nearly a century later, grew up in Carlinville during the 1870s. She remembered town elders dating events before and after the Great Snow, and in her autobiography, *Earth Horizon* (1932), she uses the storm to mark her own place in a region's unfolding history. Like the town chroniclers, she visualized the passing of time punctuated by moments, auspicious and otherwise, which marked the lives of her ancestors. *Earth Horizon* opens with a personal image that captures her sense of history. She sees her great-grandmother Polly MacAdams Dugger bidding goodbye to her home in Tennessee and clambering into an ox-cart headed to the wilds of Illinois—and to a future that became Mary Austin's birthright.

Polly Dugger's westward trek repeated itself two generations later when Austin's widowed mother, Susanna, or "Susie" (1842–96), dismantled the dark, overstuffed house in Carlinville and with her daughter and youngest son, George (1877–1933), set off for California.[2] To mother and daughter, who agreed on little else, their uprooting recapitulated the great-grandmother's courage, though Susanna's eldest son Jim (James Milo Hunter, 1866–1917) had led the way the year before and waited for them in Southern California. The year was 1888 and, in contrast to Polly Dugger's family, the Hunters traveled "tourist" on the railroad, which meant that they had Pullman accommodations without the dining privileges, green plush, or porters. Like other "Pullman pioneers," they carried a hamper with tin compartments and ate as their iron horse clattered by some of the few remaining buffalo grazing on the prairie.

Averaging a little over twenty miles an hour, the train typically stopped three or four times a day for water and fuel and for passengers to stretch their legs. The Hunters' route brought them through Denver, where they visited relatives, and across the Great Basin, which introduced Mary Hunter to the vast desert lands she came to love between the Great Salt Lake and Sacramento Pass. In San Francisco the travelers stayed at a boarding house run by more relatives, and from there sailed on a coastal steamer, by way of Santa Barbara, to Los Angeles. They found Jim working as a druggist's assistant in Monrovia, one of the half-born foothill towns east of Pasadena. Reunited, the family intended to homestead in the San Joaquin Valley where, they confidently believed, rich farmland was theirs for the asking.

That October, Susanna Hunter and her three children joined a wagon caravan that took them from the garden paradise of Pasadena—a town already known for the lavish estates of patent-medicine millionaires—across the San Fernando Valley and north to the Tejon Pass. For Mary Hunter, aged twenty and newly graduated from college, the hundred-mile, eight-day trek offered postgraduate studies in Southern Californian flora, fauna, topography, and architecture. Beyond the outskirts of Los Angeles, adobe ranch houses replaced jerry-built bungalows, and aromatic groves of imported eucalyptus gave way to wild oats, knobby grapevines, prickly pear, and copses of live oak on sunburned hills. The vegetation could not have made the grain-rich plains of Illinois feel more distant or California more exotic. As the party followed the arroyos' paths of scorched, water-gouged earth and climbed through the whale-backed Tehachapi Mountains, Mary Hunter grew nervous. At every turn, she confronted such frightening beauty it seemed to mock her with visions of grandeur. Perhaps because of the fall light or an awareness of her own frailty, she sensed an ominous presence, "something that rustled and ran" and hung "half-remotely" in wait to leap and fasten on her vitals.[3] She described this feeling not as a waking nightmare but as unappeasable desire, a hunger for whatever lay just beyond her reach.

The convoy rested at the Tejon Pass in the early dusk, as velvet shades cast their net across the San Joaquin Valley. Astride her buckskin horse, Mary, with her oversized features, thick, dust-brown hair, and opaque eyes, looked down from the mountains toward her new home. As the winding descent allowed, she could make out the dry plain broken by marshes of green tulare reeds, which reminded her of hieroglyphs in an ancient desert. To the east she saw a nest of cabins strung together with fence posts. There were no trees, no grass, just scattered balls of sagebrush and the whitish, sandy dunes lining the hollows of the great valley. In the distance, hints of settlements spotted the bare foothills that rose in waves to the peaks of the Sierra Nevada.[4] Mary Hunter believed she had come to a land in which anything seemed possible. Trying to explain for her college journal the sublimity of this stark landscape, "where the tarantulas sun themselves on our front porch," she watched her sentences growing bolder and more personal than schoolroom grammars recommended.[5] Startled by her new voice, she sent back to Carlinville an account that in observations and style anticipated her *Land of Little Rain* (1903), the book that made her reputation.

By the 1880s, the railroad-driven land booms in the West lured a different type of settler than Mary's intrepid great-grandmother. When the Santa Fe line opened to California (in 1885) and price wars drove fares from the Missouri Valley as low as one dollar, speculators and entrepreneurs led westward an acquisitive generation of immigrants. Three or four times a day the Santa Fe and Southern Pacific trains deposited their freight of passengers; in 1887, the Southern Pacific alone carried 120,000 people to Los Angeles, the spreading city some dubbed "the seacoast of Iowa." The newcomers sought, according to an 1886 resolution by the California-Illinois Association, health, happiness, and longevity.[6] So many would-be Californians arrived they nicknamed each other by state: those from Connecticut answering to "nutmeggers," those from Illinois, "suckers." Mary thought the Illinois epithet fitting for her brother, Jim, one of thousands of midwesterners who took for granted, as a popular author wrote, that they could "do here more easily what they used to do in Illinois and Indiana—buy a farm, and with their first crop clear all expenses, including the price of the land."[7] In such a climate, con men who had earlier salted mining claims now hung oranges on Joshua trees or sold developments with names like Border City—accessible by balloon and providing views of the Mojave Desert—which sank to ghost towns in the first extended drought.

For the Hunters as for millions like them, California glistened as if gold dust hung in the air. Knowing next to nothing about the state except what they gleaned from advertisements or travelers' tall tales, or the no less tall tales published by writers like Bret Harte and Mark Twain, they arrived a generation late and more than a penny short. Without farming experience, the family intended not to buy a farm but to claim one, under the terms of the Homestead Act signed by Abraham Lincoln in 1862, which allowed any U.S. citizen or intended citizen, twenty-one years or older, to secure—for a modest registration fee and a commitment to make "improvements"— 160 acres of undeveloped federal land. Long before the Hunters arrived, however, arable Californian land had been wrenched from native Indians and Spaniards, then claimed, sold, or stolen again, and accumulated into huge tracts by the railroads or by a few wealthy men who held the keys to prosperity in the form of water rights.

California emerged, to echo Charles Dudley Warner (Mark Twain's friend and collaborator on *The Gilded Age*), as the "commercial Mediterranean" of the United States.[8] Increasingly resentful of such labels and what they meant for the misuse of the state, Austin remembered her impression that the region could not "possibly be as inchoate and shallow as . . . it appears, all the uses of natural beauty slavered over with . . . purely material culture."[9] California, because of its Gordian knot of capitalism and climate, utopian myths and heart-stopping landscape, nevertheless captivated her, as it still captivates writers like Joan Didion, at once repelled and intrigued by its endless promises.

Despite her limited experience, Mary Hunter entertained few illusions about the likely success of her fortune-hunting family who, though genteel, had never been well off. Mary's father, George Hunter (1833–78) emigrated with his older brother from the small Yorkshire town of West Gilling to Alton, where he worked as a clerk to support law studies before settling in Carlinville. A sickly man and a bookish, half-hearted lawyer, George Hunter raised prize Berkshire hogs and wanted the time to watch his pigs, trees, and children grow to maturity. After years of bad health, he died in 1878, aged forty-five, leaving Susanna to raise their four young children. His decline began with service in the Civil War when, already asthmatic, he hid from Confederate troops neck-deep in the malarial ooze of a Southern swamp. Mary remembered from childhood the ever-present smell of burning pastilles and, at night, the broken rhythm of her father's breathing or frustrated cursing. Preceded by nighttime alarms and doctors' visits, his death had been expected, even by his children, yet the strain can be gauged by Mary's preoccupation with the image of "a dark, nearly black stone house with a tower and . . . people plotting."[10]

No one anticipated the death, two months later, of her younger sister, Jennie (1870–78). Having come down with diphtheria first, Mary blamed herself for bringing harm to the only person who, as she wrote, ever loved her "unselflessly." On the day of Jennie's funeral, her mother pushed Mary away "and cried aloud on God for taking Jennie."[11] Why couldn't it have been Mary? Believing herself the most unattractive and least understood member of her family, Mary clung to the memory of Jennie's love and for the rest of her life looked back on her sister as a benign, living presence.

After her husband's death, Susanna Hunter struggled to keep the family afloat. As a widow in Carlinville who had to walk past the new "drug emporium" and the Dugger building, both owned by relatives, Susanna resented the Hunters' fall in status since the first Dugger—*Daguerre*—came to America with the Marquis de Lafayette.[12] Although George had served by popular vote as magistrate of the police, the position brought more respect than reward. He left little behind, and the allotment of his military pension and back pay gave the family only a temporary safeguard against poverty. Susanna, with her knack among other talents for trimming and pressing clothes, could turn a nickel into a dollar and a daughter into a drudge. When her mother rented herself out as a nurse, ten-year-old Mary took on the pot washing, potato peeling, and care of her two-year-old brother, George.[13] "She was always an oddity," a neighbor remembered. "She had two great braids of hair on top of her head and used to wander around the yard staring at everything. I always wanted to see down into her, but I never felt that I could. I couldn't fathom her. My husband used to look out the window at her and say to me, 'I wonder what will become of Mary. I wonder what she will be.'"[14]

Raised by her mother as a Methodist, Mary absorbed (and later rejected) the tenets of Protestant religions. She accompanied Susanna to meetings of the Woman's Christian Temperance Union, or WCTU, an evangelist group providing rare political platforms for women in the years after the Civil War. Reliving those years in her novel *A Woman of Genius* (1912), Austin has her heroine ask: "Does anybody remember what the woman's world was like in small towns before the days of woman's clubs? There was the world of cooking and making over . . . of church-going and missionary societies and ministerial cooperation, half grudged and half assumed as a virtue . . . [and] a world all of care and expectancy of children overshadowed by the recurrent monthly dread."[15] Susanna herself lost three babies. One relative remembered a picture of Susanna, knitting stockings for the children while she rocked a cradle with her left foot and read a book balanced on her right knee.[16] Not everyone had her strength or will. In Carlinville, the Hunters knew a Mrs. Rogers, who, learning she was pregnant with her tenth child, jumped to her death from the roof of a buggy.[17]

Mary Hunter had seen with what pride her mother and fellow "temperancers" wore their white ribbons and tackled, or earnestly debated, issues of poverty, sex education, and birth control in accord with the popular *Robert's Rules of Order.* From an early age, she knew the Carlinville classification of drunken states: "chicken" or silly drunk, "owl" or stupidly drunk, and "hog-in-the-gutter" drunk. She recalled the tears on her mother's face as she treated a woman whose besotted husband had "accidentally" given her a bloody bruise; and, "in one of the few natural gestures" she extended to her daughter, Susanna took her hand as they listened to the first woman allowed to speak to their congregation about a woman's right *not* to bear the children of a drunkard.[18]

Susanna idolized Frances Willard, founder of the WCTU and a leader in the suffrage movement. As president of the local chapter in 1882, she invited Willard to Carlinville to address the ninth annual convention. Austin described Willard as a terrific saleswoman with "a verse of Scripture for every type of spiritual aspiration." Part of Susanna's temperance work involved similar proselytizing. A few decades later when supporting herself on the lecture circuit, Austin came to appreciate her mother's power to move an audience: "No matter . . . how taken unawares, how privately embarrassed she might be, in public Susie was never *gauche,* never anything but simply right and dignified."[19] Her Sunday school pupils clung to memories of Susanna dressed in black alpaca and exhorting them to resist sin. Observing her mother's participation in the church and the WCTU, Mary learned how small communities of women could have a hand in shaping national policies; she later urged similar models on the Hoover and FDR administrations. When she joined the Broom Brigade, the girls' division of the WCTU, Mary vowed to keep her chastity and, lest she be taken lightly, signed a pledge with other members of a group called the Caldwell's not to marry for a minimum of five years without consent of the other signatories.[20]

Until the day of Susanna's abrupt announcement that she had served her time as wife and mother and that they were bound for California, Mary had given little thought to where she might live. In years to come she argued the regional nature of art, which grows from the artist's association with a specific landscape and its past, but as a young woman she intended to write or, if necessary, to teach, either of which she could do as well in one place as another. The first sight of the thirty-thousand acre Rancho El Tejon changed her horizons and marked the beginning of her understanding, not only about who she was, but where she needed to be.

———————•·•·•———————

In December 1888, the family settled seven miles to the north of the Rancho El Tejon, whose celebrated owner, General Edward Fitzgerald Beale, played an important part in Mary Hunter's life. Sixty-six when he met the twenty-year-old woman, General Beale could boast great wealth and a legendary past. At the request of the U.S. Army and its commander in chief, President James Buchanan, he had driven a train of camels from Texas to Fort Tejon along the Santa Fe Trail. General Beale struck friends as "a sparkling combination of scholar, gentleman and Indian fighter."[21] Ferociously independent, and quick to anger, he once challenged the commissioner of Indian affairs to a duel. Contemporaries honored Beale as a hero in the Mexican-American War, who—accompanied by his Delaware Indian servant and his friend Kit Carson—slipped through enemy lines to bring life-saving reinforcements for Colonel Stephen Kearney's starving troops near San Diego. Disguised as a Mexican, Beale took to Washington the news of gold at Sutter's Mill. His 1857 surveys of Western wilderness would prove the feasibility of a transcontinental railroad and a wagon road from Fort Defiance, New Mexico, to the Colorado River.

Before accepting his post superintending Indian affairs for California and Nevada, in 1853, Beale worked for W. H. Aspinwall and Commodore Stockton, land barons whose interests competed with those of Native and immigrant peoples. According to his biographer, Beale "sought pecuniary success with a single-minded intensity" and profited from "every government position he held."[22] As commissioner of Indian affairs, Beale had a reputation for swift punishment based on firm policies, yet he also set aside a parcel of the Rancho El Tejon—the Mexican land grant he later purchased—for the Sebastian Indian Reservation. Austin praised him for being the first government official to recognize that "it is wiser for Indians to become the best sort of Indians rather than poor imitation whites."[23] A storyteller and something of a philosopher, the young Beale had written in his journal, "Thoughts, feelings, passions and events—these are the real moral timekeepers. What is it to me the mere ticking of a pendulum!"[24] His existential positions on time and meaning in human lives underlie Austin's lifelong thinking and offered her, as a struggling young woman, the keys to her independence.

Beale fascinated her as a larger-than-life explorer (like her, he was slightly under average height) and a raconteur passionate about his country, his adopted state, and himself. Whenever Beale, who alternated between East and West, returned to his two-hundred-thousand-acre ranch, he spoke to Mary Hunter about the land and its people he had known as an administrator, proprietor, rancher, soldier, and trained naval officer. Since her father's death, Mary had been drawn to older men, among them a Carlinville scientist whose insect net and specimen case she envied as a girl. (The autobiographical heroine of *A Woman of Genius* goes out of her way to catch a glimpse of a man who reminds her of her father.) At Blackburn College Mary had surprised her family by majoring first in psychology, then botany. She would speak of having "the born novelist's identification with alien personalities, [and] the scientist's itch to understand by getting inside" things.[25] Beale understood her ambitions, and probably her need for a surrogate father. Though he had slowed down with ailments and alcoholism and had only a few years to live when Austin met him, this powerful westerner who did much to bring about modern California gave the young woman a more practical and enduring education than she received from Blackburn College.

Wary of her daughter's interests and companions, and knowing Beale's reputation for manipulating the law to acquire settlers' property, Susanna cautioned Mary about pestering their benefactor. In fact, he liked nothing better than to engage a listener with stories of California, whether past or present, truth or fiction. "A Native by the name of Lopez was working on a ditch and sat under a tree to eat his lunch," Mary quotes Beale in her journal. "He took out his knife and dug up a wild onion to eat with his tortilla and uncovered grains of gold." Beale gave her a basket once used to pan the gold discovered at Mission San Fernando; she in turn presented him with a poem she had written about wild hyacinths. Beale showed the poem to the wife of the Civil War general John Logan, who sent the young author an encouraging note. "I don't know what she knows about poetry," Mary responded. "People seem to think you just want to be praised, but I want to feel sure."[26]

Beale's daughter-in-law described life at the ranch as conducted in the Spanish style, the owner addressed as "patron" and she as "patrona," to whom their wards came for advice or justice. This aristocratic ease bore no relation to the life of the Hunter family, who had left their few comforts

behind. Staking three claims in Kern County for a total of 480 acres—
Susanna's and Jim's required tenancy, Mary's did not—they set up housekeeping on Jim's land, situated four miles southeast of the present community of Mettler Station, and made the required visits to Susanna's. "There
was something quaintly ancestral in our settling in," Austin wrote of their
one-room, calico-curtained cabin, with bunks pressed against the wall.[27] In
terms of bad luck, she was right. They could not have come at a worse time:
dry, drier, and driest, the locals described the years from 1888 well into the
1890s. In the first year of drought, she observed that "quail mated sparingly;
the second year the wild oats matured no seed; the third, cattle died in their
tracks with their heads pointing toward the dried watercourses. And that
year the scavengers were as black as the plague all across the mesa and up the
treeless, tumbled hills."[28] The Hunters' scant income came from leasing
grazing rights to nonexistent grass. Mary and young George tried to prop the
tenant cattle upright, for once the animals lay down near the settlers' water
barrels, they stayed down. It took them days to die before workers from the
Rancho El Tejon came to drag the carcasses away. According to the ranch
hands, coyotes drank the still-warm blood, buzzards perched on every fence
post, and wildcats grew bold. "It is a very squalid tragedy—that of the dying
brutes and the scavenger birds," Austin wrote in *The Land of Little Rain*. "I
suppose the dumb creatures know nearly as much of death as do their betters, who have only the more imagination."[29]

As the first six months wore out, Mary Hunter collapsed. Since she had
been unwell before the trip, Susanna attributed the "breakdown" to lingering anxieties from Carlinville. Two long periods of ill health during her
college years notwithstanding, Austin would blame malnutrition.[30] "For
settlers on the Tejon there was not as much as a mess of greens to be raised
or gathered. . . . There was no butter," and canned milk had to be "diluted
with stale water from a dry-season waterhole."[31] They ate mostly rabbits
and venison, purchased from the grizzly-looking "derelicts" they more
generously called "Mountain Men." Mary, who could not bring herself
to eat canned food or game, stumbled one day on a profusion of wild
grapes growing in a canyon, and after a week's gorging began to revive.
"Malnutrition" seems the perfect metaphor for a young woman starved for
meaningful work and affection. If nothing else, the incident brought the
realization that "there was something you could do about unsatisfactory
conditions besides being heroic or a martyr to them . . . and that was getting out to hunt for the remedy." This came as "a revolutionary discovery"
for a young lady in 1880s.[32]

With regained health and energy, she now felt plagued "by an anxiety to know."[33] Some mornings she awoke to a voice calling her to explore secret places. Her mother, repelled by the vastness of the San Joaquin Valley, preferred the social amenities of Bakersfield where summer temperatures soared to 120 degrees Fahrenheit. Then a growing town with manure-thick streets, plank sidewalks, and no indoor plumbing, Bakersfield was a notorious breeding ground for malaria and typhoid. According to Norman Angell—a young ranch hand who later won the Nobel Peace Prize—Bakersfield claimed about two thousand inhabitants, five hundred of whom were prostitutes serving the needs of men from a hundred miles in every direction.[34]

Susanna could not grasp her daughter's dislike of the town or her affinity for open air. "I am not homesick with the sky, nor with the hills," Mary wrote in her journal, "though sometimes I am afraid of them." In this she differed from Susanna and from those many newcomers to Southern California who nursed a profound nostalgia for the landscapes they had left. Mary felt homesick in her own house, or in any of the houses that Susanna called "home-like" and "beautifully furnished."[35] She saw the whole aesthetic history of the Midwest enshrined in the "whatnot," an open-shelved cabinet used to display a hodgepodge of treasures from Indian arrowheads to tropical shells engraved with the Lord's Prayer. Not only at odds with her mother, she baffled her peers, who shrugged off a young woman reluctant to dance (her personal choice and a Methodist prohibition) and preferring earnest talk to flirtation.

Looking at the new environment from her double perspective of poet and scientist, Mary compared in her journal the blue shadows of bush lupine to the rusty, brown-black shadows of sage brush. She noted the white crest of the Sierras almost floating above the flatlands, the changes in season and sunlight (the air dripped with light, and night seemed to come not from the sky but up from the land), the ways of animals and men, and how the Indians made canoes from saplings and reeds. Her explorations, alone and with others, to hunt game-birds in the tulares or to camp overnight on the road to Bakersfield, allowed an inventory of her surroundings. She roamed the Rancho El Tejon and the lower San Joaquin Valley as another woman might tend her house and garden. The sketches she made of wildflowers and sheepherders' equipment, and the photographs she took of people in the landscape, became her way of marking territory. They suggest the road not taken, a career she might have chosen as a visual artist. California had, for several decades, lured painters such as the German Albert

Bierstadt, the Scot William Keith, and before them perhaps the most compelling of American landscape painters, the English-born Thomas Moran, who confronted the majesty of Western landscapes in a way that Austin came to mirror in her writing. Family troubles and poor health aside, she knew that she had found her place in this bleached, profitless land of natural wonders.

General Beale, no longer the administrator of resettled Indians, had come to know and respect those living on his property. With the help of Beale, and later of Charles Lummis, whom she met in Los Angeles, Mary found friends among her Indian neighbors in a region where tribes shrank daily in size and power, at the mercy of any white man ready to kill or rape or steal. Within a year or two, few beside Mary—and almost never, in her mind, the Bureau of Indian Affairs—knew the customs and characteristics of California's Indians: how they had lived and how they needed to live. As the "Ishi" case suggests, not many could tell one tribe from another, or cared to do so. Only the intervention of the anthropologist Alfred Kroeber allowed Ishi, believed the last survivor of his tribe, to live out the remainder of his short life, albeit in the University of California's anthropological museum. Like Kroeber, though aggressively an amateur, Mary dedicated herself to understanding the customs (and to a lesser extent the languages) of California Indians, whose diverse tribes had long ago parceled out the region. Yet however much she learned from the writing of anthropologists or from Beale's wide experience, she learned more from first-hand observation. She encountered Indian tribes local to the southern San Joaquin, including the interior Chumash and Yokuts. A village next to Fort Tejon, she discovered, was home to members of at least four tribes; and she soon became familiar with the Serranos, Cahuillas, Gabrielenos, and Mojaves in areas near Bakersfield.[36]

Mary Hunter befriended cowboys, Basque sheepherders, and Mexican *vaqueros,* along with men like Kern River Jim, who went by one of the place names of his Yokuts people. She met Pete Miller, the renowned bear killer of El Tejon, whom tradition credited with three hundred kills; and José Jesus Lopez, a descendant of early Spanish colonists and manager of the ranch, himself celebrated for driving eighty-five hundred sheep across the Nevada desert to Green River, Wyoming, during the drought of 1879. Mary especially liked General Beale's store manager, James Vineyard Rosemeyere (sometimes spelled *Rosemyer*), and his part-Serrano and part–Gabrieleno Indian wife, who spoke both languages and sang songs of mourning during the fiesta of the Day of the Dead (Dia de los Muertos). When Jimmy "had a good horse under him, a saddle of carved leather-work, *botas,* deep-roweled spurs and a silver-trimmed sombero, [he] knew himself a handsome figure of a man." Rosemeyere gave Mary a treasured camel bell and cord from Beale's Camel Corps, which, hanging above her desk, set "in motion all the echoes of Romance."[37]

Characters from these years fill her stories. The "walking woman," for example, whom the cowboys called Mrs. Walker, roamed the southern San Joaquin with a black bag attached to a stick slung over her shoulder. The men said she was a good woman and would not allow liberties. Susanna had her doubts and said she looked suspiciously like a woman who had borne a child. Some thought the walking woman mad; others thought she made sense most days and had reasons for her solitary walking. Austin tells her story in *Lost Borders* (1909), where she also writes about an Englishman in search of a cure for tuberculosis, a husband abandoning his family to find a cache of gold, and a woman who surprises herself by coming to appreciate the maternal passions of a prostitute. The sheepherders, scum of the earth to many, won Austin's affectionate respect. In hindsight, it seems odd that when she cast herself as playwright and director she never wrote a play about the people who contributed to her book about sheepherding, *The Flock,* known as "the book of Johnny Rosemeyere" and indebted to the other sheep owners and herders "who, wittingly or unwittingly, have contributed to the performances set down in it."[38]

Among the tales Mary heard, she took to heart a story from a man named Sebastiano, a Serrano Indian acquaintance and later a character in *The Flock.* Sebastiano told her how John C. Frémont, the Western pioneer known as "Pathfinder," cheated him when he ferried Frémont safely across the flooded Kern River and got nothing for his labor. These first-hand accounts of early pioneers and California lore took her beyond other greenhorns, who knew Southern California mostly through reading Helen Hunt Jackson's popular *Ramona* (1884). The romance about a part-Indian orphan raised among the Spanish aristocracy, *Ramona* established the myth of the benign era of Spanish settlers, above all missionaries, whose presence ironically if not intentionally began the decimation of the Native population. The book's popularity drew thousands of tourists to towns where the heroine, in the manner of George Washington, had ostensibly slept—or, in Ramona's case, married.

Mary read *Ramona* but drew more from local writers, especially those publishing in the *Overland Monthly* on practical, everyday matters such as dairying in California. She determined to write her own book about the region, regardless of how long it took, and with that goal in mind she kept a notebook about sheepherding, separate from one about plants and local wildlife, and another into which she poured torrents of unconnected words like so much "automatic writing."[39] The explorer and California surveyor Clarence King claimed that his field, geology, posed religious, aesthetic, and moral issues in addition to the scientific; it trained the imagination, he argued, because one person could not look deeper into the ground than another. If not deep into the ground, Mary looked widely and intensely, training her imagination and jotting down on any scrap of paper words and images that represented a constant assault on her sensibilities. Only when she came to use these notes in her writing could she put them aside.

At the beginning of June 1889, the Hunters moved to Rose Station, a small junction eight miles south of Mettler Station and eighteen miles from Susanna's favored Bakersfield. Life at Rose Station brought some physical comfort to the family. The generous Edward Beale lent them two cows along with a dilapidated but comfortable adobe house. In exchange, Mary and Susanna were to cook for travelers passing through, while George watched the livestock. Susanna hoped to save money by selling hay and provisions, such as freshly baked bread and eggs at thirty cents a dozen. Jim bought another ten acres, speculating against the odds on future irrigation.[40] Their surroundings changed daily at the station, where migrants and tradesmen rested overnight and moved on the next day. Susanna thought that anyone stopping would think that all Californians lived in wagons. In the morning light she saw "whole families rolled up in blankets like mummies lying on the ground." She never realized that people on the ranch, and many beyond it, considered homesteaders, including genteel ones from Carlinville, Illinois, marginally superior to gypsies.

At the best of times, Mary Hunter felt herself a changeling. Her needs and tastes differed so drastically from those of her siblings and mother that she thought of herself as two separate people: "I-Mary," a confident young woman embraced by the world, and "Mary-by-herself," an outcast, as her phrase suggests, isolated from society and from her kin. It did not help that Susanna made a cult of her handsome older son. The fiercely competitive Mary resented the deference paid to Jim, who expected and got what she had to earn twice over. Taking to the role like a duck to sewerage, Jim liked nothing better than to make pronouncements about the qualities or roles of "women," knowing full well his sister conformed to none of them. Hardly docile or self-sacrificing, Mary responded by claiming areas he had staked out as his own—notably, college oratory and essay writing—and then openly pitying his failures. "I could be abased, I should be delighted to be imposed upon," the heroine of *A Woman of Genius* says, "but if I paid out self-immolation, I wanted something for my money, and I didn't consider I was getting it with my brother for whom I smuggled notes and copied compositions."[41] After Susanna's death, Mary found a scrapbook full of work she herself had written for her brother, signed with *his* name in her mother's hand.

Mary Hunter took pleasure in her contrariness at a time when women won praise for their altruism, purity, and piety. She rebelled against the strictures of her sex as well as the middle-class, Midwestern life she and writers such as Sherwood Anderson and Sinclair Lewis would pillory. Illinois friends and neighbors she labeled "Carlinvillains." Insisting that she had never wanted to be a man, she demanded a man's rights, in this case her older brother's prerogatives, and argued a woman's need for money, which she understood as power. Naturally quick herself, she took Jim's measured responses as a sign of intellectual inferiority. When looking back to these times, however, she recalled with affection their arguments about everything from Herbert Spencer's version of evolution to why oysters make pearls. "For the source of the unhappy alienations of later years," she wrote, "one must go further and deeper."[42]

Her story of the four-minute egg, told in *Earth Horizon,* captures the family tensions. Hating soft-boiled eggs, Mary asked her mother to cook hers for a minute or two before adding the others to the pot. Tending to her daughter's egg was something her mother refused to do. "Oh, Mary," she would say, "why can't you take your food like the *rest* of the family?" Or, when Mary prepared her own food: "Do you always have to have something different from the *rest* of the family?" Jim, "playing his part as the complaisant favorite," delivered judgment. " 'Somehow you never seem to have any feeling for what a HOME should be.' " Mary decided that mothers like Susanna drove their daughters away from domestic life by letting them know that "a different sort of boiled egg was more than a woman had a right to claim on her own behalf."[43]

Apportioning praise or blame about any family rarely makes sense, and it makes less sense when only one person's account speaks across a century. Unlike Mary, Jim and George left no record of their feelings, though George's pained letters to her in later years indicate how much his story differed from his sister's. Each of the Hunters had more than his or her share of hardship. Jim longed for the life of a country doctor, while Susanna, who distrusted doctors, refused to borrow the money necessary for his training.

She preferred immediate income to distant wealth—and acquired neither. George, by every account a good-natured, if scapegrace child, grew up almost like the ward of his grudging sister; he did become a doctor, with unforeseen consequences.

Still without her teaching license, Mary stayed a year at Rose Station before she found a temporary teaching position at the Old River Primary School, not far from Bakersfield. Darius Pyle, a former teacher and manager of the Mountain View Dairy, oversaw the school. The owner of the dairy, indeed of a chain of ranches, James Haggin made his fortune from moneylending and investments in Wells Fargo, the Anaconda Copper Company, and George Hearst's mining ventures. His business partner, the Bay Area politician William B. Carr, was said to belong to "a ring of mercenary bandits who steal to get office and get office to steal."[44] At the time Mary boarded with Darius and Mary Pyle in the fall of 1889, Haggin owned more than four hundred thousand acres in the Central Valley.

Mary took charge of the Pyles' three children and particularly liked their daughter Dena. For them she composed the poems that form part of *Children Sing in the Far West* (not published until 1928), including one about the Australian ladybug imported to control aphids:

Ladybug, Ladybug, fly away home,
The scale bug is down in the orchard alone,
He is eating his way to the topmost limb,
Ladybug, Ladybug, go and eat him![45]

The dairy farm, sprawling across five thousand acres, employed Swiss immigrants to tend cows and Chinese laborers to cook, garden, and irrigate. The house itself, a five-room ranch, sat on three acres of lawn and trees. The situation suited Mary so well that, when she failed to pass the licensing examination in December and lost her job, she stayed on at the dairy, contemplating a textbook about teaching and supporting herself as an itinerant tutor. To visit her new students, she drove a cart from house to house and in the process taught herself about the "intricate interrelations of land, water, crops, politics, and personal life in the great Valley." Nothing, she learned, figured so prominently in Southern California as the presence or absence of water, the evidence of which she saw in the chicanery and violence of men "skirmishing over water rights."[46]

One of the major skirmishers, Henry Miller, a friend of General Beale, was a slow-mannered, German immigrant given to business suits, cowboy boots, a diamond tie stud, and the exclamation "Chesus!" He began his American life as a butcher's assistant in San Francisco. After cornering the beef trade, he and his partner, another former butcher named Charles Lux, bought huge tracts of land for grazing, one hundred thousand acres near Los Banos alone. People claimed that Miller, whose holdings were said to equal the area of Belgium twice over, could travel from Idaho to Mexico, camping each night on his own land. As chief of the San Joaquin and King's River Canal and Irrigation Company, he controlled—along with men like Haggin and Carr—the price *and* availability of water to small farmers. Miller and Lux had come into conflict with Haggin and Carr ostensibly over a piece of swampland on the Kern River west of Bakersfield. The real issue came down to water, and so did the ensuing court case that lasted from May 1879 through multiple appeals to its inconclusive end in 1886. The courts offered little help and were, in any case, beyond the means of ordinary farmers. As an old man, Miller would say that *Lux v. Haggin* had cost him twenty-five million dollars. For observers seeking to protect their own interests, the case, which managed to legitimize competing water-law systems—the English riparian law (of riverside ownership) and the Spanish doctrine of appropriation based on prior use—underscored the confusion of the state's water-distribution policies.[47]

While farmers protected their ditches with shotguns, employees of the land barons destroyed dikes and tore out water gates. Elmo Pyle, a member of Mary Hunter's adopted family, found himself looking into the muzzle of a settler's gun when he went out to mend a gate. Battles over water affected everyone. Even John Muir, his name synonymous with conservation, supported the so-called reclamation of the San Joaquin Valley. The term essentially meant *claiming,* rather than *re*claiming, or more accurately, the grabbing of land that may or may not have been arable. Writing for the *San Francisco Bulletin* in 1874, Muir argued that irrigation mimicked the natural flooding process, whereas failure to irrigate "degraded" the land by allowing "atmospheric weathering." It appeared to Muir that "all the physical and moral brightness" of Tulare Basin landowners flowed "directly from a ditch," and he predicted that "true homes embowered in trees and lovingly broidered with flowers" would eventually replace "cheerless shanties."[48] Muir's comments illustrate some of the personal and public complexities of reclamation—and how its supporters tended to couch their arguments in platitudes about home and progress.

In their modest way, the Hunter family's fortunes speak to larger issues of the arid West, where the confiscation of land and rerouting of water made multimillionaires of those with the luck or daring to steal what they could not buy. As Mary soon learned, the prefix *pa* in Northern Paiute means "water," the key to survival for Indian tribes and for those who came after. With few accessible lakes or, in the south, year-round rivers and creeks, the Hunters and other newcomers relied for water on the uncertain rainy season from November to March. According to Austin, many home-steaders believed that wherever enough people settled, an irrigating ditch magically followed. She suspected that "pipe-dream" to be driving her brother and their neighbors, the would-be developers reduced to gamblers. Water controversies would play a continuing and at times a central role in Austin's life, including her literary life. She published *The Ford,* her novel about these issues, in 1917.

During the two years she spent at Mountain View Dairy, Mary saw little of her family, who had moved closer to Bakersfield. She had clashed with her mother when Susanna invested her share of the family's shrinking cap-ital in a farm that Susanna and Jim owned jointly. Angry about the waste of money, Mary believed that her overworked mother should move to Los Angeles where she had relatives and that George should enroll there in a Methodist college. Susanna and Jim had intended to make their first year's mortgage payment on the farm from the sale of grapes, which in their in-nocence they supposed to be raisin, not wine stock. Out came the vines, and with them Mary's hope of at least a small nest egg or dowry. Austin compared the relationship between the mother and son to a bad marriage. She avoided Susanna until the eve of her wedding in 1891.[49]

───────────── ◆ ─────────────

When Mary Hunter agreed to marry Stafford Wallace Austin (1861–1931) in the summer of 1890, she surprised no one more than her mother. She was not conventionally attractive with the "wax-doll prettiness" valued in that era, and to Susanna she seemed an ungainly and isolated girl destined for "spinsterhood." In retrospect, Austin did not accept that she had been as homely or awkward as her family led her to believe. *Intense* she could understand, and overly sensitive, but not, as Susanna charged, unfemi-nine, immune to the wisdom of pleasing, or fundamentally unfit for mar-riage. "What would I do with the people after I have drawn them to me?" she had asked.[50] In *The Basket Woman* (1904), a book of Indian tales for children, Austin makes a parable of her experience. "You should try to be natural," the meadowsweet—sounding like Susanna Hunter—tells the little sugar pine, "do not be so stiff, and then everyone will love you though you are so plain." The flowers chime in, "If only you were not so odd." The sugar pine protests, "I would do very well as I am if they would let me be happy in my own way."[51] Now, optimistic in her hope or inexperience, she decided that love would come naturally in marriage. Years later she would write of a woman author in her story "Frustrate" (1912), who, if she "had known a little more, just a very little," might not have gone through with her wedding.[52]

Seven years older than his fiancée, Wallace had grown up on a sugar plantation near Hilo, on the island of Hawaii, where his father served as a high-ranking government secretary before losing the bulk of his fortune in 1885. His mother's family traced roots back to the Revolutionary War hero Edward Clark. Wallace, a graduate of the University of California, Berkeley, was shy and noncommittal, which may explain why people thought him absentminded. Dena Pyle, only ten when the Austins courted, remembered Wallace as "a strange man, a million-dollar dreamer," and may have known that, like Jim Hunter, Wallace speculated in land.[53] The Pyles referred to Wallace and his fellows as "remittance men," those paid by their families to keep their distance. Intellectually inclined and fascinated by winemaking, Wallace seemed superior to Mary's other suitors, among them a cheese-maker who worked for a company dairy, a locomotive engineer, and an ex-cowboy turned farmer.[54] Wallace might have reminded her of her father, whom she idealized for his "fine intellectual attainments," "rare conversational powers," and "remarkably retentive memory—a man to whom it was a pleasure to listen."[55] The couple, who shared an interest in botany, met at the home of friends at a time when men in the West outnumbered women fifteen to one. (During the 1870s only half the men in California could expect to marry, and those who did ran the risk of losing a wife to a better prospect.) Statistics mattered little to Wallace, who was smitten by the intellectual young woman, while she appreciated a man with whom she could talk. Alienated from her family and with few friends, she was also at a kind of crossroads. Still without her teaching certificate, she learned in July that the Haggin firm, which had been selling off parcels of land in the area to people like Wallace, intended to close the dairy and evict her adopted family.

After a short courtship, which consisted of buggy rides and conversations on the dairy lawn, Mary went home to her mother's house to be married. "My family thought I was doing well to marry Henry," her character says in "Frustrate." "He had no bad habits, and his people were well-to-do; and then I wasn't particularly pretty or rich. I have never been very popular with young men; I was too eager. Not for them, you understand; but just living and doing things seemed to me such a good game."[56] The wedding took place the evening of 19 May 1891. Over fifty people attended, with Austin's student, Dena Pyle, as the single bridesmaid. Jim Hunter served as best man. The Austins' wedding photograph shows the bride and groom in profile with their shoulders touching and eyes not meeting: he sporting wire-rimmed glasses and cropped handlebar moustaches of the day; she with curling bangs, dark brows, and a bit of festive white lace pinned to her drab shirtfront. The bride and groom did not exchange rings. Wallace gave Mary a velvet box containing a pearl-handled pen, which she valued more than a pearl necklace: "it means I am to go on with my writing."[57]

The couple took a three-day honeymoon before returning to their new home, a one-story board-and-batten house, to be at some imaginary time surrounded by alfalfa fields and vineyards. Taking her husband at his word, Austin devoted her days to writing, so much so that the dishes piled high enough to shock the sensibilities of neighbors. Dena Pyle remembered the new bride washing dishes in a trance. She'd "look out the window and not know whether she had a cat or dish in hand."[58] After barely four months, the Austins admitted failure and gave up farming. Early in 1892 they moved to Bakersfield, where Wallace got a job with an irrigation company and Austin wrote her early stories "The Mother of Felipe" and "The Conversion of Ah Lew Sing," a spoof about religious hypocrisy and, more seriously, traffic in Chinese women.[59]

From the beginning, Austin naively assumed that she could earn a living by writing. Apart from Bret Harte and Mark Twain, few writers maintained themselves and their families without inherited wealth, or success with plays or lectures, or plain good luck. Harte, having accepted ten thousand dollars a year to write exclusively for *The Atlantic Monthly*, wrote little and lived to see his literary coin drop to almost nothing. Twain's lectures, and his wife's allowance, supported their lavish Connecticut house at Nook Farm, while William Dean Howells, one of the era's most prolific writers, drew a steady $5,000 salary editing *The Atlantic* and later a guaranteed $10,000 (or well over $200,000 in today's dollars) for writing a novel a year and a column for *Harper's Weekly*.[60] Harper & Brothers also put him to work soliciting and reading manuscripts.

Austin began to understand that good writing did not guarantee either income or readership. The experiences of the last two years had sharpened her awareness of the world and her sense of who she was. Determined to write about the West, she concentrated on sorting out her voluminous notes on Spanish folklore and winnowing lists of adjectives; she wanted "to find the exact word for the cries of mules—'maimed noises,'" she called them in *The Land of Little Rain*—or "the difference between the sound of ripe figs dropping and the patter of olives shaken down by the wind."[61] When she looked back at these early writings, Austin singled out an unlikely model, the Indian-born Englishman, Rudyard Kipling. In the year of her marriage, the twenty-four-year-old Kipling, after thousands of miles of traveling throughout the United States, published (like Charles Dickens before him) a book called *American Notes*. Kipling, who decried the West's unchecked growth and waste of natural resources, appealed to Austin because of his language and his method. She had never read any short stories resembling "their slightly mocking detachment, their air of completely disengaging the author from any responsibility for the moral implications of the scene." Kipling's "strange and far away" tales set a standard for Austin's own.[62]

"The Mother of Felipe," Austin's first published story, appeared in the *Overland Monthly* for October 1892. It begins panoramically with a description of Antelope Valley, which Austin calls "a country to be avoided by the solitary traveler, with its hard, inhospitable soil, and its vast monotony of contour and color. A country sublime in its immensity of light, and soft unvarying tints—fawn, and olive, and pearl, with glistening stretches of white sand, and brown hollows between the hills, out of which the gray and purple shadows creep at night. A country laid visibly under the ban of eternal silence." (Lying due north of Los Angeles, Antelope Valley today contains the cities of Palmdale and Lancaster and a large military base.) Dropping to a close-up focus, the narrator follows a train of wagons belonging to "the class commonly styled 'Greasers,'" their "mixed origin plainly visible in the dark hue of the skin, the crisp, coarse hair, the high-arched foot and the Madonna-like outlines of the women's heads."[63] Driving the last wagon is a woman, the mother of the dying Felipe. Like Kipling, Austin tends to avoid judgments about her characters and their world. Her oracular if sometimes ironical tone grants her characters dignity without hiding their foibles. This first story differs from, say, Bret Harte's local-color sketches in its lack of sentimentality and condescension; at the same time, Austin's storyteller speaks with intimacy about people like Felipe's mother and the solitary places in which they find themselves. Her understated compassion for the mother, as for the eccentrics, lost souls, and other dispossessed people she came to write about, seems in a distant way a reflection of herself as outsider. Her kin were not the Hunter family, and in time not her husband, but the strangers who lit her imagination.

Adding to the problems of intimacy usually faced by newlyweds, neither Mary nor Wallace felt comfortable in Bakersfield, where they claimed that neighbors despised them for their college educations. Mary certainly craved better company, especially the writers, editors, and intellectuals she associated with San Francisco. To please his wife, Wallace appealed to his brother Frank, who proposed that they join him in San Francisco where the brothers could work together on a water-reclamation project in the Sierra Nevada. Wallace went first, and Mary followed soon after.

Ina Coolbrith, the first poet laureate of California, called San Francisco the "City of mists and of dreams!"[64] A businessman would have described it as a major financial center since the gold rush days, and it was already by 1860 the fourteenth-largest city in the Union. Religious zealots railed at the unholy city deserving the wrath of an angry god; many believed the 1906 earthquake an appropriate punishment. With a reputation for saloons, sex, and anarchy, San Francisco also offered restaurants such as The Poodle Dog and Delmonicos, where, it was said, Society dined with her husband on the first floor and trifled with her reputation on the second. Whatever happened on the third, where dining rooms served as supper bedrooms, spoke for itself. Mrs. Frank Leslie reported in 1877 "that in other cities the *demi-monde* imitates the fashions of the *beau-monde,* but that in San Francisco the case is reversed."[65] Yet the city outdid Los Angeles in ways beyond unbridled drinking and sexual license; it boasted (with due deference to the much-married Mrs. Leslie) a nascent *society,* and society's backing of institutions like the Opera House.

San Francisco had long featured writers and editors such as Mark Twain and his then friend Bret Harte, contributor and first editor (in 1868) of the West's best-known literary magazine, the *Overland Monthly.* To Austin, as to Frank Norris, her near but unmet neighbor on Telegraph Hill, the city appeared a literary and artistic mecca. Twain, Harte, Ina Coolbrith, and Ambrose Bierce believed they had established a Western literature. Jack London, Frank Norris, and Mary Austin, who was asked to join the editorial staff of *Out West* in 1902, helped prove them right. Then there were the popular if now overlooked contemporaries, such as Charles Warren Stoddard, once Twain's secretary and cofounder of *The Californian,* an early literary weekly. Stoddard's friend, the poet Joaquin Miller, wrote lines that "boomed with the pomposity of a brass band; floods, fires, hurricanes, extravagantly blazing sunsets, Amazonian women, Mark Twain [and] the thunder of a herd of buffaloes."[66] After Coolbrith persuaded Miller that the muses would not welcome anyone called Cincinnatus, he shed his given name and, with her encouragement, rewrote his poems. Keeping the beaded moccasins and sombrero, "that great vulgar fraud," in the words of another eccentric, Bayard Taylor, cast off his jailhouse past and Indian wife to dub himself the "Byron of the Rockies"—before his elevation to "the Poet of the Sierras."[67]

Ina Coolbrith attended to many writers in the Bay Area. A generation older than the twenty-three-year-old Austin, she welcomed the young writer who sought advice about publishing. When Austin crossed the threshold of the Oakland Free Library on Fourteenth Street, she found its beautiful librarian, with long tendrils of curly light hair and dangling earrings, sitting on her chair as if it were a throne. To a small boy in short knee pants, Jack London, Coolbrith had been a "noble goddess." Isadora Duncan, another Californian, believed her father fell in love with the woman who, in Duncan's words, had "eyes that glowed with burning fire and passion."[68] To Austin, appropriately, Coolbrith had the look of someone "accustomed to uninhibited space and wide horizons."[69] A descendant of the Mormon leader Joseph Smith, Coolbrith had been driven, like other Mormons, from one state to another, eventually emigrating from Illinois to Southern California, where after the death of her only child and a scandalous divorce from an abusive husband, she changed her name. In the years between she had achieved celebrity. Referring to Coolbrith, Charlie Stoddard, and himself, Bret Harte quipped:

> There is a poetic divinity—
> Number One of the "Overland Trinity"—
> Who uses the Muses
> Pretty much as she chooses—
> This dark-eyed, young Sapphic divinity.[70]

Austin found her "entirely kind and matter-of-fact," and the generous Coolbrith taught her how to prepare her first manuscript for the *Overland Monthly.*

At the time she worked on "The Mother of Felipe" in Bakersfield, Austin learned to her surprise that she was pregnant. However unexpected the news, she promised herself that she "would give birth to the smartest child that was ever born."[71] She doubled her working hours, hardly eating or sleeping. "Secure in the traditional preciousness of the young wife and expectant mother," she did not object when, after two short months in San Francisco, Wallace proposed their moving to the Owens Valley in Inyo County. "Paper and pencil could be had there as well as anywhere," she once again consoled herself. She did not know about the risky and under-financed nature of the water project, or that the brothers lacked "any experience whatsoever of the work in hand."[72] For the next seven years she would make her home in the long, high valley and the region she named "the land of little rain."

two

OWENS VALLEY

1892–1900

> The best of all ways is over the Sierra passes by pack and trail, seeing
> and believing. But the real heart and core of the country are not to be
> come at in a month's vacation. One must summer and winter with the
> land and wait its occasions.
>
> MARY AUSTIN,
> *The Land of Little Rain, 1903*

IN SUMMER, TO VISIT HER mother, Austin rode the worn, rocking stage-coaches that advanced in eighteen-mile relays from Keeler, at the head of Owens Lake, to the town of Mojave, where she boarded the Southern Pacific train for Bakersfield. In a phrase that captures the distance and division among people living in the same state, locals called their journeys to the San Joaquin going "over beyond," as though the train were a chariot and Bakersfield the site of pearly gates.[1] It was the first, rough stretch to Mojave that Austin liked best. She made a point of engaging the open-air seat beside the driver to avoid the cramped company of liquor salesmen, mining engineers, prostitutes, tuberculosis patients labeled "lungers," and old-timers who had made and lost or never found their fortunes. Drivers welcomed the young woman who came equipped with baskets of fruit and chocolate layer cakes. The coach journey took twenty-six hours, plenty of time, as Austin's *Lost Borders* testifies, for exchanging stories. The desert land they traveled struck Austin as a place of endless storytelling, where mirages were magical and the ghosts of men murdered for gold or silver palpably real. Here she expected the improbable to happen, as it did happen on one of those coach rides to Mojave.

Because she had grown accustomed to men hungry for the company of women and staring at her when they stopped to eat and change horses, this man's request came as no surprise. The superintendent of a mine ("call it the Lost Burro Mine—there was one of these in every district") asked if she would spend a day with his unhappy mother, yearning for another woman's company.[2] Intrepid as she was, Austin obliged. She had wanted to see the remote mine and relished the idea of a detour. Four hours later, it dawned on her that she had been kidnapped. The man had no lonely mother, it turned out, except the one at home in Philadelphia or Poughkeepsie; he did have a camp full of miners desperate to see a "lady." "You know what they will do to you if I tell them I have been insulted?" Austin warned her kidnapper. Frontier chivalry, which did not extend to Indian women or women with a reputation, called for violent retribution. Even in a town as wild as Bodie, California, "the wickedest and most tumultuous city in the entire American West"—as in Mark Twain's "The Bad Man from Bodie"—a woman's honor supposedly remained sacrosanct.[3] "I *will* tell them that," the young woman threatened her abductor, "unless you do exactly as I tell you from now on."[4]

Lost Burro Mine lay among the newly developed gold-and-silver deposits around Johannesburg, named wishfully for the South African city atop the world's largest reserves. Today, abandoned freight cars and rusted equipment remain strung across the desert, the signposts of dead ambitions and "the great mining days, whose trail went up like smoke."[5] As they approached the camp, Austin saw a host of shaven and clean-shirted men waiting to greet her. For the last hour they had watched her wagon inch up the switchback grade to camp. At dinner, Chinese cooks served six desserts, three of them variations of bread pudding. It might well have been Christmas day. Excused from duty, men on the graveyard shift joined their fellows in the mess hall, where the guest of honor sat on a long platform, holding a staff like a fairy godmother. Two or three women, probably camp followers, stood as if invisible at the outskirts of the room.

After cowboy songs, card tricks, and an imitation of a sword dance, Austin recited favorite poems, including some she had written. The evening ended in a medley of sentimental songs as the lady made an exit worthy of the actress Ellen Terry. When she remembered the old Mojave stage and her visit to Lost Burro Mine, Austin wondered if the new highway blighted with gas stations and hot-dog stands marked any improvement over the old coach road rich in its wealth of desert lore.

In years to come, Austin made light of being shanghaied and felt nostalgic about a vanishing world; as a young woman she nursed a "sacred rage" about her exile in the high desert.[6] "To think how little help I had, how much of what should have been help was turned to torture, in breaking away from the practical and literary restraint of the period. When I think of the long stale years in the hot dull little town [Lone Pine], I could weep, only I am too angry to weep"[7] "Little towns" would have been more to the point, for she lived in three of them: Lone Pine, Independence, and Bishop, outposts along the eastern face of the Sierra Nevada. To the rest of America, places like Lone Pine and Bishop—which had no electric lights before the turn of the century—seemed part of an earlier America than the one that celebrated the World's Columbia Exposition in 1893 or that took sides in the murder of striking workers and Pinkertons at Andrew Carnegie's steel mill in Homestead, Pennsylvania. Feeling trapped, isolated, and parochial, Austin in these years had little to say about national events and causes, or about politics, except as they related to local water issues or the treatment of American Indians, a topic that occupied her in the high desert almost as much as her writing.

For a hundred miles, the twisting Owens Valley runs roughly adjacent to the area of King's Canyon, Sequoia, and Yosemite national parks, with the mountain fortress of the Sierras rising between. Mount Whitney, over fourteen thousand feet high, commands the valley from above Lone Pine. To the east lies a less rugged range called the White Mountains near Bishop, the Inyo Mountains near Lone Pine. From the Owens Valley to the Mojave Desert and Death Valley, the land rises and falls and eventually drops from about four thousand feet to below sea level. Choosing the northerly and roundabout train route in 1892, the Austins traveled three days—stopping overnight in Reno and Sodaville, Nevada—to reach their new home, named for the solitary tree that once marked the entrance to Lone Pine Canyon. The last leg of their trip, by way of a narrow-gauge railway, followed the course of the Owens River, soon to be the target of the famously bitter struggle over water rights.

Founded as a supply depot for the Cerro Gordo Mine in the 1860s, Lone Pine in the 1890s served farmers needing a steady supply of water, which the Austin brothers aimed to provide. Wallace moved his uncomfortably pregnant wife into the Lone Pine Hotel while he and Frank turned to the construction of an irrigation ditch from Owens Lake. The project was hazardous—repositioning rock with shovels and mule-drawn scrapers— and a gamble, since spring floods could wipe out months of work.

Two weeks passed much as they had when Mary Austin first arrived at the Rancho El Tejon. She talked to older residents who remembered lucky strikes, stagecoach bandits, and the time when townspeople drove the help-less Paiutes to drown in "the bitter waters" of Owens Lake. "There were In-dians who had stories to tell of the last great struggle between Paiutes and the Southern Shoshones and of the gathering-up of the clans when Edward Beale became Indian Commissioner. . . . Older and older there was myth and legend, and . . . strange outline ruins of forgotten villages in the black rock country."[8] For their father, the Paiutes claimed the mythical Coyote, he who went swimming as his wife gave birth and returned to find the home-liest of children, his beautiful offspring having scampered off in every di-rection. "You are scrubby-looking," he told those who remained, "but you will be greater than those who went away."[9]

Austin's passion for Indian lore barely outweighed another, the lives and traditions of Mexicans and other Spanish-speaking peoples. In Lone Pine she could stroll beyond the dusty, cottonwooded main street, with its tum-bledown buildings and two saloons, toward the Mexican quarter, a place of white adobe walls sporting ropes of reddening chilies. Here she learned to cook chicken with chili, soup and meat balls with chili, and a sauce for en-chiladas made of tomatoes, onion, grated cheese, and olives—with chili. If the Greeks boasted wine and olives as symbols of civilization, the local Mex-icans pointed to the chili-laden tamales and enchiladas of Austin's friend and unofficial Spanish teacher, Señora Josefa Maria de la Luz Ortiz y Romero.

Not long after the move to Lone Pine, Austin returned from one of her daily walks to find a trunk, her own, dumped unceremoniously outside the hotel. The Austins and their belongings had been evicted. With no money to pay their overdue bill and Wallace away on the irrigation project, she could think of nothing except to use the trunk as a seat. She sat for hours, exposed to the stares of passers-by and trying not to break down. At last a kindly woman stopped and told her of a boarding house on the outskirts of town where she might find lodging. After a sweating walk in the afternoon heat, which built with her frustration, Austin presented her bedraggled, preg-nant self to Mrs. Dodge, the German landlady of a farmhouse-sanatorium catering to men with lead poisoning, otherwise known as "miners' rot." She persuaded Mrs. Dodge, whose cook had recently quit, to let her make the day's pies. As she cut butter into flour, rolled dough, and crimped edges, she railed against her husband. When Wallace found his wife that evening, she had become a different woman. She continued to follow the routines a young wife does for a husband who comes home and expects to be fed, but now a dull sense of duty had taken the place of respect.

Introduced to Wallace, the landlady smelled a rat. " 'You don't look like you was goin' to be able to earn your board and his'n," she said.[10] Austin remembered that her mother had taught her to sew, and Mrs. Dodge relented. The next three months, between baking and mending, Austin listened to the stories of fellow boarders and to the man of the house, Mr. Dodge, who spoke in strings of idioms salted with blasphemies from the mining camps. Austin learned them all. Lupe, the common-law wife of a gambler named Bill Withrow (the one man beside Wallace in town to wear starched shirts) taught her Spanish songs and dances. Together they collected a shoebox full of bats, in whose mouths they stuck miniature lighted cigarettes before setting the creatures free. Lupe thought that ill luck, sickness, and spite fled with the bats, and Austin, who listened sympathetically to almost anyone, took her seriously. Surprisingly, Austin thought herself a slow learner, because, as she said, she needed time to know things in her bones. People, especially outcast people, she knew with uncanny quickness.

According to popular mythology about the West, Austin should have had room to express herself in the open spaces of the Owens Valley. She lived, however, in raw towns begot by greed and fed by the railroads, where standards for womanly behavior matched the strictness of those in Boston, Massachusetts, or Carlinville, Illinois. Since she spoke freely and cared little for the distinctions society prescribed, the locals thought her odd. No matter how much men like those at Lost Burro Mine showed their respect, her neighbors felt less threatened by Lupe—whose lovers had fought for her with knives—than by a "lady" with a mind of her own.

In September 1892, Austin traveled to her mother's house in Bakersfield to await the birth of her baby, leaving Wallace, at loose ends after abandoning the irrigation ditch, to camp outside of Lone Pine. As she felt her baby move and contemplated its future, she already weighed the pros and cons of divorce. Her family would reluctantly take her back, yet to what avail? They offered at most grudging affection and despaired of her ambitions. Though divorce was becoming more common—and the subject of fiction in William Dean Howells's *A Modern Instance* (1882)—a divorced woman still faced censure. Western chivalry did not extend to erring wives, and irreconcilable differences held no sway in the court of public opinion that turned a blind eye on drunkards and wife beaters. Not so much as hinting at such abuses, Austin could only cite incompatibility or differences in temperament. Wallace shared many of his wife's values, above all respect for the natural world and a passion for hiking, climbing, and camping in the mountains. Apart from being the father of their soon-to-be-born child, he also took pleasure in her work. Like anyone torn between conflicting emotions and impossible choices, Austin wavered, regretting their failure to come together as a couple and, in less despondent moods, hoping that once she and Wallace learned to talk together, they might come to an understanding. The problem remained: what then?

Yet for all her good intentions, Austin could not forgive her husband the humiliations she endured in Lone Pine. She would say that "having grown up on a carelessly kept plantation," with a sense of social superiority that "accrues to Nordics living among brown peoples," he knew little about the kind of economies that had allowed the Hunters a measure of gentility. He made his wife feel vulgar when she broached the topic of money and could not understand why she promised to pay creditors rather than declare bankruptcy. Without her knowledge he had, after their farming debacle, secretly incurred more debt, which creditors expected her mother and brother to assume. Austin felt more bitterness toward Wallace when she learned that he had declined the job of principal at the local school. According to Mrs. Dodge, his refusal had triggered their eviction from the Lone Pine Hotel. When asked why he had not prevented his wife from being evicted, he replied, "How would that have helped?"[11]

The couple's disagreements about money reflected deeper incompatibilities. Olivia Lattimore in Austin's *A Woman of Genius* (1912) says of her marriage that "young things we were, who had not fairly known each other as man and woman before we were compelled to trace in one another the lineaments of parents, all attention drawn away from the imperative business of framing a common ideal, to centre on the child."[12] Just as disenchanted with her own marriage, Austin blamed her mother—and the age in which she lived—for her ignorance about sex. To one witness, she and Wallace appeared unconnected from the beginning of their courtship, and whether from natural reserve or inbred manners, seldom touched or talked about each other. Another couple might have fallen back on passion when talk failed. Not these two. Austin hoped that she and Wallace might build a marriage on an intellectual basis; she had not plumbed the depth of his reticence. "He never once came toward her," she would write; "was most silent when there was most need of talking; absent when there was the sharpest demand for his presence. . . . Once he had given himself to me, my husband never looked at another woman; but also he never looked with me at any single thing."[13] In her story, "Frustrate," the narrator says of her husband, "I . . . wonder if he has the least idea how disappointed I am. I even have days of wondering if Henry isn't disappointed, too."[14]

On 30 October 1892, Austin gave birth to a daughter she named Ruth. Nothing could have prepared her for the agony. At one point, the doctor left for several hours to amputate a man's leg crushed in an accident. Nine days after Ruth's birth, Susanna demanded that her bedridden daughter show some spirit and get up. The next months would be one long torment. "I know now," Austin wrote in 1927, "that I did not have proper medical treatment, but at the time nothing much was thought of such things. My memory of the first seven or eight years of marriage is like some poor martyr's memory of the wheel and the rack, all the best things of marriage obscured by a fog of drudgery impossible to be met and by recurrent physical anguish."[15] Afflicted with what might now be diagnosed as postpartum depression, she had come "to the end of her . . . resources" but not the end of her suffering.[16] Intense chest pains related to the strain of Ruth's birth would later be diagnosed as angina, though Austin may also have suffered, like her father before her, from asthma, aggravated by the high altitude of the Owens Valley.

One temporary palliative arrived with the November 1892 issue of *Overland Monthly*, which featured "The Mother of Felipe," her first published story. The magazine paid three dollars a page upon publication, and Austin, still recovering at her mother's house, sent twelve dollars, her entire earnings, to Wallace at Christmas. The new year brought another change in fortune. Setting aside his aversion to teaching, Wallace found employment in a district school at George's Creek, a few miles from Lone Pine. He had not yet seen his daughter and, with Ruth nestled in a market basket, Austin boarded a train that would take her back to Inyo County—"that ragged edge of the world"—and to a husband who, for all she knew, had changed as much as herself in the last six months.[17]

If Austin sensed from the beginning that something was not quite right with her baby, she feared that asking might make it true. The acerbic, alcoholic Dr. Woodin attended mother and daughter through the early months. He and Austin whiled away chunks of time playing poker, as he waited for her to come to her own heartbreaking awareness. Ruth suffered from a mental disability—never diagnosed—that delayed her speech and made her behavior unpredictable. During the first year of her daughter's life, Austin reminded herself that children develop at different rates. Lingering problems from the excruciating birth and what she saw as her own unfitness for childbearing finally prompted her to ask Dr. Woodin if she were to blame for Ruth's deficiencies. He tried to reassure her that the cause was genetic, that whatever had happened predated Ruth's birth. Remembering the forty-eight hours she had struggled in labor, she found his consolation hard to believe.

In her autobiography, Austin circles around her daughter's infirmity, the hurt and guilt of it still raw after a quarter century. She remembers lying sick in bed and watching one of the Paiute women who occasionally visited breastfeed Ruth along with her own child. Two or three years later, when Ruth had not begun to speak as she should, that same woman came "all the way to Lone Pine to bring her dried meadow-larks' tongues, which make the speech nimble and quick."[18] Neither Paiute remedies nor the ministrations of doctors had any effect. Though Ruth did learn to communicate with her mother and to play with children who soon outstripped her, those who knew her understood that she would never be able to function independently.

Ruth's condition helps to explain Austin's later obsession with questions of heredity. In the early 1890s, people still considered a child's developmental difficulties the result of a parent's moral degeneracy—a drunken father, for example, or a promiscuous mother. In years when state governments passed laws preventing people with disabilities from marrying and having children, forced sterilization was not uncommon. Toward the end of the nineteenth century, the eugenics movement, named by Charles Darwin's cousin, Sir Francis Galton, concerned itself with issues of human engineering and hierarchies of race and intelligence. In "Hereditary Character and Talent," Galton had argued: "If a twentieth part of the cost and pains were spent in measures for the improvement of the human race that is spent on the improvement of the breed of horses and cattle, what a galaxy of genius might we not create! We might introduce prophets and high priests of civilization into the world, as surely as we can propagate idiots by mating *cretins*."[19] In the same article Galton predicted that the temperament of the American Indian, widely considered melancholic and antisocial, would lead to the demise of the race. As late as 1935 the Nobel Prize recipient Alexis Carrel, in concert with Nazi policies, advocated death by gassing for criminals and the mentally disabled.

Ruth may or may not have been the main prompt to Austin's preoccupation with eugenic hypotheses and their application to minority populations. Certainly the prevailing views about disability led her to distrust science, or social science, of the early century—which dealt generically with American Indians, Chinese immigrants, African Americans, Jews, women of all sorts, and the physically and mentally handicapped. Biased and hierarchical science challenged her sympathy for the dispossessed Paiute and

Shoshone neighbors she had come to admire. It also prompted her inquiries into the nature of genius, the sources of inspiration, and the workings of art. Science, nevertheless, could do nothing to improve Ruth's condition. Not only did Austin bear and raise a handicapped child, she lived with the sad fact of her daughter's incapacity to grow up happy and self-sufficient. How much she believed in genetic inheritance—or Galton's eugenics—seemed to shift with the circumstances. She blamed her husband for Ruth's problems but clearly suffered for her own imagined guilt, and she can never have underestimated the consequences of that grueling and dangerous birth.

Through the first years of Ruth's childhood, Austin felt increasingly comfortable with those whom polite society overlooked or scorned. She joined Paiute women digging wild hyacinth roots on the mesa and learned from them which plants should be eaten and which reserved for medicine. (She devoted one of her notebooks to folk remedies for kidney trouble, teething babies, and fevers.) Her education extended to catching quail with a snare made of long hair and "tickling" trout from a stream. On one expedition, she almost lost Ruth to an eagle, which first approached the trout she had caught, then darted for the child asleep under a sage bush. Austin, by her own account, beat back the screaming bird with a hoe, and—her bloody arms still hurting—served Wallace trout for supper.

In 1894, Wallace, the newly appointed superintendent of Inyo County schools, accepted a better paid teaching position back in Lone Pine. Before finding permanent lodging, the family homesteaded on the mesa between monolithic red-orange rock forms called the Alabama Hills (named by Southern sympathizers for the battleship *Alabama*). Austin pursued her friendships with itinerant shepherds, some of whom she knew from her Rancho El Tejon days, and with local characters, including an Irishman named Fitz who talked nonstop about Napoleon Bonaparte and unloaded his pistol in any hotel refusing entry to his Indian wife. Austin met English travelers recuperating from tuberculosis or vacationing in the area, as well as miners from the eastern states, some of whom in flusher days had listened to Christine Nilsson sing in New York's Academy of Music. That fall, the Austins moved into town next to the saloon where Lupe's lover, Bill Withrow, shuffled cards and kept an eye open for tenderfoots.

Austin had kept Ruth's condition secret from her mother, guessing and dreading what lay ahead. "I went every summer," she writes, "to visit my mother, being in great need of her, and yet somehow always failing to make a vital connection."[20] Trying to please Susanna, she wrote a number of pieces using her mother's given and maiden names—Savilla Graham—which won no maternal thanks. Though Susanna avidly read *The Atlantic Monthly* and *Harper's,* she curtly dismissed any congratulations about her daughter's work: it was, she said, beyond her. The little celebrity that Austin began to earn as one of California's new writers alarmed her mother and infuriated her older brother. When interviewers sought her opinion about the treatment of juvenile delinquency or the regulations of marital relationships, Jim ordered her to obey what he called "domestic propriety."[21]

If, in such a climate, Austin found it awkward or unbearable to broach the subject of Ruth's troubles, that alone cannot explain the way she and Wallace chose to announce their plight. Without warning, they asked friends traveling to Bakersfield to deposit Ruth at her grandmother's for an extended visit. "I don't know what I expected," Austin later wrote, "that she would discover the truth; . . . that she would come to me and that we would weep and console one another." Instead she received a letter from Jim demanding that they fetch Ruth immediately. Wallace agreed to make the journey. No one, not Wallace or Austin or the rest of the Hunter family mentioned Ruth's condition until a letter arrived from Susanna with this message: "I don't know what you've done, daughter, to have such a judgment upon you."[22] Austin never spoke to her mother again.

In 1895, without money and committed to providing lifelong security for Ruth, Austin accepted a teaching position in the town of Bishop, about sixty miles north of Lone Pine. She may also have considered the remove to Bishop as a temporary escape or a trial separation from her husband. Either way, she met with frustration. Boarding in the Drake Hotel on Main Street, she had not considered how to fulfill her teaching responsibilities *and* care for Ruth, who frequently erupted in tantrums. Ruth hurt herself running wildly in small quarters, and Austin's desperate ploy of strapping her in a chair quickly sowed gossip among those, like Susanna, predisposed to see the girl's condition as God's punishment of the mother. When she went off to work, Austin left Ruth unattended; returning, she met with belligerent silence the few caring souls who took it upon themselves to tidy up after the child. In *Lost Borders,* Austin wrote from experience about her dead protagonist: "Emma Jeffries had taken death as she had taken everything in life hard. She had met it with the same bright surface competency that she had presented to the . . . affliction of her crippled child; and the intensity of her wordless struggle against it had caught the attention of the townspeople and held it in a shocked curious awe." Lonely in a place "where so little ever happened that even trouble was a godsend if it gave you something to talk about," Austin at first found no friends or confidantes in Bishop—and scarcely any sympathetic strangers.[23] She did eventually find a temporary home for Ruth with a childless couple named Frager.

Austin's situation recalls that of a fellow writer and soon-to-be friend, Charlotte Perkins Gilman, who, struggling with severe depression after giving birth, awarded custody of her daughter to her husband, the painter Charles Walter Stetson and Stetson's second wife, Grace Ellery Channing. "To hear what was said and read what was printed," Gilman wrote, "one would think I had handed over a baby in a basket . . . , but in companionship with her beloved father she grew up to be the artist she is, with advantages I could never have given her. I lived without her, temporarily, but why did they think I liked it? She was all I had. . . . What were those pious condemners thinking of?"[24] Austin, who might have asked the same question about those who thought her an unfit mother, tended to be more oblique. There were, she said, "so few people who ever had the courage to know about my Ruth."[25] Austin admired Gilman "for the freedom from convention that left her the right to care for her child in what seemed the best way." Unlike Gilman, she had nowhere to turn for financial support, and, after teaching all day, little or no energy left for her writing.

Thanks to several new and unexpected acquaintances, the gossip about Ruth's care gradually subsided. She met the Wattersons, well-to-do sheep ranchers, whose children she taught. Largely because the Wattersons took Ruth in stride, Austin could relax with them. Weekends at their ranch, as Ruth played happily outside, she gathered herself together. Not just supporting her at a bad time, the Wattersons serendipitously contributed to the lyrical style that would become Austin's trademark in books like *The Land of Little Rain* and *Lost Borders*. She had been thinking about how to tell a story in brief, suggestive increments when she happened to watch the Wattersons' dogs respond to calls and gestures that could not possibly convey the shepherd's full meaning. If a flick of the wrist meant "Sheep missing on the left; go and find them," what possibilities, what power, must there be within a single phrase of her own?[26] From sources like the canny sheepdogs and their masters or the skilled storytelling of Native Americans, Austin found the premise of her books: that patterns of speech and gesture reflect underlying social and cultural realities, along with the tangled complexities of human experience.

During her first year in Bishop, Austin entered into friendship with a Miss Williams, a teacher at the Indian school, and with another family of sheep ranchers named Birchim, who lived near an encampment of Paiutes in Round Valley and whose son, a student of Paiute culture, could repeat chants and stories. Williams sharpened Austin's awareness about government policies that made it a crime for Indians to speak their own language, practice their religion, or wear traditional dress. The law singled out males by prohibiting them from having the shoulder-length hair that confirmed their manhood. Then there were the notorious Indian schools, with policies that favored boys over girls and turned the girls into dishwashers, seamstresses, and launderers. In some schools, children were chained to beds, fed on maggot-infested meat, beaten, and forced to carry heavy cordwood. Austin took some consolation in the fact that students at Williams's school at least had contact with their families and tribe, which, in turn, had to adjust to changing conditions, including the realities of intermarriage.

"A Case of Conscience" addresses social and ethnic conflicts in the tale of a tubercular Englishman, Saunders, who falls in love with a Shoshone woman named Turwhasé. After several years, Saunders learns that his lungs have miraculously healed and must decide whether to bring his two-year-old daughter back to England; he does not consider bringing the mother. Saunders's Anglo-Saxon sense of "duty" decides the case. Without consulting Turwhasé, he steals the child away, begins a long, slogging journey, and finally reaches a town. There he confronts his failure. He cannot bear the thought that "men, white men, mining men, mill superintendents, well-dressed, competent, looked at the brat which had Shoshone written plainly all over it, and looked away unsmiling." By the time Turwhasé tracks him down and demands her child, he is only too glad to hand back to her the little "prehensile" body.[27] Without hammering a moral, the story takes the form of a parable, in which virtue prevails and false honor reveals itself as cowardice, while Native decency overcomes pseudo-civilization.

Austin spent a great deal of time at the large Bishop campoody (also "campodee" or "campoodie"), Mark Twain's coinage for an Indian village that, to Austin, suggested a communal way of life. There she observed grandfathers settle themselves into their favorite places, roll a cigarette, and, after a satisfying smoke, enter into storytelling. All these "one smoke" stories began with Coyote and with the same first line: "Once long ago when we were all the same . . . ."[28] The Paiutes, who normally kept their tribal names secret, especially from federal census takers, honored Austin with a tribal name, See-goo-chee, the woman-who-gives-good-things-to-eat.[29] She credited her natural sympathy for these neighbors to what she called her own "far-off and slightly mythical Indian ancestor."[30] During her time in Bishop, two young girls who had stayed behind to sweep out the school-house were raped by a group of white men—some from the town's "best" families—who received no punishment. Austin condemned these rapes, which were treated as pranks and ignored as "mahala chasing."

To put such abuses in context, it had been a mere five years since December 1890, when three hundred Indians died at Wounded Knee, and if that battle marked the so-called end of the Indian Wars, it aggravated the social and racial hatred that Austin encountered in the Owens Valley. Perhaps because of her loneliness or sense of injustice, she felt increasingly drawn to campoody neighbors, especially their rituals, which, combined with borrowings from other religions and the Methodist teachings of her childhood, helped to satisfy her spiritual longings. Not, however, without consequences. Though she went so far as to renew her membership in the Methodist church, the plight of Indians (and Mexicans) brought Austin to the realization that she could no longer call herself a Christian.

She found her closest companion not in the campoody but in the town she hated. A young woman doctor, Helen MacKnight (later Doyle), or Dr. Nellie, as the locals referred to her, had been a pupil at the Inyo Academy, where Austin now taught English, art, literature, and calisthenics. After medical school in San Francisco, MacKnight came back to live with her abusive father, who had deserted her mother in Connecticut and saw his doctor-daughter as a meal ticket. Like Wallace Austin, MacKnight's father suffered from gold-dust fever. He was a surveyor, who once named a mine for his daughter, in lieu of child or spousal support.[31] The doctor made her rounds in a two-wheeled cart, navigating roads blocked by fallen boulders and barbed-wire gates. Like other women doctors—they were still a rarity—MacKnight had been the butt of jokes and sexual innuendos and was shunned by male colleagues who refused to consult with her. A few near-miraculous cures and the successful delivery of twins finally endeared her to the community. Living in her office, which doubled as dispensary, MacKnight owned one of the town's few washtubs. Austin would drop by evenings to sit before MacKnight's stove and read aloud the stories she had written. Decades later Austin agreed to write an introduction to her friend's autobiography, *A Child Went Forth* (1934), and MacKnight, still fascinated by the "small, plain, brown woman, with too much hair, [and] always a little sick," revisited the Bishop days in *Mary Austin: Woman of Genius* (1939).[32]

Austin returned to Lone Pine at Christmas, 1895, to find Wallace's mother and sister visiting and her husband in crisis. Teaching remained as much a torment as ever to Wallace, who dreamed of "getting into something"—though he did not know what that something might be. "There was a spell of the land" over him, Austin wrote, which worked on him like the most beautiful woman. "It was proof against all prior claims, and required no justification. It is the way Beauty works to set up in men the desire to master and make it fruitful. But it is the restraining condition of Beauty in the arid West that man cannot simply appropriate individual holdings of it." She adds that when men like Wallace began to talk about their claims and the riches to come, their wives looked "at one another with sharp—or weary—implications of exasperated resignation."[33] Resignation came hard for Austin, who determined somehow to get Wallace or herself away from his beloved Inyo County.

Life, as if conspiring against her, hit hard in the summer of 1896. Her mother wrote to inform her about an illness, saying nothing about its severity. With as much pride and stubbornness as her daughter, Susanna had apparently kept silent since her vicious letter following Ruth's stay. This letter, with its understated urgency, laid Austin low. When she received Jim's telegram summoning her home, the triweekly stage had already left. She decided to take a later train that wound a longer route by way of Reno. About dusk on the day of the telegram, Wallace coaxed his fretting wife out of the house while he fed Ruth and put her to bed. Too tired to resist, Austin slumped on the front stoop. In the third-person account from her autobiography, Susanna appeared to her in the twilight, "all in white as Mary recalled her when Father was still a young man, with a rose in her hair, pink and sweetly smiling. . . . She said there was no need for Mary to take the train now, since everything was well with her, and Mary believed her." Austin told Wallace she would not be going to Bakersfield and fell asleep. The next morning, she woke in tears to receive another telegram announcing her mother's death. Jim quoted Susanna's surprising last words to Jim: "Take care of Mary." Whatever their differences, Austin acknowledged the profound effects of her mother's loss. She would never have the opportunity to prove herself to Susanna or feel the motherly comfort of her arms. "There is an element of incalculable ravening," she wrote, "in the loss of your mother; . . . there is the psychic wound, the severed root of being."[34]

She grieved for all her mother had and had not been, for her own failure to please, and for the energy spent in sustaining anger. Austin's autobiography and letters show how her mistakes, losses, and self-doubts had to be counted like beads on a rosary until the multiple tellings and retellings muted the ache for a time. In the months following Susanna's death, Austin reflected on the whole vexed question of what it meant to be a woman. If fiction has anything to say about its author's life, Olivia Lattimore, the heroine in *A Woman of Genius,* mirrors Austin herself. Like Olivia she saw herself battling women such as Pauline Mills, a middle-class wife and mother who requires other women to conform to a soul-killing, self-congratulatory pattern of respectability. "Under disguising names of womanliness, of tact, of religion even, this humiliating necessity, this compulsive fear goes through all our social use like mould, corrupting the bread of life."[35] Drawn to women like Charlotte Perkins Gilman and Susan B. Anthony, Austin decided she must renounce the power of pleasing, loving, and helping, as an older generation had renounced crinolines.

She came back to Wallace and Lone Pine, in the fall of 1897, to find that money problems had worsened and that she had little choice except earning more to reduce the family debt. She reckoned a decade to pay "on the nail" for the unfettered, debt-free future she demanded. Then, before the school term ended, and without consulting his wife, Wallace accepted a position as registrar of the Desert Land Office at Independence, a smaller town about fifteen miles north of Lone Pine. Austin agreed to take on his teaching responsibilities along with her own. Though finally qualified to teach grammar school in Inyo County, she had earned her certificate with her lowest score in composition—forty-four out of fifty.

Her return to Wallace had been indirect, by way of San Francisco and Oakland. It did not escape the townspeople that her homecoming followed a long stint in a San Francisco hospital, recovering from an unspecified illness that interrupted her school year. Not only did neighbors gossip about the illness and her overlong absence, they charged that her assisting in Wallace's school smelled of nepotism. Their opinions may not have mattered to Austin, who would remember for the rest of her life the visit she had paid in Oakland to her hero, the Harvard psychologist and philosopher, William James, whom she knew as the author of *The Principles of Psychology* (1891) and *The Will to Believe and Other Essays on Popular Psychology* (1897). In the years he worked toward *The Varieties of Religious Experience* (1902), he and Austin shared an intense curiosity about the nature and existence of God, the possibility of survival after death, and the lessons inherent in diverse states of consciousness. When Austin met James, she was twenty-six, he fifty-eight. As a young man he had an Errol Flynn profile, but with a receding hairline, extraordinarily high forehead, and permanently raised left eyebrow, he looked like the affable scientist he had since become. Austin might not have planned her wardrobe as carefully as Edith Wharton planned hers for a first meeting with James's brother, Henry. If she did, the women's frilled clothing of the day would have lent her wistful face a matronly cast. She tended to wear her hair tightly pulled off her face and pinned up, which highlighted the fullness of her lips and the dark sweeps of brow nearly meeting above her wide-set eyes. She had the courage or cheek to call on James at his hotel and he, with a soft spot for women, promptly agreed to see her.

Psychology had made important advances in the last half century, thanks to the German Karl Eduard von Hartmann, the Frenchman Jean-Martin Charcot (a teacher of Sigmund Freud), and the Englishman William Benjamin Carpenter (who led the way in fields of "mental physiology," along with "marine biology"). But relative to biology, say, or physics, psychology remained in its infancy. Whereas some psychologists still pursued outdated areas such as phrenology, reflexology, or newer models of associationism that relied on John Locke's model of the mind as a blank slate, William James, like Carpenter, sought a biological basis for mental science without negating the function of free will. He popularized his field with personal essays written in lucid, conversational prose—which he thought his novelist-brother might profitably emulate. James's brilliance for Austin lay in statements he made, for example, in the essays that formed *The Will to Believe* about religious faith and spirituality. Like James, Austin wanted to believe in a world where truth could be comprehended and goodness existed; otherwise, moral choices lost their import. She later dismissed Freud's categories of the id, ego, and the superego as empty and belittled his followers as amateur astrologists. In an essay, "The Kitchen Complex" (1920), she indulges in this light satire: "It is not until you have occasion to comment on the weaknesses of your friends without at the same time causing them to lose their tempers, that you fully appreciate the contribution of psychoanalysis to modern thinking. You can always say they have complexes which are always supposed to have happened to you in your extreme youth, and somebody else is to blame for them."[36]

Although by now a recognized author, with recent stories appearing in the *Overland Monthly*—"The Wooing of the Señorita" and "The Conversion of Ah Lew Sing" (March and November 1897)—Austin wanted and still thought she lacked an essential understanding of her process of writing. The meeting with James freed her for new directions. "The beginning of an intelligent method for my work," she wrote, "was a long talk I had with William James, in which he said, and afterward said in one of his books, I think, that the secret of creative thinking lay in that vast area of the mind which, for want of a better word, we call the sub-consciousness. From that time I began to treat my mind as part of the whole Mind, and to try to reach those attributes of the Mind which deal with the sort of thing I want to do."[37] The relationship she intuits between private reverie (the work of the unconscious in dreams or semiwaking states) and artistic expression (the disguised and public form of fantasy) would continue to interest James, as it did Freud. When Freud, the maligned author of *The Interpretation of Dreams* (1899) and "Creative Writers and Day-Dreaming" (1908), lectured at Clark University in 1909, William James entertained him, walking through the gardens while stricken by excruciating bouts of angina.

From her visits to the Bishop campoody and her relationship with a Paiute healer named Tinnemaha, Austin came to believe that the world evaded the best of logic; it had to exist on faith. From Tinnemaha, Austin discovered prayer to be an inner process "expressed in bodily acts, in words, in music, rhythm, color, whatever medium served the purpose, or all of them."[38] Since her undergraduate days at Blackburn, she had been moving both toward and away from formal scientific studies, as her engagement with eugenics suggests. Committed to empirical observation and careful description, she also felt part of the "world mind," to use the phrase of Josiah Royce, the California-born idealist and friend of William James. For Royce, "world mind" meant a separate, all-embracing creative force or logos. Austin would take the title of her autobiography, *Earth Horizon,* from a "Rain Song of the Sia," in which a wanderer seeks "the Sacred Middle," where all horizons are equidistant and the mind can be at rest.[39] At the same time, she employs a word forever associated with William James, calling herself a "pragmatist" in religion who "temperamentally demanded that something more should come out of mystical experience than the mere ecstatic notice of its taking place." One had to go to the circus to enjoy it.[40]

Austin *knew* that as a young child she had experienced a mystical episode, and that, too, made her leery of strictly scientific explanations of the universe. Standing under a walnut tree, the girl and wind and tree and sky had come "alive together with a pulsing light of consciousness."[41] As an adult, she had visions of Christ, which she usually describes not as mystical so much as the natural consequence of an open mind or the result of prayer. She believed she could adopt the character of another person, an Indian woman, for instance, and slip across boundaries of ego until the process seemed second nature. She carried this thinking into her writing by trying to feel or in a sense live a story before she wrote it. As she worked on her first novel, *Isidro,* she wanted "some account of a place far inland, a two days ride."

> I was living in Inyo [she recalled]. I tried a common device with me, that of sending my subconscious self at night to try and find the facts I wanted. I tried this for several nights with no sensible results. I could remember nothing whatever. So I supposed that I should be obliged to invent. A week or so later when I began to write that chapter, I found something very good came quite easily. I did not at that time suspect its veridicality. I called the place I described Las Chimineas, the chimneys. A year or so after the story was published I met a woman who reproached me for saying that I did not know the country described, as I had accurately described a place known to her as the 'pinnacles.'"[42]

Such coincidences formed part of her everyday reality. In 1919, she would tell a correspondent that religious experience "is nothing more or less than a subconscious view of Truth or Oneness or the Universe, or whatever you . . . call it. Let us just say God for short."[43] She associates these extra-rational experiences with acts of prayer but also with the license she took from her conversation with James, as if he allowed her to think in new ways. Austin left James as the sun set and lights came on across the San Francisco Bay, reassured about her thinking and her ability to hold her own. James in turn sent her a list of recommended reading, including his Oakland lecture "Power through Repose."

Austin had been given a glimpse of the lives led by artists when she went, in the summer of 1899, to the flamboyant Charles Lummis's perennially open house in Los Angeles, then a city of a little more than fifty thousand inhabitants. She rented a place not far from the Lummises, whose stone and adobe house, called El Alisal, sat in a sycamore grove on the west bank of the Arroyo Seco. From his garden, Lummis could look up and down the usually dry riverbed and out across a broad reach of canyon, with hills that were lush green in winter and burned sandy brown in summer. The house lay about three miles to the northeast of downtown Los Angeles, or as Lummis would have said, three miles from Olvera Street, site of the early Spanish settlement. El Alisal, construction of which lasted fourteen years, reflected its owner, a man with ambitions that seemed to require an entire ranchero. Lummis was as committed as Edward Beale and Mary Austin to promoting Mexican and American Indian causes. A prodigious collector and the guiding spirit for the Southwest Museum, he designed El Alisal with every room opening on a central patio, in the middle of which stood a magnificent sycamore he called El Alcalde Mayor. The author and editor of the omnibus *Land of Sunshine* since 1893, Lummis said that "any fool can write a book and most of them do, but it takes brains to build a house."[44] When Austin first visited El Alisal, it consisted of one finished large room; the other rooms remained rough huts. The house grew with Lummis's ambitions. Today it remains as a state monument, intact and cared for, though unfortunately close on its eastern side to the rush of traffic along the Pasadena Freeway. The Southwest Museum, on a nearby hill, has become the Southwest Museum of the American Indian, a satellite of the Autry National Center.

Austin went to Los Angeles ostensibly to consult doctors about Ruth; in fact to stay in the city if she could find employment, as she did, by giving lectures to prospective teachers on Western nature study. She hoped for enough money to allow Wallace to give up his registrar's position in Independence. During the next year, she became a fixture at the Lummises and a lifelong friend of Charles's second wife, Eve, then pregnant with a third child. The Lummises' domestic arrangements intrigued Austin. Charles's first wife, a physician named Dorothea Rhodes, had stepped aside when her husband fell in love with Eve Douglas. Eve made the same offer when she found out that Lummis had lied to her about his relationship with Dorothea. The women visited one another, no doubt commiserating about Lummis' habitual womanizing. "My heart is so full of bitterness toward my husband," Eve would write in 1905. "I always envy those people who have troubles they can mention."[45] If Austin counted both women among her friends, Charles Lummis outdid her by dedicating *The Land of Poco Tiempo* "To Eva and Dorothea."

People gathered at El Alisal "to be met; to be challenged or to challenge; to be identified and remembered." [46] Guests from across the United States and Mexico conversed in Spanish, French, and English, while their host led the singing of Spanish ballads—between courses served by moccasined Mojave servants. Lummis represented, in his opinion and that of many friends, the center of literary activities in Los Angeles. Through him, Austin met Charlotte Perkins Gilman and Grace Ellery Channing, an editor for a time of the *Land of Sunshine* and a friend in whom Austin would confide. Lummis often entertained contributors to the magazine, among them Edwin Markham, famous for his proletarian poem "The Man with the Hoe"; William Keith, the painter; and Frederick "Fred" Webb Hodge, the author of *A Handbook of American Indians North of Mexico,* who for decades to come generously shared his knowledge with Austin. On return visits to Los Angeles, either to lecture at the normal school (now the University of California, Los Angeles) or to see the Lummises, Austin would meet the reformer Jane Addams, as well as local eccentrics such as Harrison Gray Otis (credited with introducing the finger bowl to Angelinos), and Lummis's detested rival, the handsome George Wharton James, editor of the *Mt. Lowe Echo,* and a Lothario who lost his Methodist ministry for adultery.

At a critical time, Lummis provided a model for Austin's career. Thirty-one years old, she had yet to publish her first book. Lummis, at forty, had published eleven, including *The Spanish Pioneers* (1893) and *The Man Who Married the Moon and Other Pueblo Folk-Stories* (1894). A Harvard-educated writer and more than amateur ethnologist, he had begun his career as a reporter-editor of the *Scioto Gazette* and made his reputation by walking from Chillicothe, Ohio, to Los Angeles to accept a job with the Los Angeles *Daily Times.* He dedicated *A Tramp Across the Continent* (1892), a mixture—in the wake of Mark Twain's *Roughing It*—of tall tales, self-puffery, and travelogue, to Twain's friend Charles Dudley Warner, himself an author and editor. Partially paralyzed by a stroke in 1887, Lummis spent five years recovering on a New Mexico ranch among the Indians of Pueblo Ysleta. There he met Eve, who, visiting her sister from Connecticut, volunteered to nurse the invalid. After archeological expeditions to Peru and Bolivia, in 1892, Lummis returned to Los Angeles to begin anew. He collected folktales and transcribed or recorded nearly a thousand old Spanish and Indian songs. In 1905, the board of the Los Angeles library elected him city librarian. He served five years, "eagerly grasping the opportunity to brand the city's books as if they were cattle, to stamp warning notices on such reference works that he considered untrustworthy, and to write annual bombastic reports," all of which cost him his job.[47]

The clean-shaven, perennially tanned Lummis, nicknamed Don Carlos, wore beaded belts, wide-brimmed hats, and sometimes a red serape. He had, a would-be acolyte noted, much of the poseur in him.[48] A less sympathetic critic wrote:

My name is Lummis, I'm the West!
For culture I don't give a hang;
I hate the puny East, although
I can't conceal my Yankee twang.
My trousers they are corduroy,
Ditto my jacket and my vest;
For I'm the wild and woolly boy.
My name is Lummis, I'm the West!
Who first beheld the Indian race?
Columbus, say you? 'Tisn't true.
I was the first to see his face;
I've had him copyrighted too.
I am the mountains and the sea,
I am the salty plain between;
You've seen the orange crop; That's Me,
I did it with my magazine.[49]

Lummis summarized his own career in this way: "For nearly forty years I have been writing in and of the million square miles which include New Mexico, Arizona, Southern California, and adjoining parts of Colorado, Utah, Texas, and Northern Mexico—an area to which I was first to apply, over a third of a century ago, the generic christening by which it is now commonly known—THE SOUTHWEST. My books were the first to make widely known most of the marvels of that incomparable Wonder Land."[50] Writing his own epitaph, he was more modest:

He founded the Southwest Museum
He built this house [El Alisal, which holds his ashes]
He saved four old missions
He studied and recorded Spanish America
He tried to do his share.[51]

Lummis's editorship of the *Land of Sunshine* made him an arbiter and to some extent a shaper of Western literature. For each issue of the monthly, he wrote a column of brief "book notes" in addition to at least one feature-length article and an editorial ("The Lion's Den"). He also organized the league of Western writers, through which members held stock options in the *Land of Sunshine* and provided a steady stream of contributions. Lummis and his circle intended the magazine's Western themes to rival the content of Eastern magazines such as *The Atlantic Monthly* or *The Nation*, which Lummis admired. *Land of Sunshine* shamelessly promoted all things Californian, especially its history and contributions to the arts and sciences. A typical number, for February 1896, contained articles on serape weaving, Los Angeles's Chinatown, and architecture unique to the Southwest. A photograph of the decaying mission at San Juan Capistrano served as the frontispiece; the caption read, "How Our Landmarks Are Going."[52] An accomplished photographer, Lummis packed photographs into feature articles on Western painters and ethnologists like John C. Fillmore, who pioneered the field of aboriginal folk music. Every number included a column called "The Angle of Reflection," directed at women. Lummis printed monthly accounts of two organizations he founded: the Sequoia League, which bought land for the Natives of Warner's Ranch; and the Landmarks Club, which pushed for restoration of Spanish missions such as San Juan Capistrano and St. Luis Rey.

Much as Austin's interests in Native and Spanish societies paralleled those of Lummis, her approach differed from the outset. He saw himself her mentor, addressing her as "dear child," and also as her rival, at times assuming a tone she found—as others found hers—presumptuous or offensive. "If you are 'not in the least ashamed of your ignorance of Spanish derivations' then you ought to be," he scolded her in 1904. "If you want to take a historic period, or a geographic setting, to make fame or money, for you—or even—let us say, in the very extreme of liberality, to fulfill your mission toward rounding out literature—you are entitled to give them a fair bargain. . . . When you use Spanish names, it is your business as a decent woman, and as a writer, to have them right. . . . What would you think of yourself if, as a Californian, writing of California, you described seasons as they are in New England?"[53]

Austin thought that Lummis grew to dislike her because she "did things he tried and couldn't. I don't think it matters," she told a friend. "His work was less important than he'd like to think it, but probably all of our work is like that."[54] She "felt that he placed too heavy an emphasis upon the lesser achievements; on working too many hours a day; on sleeping too little; on drinking too much; on his wife's translations of Spanish manuscripts."[55] Their shared passion for Native and Mexican art and history aside, Lummis needed to be the impresario of literary Los Angeles; Austin wanted power as a writer. Lummis anticipated and encouraged Austin's work, yet he never wrote a book comparable to *The Land of Little Rain,* the achievement of which he had the generosity to recognize. From the earliest of her stories, Austin had a consciousness about her material and storytelling that Lummis never found. "The Wooing of the Señorita," which makes fun of "a man of ideas" who goes to California to test his theories about the superiority of savages, shows Austin's grasp of her own precarious role, and perhaps hints at Lummis's excesses.

Though irritated by Lummis, she remembered gratefully the years of her apprenticeship with him and with his like-minded friends who believed in her talent. Long after many of Lummis's circle had fallen from public notice, Austin wrote to Eve: "You remind me . . . that I once said that my friends were jealous of me. If I said that what I meant was merely the friends who began to write when I did, whom I afterwards passed on the way towards success; and that was always sad to me, because no one would have liked better than I that all of us should have gone along together."[56] The Lummises and their friends not only gave her professional support, they legitimized what Wallace, with many of her neighbors in Lone Pine and Independence, considered to be downright oddity. "I couldn't talk to Mr. Austin about experiences into which he never entered, nor wished to enter. He was of course kind about going through the motions of listening to me talk *about* my artist life, but I suspect that at heart, though he was too much of a gentleman to say so, he also thought them 'queer.'"[57] Lummis credited her ways of seeing and experiencing life and pushed her thinking. If to some of his friends she appeared naive, most agreed that when this woman with tragic, brooding features entered a room and spoke in a rhythmic prose all her own, she filled the space. Her time with the Lummises allowed her resolve, as she wrote in an early diary, not to be "afraid to fear, nor ashamed of any of the motions of life."[58]

At the end of the school term, Austin learned that the normal school wanted to renew her contract. "Would Wallace come to Los Angeles?" she asked, "the opportunity wouldn't stay open indefinitely. But strangely he didn't see it that way; he had not been all this time seeing it that way . . . he had given himself the more completely to Inyo."[59] Austin reluctantly agreed to join Wallace in Independence—a town of a few hundred residents—with the requisite two saloons, one hotel, and a store crammed with spools of wire, ammunition, ladies' hats, and tools. When it rained, the creek that ran through town turned the wagon-trafficked streets to mud. Life in such towns was "deadly, appallingly dull," she wrote. "The stark house, the rubbishy streets, the women who went about in them in calico wrappers, the draggling speech of the men, the wide, shadowless table-lands, the hard, bright skies, and the days all of one pattern, that went so stilly by that you only knew it was afternoon when you smelled the fried cabbage Mrs. Mulligan was cooking for supper."[60]

Austin would live in Independence seven years, five of them in a brown, wooden cottage they built on Market Street in 1900. The county seat, Independence had been restored after an 1872 earthquake toppled the court-house and most of the town's predominately adobe houses. The Austin house—still one of the town's most attractive—had a study, the first of many Mary would call a "wickiup" or shelter, and a fireplace she built herself with rock from Fort Independence.

three

INDEPENDENCE

1900–1905

There it is, take it.

WILLIAM MULHOLLAND, 1913

Untamed and barren, lone the valley lies.
Forego, O River, all the wrong you do her,
Hasting your waters to the bitter lake,
Rise from your reedy marges and subdue her,
So shall the land be fertile for your sake.

MARY AUSTIN

"Inyo," Overland Monthly, 1899

IN PREDAWN DARKNESS ON MAY 21, 1924, almost twenty years after Mary Austin left the Owens Valley, a convoy of cars made its way from the small town of Bishop to a point fifty miles south, near Lone Pine. The forty or so men who dynamited the Los Angeles aqueduct that day considered themselves ordinary people—husbands, fathers, merchants, and ranchers—forced to defend their property against the water-guzzling Goliath of Los Angeles. On November 16 of that same year, seventy men, led by the banking brothers Mark and Wilfred Watterson, once again left Bishop, this time to seize the aqueduct at the Alabama Gates spillway. A former worker at the aqueduct removed protective equipment, opened the flood gate, and allowed the water to flow back into the depleted Owens River. When William Mulholland, chief engineer of the Los Angeles water department, sent armed detectives to break up the demonstration, they confronted the Owens Valley sheriff. If they valued their lives, he told them, they had better leave.[1]

News of the occupation spread quickly, making headlines as far away as Paris. Even the *Los Angeles Times,* an advocate for the city's water strategy, portrayed the gun-toting activists as victims. By the third day, as many as eight hundred sympathizers had gathered from Bishop, Lone Pine, and Independence in support of their threatened communities. "If I am not on the job," a poster at the main Bishop crossroads announced, "you can find me at the aqueduct."[2] The standoff took on the spirit of a county fair. On the fourth day, Bishop's grocers hosted a barbecue, and Tom Mix, filming a Western nearby, brought over his crew and mariachi band. A day later, with the governor agreeing to mediate what newspapers dubbed California's Civil War, the siege ended. Thinking they had won the battle, at least the publicity battle, the protestors lost the war, which metamorphosed into a court case and dragged on so long it recalled *Jarndyce v. Jarndyce,* the interminable lawsuit at the heart of Charles Dickens's *Bleak House.*

In 1927, following another series of explosions that destroyed parts of the aqueduct—now nicknamed "the Panama Canal of the West"—Los Angeles detectives illegally imposed martial law on the Owens Valley. Soon after, the Wattersons' Inyo County Bank failed, and the brothers received ten-year prison terms in San Quentin for embezzlement. Many believed they had been framed. Guilty or not, their downfall marked the beginning of the end for the men and women hoping to keep the water where they believed it belonged. "Such tearing down!" an old friend of Austin lamented. "People selling—or not knowing whether to sell. Wanting to keep their homes and yet afraid of what the City will do to them if they dare to refuse the City's price. We have signed up. Oh—I wish you would come back and learn the facts and in your Heaven given way—write of our valley—our people and our sorrow. THEN THE WORLD WOULD KNOW WHAT HAPPENED TO US!"[3] Willie Arthur Chalfant, long an opponent of Los Angeles as editor of the *Inyo Register,* gave his estimate of the situation in a 1932 letter to Austin: "Suffice it to say that Los Angeles has now almost a free hand in Owens Valley. It now owns probably 95 per cent of farm property and at least 80 per cent of town property. There is no foundation for hope of any come-back. . . . The valley has become a sad wreck."[4] By this time, too, William Mulholland had been disgraced, not for taking the Owens Valley water, but for the failure of the St. Francis Dam, his own pet project, which collapsed with devastating consequences on the first day it held water.

As a resident of Independence in the early 1900s, Austin knew Chalfant and the Wattersons, whose parents had befriended her in Bishop. She became something of a spokeswoman in the early days for those fighting the

Los Angeles takeover, and, with her husband, she mounted a case against Mulholland and Fred Eaton, former head of the city's water company and mayor of Los Angeles from 1898 to 1905. The struggle by the Owens Valley inhabitants, including the later dynamiting of the aqueduct and the downfall of the Wattersons, highlights why so many people define the West less in terms of open land and space than by inches of rainfall or the damming and diversion of rivers. "The West's ultimate unity," Wallace Stegner writes in *The Sound of Mountain Water,* "is its aridity."[5] From the days of John Wesley Powell to those of Stegner, from the early reclamation projects to the draining of the Colorado River, water has been in the sights of every politician, farmer, industrialist, and environmentalist in the Western United States. Austin, who saw the struggles for water firsthand in the San Joaquin and Owens valleys, wrote about the topic as early as 1900 and came back to it throughout her life. Her first book, *The Land of Little Rain,* pays tacit tribute to the water issue, except that, like John Van Dyke in her time or Marc Reisner in our own, Austin wanted no "Cadillac Desert" and no city or state appropriating the waters of another region. There came one late exception when, responding to a request by the state governor, she criticized California and supported her adopted New Mexico in its bid for a share of the Colorado waters.

———————————— ·•◦•· ————————————

In the last decade of the nineteenth century, farmers of the Owens Valley dreamed of irrigated fields and rows of fruit trees and looked confidently toward the future. Not Mary Austin, whose ambitions lay elsewhere and who went to Independence as if into exile. "She was so far above the average person in most small towns," remembered one sympathetic observer, "that instead of appreciating, they criticized her."[6] In her published writing, Austin can find endearing absurdity and small kindnesses in places like Independence, but living in the town she fictionalized as "Maverick" seemed intolerable. The real name of her new hometown seemed a taunt to someone who felt she had never exercised her own *independence*—or the cultural pleasures it could bring. She had seen two plays, and those as a child without the knowledge of her parents. Nor had she been to an opera, seen "a good picture," or heard "good music." Independence had "no library in town, not many books of any sort."[7] As she began to earn more from her writing, she would make up for the lack of books, yet even books reflected her isolation. "I can think of no happier arrangement," she wrote, "than to be shut away in a room lined with books from floor to ceiling, and with no opening except some place where food could be brought to me and taken away."[8]

Once again she gathered around her a few staunch friends, among them the Gunns, who owned the Murietta Mine, and the Webbs, who ran a cattle ranch. In the first months, however, she remained the outsider, the writer and perceived eccentric, the troublemaker. Townspeople called her a shrewish wife to the long-suffering Wallace. Nothing went unnoticed in Independence, especially a woman glimpsed through a window railing at her husband—and worse. An angry group of women delegates called on her to explain why she participated in Indian dances and presented a cake at Chinese New Year to the young man who did her laundry. Bishop, Independence, and Independence Creek each had small Chinatowns, residents of which, like American Indians, lacked civil rights when whites accused them of crimes, destroyed their property, or resorted to murder. The *Inyo Register* campaigned to purge the Owens Valley of thirsty Angelinos, but also of Chinese laborers, as soon as others could take their places. "Negroes," ran an article as early as 1886, "will be employed at once in preference to Chinese; the people want to get rid of these pests."[9] In such a climate, Austin's new-year's cake, which the recipient proudly displayed on Main Street, might as well have been a stick of dynamite. She invited further scandal when the Methodist minister censured her for teaching the Bible as a book having literary origins.

Austin arrived in Independence impatient with small-town limitations and—because she knew what ailed her child—increasingly hardened against her husband. Her sister-in-law, moved by Austin's self-recriminations, had written to disclose other instances of mental impairment in the Austin family. When Mary Hunter agreed to marry Wallace, she had made a full disclosure of her past, listing abnormalities in the Hunter-Graham lines. She insisted that her husband's deceit, or evasive silence, amounted to nullification of their marriage contract. Whether she assumed direct connection between inherited tendencies and Ruth's troubles, she did not say. She blamed Wallace as if he hid the inevitable from her, and she would later argue that engaged couples should register with a bureau to ensure genetic compatibility. Practically, she was forced to abandon hope that an operation would improve Ruth's speech and motor coordination; she also contended with

Wallace's reluctance to institutionalize the child, an act he regarded as immoral.

Although husband and wife occupied separate emotional worlds, both wanted and failed to have a second child. Austin once bragged that she would have been equal to bearing five children—this despite Ruth's excruciating birth, Wallace's family history, and her own thwarted ambitions. Wallace's hope for a larger family made better sense. He remained invested in the marriage and, like so many before and after, believed in the power of children to solve marital problems. Against his better judgment, for example, he agreed to let Ruth board with friends of Edward Beale, called the Skinners. Determined to keep his family intact, Wallace continued to support his wife's writing, freeing her as much as possible from household chores and the oversight of Ruth. He hired a typist to reduce the time his wife spent transcribing drafts. One friend remembered his bringing her breakfast in bed so that she could continue working. The paradox of their angry scenes and misunderstandings set against the snug image of Austin tapping her five-minute egg or sprinkling sugar on her oatmeal underscores the difficulty of knowing any marriage from the outside.

Austin would complain bitterly about her husband's disregard for her feelings and health, and still more about his lack of originality, yet she told her publisher that much of her outdoor life amounted to "assisting" Wallace's fieldwork. She ridiculed his knowledge of plants—he was now a botanist and registrar of the U.S. Land Office—and praised him for help with proofreading and for trying to sell her work.[10] Wallace did more than that. "Little Pete," the shepherd Austin met on the Rancho El Tejon and mentions frequently in her early books, wrote a letter to Wallace, not Mary, about meeting to observe the sheepshearing.[11] In other words, he helped with his wife's research, in this case at a time when she was working headlong on her manuscript of *The Flock*.

Wallace loved his new work as much as his wife loved hers, and as botanist-registrar played a role in the development of the region. He lobbied the federal government, for example, to build a trail "over the range at Whitney, which would make a short hike from Owens Valley to the grand Kern Cañon country and thence on by direct route" to Visalia.[12] Though Austin described her marriage as torment, she and Wallace seemed in some ways closer than before, bound by their common investment in her career and the miserable child who tore them apart. "Where shall life find radiance if love depart?" Austin asked in a poem from around 1899, which ends with an echo of William Wordsworth:

And we shall walk together hand in hand,
And hear again the voice of wind and stream,
Amid fair meadows in that lovely land,
Shall find again the glory and the dream."[13]

It was shortly after the writing of this poem that Austin and Wallace set private differences aside to embroil themselves in the public contest for the Owens Valley water. Around the turn of the century, Inyo County, advertised by the local chamber of commerce, the county board of supervisors, and the horticultural commissioner as "the Switzerland of America," experienced a boom in population. Land prices rose accordingly, and residents hoped to profit from a 1902 reclamation act, sponsored by Senator Francis Newlands, for the development of Western water projects. Engineers scouting the area estimated that a dam and reservoir could increase the number of irrigated acres in the valley two- to threefold.

Quick to respond, farmers speculated, believing they invested in a richer future by giving low-priced options on their land to self-described government officials. Learning they had indirectly sold to officials representing Los Angeles—a city desperate for water and unprepared for another drought or population boom—they panicked. Citizens meeting in Bishop formed a committee to ask the U.S. secretary of the interior to investigate. "We believe," they wrote, "that the officers of the Reclamation Service are, and have been, using their services to acquire the water rights of this valley for the City of Los Angeles instead of for the reclamation of arid lands. If this is accomplished it will mean the eventual ruination of this beautiful valley and conversion of the same into a barren waste of desert."[14] Neither of the Austins served on the committee; as registrar of the U.S. Land Office at Independence, however, Wallace wrote to President Theodore Roosevelt requesting that the federal government probe "the whole outrageous scheme." He singled out Lippincott, the supervising engineer of the U.S. Reclamation Service, and his business associate, Fred Eaton, for special blame: "Mr. Lippincott while drawing a large salary from the Government was employed by the City of Los Angeles to assist in securing this water for the city. . . . With his connivance Mr. Fred Eaton came into the valley and purchased all the patented land within the Government's reservoir and its riparian rights along the Owens River."[15]

Eaton eventually realized half a million dollars on options acquired for as little as fifteen thousand; he made another hundred thousand from his commissions as sales agent in the transfer of Owens Valley properties to the city. Wallace felt duped and betrayed. He had carelessly allowed Eaton access to records, among them rights-of-way, without demanding a letter of authorization. Coincidentally, Wallace's brother Frank had first invited Eaton to the region in 1892, the year Eaton envisioned bringing water to Los Angeles, the population of which had since grown from a mere 50,000 to 200,000 inhabitants.

Deceived about the connection between Eaton and Lippincott, and previously trusting the Reclamation Service, Owens Valley residents "could not believe," as Wallace put it, "that a plan to rob the valley of its water and turn down the Government's irrigation project was being carried out with the consent of the Supervising Engineer."[16] Wallace and a former Bakersfield newspaperman, Congressman Sylvester C. Smith, tried to broker a compromise by which Los Angeles would have domestic use of the Owens River without the rights to irrigate the San Fernando Valley. Their plan failed when Theodore Roosevelt, a Progressive who believed in serving the largest number of constituents, intervened to delete the no-irrigation rider from a bill that would have made it law.[17]

Wallace had another ploy for thwarting Eaton's scheme. He and William Rowan filed a claim for two hundred thousand inches of water near the intake to the aqueduct, with the understanding that the land would be given later to the Reclamation Service or a community-owned company called Associated Ditches.[18] To a friend in Bishop, Austin declared:

> There is not a word of truth in the childish and scurrilous stories that Mr. Eaton has spread about my husband. . . . What my husband really did was to present the filing to the People of Inyo to help them in defending their homes. Mr. Eaton was told this but he was simply unable to understand how a poor man like my husband could give away a right he had just been offered money for, and invented the other story to account for it. . . . One thing the desert has taught us and that is that we can always afford to be poor, that is if you can call a man poor who can give away a $5000 water right.[19]

If the lady protests too much here, that may reflect her dilemma: the struggle between loyalty to a husband she did not respect and the cause she did not want to lose. Or perhaps she had her own doubts about Wallace, who, recognizing a lost cause, may or may not have thought to make his own fortune from the ebb and flow of Owens Valley waters.

The *Los Angeles Times,* which reported Wallace's filing, gleefully recounted his altercation with the editor of a Bishop newspaper, the *Independent.*

Wallace called the man a "stinker" for questioning his wife's veracity, whereupon the editor "promptly whacked the novelist's husband in the eye turning it the hue of a thundercloud." The sheriff had to separate the two. "It was a wild war dance, but no more damage was done."[20] Wallace's plan for a water cooperative need not be seen as a utopian fantasy. Riverside, then California's unofficial orange-growing capital and one of the state's booming areas, had remained the arid Jurupa Ranch until a communally owned canal brought mountain water to the groves.

Austin drew on personal experience when she used the Owens Valley saga for *The Ford* in 1917. In this novel, land barons conspire with San Francisco officials to rob the "Tierra Longa Valley" of its oil and water, aided by small ranchers beset by drought and eager for a windfall. The story follows the sliding fortunes of the Burkes, who sell their land for someone else's profit. "Capital went about seeking whom it might devour," Austin writes, "yet such was their strange illusion about it that they believed that if once they could lay hands on it, Capital could be made to run in their harness, breed in their pastures. To those who owned Capital, and set their brand upon it, it ate out of the hand, but its proper nutrient was the content of poor men's pockets."[21] Reminiscent of *The Octopus: A Story of California* (1901), Frank Norris's story of the conflict between wheat farmers and the Southern Pacific Railroad, *The Ford* depicts oil derricks as "half-formed, pre-historic creatures feeling their way up from the depths to light, leaning all together with the slight undulations of the land, and seeming to communicate in low, guttering blubs and endless creaking, as though they plotted to tear loose at any moment and stamp out the little hordes of men who ran perpetually about."[22] Austin's novel questions the inherent right of anyone to land seized from its first inhabitants or granted by the Spanish crown. She would work on *The Ford* as war swept Europe, a dozen years after Eaton and his men had acquired enough parcels of land, through legitimate land purchases and ethical shenanigans, to secure the Owens Valley water.

During the early years of the controversy, Austin wrote articles for the *San Francisco Chronicle* decrying the practice of what amounted to manifest destiny by Los Angeles (and San Francisco, which dammed Hetch Hetchy, the sister valley to Yosemite). "I suppose your feeling is that if you with other residents of the valley are compelled to march in chains behind the triumphant car in Los Angeles, you will do so," a sympathizer wrote, "but you will be hanged if you . . . sing during the procession."[23] *Howl* might have been a more appropriate word. A headline in the *Inyo Register* shrieked "Los Angeles Plots Destruction: Would Take Owens River, Lay

Lands Waste, Ruin People, Homes and Communities." "I know this people," Austin told readers in another article, "and I promise you there will be entered against the city of Los Angeles incalculable forces, intangible and immeasurable by any standard known to them, maddening meekness which seems to surrender and rises up over night to confront you in its original proportions, obstinate reprisals carried long past the point where they are supposed to pay."[24] Notwithstanding that the editor of the *Los Angeles Times* called her hysterical, the movement of guns into the Owens Valley and the dynamiting of the Los Angeles aqueduct twenty years later proved her right. In the words of Elsie Watterson, sister to Wilfred and Mark: "If the Los Angeles Aqueduct whose waters spring so crystal clear from the snows of the Sierras, could reflect the tragedy of Owens Valley, that stream would run red from its very beginnings—red as the heart's blood of a valiant people!"[25]

Owens Valley waters flow parallel to Highway 395 down to the Mojave Desert, before being pumped to an ever more thirsty Los Angeles County, its population now a hundred times bigger than at the turn of the twentieth century. By a twist of historical irony, the people of Los Angeles once again transformed the Owens Valley, not as the principal legatees of its water, but into, after all, another Switzerland, a place for skiing and mountain climbing—and an escape from the polluted and overcrowded city that valley water made possible. There is yet another, more surprising, twist. To settle a 1972 lawsuit initiated by Inyo County, Mayor Antonio Villaraigosa of Los Angeles announced in December 2006 that his city will, at last, allow some of the water to flow again through the bed of the long-dry Owens River. The city will retain most of the water, but has at last made a concession to wetlands and wildlife.

When Austin moved to the Owens Valley, she had so much to write about that she spoke of "the pressure of knowledge, all the knowledge in the world, pulsing just out of reach." It welled up inside her, "aching intolerably to escape."[26] Periods of writer's block would come later. Her work sold well, and in the "right" places. Her poems and stories could be found in widely circulated magazines for children, such as *Youth's Companion* and *St. Nicholas,* as well as *Cosmopolitan* and *Munsey's.* For her first *Atlantic Monthly* story she earned thirty-five dollars; for others, eight dollars a page.

Poems in the *Overland Monthly* brought ten to fifteen dollars, and stories twenty-five to thirty dollars. She broke into *The Atlantic Monthly* with "A Shepherd of the Sierras" (1900), and followed it with "The Last Antelope" (1903). The editor, Bliss Perry, said that though he took a risk accepting "nature books" for serialization—they seldom paid the cost of publication—he did not think of her writing in terms of dollars returned. Her books belonged to a growing literature of California that drew attention to the "exotic" (meaning Indians, Mexicans, and early Spanish colonists), yet there had never been anything quite like it.[27]

Austin had, by the time she wrote *The Land of Little Rain,* found her subject and learned her craft. She finished this welcoming, open narrative in Independence and published parts of it in *The Atlantic.*[28] A passage from her book suggests that in certain moods she could reconcile herself to the region if not to the town itself. "Is it not perhaps to satisfy expectations that one falls into the tragic key in writing of desertness?" she asks. "In that country . . . it is possible to live with great zest, to have red blood and delicate joys."[29] Simultaneously personal and exalted, *The Land of Little Rain* launches the experimentation she sustained throughout her career. Its language owes something to the King James Bible, to Ralph Waldo Emerson (a favorite of her father), and to oral folk traditions, which form "a background . . . such as you find taken for granted in fairy tales"—or in the best short stories.[30] "You may reach my country," she writes, "and find or not find, according as it lieth in you, much that is set down here. And more. The earth is no wanton to give up all her best to every comer, but keeps a sweet, separate intimacy for each. But if you do not find it all as I write, think me not less dependable nor yourself less clever."[31]

As her editor knew, Austin was not the first or only writer to appreciate dry and sparsely populated spaces. Cabeza de Vaca, the first European to explore and extol the Southwest, inspired his sixteenth-century countrymen Hernando de Soto and Francisco Vásquez de Coronado to believe in cities of gold. Nineteenth-century adventurers like Sir Richard Burton had written about the deserts of North Africa and Arabia; and closer to home, George Wilkins Kendall about the territories explored by the Texan Santa Fe Expedition of 1841. Two years before Austin's book, John Van Dyke, a lawyer turned librarian and art historian, went to the Arizona desert lands to cure his asthma; he stayed to explore the region and, in 1901, published *The Desert* to surprising critical and financial success.

Van Dyke challenged the assumption of the desert as wasteland and approached it from the perspective of an impressionist painter. *The Desert* appeals to a certain aesthetic snobbery. Readers "must begin by admiring the Hudson-River landscape," Van Dyke insists, before matriculating as connoisseurs of the arid western "desolation"; the Indians themselves, those who have lived upon the land for centuries, fail to see the ledges of copper infused with turquoise, the terra-cotta buttes and sands stained rose and violet, or the silvery sheen of mesquite, nor do they comprehend the larger implications of the desert, which offer fables for living. Van Dyke, a social Darwinist, asserts that "everything [in the desert] is at war with its neighbor, and the conflict is unceasing."[32]

Ways of looking, quite apart from the connoisseur's relationship to his material, distinguish Van Dyke from Austin. Readers of *The Desert* might suppose that the land can best be appreciated—and by extension, entrusted—to those who share its author's sensibility. The risk here lies in conceiving public lands as middle-class adventure parks or outdoor museums reserved for the discerning few. In sharp contrast, Austin sees the land and its uses as if from the inside out, and as inextricably linked with human life. The English iconoclast Raymond Williams echoes her thinking when he writes that men and women have mixed their labor with the earth, "with its forces too deeply to be able to draw back and separate either."[33] The American iconoclast Edward Abbey takes a different approach. In his introduction to an edition of *The Land of Little Rain* (grudgingly acknowledging Austin as his predecessor), Abbey wrestles with issues of people in the wilderness. A man of few pieties, he could approach a John Muir–like spirituality, but in his startling 1950s descriptions of southern Utah he speaks as a belligerent solitary in the desert lands he describes. Austin, by contrast, attends almost as much to the inhabitants as to the place itself.

In a similar way, the composition of Austin's book differs from Van Dyke's. His might be called a cross between travelogue and meditative essay; hers a series of interwoven stories about the region "between the Sierras south from Yosemite—east and south over a very great assemblage of broken ranges beyond Death Valley, and on illimitably into the Mojave Desert."[34] Indians, she writes, have a better name for the region; they call it the "Country of Lost Borders." Austin would describe this region as a wilderness that is as much psychological as physical, "where the borders of conscience break down, where there is no convention, and behavior is of little account except as it gets you your desire."[35] Austin believed that places carry their own storylines, which in turn shape people's thoughts and actions, if not their destinies. In *The Land of Little Rain* she cautions readers that "the manner of the country makes the usage of life there, and the land will not be lived in except in its own fashion."[36]

No less than Van Dyke, Austin recognizes the dangers of the desert, where "nothing so large as a man can move unspied on." Her desert jars with the croaking of scavenger birds and the cries of thin, "tormented" forests.[37] The fauna, human and otherwise, nevertheless matter as part of a larger orchestration. In Death Valley, the very "core of desolation," hundreds of species find a way and possibly a will to survive—often through cooperation. She finds courage in her characters, a way of proceeding through life that reminds her of the ancient Greeks. Men like Three Finger Wilson endure without sniveling, renounce without self-pity, and die without fear. Like the pagan gods she lumps together with the beasts and St. Jerome, they topple social pecking orders. As a writer Austin never worked at the remove of, say, Henry James, watching (to borrow his metaphor of the house of fiction) from assorted windows the distinct prospect through each. She claimed a setting or a story after she grasped it kinesthetically, walking her neighbor's field, chatting with gamblers, or grinding spices for tamales. In this she resembles her soon-to-be friend, Jack London, whose visceral immediacy parallels her own. But as with Van Dyke's, London's writing draws on the theories of Darwin and Friedrich Nietzsche to depict life as a battle for dominance, while Austin presents the natural world as at once unforgiving or indifferent *and* nurturing.

Taking her materials from a variety of sources, Austin also chose with care. When one of the Watterson sisters, Isabel, told her about the end of Little Pete's life, she expected Austin to use it. Austin balked. Pete had been living with a half-breed woman, the daughter of a notorious robber and highwayman, whom he sheltered from drunken Basque shepherds. When the woman became pregnant, Pete "said he knew he was responsible for her condition and as he liked her, he wasn't going to send her back to those 'devilish Basques and Indians' and so he took her with him." Townspeople looked down on him "because of the woman," and he, caught in a moral dilemma, could neither leave his children nor "take them from their mother." Choosing to end his life, Pete "was found with a bullet hole in his temple in a cellar he used as a store room." He left a hundred dollars to the woman and twenty thousand to his two children.[38] Much as Austin had delighted Pete by telling stories about him, in *The Land of Little Rain* and *The Flock,* she chose not to tell this one, which may have been too close to the bone or unfair to a friend, or simply not *her* story of the West. Theodore Dreiser would have focused on Pete's social displacement, Jack London on his body's ironic return to the hills he deserted. Austin's imagination, disposed to see a "conscious unity in all things," led her to parse, as she puts it in *Earth Horizon*, "the fine moralities of nature."[39]

Austin's narrative voice reflects the paradoxes she discussed with William James. She liked to distinguish between stories, which tell "how life itself gets accomplished," and myth, the portrayal of invisible life forces at work in human endeavors. In *The Land of Little Rain,* she manages to bring the two together with anecdotes about local characters—among them Salty Williams, who drove a team of twenty mules from the borax marsh to Mojave, and Timmie O'Shea, lost for three days without water on Armogosa Flats. Her desert is a place where plants, animals, and people struggle for existence and where the line that separates humans and nonhumans blurs. A "pocket hunter," or prospector, ignorant of "how much he depended for the necessary sense of home and companionship on the beasts and trees," might as well be a badger or a gopher.[40] Whatever their instinct urges, travelers should be warned to follow the old water trails of the desert's aboriginal creatures. "Man is a great blunderer going about in the woods," she writes, "and there is no other . . . makes so much noise. . . . The cunningest hunter is hunted in turn, and what he leaves of his kill is meat for some other. That is the economy of nature." Unlike man the scavenger, she concludes, "no wild thing leaves a like disfigurement on the forest floor."[41] Men and women for Austin resemble the world they inhabit, at once heroic and generous, blundering and crude.

At the same time, *The Land of Little Rain* presents a way of being in the world that respects the rights of others to share that world. In what became a hallmark of her work, *The Land of Little Rain* depicts people thought to be either alien or approaching extinction: a Paiute "campoody"; a Bret Harte town she calls Jimville; and El Pueblo de Las Uvas, "the little town of the grape vines" that celebrates both Mexican Independence Day and the Fourth of July. In presenting Lone Pine and Bishop as they were, segregated like the town of Las Uvas into ethnic communities, she wrote against the grain, or at least against the explosion of sentimental romances endorsing an unexamined vision of the United States.[42]

Written during and after the Spanish-American War, a world away, *The Land of Little Rain* appeared three years into the twentieth century. It was in a sense both a timely book and a book separate from national or world events—if not entirely from millennial visions. Austin understood herself to be working in a realm that went beyond the merely realistic. Since her encounter with the invisible predator-spirit on her hundred-mile trek to the

Rancho El Tejon, she apprehended something ultimately elusive in the land itself. It struck her as a form of unappeasable desire, an "insistent experiential pang for which the wise Greeks had the clearest name concepts . . . fauns, satyrs, the ultimate Pan. Beauty-in-the-wild, yearning to be made human."[43] Like her early benefactor, General Beale, she might have substituted "existential" for "experiential." The desert, which upsets time no less than human self-importance, demands the untenable choices made by men and women in the plays of Sophocles, the novels of Albert Camus, and the lives of people such as Mary and Wallace Austin.

To the degree that *The Land of Little Rain* proposed a new consciousness about the desert and those who live there, it gave an original—and dynamic—vision of the "West" tied to shifting notions of individual freedoms and responsibilities and to an understanding of people in their relation to the land. Austin valued a regional attitude at odds with "Eastern" thinking, manners, and traditions. She puts it this way: "Says the East, judiciously: 'That has never been done before; better not try it.' Says the joyful West: 'That has never been done before; let's try it!' "[44] Austin's West, or *Wests,* embraced the Southwest, Northwest, and California Coast; cities like San Francisco; communities like Carmel; and eventually industries or illusions like those of Hollywood, each producing a different cultural or spiritual ethos. Her thinking was seldom monolithic or inflexible. She knew that any or all labels, like the borders in her fiction, have a way of breaking down—as do definitions of "Western" writers, which seemed to baffle her. She had no trouble including Owen Wister as a Western writer, though *The Virginian,* a 1902 novel, weds East and West through the courtship of a gentleman cowboy and a Vermont schoolmarm. She struggled to claim Jack London, whose theories of race grew from a commitment to an "Anglo-Saxon" America, and she could say that works like Twain's *Adventures of Huckleberry Finn* or Sinclair Lewis's *Babbitt* were born "of resistance to regional interests and influences."[45] As a rule, she fell back on citing the particulars of place and the books that captured them as signs of Western, or regional, literature, which in its aggregate made up a national literature. Regional for Austin, as for someone like Faulkner, did not mean parochial.

Whether unafraid of contradictions or embracing paradox, Austin included everything in her writing from local gossip to legends to common experience and values. No wonder many of her neighbors objected, damning *The Land of Little Rain*—which attracted tourists and gave a name to their region—as a pack of lies. Beyond Independence and Lone Pine, however, the response to her book could not have been more flattering.

Californians linked her name with Edwin Markham and, more pertinently, with Mary Hallock Foote, the writer-illustrator Austin greatly admired. A sophisticated easterner who followed her engineer-husband from one mining area to another—New Almaden, Santa Cruz, Leadville, Grass Valley—Foote lives again as the courageous grandmother in Wallace Stegner's novel, *Angle of Repose* (1971). After reading *The Land of Little Rain*, Foote welcomed Austin as Emerson had welcomed Walt Whitman: she praised the book's unique voice, "the reserve, the power of instantaneous presentation, its nervous, rich, sensual speech straight at the mark—and a something besides that is pure woman."[46] This in a banner year for American literature, which, besides *The Land of Little Rain*, saw publication of Frank Norris's *The Pit*, W. E. B. Du Bois's *The Souls of Black Folks*, Henry James's *The Ambassadors*, and Jack London's *The Call of the Wild*.

Wallace Austin took great pride in his wife's accomplishment, and how could he not, given its public reception? To the editor of the *Mt. Whitney Journal*, he boasted that "*The Land of Little Rain* has met with very favorable mention from one end of the country to another."[47] Critics immediately recognized Mary Austin's power. One reviewer insisted that none of E. Boyd Smith's accompanying illustrations "bring out the country with its human and animal dwellers as does a single paragraph of Mrs. Austin's work. Indeed such illustrations of such fine descriptive work as hers seem almost an impertinence."[48] The praise continued throughout her lifetime. Carl Van Doren wanted to grant her an honorary MAE—Master of the American environment. Van Wyck Brooks compared her to Balzac and Tolstoy for grasping the nature of the desert as "absolutely and familiarly" as they had "grasped society, as no novelist perhaps can grasp a society as kaleidoscopic as ours."[49]

———— • • • ————

Austin had surprised friends by dedicating *The Land of Little Rain* to Eve Lummis, her "comfortress of unsuccess." Overlooking Wallace's claim, they thought the dedication slighted Eve's husband, Charles, Austin's affable nemesis. Austin, already close to Eve, felt more so since the death of Eve's young son Amado from pneumonia. He and Ruth had been playmates, and at the very hour he died, Austin said, Ruth announced that Amado asked her to go for a walk with him a long way off.[50] "It is no more than fitting," Austin told Eve, "that this book should be dedicated to you since you are the first western woman I met capable of inspiring me either with affection or a very great measure of respect."[51]

Prior to the appearance of *The Land of Little Rain,* Austin had begun to spend more time in Los Angeles, where Charles Lummis still held sway; and in San Francisco, a city of about 450,000 at the turn of the century (almost twice the size of Los Angeles), where once again she extended her contacts with literary people. She met Charles Moody of *Out West* (formerly Lummis's *Land of Sunshine*) and sought the friendship of well-heeled intellectuals. In San Francisco she also reconnected with friends from Los Angeles, especially Eve Lummis, who in turn introduced her to the historian Theodore Hittell and his family. The Hittells—they remained lifelong friends—welcomed Austin into their circle, which included Ina Coolbrith, midwife of *The Land of Little Rain,* Edwin Markham, Charlie Stoddard, and William Keith. She also met the naturalist and unlikely matchmaker John Muir, who had no more success finding a husband for his friend Ina than he would fighting, valiantly, to save the Hetch Hetchy Valley. Austin met Muir once, long enough she thought to dismiss him as a "naturist" and to resent his habit of lecturing, though she herself talked at people in later years and grew equally certain about her own ideas. Because of Muir's unmatched persuasiveness— and his founding of the Sierra Club (1892)—mountain climbers, explorers, botanists, hunters, fishermen, and collectors of Indian crafts made their way to the eastern Sierras and to Independence, some of them hoping to meet Mary Austin.

Soon after publication of *The Land of Little Rain,* Austin had begun writing the novel that became *Isidro,* which, with a change of heart, she could now dedicate affectionately to her brother Jim; and she finished *The Basket Woman, a Book of Fanciful Tales for Children,* which her publishers compared to Rudyard Kipling's *Jungle Book.* The comparison pleased Austin but prompted a rebuttal from Charles Moody, who thought her book more like Hans Christian Andersen at his best. As Austin worked on this second book, a neighbor girl named Helen Gunn often came over to play with Ruth. In part because Austin still hoped that the presence of other children would stimulate her daughter, she gave parties for Helen and her friends, teaching them—Carlinville's—social niceties, such as how to pay calls and make conversation. In 1931, Helen would write to her, "As the years roll by I understand more and appreciate more deeply the things you did for us when we were girls . . . and the kindly hand that led us has always been a treasured memory to me."[52] These children served as the first audience for *The Basket Woman;* the second audience, Bliss Perry's daughter, lived in

Boston. *The Atlantic* editor asked his twelve-year-old for a reader's report before accepting two of Austin's stories for the magazine. Miss Perry gave her approval.

Believing that contemporary society should learn from its Native peoples, Austin appropriately centered *The Basket Woman* around the education of a young white boy named Alan. At the beginning of the volume, Alan fears Indians, having heard frightening accounts of their violent history and excuses for their present misery; by the end, he respects, even prefers the people his society scorns. Austin complicates the structure of her book by having the Basket Woman guide Alan as he innocently prompts her to recover her pride and assert her history.

The Basket Woman recalls Seyavi in *The Land of Little Rain,* who weaves baskets for love and sells them for money. With the coming of night, Alan steps into the Indian woman's basket and into another consciousness. He leaps mountains and centuries, slipping back and forth in time to understand what lies beyond the mean life of the campoody. In the process, he comes to know the woman he first feared as a creator, savior, and surrogate mother. In one story, this weaver of baskets and human lives rescues the lost boy by going "straight to the point where she saw the [buzzards'] black wings hanging in the air." He wakes to see his mother kissing the Basket Woman. The kiss, linking the women and their cultures, opens to Alan the rich world that Austin associated with the borderlands of art: "he was Alan, and yet it seemed, without seeming strange, that he was the boy of the story who was afterward to be called the Fire Bringer."[53]

The Basket Woman concludes with a parable titled "Mahala Joe," inspired by Joe Eugley, a Paiute at Big Pine who dressed like a woman. Austin reimagines Joe's skirt as a badge of courage, testimony to his oath never to fight against his white blood-brother in an Indian war. Long after Mahala Joe might have thrown off women's clothing, he endures or rather wears his sentence much as Hester Prynne wears her scarlet letter. The brother for whom he does penance knows nothing of it and probably never will. He has left the valley long before. If Austin offers a moral, it might be that we have a choice whether to live as principled men and women or as coyotes—in this case a name for ambivalent spirits and for white men who hang around Native women. The artist, as Austin shows in "The Coyote-Spirit and the Weaving Woman," can transform a beast into a man by imitating his best nature. Such power also makes the artist a pariah. The coyote-spirit's wife warns him that "one cannot be too careful" about those said to associate with spirits. Agreeing with her, the man who had once been a coyote reveals himself as, after all, only a man. But then, Austin seems to ask, can any man be more than illusion?

The Basket Woman, which creates indeterminate space and time by interspersing folktales with firsthand accounts addressed to "you," the reader, shares with American Indian literature an emphasis on alternate realities, community, sacred places and practices, nature, and storytelling. Its third-person point of view sets a boundary between the author and her stories and restricts what we know about her characters' consciousnesses. Throughout her career, Austin insisted that she did not speak for Native peoples, that her knowledge had limits. She nevertheless considered her stories to be true because her sources, like the Basket Woman and Kern River Jim, told and believed them. As the subtitle to *The Basket Woman*—*a Book of Fanciful Tales for Children*—suggests, her Indian stories are at once translations from and tributes to the Indian peoples she admired. In her own estimate, she was a broker. Without characterizing herself a "realist," Austin cared about authenticity, which for her meant accuracy of both spirit and details.

At the time of *The Basket Woman,* she was not in competition with Native writers. Her contemporaries wanting to read American Indian writing in the 1880s would have found few examples beyond Sarah Winnemucca's *Life among the Paiutes: Their Wrongs and Claims* (1883). (In 1904, Charles Alexander Eastman would publish *Indian Boyhood* and *Red Hunters and the Animal People;* two years later the public could read *Geronimo's Story of His Life,* told to and edited by Stephen Melvil Barrett.) The daughter of a Paiute chief and medicine man, Winnemucca translated for the U.S. government during negotiations with the Paiutes and Shoshones; she also testified before the secretary of the interior and the president of the United States, Rutherford B. Hayes. Billed as "The Princess" and dressed in buckskin, she lectured about the perfidy of Indian agents. Powerful friends such as the suffragist Elizabeth Peabody and her sister, Mary Mann, the widow of Horace Mann, helped secure Winnemucca subscriptions to publish *Life among the Paiutes* and promoted her book. For all the contemporary support, Winnemucca's anomaly of a work—a blend of autobiography, history, and impassioned plea for sympathy—has not fared well with historians skeptical about its accuracy and distrustful of a document that smacks of self-aggrandizing or appeasement. Austin, who owned a copy of *Life among the Paiutes,* has been criticized for overlapping reasons, including her portrayal and boosting of Native peoples and her inflated claims of authority. Both charges ignore Austin's determination to make Indian poetry and narratives known through whatever means necessary in years when little else was available.

Austin appealed to a growing audience for things "Indian." At the turn of the twentieth century, the American public's fascination with "primitive" peoples, especially American Indians, had grown inversely to their annihilation. The paradoxes went back several generations. The rediscovery, for example, of Mayan ruins in Central America after 1839 had coincided with the Western explorations of John Charles Frémont and Kit Carson, friends who differed about treatment of the Indians but ultimately joined forces against them. The discovery of gold at Sutter's Mill in 1848 led at least indirectly to California statehood, along with great increases in population and to death by murder, warfare, and attrition of Californian tribes. The new state's Native population dropped from 120,000 in 1850—the year before the governor endorsed a policy of extermination—to fewer than 20,000 by 1880. In 1879, the Carlisle Indian School began its mission of assimilation, and Helen Hunt Jackson's *A Century of Dishonor,* published in 1881, galvanized reformers critical of the government's treatment of American Indians.

The next half-dozen years saw a boom in organizations—the Indian Protection Committee, Indian Rights Association, Women's National Indian Association, the Smithsonian Institute's Bureau of American Ethnology, and the American Indian Defense Association—initiated by "friends of the Indian" and aimed at preserving their customs and their land. Yet in a single year, 1891, the federal government offered nine hundred thousand acres of Indian land to white settlers. That same year, the ethnologist Alice C. Fletcher described the followers of the Paiute prophet Wovoka, whose teaching combined Christian and Native beliefs, as appealing "for the preservation of their race, to the God of their oppressors."[54] Wovoka's "Ghost Dancers" had been told that ritual dancing would bring back the dead, revive the buffalo, eradicate whites, and return the land to its true people. They died at Wounded Knee in the belief that clothing worn during the dance ceremony could ward off bullets and disease. The year following publication of *The Land of Little Rain,* thousands of visitors to the St. Louis World's Fair lined up to see Geronimo on exhibit. He signed photographs and sold his autograph for ten, fifteen, or twenty-five cents, learning, as he wrote in *Geronimo: His Own Story,* the good and the bad ways of white people. Not until the 1924 passage of the Indian Citizenship Act did American Indians win the right to vote in national elections.

Austin stood apart from her government, her neighbors, and the anthropologists who discounted the psychology of American Indians as instinctive, their myths and religions superstition. In method she was influenced, or more accurately, reassured, by the Englishman Sir James Frazer, author of the monumental *Golden Bough* (1890–1922). Originally two volumes packed with materials about religious beliefs and practices, magic, and rituals from across the globe, it eventually swelled to twelve volumes. Frazer intended, as he says in his preface to the third edition, "to explain . . . the legend of the Golden Bough, immortalized by Virgil, which the voice of antiquity associated with the priesthood."[55] For all its influence on psychology and literature, anthropologists disowned Frazer's work. Among other problems, they pointed out that, unlike modern ethnologists, he remained in his library compiling unreliable texts and the reports of untrained observers.

The sway of *The Golden Bough* and Frazer's methodology can be seen in Austin's 1931 introduction to Frank Hamilton Cushing's *Zuni Folk Tales,* in which she claims that "it did not occur to any ethnologist of thirty years ago that the Zuni Folk Tales had proceeded directly out of that complex of intellectual perceptivity, emotional need, and aesthetic insight which is the matrix of all literatures."[56] In other words, the ethnologists' claims were barren, those of Frazer and herself reliable—not to mention readable. Again following Frazer's expansive theories, she noted in an introduction to George William Cronyn's anthology of songs and chants, *The Path on the Rainbow,* a close resemblance among American Indian, Greek, Japanese, and Imagist poetry.

With the years, Austin grew increasingly resentful about the professionalizing of fields like anthropology, which came to bar the gifted amateurs responsible for its development and success. If not a trained anthropologist, Austin had witnessed Paiute ceremonies and translated songs with the help of tribal elders: "I have had old men sit for hours with me, considering the whole content of a word or a phrase, taking the words apart, resorting to sign language sometimes to explain them, quoting from songs and ritual otherwise unknown to me, in short, behaving like other scholars on the trail of an intellectual interest. There is, indeed, an almost Chinese indefatigability of pursuit of the last scrap of meaning which has sometimes taxed my own endurance."[57] Brought up in an age when scientists studied the bumps on people's heads to determine character or more insidiously attributed low intelligence and immorality to people of non-European descent, she had the independence of mind to ask, "What is a race but a pattern of response common to a group of people who have lived together under a given environment long enough to take on a recognizable pattern?"[58] Quick to ridicule myths about European superiority and the legitimacy of colonial conquest and expansion, Austin made a point, lost on most contemporaries, of distinguishing between the customs of different Indian tribes. She would assert in an article for the *Yale Review* that "Indian life is never the static affair that popular notion describes it" and would also brag that she could teach Sigmund Freud a thing or two about totems.[59]

Ethnographers have come to accept what she intuitively knew as a writer: that tales, often adopted from other tribes, change according to the narrator's imagination, which for Austin made them all the more valuable: "if they have your speech or you theirs, and have an hour to spare, there are things to be learned of life not set down in any books, folk tales, famine tales, love and long-suffering and desire."[60] However much she may have romanticized the traditions of American Indians or drawn at times on stereotypes, contemporary readers already considered Austin an authority. A 1905 article in the *Saturday Evening Post* described her as someone who "nurses" the Indians, "helps the women in their hours of greatest stress, combats their superstition, adjudicates some of their quarrels, encourages them in their Native arts and finds a market for their wares."[61] To her publisher, she explained her creed. People had misrepresented her work among the Indians: "They tell me things because I am really interested and a little for the sake of small favors but mostly because I give them no rest. . . . Says my friend, Kern River Jim; 'What for you learn them Injun songs? You can't sing um, You go learn songs in a book, that's good enough for you.' Nevertheless I have been able to do them as much good as they have done me."[62] Austin's main contribution to the recognition of Indian poems, songs, and dance rests on her bridging seemingly antagonist traditions, oral and literary, or Anglo-European and American Indian. In this she carried on the great traditions of Henry Schoolcraft and Lewis H. Morgan, the early nineteenth-century pioneers who saw in the culture and imaginations of American Indians what Austin, without their guidance, discovered for herself. Her aim at this time in her life was, to invoke her later friend, Joseph Conrad, less to do good than "to make people see"—and see what very few had seen before. It was also to escape the high valley she had lived in for too many years, and to make radical changes in her marriage, her career, and the place she called home.

four

CARMEL

1904–1907

How white the beach at Carmel was that day!
Woman white and curving
　　round the discarded sapphire-shot silk dappled
　　heap of her garment
That lisped and lifted, bowed full
　　to the wondrous long line of her,
　　lapsed and revealed her.
Behind us the dunes breasted shoreward,
　　trumpet shaped minulus
　　and apple-hued sea grass.
Low on the foreshore, Jack London and Sterling
　　and I together.

MARY AUSTIN
"Three at Carmel," 1928

ONE EVENING IN JULY 1904, Mary Austin strode into Coppa's restaurant on the arm of the poet George Sterling. A favorite San Francisco hangout, Coppa's sported crimson walls, capped by a frieze of black cats, and gas chandeliers, which gave the restaurant the aura of a Parisian art gallery or Left Bank brothel. "One dined so very well at Coppa's," Austin later reminisced. "Such platefuls of fresh shrimps; such sand dabs and crisp salads; such almond tartlets" and such "dago red."[1] The wine must have been especially seductive to someone raised by and as a Methodist temperancer.

Sterling, the so-called King of Bohemia—his sculpted features and "Indian build" won as much praise from women as his poems—introduced Austin to the regulars, all of them his close friends.[2] They included Jimmy

Hopper, a lawyer turned writer, who in Austin's words resembled a Breton sailor with the hair of a Fra Angelico angel; the exuberant painter, Xavier "Marty" Martinez, attired in his signature red tie and velvet beret; Harry Lafler, poet-editor of the San Francisco literary magazine *The Argonaut;* the lovely and tragic poet, Nora May French; Vernon Kellogg, a Stanford scientist and the one academic accepted by the group on equal terms; and Bertha and Perry Newberry, she an aspiring playwright, nicknamed "Buttsky" because she scrounged half-smoked cigarettes, he a man of many trades—probation officer, businessman, journalist, poet, actor, and for a time mayor of Carmel.

Since the days when Mark Twain and Bret Harte set the standard, bohemians like Sterling ranted at respectability and ranted by choice in Coppa's on Montgomery Street. They decorated its walls with self-flattering verse, witticisms, cartoons, and bad puns ("paste makes waist") and drew tourists to see the art and watch the patrons, who were nothing if not flamboyant. Martinez, working Sundays for his lunch and wine, painted the black cats and also the murals, one a parody of the Last Supper, which featured Sterling wearing a crown of olive leaves and Martinez as host. "Aristotle," "Perry Newberry," "Lafler," "Sappho," "Sterling," "Verlaine," "Dante," "Martinez," "Villon," "Buttsky"—these names, inscribed horizontally, composed their Temple of Fame.[3] Half a century before the appearance of Jack Kerouac and Allen Ginsberg, the bohemians of Sterling's generation saw themselves as brilliant, rebel outsiders.

Martinez had studied with the bad boy of art, James Whistler, who took John Ruskin to court for likening his painting, *Black and Gold—The Falling Rocket,* to a pot of paint flung with Cockney impudence in the public's face. (He was awarded a farthing in damages.) Charlie Stoddard and Joaquin Miller had traveled to London in the 1890s to witness the lives of English bohemians, as if modeling themselves on younger brothers in revolt. They might have gone to Paris, where bohemianism had its birth—and its apotheosis in Puccini's 1896 *La Bohème,* a favorite with the Newberries, who belted out duets for a glass of wine. By the turn of the century, the Bohemian Club that Twain and his friends founded no longer required initiates to be poor, having slipped toward its future as a watering hole for the wealthy and powerful.

Looking around the table that night, Austin saw relatively young men and women, proud of their differences, restless in traditional settings, and determined to live as writers and artists. A duckling surprised to find herself a swan—and much deceived—she felt connected with her own kind.

Sterling's friends, on the other hand, saw a Midwestern matron who talked too much. According to Jimmy Hopper, she didn't have a chance. The group took one look at her square face and stout body and, through a series of secret hand and foot signals, gave thumbs down. Although she knew everything about the desert and wrote "beautiful stuff," Hopper said, she wasn't pretty.[4] Because Sterling prided himself on being a gentleman, Austin never knew of her blackball. The next day, her silently penitent friend escorted her to Portsmouth Square, where they filled a galleon with violets at the Robert Louis Stevenson memorial, then feasted on tea and kumquats.

The evening at Coppa's would have consequences for both Austin and Sterling. After her visit and the delight of promised friendships, she returned for many months to Independence and a marriage now reduced to short encounters in the form of silence or excessive politeness. Independence, "precisely the town," as she wrote, in which her "married adventure" should come to an end, made plain "at last that her husband could not be served, that he was to be accepted and extenuated; that he had . . . no plan either for himself or their common way of life."[5] Starved for companionship, Austin found it increasingly annoying to use Independence as a base camp from which to pay visits to Los Angeles and San Francisco. Although *The Land of Little Rain* earned her the respect of other writers along with Eastern critics, newfound fame made her more of a local oddity. Sometimes she doubted her achievements. There was so much to experience if she were to write the books that seemed just beyond her reach. Soon she yearned for any place other than "the long, brown land" of the Owens Valley. When Wallace opposed her leaving again to teach in "one of the northern normal schools," their marriage came to an overdue crisis.[6] At wit's end, he offered to let her go, to live apart for another year. Wanting a permanent separation, Austin refused.

In January 1905, over Wallace's objections, Austin placed Ruth in a sanatorium, where (as she wrote in *Earth Horizon*) "the difference between herself and other children . . . would not be felt, where it would not be known. Here the inability of other people to bear her cross would not be taxed; where one could say if questioned, 'We have lost her.'"[7] She could only hope that the institution—highly recommended and located in Santa Clara, next door to San Jose and not too distant from Carmel—served Ruth well. With a credentialed medical staff and teachers advertised to train and care for "the feeble-minded," it offered at least an alternative to the vagaries of private boarding. Austin had to live with charges that she abandoned

Ruth and then ignored her. Her letters tell a different story. Not only did she pick the facility with care, she visited her daughter when possible, attended to her needs, and saved what little money she had against the possibility that Ruth would outlive her. As her letters also testify, she bore the consequences of the decision for the rest of her life.[8]

Who first imagined Carmel as a desirable place to live remains a matter of legend. Apart from Fray Junípero Serra and his followers, or temporary groups of Portuguese or Chinese whale hunters and Mexican fishermen, scouting credit might be given—as Austin believed—to Robert Louis Stevenson. Suffering from tuberculosis and pining for the married woman who would become his wife, Stevenson spent several despondent months on the Carmel coast in 1879. He appreciated the Spanish qualities of "the ancient capital," Monterey; the wildness of Point Lobos to the south; and the prospect of Carmel Valley, "bare, dotted with chaparral, overlooked by quaint, unfinished hills."[9] Another Scot, William Martin, settled with his family at the mouth of the Carmel River, nostalgic maybe for the terrain of his homeland.[10] After a research visit in 1880, the scientist David Starr Jordan, Stanford University's talented first president (from 1891) and a charter member of the Sierra Club, announced that of all California's coastal areas, he found "the most picturesque and most charming the little bay of Carmelo."[11]

A decade later, Austin's near contemporary, the eye-catching, exasperating Gertrude Atherton, admired the splendor of Carmel, where "the breakers leapt and fought" and the "Carmel River sparkled peacefully beneath its moving willows."[12] Atherton saw Carmel as a mine of literary lore and arrived with a project in mind. She enlisted the help of several elderly and puzzled Mexican women (who refused costumes) and staged a midnight tableau at the shore to help imagine her 1894 novel, *Before the Gringo Came* (later called *The Splendid Idle Forties*), designed to exploit the sublimity of the landscape and the romance of a lost civilization.[13] Unlike Austin who revered the missions, Atherton sniffed that there could be no "structure on earth colder, barer, uglier, dirtier, less picturesque, less romantic than a Californian mission."[14]

Between the visits of Stevenson and Atherton, speculators had planned to make Carmel a tourist center or a religious community, neither of which quite materialized. Except for a few dozen buildings and two small hotels, the village offered at the turn of the century little more than the solitude and the views, which included the badly "restored" ruins of Father Serra's mission, San Carlos Borromeo. The setting sufficed for James Franklin Devendorf and his partner Frank H. Powers, who bought up the available land and joined forces in 1903 as the Carmel Development Company. Carmel owes much to the foresight of these men, who brushed aside earlier failures and found a way to put people above profit. "Though I'm a businessman," Devendorf would say, "I'm glad to see one town refuse to be bossed by the business elements. I'd rather see purple pavements than factories in Carmel. I might have been a millionaire, but I'm glad I sold the land cheap to poets and painters who were glad to plant my trees."[15] Powers, an affable San Francisco lawyer and president of the company, remained an attentive silent partner. Devendorf, secretary and manager, transformed Carmel into a retreat for Bay Area intellectuals. Devendorf recruited people with "brain power," especially artists and teachers needing a place to recoup their energies. With exceptions like Stanford's Vernon Kellogg and David Starr Jordan, the artists—most of them writers—came early, the school teachers and professors followed, and the suburbanites finally inherited.

But from the beginnings there were two communities in Carmel, a variation on town and gown; and while the writers' community, shifting in people and purpose, flourished for the next twenty years, the village came to espouse the commercial and middle-class values its founding bohemians had hoped to escape. In deference to Mrs. Devendorf, Carmel remained officially a dry town, though apparently no one alerted Sterling and his friends. More surprisingly, it welcomed African Americans like E. A. Foster, a woman from Michigan who bought one of the first lots in the colony. During the first years, lots sold for as little as fifty dollars, rarely more than a hundred, with five dollars deposit and payments of five dollars a month. The colonists helped themselves to local wood, rock, and anything else not nailed down.

Trying to sort out her own history with Carmel, Austin recalled an early interview for a San Francisco newspaper, in which she had spoken enthusiastically about her determination "some day to have a home there." When she met Sterling, his "first personal remark was that he, too, meant to settle somewhere about Carmel Bay, with no more delay than the building preliminaries called for."[16] Carey McWilliams, the California historian and a friend of both Sterling and Austin, claimed that "the original settlement was the inspiration of Mary Austin, contrary to the legend which always named George Sterling. . . . Frank Powers, who owned most of the property, called on her and suggested that the place be developed as an art colony."[17] Powers, a member of the Bohemian Club, would likewise have supported his friend Sterling's move to Carmel.

Given Austin's and Sterling's personalities, it is not surprising that both claimed to have sighted land first—and that, for all the chest pounding and preening that went on at Coppa's, people disagreed about the date of the Austin dinner or who attended it. In one version she met Sterling after he praised *The Land of Little Rain,* and they visited Carmel together. In another, Austin's own, the two met before she went alone to Carmel, not seeing her new friend again until the summer of 1905—when she was in fact elsewhere. However mixed the recollections, her discovery of the place and her friendship with Sterling brought Austin to the West's most celebrated colony. He arrived in the summer of 1905; she in the early weeks of 1906. Her piecemeal but vivid remembering in *Earth Horizon,* and her impressions in articles and poems like "Three at Carmel," speak to the emotions of those years as she struggled to begin an independent life and build a career.[18]

Austin came to Carmel with wounds to heal, and so did Sterling. By 1905 he had been married for nine years to the Junoesque Caroline "Carrie" Rand, formerly a secretary in his uncle's real-estate business. He had, with the aid of his friend Jack London, philandered and drunk his way through the last several years and had come to understand "probably better than anyone else with whom Jack was acquainted . . . what he meant by the 'white logic' of John Barleycorn."[19] A nonsmoker who swore off coffee and swearing itself, Sterling never for more than a few months swore off alcohol. He had equal difficulty as a sometimes proud, sometimes contrite womanizer, who, as his wife discovered, kept a room in San Francisco for assignations. Carrie presented him with an ultimatum in the guise of a fresh start. Hoping that a change of place would lead to a change of behavior, the couple determined to try again in Carmel.

Though Sterling proclaimed city life the badge of true bohemianism, he imagined a rural colony where like-minded artists could enjoy the pleasures of friendship in a natural setting. Carmel seemed the perfect place. The Arts and Crafts house he (or rather two of his friends) built of redwood, with a loan from his tycoon uncle, included a thirty-foot living room and a stone fireplace with a view toward "the lilac-colored crests" of the Santa Lucia Mountains.[20] In his own soil, Sterling, nursing his conscience, hoed and dug a flourishing garden. "I must raise vegetables, Belgian hares, hens and the fruit of their wombs, squabs and goldfish, 'keep a bee,' raid mussel reefs, and cultivate a taste for rice," Sterling wrote to his friend and supporter, Ambrose Bierce—"not to mention cold water and 'just one girl.'"[21] Bierce—whose fierce white eyebrows and sharp tongue unnerved Carrie— had himself a reputation for being chased, if not hounded, by women, notably Gertrude Atherton. After a long and unsatisfactory flirtation with Bierce, Atherton publicly labeled him a prudish and hypocritical Don Juan, a phrase belonging in his own *Devil's Dictionary.*

The acerbic Bierce, remembered for such stories as "An Occurrence at Owl Creek Bridge," called Sterling the self-appointed "high panjandrum" of the Carmel colony, and few would have disagreed.[22] Coaxing friends from Oakland and San Francisco, Sterling first converted his fellow hedonist, the German-born photographer Arnold Genthe, renowned for his searching portraits of men and women in San Francisco's Chinatown. Genthe built his own redwood house shortly after Sterling's. Mary Austin came next. Soon there followed the likeable Jimmy Hopper, along with the minor writer and lady's man with a propensity for dueling, Harry Leon Wilson; and Harry Lafler, who fell in love with the troubled Nora May French (they called her Phyllis). There "is a side of me that finds an ugly fascination in cigarette smoking, heavy perfume, [and] purple loves," French wrote to her suitor. "You have come very near, with your flowing locks, your sonnets and your pettiness, to being a type I have always hunted with sarcasm and an ax."[23] Tubercular and probably suffering from bipolar disorder, she would be the first of Carmel's suicides. "I fancy that all sensible people will ultimately be damned," she told Lafler, who added that line to Coppa's wall.[24]

Within a few years, the Carmel colony greeted Sinclair "Red" Lewis and the reporter Lincoln Steffens; the writers Alice MacGowan and her sister, Grace MacGowan Cooke; Charmian, and later Jack London; Herbert Heron (founder of Carmel's Forest Theater); and Frederick Bechdolt (muckraker, gold miner, and writer of Westerns), whom Sterling declared the one thoroughbred bohemian of the group. Some members of the growing community remained visitors more than residents, among them Marty Martinez, who came to teach in summer months but lived in the established painters' colony in Monterey, where Charlie Stoddard dragged out his last whiskey-steeped years. Martinez had known Sterling and Jack London in San Francisco, and before that in Oakland. London and Sterling had been friends before London left his first wife, Bessie, and for a time the two men lived in nearby Piedmont, enjoying the company of Stoddard and Joaquin Miller, whose house up the hill was open to both. Besides their passion for Oakland's bars and brothels, they had gathered at Miller's in past years to debate Jack London's positions on art and socialism.

Among the eccentric personalities in the Carmel group, Austin insisted, "George Sterling was easily the most arresting figure."[25] At once a brooder and an extrovert, the mercurial Sterling could be charming and distant, or charming one day and physically absent (or present and unresponsive) the next. He embodied all the wit and intelligence Austin found missing in the broad American society that she, too, believed unfavorable to literary life. In 1903, the year of *The Land of Little Rain,* Jack London won international fame for *The Call of the Wild* (he was, Austin said, already "sagging a little with the surfeit of success"), and Sterling published his first book of poems, *The Testimony of the Suns,* an attractive, if self-conscious volume that cast the mold for most of his later poems.[26] A mix of Keats and Tennyson, with a hint of Baudelaire in *Fleurs du Mal,* Sterling's poems already seemed out of date in years when poets as unlike as Thomas Hardy, William Butler Yeats, Robert Frost, and the young Marianne Moore worked their magic. Moore damned Sterling's poems with faint praise, calling them elegant but eclectic leftovers, and her judgment reflects a common response. Despite the acclaim given *Testimony of the Suns,* Sterling's reputation remained a Western phenomenon. Much as San Francisco readers admired his poems, he never won a national, which then meant an eastern, readership. Whenever he took trips east to win over editors and critics, he typically ended his stays in misery, destitute and eager to leave New York or Connecticut, where he grew up, to lick his wounds in California.

In 1906, Sterling turned thirty-six, as did Austin, who came to Carmel determined to fulfill a long-stifled passion for *life*—without hindrances to her work—in a place as beautiful as any she had seen. "When I first came to this land," she wrote, "a virgin thicket of buckthorn sage and sea-blue lilac spread between well-spaced, long-leaved pines. The dunes glistened white with violet shadows, and in warm hollows, between live oaks, a wine of light had mellowed undisturbed a thousand years."[27] Austin and her colleagues associated that light with ancient Greece and with what they saw as Carmel's magical ethos. Serious or not, Sterling transformed his backyard into a semisacred grove, with a stone fire pit for an altar and the skulls of horses and cows marking his outdoor temple. Local residents referred to milk repositories, scattered throughout the community, as "shrines." The critic Van Wyck Brooks felt as though he were immortalized in Carmel: "this Arcadia, outside the world in which thought evolves . . . for there was something Theocritean, something Sicilian or Greek, in this afternoon land of olive trees, honey-bees and shepherds."[28] As the Victorian Lawrence Alma-Tadema painted his English contemporaries in Roman dress among ancient ruins—or scantily clad in Turkish harems—the "Carmelites" imagined themselves in Grecian groves and pagan disarray. Arnold Genthe remembered Sterling, "proud of his classic contours," scrambling "to the top of a cliff in his bathing trunks. Somewhere or other he had procured a trident and stood silhouetted against the sky while Jimmie Hopper took his picture."[29] Austin re-created the mythical, if not the playful, atmosphere of Carmel in the land of Pan she drew for her novel *Outland* (1910).

A few days after Austin bought her first house in Carmel, on 5 March 1906, Wallace arrived for a visit. Elsie Martinez, the irreverent wife of Marty Martinez, remembered him as "a small amiable man who adored [Austin], thought she was the greatest genius who had ever lived and waited on her hand and foot"—for which the Carmelites called him "Mr. Mary" behind his back. His visit underscored the couple's incompatibility as well as the affection each felt for the other. To Blanche Partington, a theater reviewer for the *San Francisco Call* and a close friend of Sterling and London, with whom she had an affair, Austin explained, "I have only managed to love one man for fifteen years by not obliging myself to love him every day. . . . Hearing that my husband had come up unexpectedly to the convention at Santa Cruz I left town like a streak and hit the trail for Carmel where Stafford [Wallace] joined me. We have had a delightful visit—nicer even than if we had not been married."[30] This is one of her rare tributes to Wallace—and one version of the story. Years later, writing to Charles Lummis, she called her separation from her husband "a protest against the indignity [of his not confessing his "flawed" heredity]. For though my marriage was not satisfying in any particular, I am too thoroughly a democrat to have left him without his full consent unless there had been something like this."[31] That did not interrupt her correspondence with Wallace, who in turn sent her birthday greetings, invited her to Death Valley, where he worked, did research for her autobiography, and once, after a round-the-world trip, brought her a shawl from Kashmir.

Wallace found her attractive, a quality few of her photographs confirm, and definitely not what impressed the crew at Coppa's. Yet many people show badly in photographs, just as they change over time and according to how we see or want to see them. In 1906, according to Elsie Martinez, Austin "was a little tiny thin thing, as thin as a string with a mass of beautiful hair which she took down to show all of us. She was as large as a tank before she died."[32] The various descriptions of her speak of an expressive face, which in certain lights shifted from plain to handsome. As Austin wrote of the eponymous character in her story "The Walking Woman," "she really did have a twist to her face, a sort of natural warp or skew into which it fell when it was worn merely as a countenance, but which disappeared the moment it became the vehicle of thought or feeling."[33] Edith Wharton maybe captures Austin's situation when she writes of her heroine in *The Touchstone* that she missed being loved "by just such a hairbreadth deflection from the line of beauty as had determined the curve" of her lips.[34]

Austin's life in Carmel began by filling simple needs. She left poems and reminiscences about the colony and a "garden book." She did not leave twenty-two pages called "The Truth (But not the whole Truth) about Mary Austin. Written at Carmel-By-The-Sea, Begun March 17, 1906," which she or someone else cut out of a notebook, no doubt to tease her biographers. Still, it is not hard imagining a day in her new life—once Wallace had left and she found her routines. Let's say that she rises early, listening to heavy surf on an unusually warm and clear February morning. Sauntering in her loose robe to pick up milk at the "delivery point," she stares at the Pacific as row after row of white breakers thunder toward her, crashing against the rocks to her right or foaming along the beach while the outer waters lie still and dark. An adventurous cook, Austin returns to inspect her kitchen garden, and after a simple breakfast she plans her day's work. She has not yet arranged for her new "wickiup," an open-air platform resting among Monterey pines that amused her friends and drew sightseers. She writes this morning at her kitchen table, dressed still in her robe, and has arranged for her lunch to be delivered from the Pine Inn, where dinners, subsidized by Devendorf's company, cost forty cents. With dances at the bathhouse—looking seaward from the foot of Ocean Avenue and offering towel and dressing gown at twenty-five cents—or watching for winter storms, or talk that seems as tonic as the pounding of the sea and the wind in the trees, life cannot be much better. And this is a night for a party at the beach.

Picture a cool, starlit evening and most of Austin's new friends, among them guests from Monterey, arriving for the feast. There is to be drinking and eating, along with the work. Sterling and Jimmy Hopper, or Jack London, fill bags with mussels and clams, while others pound the community favorite, abalone, into an edible delicacy for "Thackeray stew," named for the English novelist's "Ballad of Bouillabaisse." Austin takes her turn, and joins in singing "the abalone song," a key part of the ritual. London catches the atmosphere of these occasions from the perspective of distance—and the medium of fiction—in *The Valley of the Moon,* his own tribute to Carmel and to the stereotypical but sympathetic "American" characters, Saxon and Billy, who temporarily join the Carmel colony after escaping the strikes and violence of 1906 Oakland:

> We sit around and gaily pound,
> And bear no acrimony,
> Because our ob—ject is a gob
> Of sizzling abalone.
>
> Oh! Some like ham and some like lamb,
> And some like macaroni;
> But bring me in a pail of gin
> And a tub of abalone.[35]

One dark night—call it this night—Austin walks home a little tipsy, though she denies it, attentively followed by Hopper, whose guidance she refuses. Hopper will tell with delight the story of her banging into tree after tree, all the while protesting that she can walk that way blindfolded. And so, as Pepys would say, to bed, and another day in Arcady.

Austin's intense first year in Carmel depended on Sterling. She spent long hours with him, and, as her essay "George Sterling at Carmel" and "Three at Carmel" make clear, she felt they had a close kinship. After walks around "the jaws" of Point Lobos (not yet associated with Robinson Jeffers, a later Carmelite), drenched from the "smoking foam," they would sip steaming mugs of tea and talk "ambrosial, unquotable talk."[36] Sterling's 1907 poem "The Rack" held special meaning for her, as for the other women to whom Sterling may have dedicated it:

> The sin we could not sin!
> Yes! Tho infernal art
> Goad the remorseful heart,
> Till primacies of pain
> Within this bosom reign,
> First of their legion, first,
> Is that unsated thirst!—
> The pang of lips unkissed,
> The racks of raptures missed![37]

From the outset, eroticism filled the air at Carmel. Van Wyck Brooks later described the colony as "a wildwood with an operatic setting where . . .

curious dramas were taking place in the bungalows and cabins, smothered in blossoming vines on the sylvan slope."[38] A headline in the *Los Angeles Times* proclaimed the town a "hotbed of soulful culture," a "vortex of erotic erudition."[39] Ambrose Bierce, who spent little of his time in Carmel—or anywhere else—disliked the sexual license in the colony and the decadence of his friends' lives. He stayed mainly in San Francisco, which he described as a paradise of ignorance.

Helen MacKnight Doyle thought that Austin wanted a great passion, and very likely she did. She had no patience with the free sex or the countless hours the colonists spent debating the relationship between sex and creativity—which London and Sterling insisted to be causal, as in "no sex, no good writing." Austin claimed not to need a love affair in order to write.[40] She wanted passion without the arguments, and in a limited way she found it with Sterling, who, while appreciating her, seems not to have pursued her as a lover. Austin made no complaints, believing that Sterling could speak with her as with no other woman precisely because he was not physically attracted.

Though Austin found good friends in Carrie Sterling, Jimmy Hopper, Nora May French, and later, Robinson Jeffers, issues of sexuality may have separated her from the community as they had separated her from the regulars at Coppa's. She loved the company, the dinners, the entertainments as much as anyone, but unlike Sterling, for example, she went to Carmel to work. Charmingly aware of his own failings, Sterling wrote in his first year at Carmel one verse drama, aptly if ironically entitled *The Triumphs of Bohemia*.[41] He published his "Wine of Wizardry" in 1907 (and a volume of poems with that title in 1909), which Bierce puffed extravagantly enough to ruin what remained of Sterling's reputation.[42] London and Austin probably wrote more in the next few years than the rest of their confederates put together (though Frederick Bechdolt hammered out the Westerns and Hopper was a steady writer). Oddly, while Austin preferred Sterling to London, she thought that much of the drama and eroticism of the community emanated from London, a man of sharp contrasts and conflicts whose greyblue eyes seemed at once to look into a person's soul and beyond. Sterling affectionately called him "Wolf" and answered himself to "Greek." As Austin said about men she found attractive, women "threw" themselves at London. For many of those who have looked back on the Carmel colony, including at times Austin herself, London looms as a focal personality. Yet for all the fond remembering, he visited Carmel only sporadically, and seldom if ever for more than a week. His journeys to the South Seas, his writing, and his health-damaging labor on the Glen Ellen farm (the "Valley of the Moon") kept him away.

Austin knew Jack London through Sterling, as she came to know someone like Ambrose Bierce. Bierce, who had looked forward to meeting her because he liked her work, did not like Austin in person. She would later describe him as a kind of vampire feeding on Sterling, who felt it necessary to keep the extent of his artistic collaboration with London secret from his mentor. Although London and Austin met and corresponded as equals, their relationship remained one of mutual respect, made possible through the offices of London's "mate," as he called his second wife, Charmian, who played a role similar to that of Eve Lummis in negotiating between Austin and her husband. For all her tact and pains, Charmian drew criticism from her husband's friends, including those at Carmel; they called her overbearing. If it seems odd that Austin should include London with Sterling in "Three at Carmel," the poem shows her admiration for the man who, like herself, loved Sterling, and for the writer whose success she admired and may have envied.

"Three at Carmel" is a poetic snapshot told with the remembered magnificence of the coast and the three persons, taken in a rare moment of friendship and accord. (An actual snapshot includes the "three" in company with the Hobbit-like Jimmy Hopper.) Her poem is a memorial of loving nostalgia for a place that gave her what she had never before found, yet found now with unexpected liabilities. Like "George Sterling at Carmel," the poem suggests what never quite happened: close or at least lasting friendships and collaboration or shared ambitions among those who gathered in this self-conscious Bohemia. Austin writes in *Earth Horizon* that the thing she "suffered from in the middle nineties had been loneness"—not *loneliness,* which she thought an indulgent state of mind, so much as separation from what she needed. Did she, or anyone, end that loneness in Carmel? A bizarre accident would take Harry Lafler's life. Driving home from Big Sur in the fog, he leaned out the window and an oncoming vehicle decapitated him. The Sterlings' house never regained its magic after Nora May French died there in 1907. Distraught about another of George's affairs, Carrie left Sterling in 1913, and five years later, while listening to Chopin's *Funeral March,* she swallowed, like French, a fatal dose of cyanide. Miserable himself in 1926, Sterling chose the same painful route—in lieu of a scheduled speech at the Bohemian Club. Looking back in her autobiography, Austin would write, "California had slipped away from me. Sterling's death and other changes at Carmel had made of it a faded leaf, pressed for remembrance."[43] It had, as she knew, slipped away long before Sterling died.

The Carmel community, important in its own right, reflects the spate of latter-day Brook Farms springing up across the United States in the early twentieth century. From New England to Florida and the Midwest, groups of young intellectuals left the cities to join cooperative groups in country places.[44] Many of these colonies were not, like Carmel, built or occupied by artists. California alone had dozens of religious and political (usually socialist) groups, nearly all underfinanced and short-lived. What they shared amounted to a common dream of benign exile with great work to be done. The socialist Upton Sinclair, for example, bought his own building to create Helicon House, near Englewood, New Jersey, a utopian residence that applied principles of child raising and equality to communal living (without, Sinclair insisted, a hint of sexual misbehavior). He moved with the McGowan sisters and other members from this group to Carmel after Helicon House burned down.

Adopting compatible or overlapping if not necessarily similar values, such colonies emerged across Europe as well as the United States in the years between 1900 and 1930. D. H. Lawrence, who would accept an invitation from Austin's future friend, Mabel Dodge (later Luhan) to visit the colony at Taos, New Mexico, met his wife in another, more famous community. Frieda Lawrence, lover and supporter of Otto Gross—an intellectual George Sterling who advocated and practiced free and open sexual relations—followed Gross to Ascona, a Swiss community built on the "mountain of truth" near Lake Maggiore on the Italian border. Women like Frieda admired Gross's insistence on equality, especially women's, as well as the larger political and intellectual concerns that dominated Ascona and played out uncertainly, if at all, in Carmel, where Upton Sinclair, with his social blueprint and intellectual zeal, proved the exception. Founded in 1900, the Ascona community drew émigrés from across Europe escaping the industrial and military regimes they deplored and seeking Arcadian ideals at the foot of the Alps. Carl Jung, Hermann Hesse, and hundreds of others made their pilgrimage.

The parallels with Carmel, or Monterey, suggest the extent of this cultural movement taking place in the years before what, to many Asconans, seemed the inevitable onset of the Great War.[45] Residents of both Carmel and Ascona saw themselves as the new Athenians in a commercialized and self-destructive world, but not for long. Most, like Austin, found no permanent answers in their utopias, which were always transitory. Carmel could not give Austin heartsease or good health, and for reasons of health her connection with the colony remained brief: a year or two in its halcyon days before and after she bought property on Lincoln Street (with money from the house in Independence); then visits sandwiched between travel abroad, or time in San Francisco and New York, before she sold her house in 1924.[46] The short and interrupted stays made Carmel no less a turning point in her life.

Her search for health, or what she called her place to die, took Austin to Europe in the coming years. Returning, she would find Carmel's once empty streets a honeymoon haven lined with house names—Driftwood, White Caps, Green Breakers, and Surf's Echoes—that would have made the original Carmelites cringe. Austin, who predicted the transformation of the Owens Valley, anticipated an end to Carmel as she knew it. As so often, her sense of impermanence took on a grander perspective. Looking at a red-wood she had just planted, Austin realized it would "not be allowed to live out its five thousand years. Even if I succeed with it, it can be but for thirty or forty years at best," she wrote in her garden journal. "And all the time I know and the sequoia knows that it will be cut off in its prime, yet it will grow on undisturbed by that."[47] She might have been thinking of Henry David Thoreau: "The trees were so grand and venerable that they could not afford to let them grow a hair's breadth bigger, or live a moment longer to reproach themselves."[48] Carmel changed faster than Austin envisioned, so fast that in the 1920s Lincoln Steffens's young wife would rechristen it "Too Many Lampshades by-the-Sea."[49]

Those gathered at Carmel and Ascona tended to lead divided lives. The German-born Asconans spent time in Schwabing, the bohemian section of Munich, and the Carmelites frequented San Francisco. Carmel did not offer publishers and literary opportunities, or city attractions like Coppa's, and most residents had friends in the Bay Area or, like Sterling, temporary jobs when needed. They used the city, much like modern commuters, for necessary business and intermittent entertainments. On 17 April 1906, for example, Enrico Caruso sang in a production of *Carmen* at the opera house, and John Barrymore performed in a local theater. Austin saw neither Caruso nor Barrymore that night, but like them she was unlucky enough to be in the city on 18 April, the day the earthquake struck.

Anyone who felt the huge tremors—which in forty-seven seconds wrenched the land as far away as Los Angeles and knocked down chimneys in Carmel—felt the dread of a world no longer stable. Along the San Andreas Fault much of California split wide open, then closed again, with the western side displaced sixteen feet to the north. Caruso vowed never to come again to a place "where disorders like that are permitted."[50] The city's fire chief died the day of the earthquake, leaving a lesser man in charge of a job that perhaps no one could have handled. City Hall, erected largely on the stones of corruption, fell to pieces. Coppa's restaurant, on Montgomery Street's unstable land, was one of countless casualties. Pavements rose up like waking dinosaurs, streetcar rails twisted free, and, with water mains damaged beyond use, flames soon leapt across the city like forest fires. Wooden structures, built to move with earthquakes as bricks would not, seemed intact one minute and vanished in smoke the next.

In panic, Austin called her brother George. Both may have remembered that, thirty-five years before, their father worked to relieve victims of another great disaster, the 1871 Chicago fire. Having premonition of the quake, Austin had moved the day before from the Palace Hotel, which burned, to Theodore Hittell's house on the edge of the inner city. Austin's friend and advisor, Ina Coolbrith watched the spreading fires and unrewarded efforts of firefighters as she struggled through massing crowds to Fort Mason and the relatively untouched northwest of the city. In the aftermath of the disaster, Coolbrith wrote "San Francisco—April 18, 1906":

Gray wind-blown ashes, broken, toppling wall
And ruined hearth—are these thy funeral pyre?
Black desolation covering as a pall—
Is this thy end—my love and my desire?[51]

Coolbrith lost all her manuscripts, indeed all her possessions, when her house on Taylor Street burned to the ground. She managed to save her two cats. "Imagine," she wrote a friend, "your home with every article it contains swept from you, and you left with not so much as a comb or hair pin or common pin except what might be on your person."[52] Coolbrith especially lamented the burning of the Bohemian Club's irreplaceable library, where she worked, with its treasures of Californian documents, maps, historical accounts, and literary works. Friends offered her shelter. Austin urged her to stay as the Newberrys' guest at Carmel's Pine Inn. "You and I have never had the opportunity to become properly acquainted," she wrote.

"Come and sit in my wickiup and write a poem, and we will walk by the sea and talk and talk."[53] Although she could not perform her usual work, the Bohemian Club doubled Coolbrith's part-time salary to a hundred dollars a month, and friends, including Austin, Sterling, Hopper, and London, brought out a subscription volume to provide her more income.[54]

Austin's response to the earthquake, a personal essay titled "The Tremblor," appeared in David Starr Jordan's *The California Earthquake of 1906* (1907), a book that included chapters by several friends. She confesses that there are three things she will "never be able to abide in quietness again— the smell of burning, the creaking of house-beams in the night, and the roar of a great city going past." Her account gives a sense of growing fear, her compassion for those who suffered, and the enormity of the events themselves: "The appreciation of calamity widened slowly as water rays on a mantling pond. . . . Almost before the dust of ruined walls had ceased rising, smoke began to go up against the sun, which, by nine of the clock, showed bloodshot through it as the eye of Disaster. It is perfectly safe to believe anything anyone tells you of personal adventure; the inventive faculty does not exist which could outdo the actuality; little things prick themselves on the attention as the index of the greater horror." Recalling the bright, almost illuminated red of a potted geranium "undisturbed on a window ledge in a wall of which the brickwork drooped outward, while the roof had gone through the flooring," she pans to a wider view of "Market Street Wednesday morning, in the district known as the Mission," where "cheap man-traps folded in like pasteboard." From these, "before the rip of the flames blotted out the sound, arose a thin, long scream of mortal agony."[55]

"It was all like this," she writes, "broken bits of human tragedy, curiously unrelated, inconsequential, disrupted by the tremblor, impossible to this day to gather up and compose into a proper picture."[56] In fact, she composed one of the best:

> Before the red night paled into murky dawn thousands of people were vomited out of the angry throat of the street far down toward Market. Even the smallest child carried something, or pushed it before him on a rocking chair, or dragged it behind him in a trunk. . . . All the women saved their best hats and their babies, and, if there were no babies, some of them pushed pianos up the cement pavements. All the faces were smutched and pallid, all the figures sloped steadily forward toward the cleared places. Behind them the expelling fire bent out over the lines of flight, the writhing smoke stooped and waved, a fine rain of cinders pattered and rustled over all the folks. There was a strange, hot, sickish smell

in the street as if it had become the hollow slot of some fiery breathing snake.[57]

Evoking the inferno she saw and heard and smelled, Austin writes about the responses of ordinary people. She credits their surprisingly good manners, their wry humor in snippets of conversation, as when one man responded to her calling the conflagration her "judgment day." "Aw!" he said, "it looks like hell!" In the parks where she watched other refugees huddled on the damp grass with hardly any bedding, food, or water, they laughed "the laughter of unbroken courage." The stoicism reminds her of her favorite theme. "Right here [in Jefferson Square], if you had time for it, you gripped the large, essential spirit of the West, the ability to dramatize its own activity, and, while continuing in it, to stand off and be vastly entertained by it." By this time she has, if not mythified the people of San Francisco, moved from her own private perspective to a kind of collective telling. "Everyone tells you tales like this," she writes, as if in everyone's voice.[58]

Her essay suggests the widening range of Austin's work in these years, and the energy she brought to it. She won a reputation for different kinds of writing, including bread-and-butter stories for magazines. Her books, too, appeared in rapid succession. Between *The Land of Little Rain* in 1903 and her move to Carmel, Austin had published *The Basket Woman* and *Isidro* and worked on *The Flock,* published in 1906. *Santa Lucia* came out in 1908, followed by *Lost Borders* in 1909 and the fantasy *Outland* in 1910, written with or possibly inspired by George Sterling, who invented dozens of plots and freely presented them to his friends. Jack London offered to pay Sterling—and did charitably pay the young Sinclair Lewis—for plots he may not have meant to use.

Among Austin's books, *Outland,* because of its setting, and *Isidro,* because of its subject, seem the real fruits of her time in Carmel. A historical romance, *Isidro* pays tribute to the lost times of Spanish California. Its titular hero, a young *hidalgo,* commits himself to the church until his journeys bring him together with a handsome young "lad," who eventually emerges as a beautiful young woman, heir to a great fortune. Murder, theft, ambition, gossip, unexpected (yet expected) turns of fortune, Spanish manners, Indian fights and rights, all combined to make Austin's one such foray a popular success. While Carmel and Monterey provide the main settings, the story sprawls over Alta California in the generation after Father Serra and before the gringos came to take the land. Austin's pleasure in the land included its history, which drives the story of *Isidro.* "In a cove of quietness back from the bay, between the mountain and the Point of Pines, stands Carmel, otherwise the Mission San Carlos Borromeo, established by that great saint and greater man, Fray Junipera Serra, for the salvation of souls and the increasing glory of God."[59] Places and people mattered to Austin, who admired the mission era of old California as she admired the ancient traditions of American Indians. In *Isidro* she writes about both, playfully commenting on the church's feminization of priests (they wear dresses), and more caustically on its treatment of Native peoples (flogged escaping the mission) and its subordination of women. "Do women become priests ever," the ironic heroine asks.[60] Near the end of the novel, Marta, an Indian convert to Christianity, sacrifices her life for her scapegrace son: "She took no care of what might happen to herself. . . . God's priests should so carry salvation to men."[61] In this, her first novel, Austin writes with the authorial intimacy and historical zeal of a Walter Scott or Robert Louis Stevenson, who, as Austin was well aware, described the Carmel coast for settings in *Treasure Island.*

Austin's borrowed materials for *Isidro* include reports of a local crime (a shepherd's murder of a rancher), which drives some of her plot; and the story of a misanthropic trapper, Peter Lebeque (from an Edward Beale story), whose name and disposition she took for her heroine's quasi-guardian. Austin offers a self-consciously historical spoof, including clever rewriting of Shakespearean comic scenes in which loquacious heroines playing men's parts force couples through the witty torture of hidden or shifting sexual identities. The primness of her language, breasts as "female amplitudes," adds to the humor and to the relationship between the epicene hero and the sharp-tongued girl-as-boy—she calls herself El Zarro, "the thorn"—as they stumble toward the obvious conclusion. Austin pushes the limits of polite fiction with titillating scenes of homosexual embraces, miscegenation, and near rape, as when Marta's son kidnaps El Zarro, whom he knows to be a woman: "At every shift of the rider the girl struggled shrewdly, but neither wept nor cried out. Once he spoke to his horse and she grew instantly quiet. He trembled through all his naked body at the sudden loosening of the tension of hers. Had she recognized his voice? was this the quiescence of submission? They rode; he felt her breast heave and fill under his hand; the weight of her body was sweet upon his arm. . . . His passion had reached that state where it was necessary for his ease to know how she stood toward it."[62]

Isidro, which had a larger first run than any other of Austin's books, indicates—beyond the articles and stories for magazines—the future pattern of her work. Throughout her life she kept articles and book ideas, along with her voluminous notes, ready on the back burner. The assortment of projects may have left Austin herself unsure about the kind of writer she was or preferred to be, and it damaged her reputation by inviting readers to judge each new work in terms of its contrasting predecessors. She seldom followed one book with anything similar, partly because the previous book had not sold enough, partly because she continued to experiment and explore new avenues.

She followed *Isidro* with *The Flock,* a book conceived as a companion to *The Land of Little Rain* and begun in Bakersfield, where she stayed after the death of her sister-in-law, in early December 1904. At the time, Austin had provided fodder for town gossips by spending several unchaperoned days at the Rancho El Tejon—and more importantly, renewed her acquaintance with the landscape of the southern San Joaquin. *The Flock* focuses on these grazing lands where she had lived so long and observed so intimately. It is at once a complement to *Isidro* and a contrast: filled with extraordinary descriptions of landscape, bred in history, idiosyncratic in whatever genre it most nearly approximates, and at the same time so unlike *Isidro* that it suggests a different imagination.

In subject *The Flock* connects with the writings of John Muir, whom Austin had met and disagreed with in the house of their mutual friends, the Hittells. Five years after publication of *The Flock,* Muir issued what seems to be a rebuttal of Austin. Muir had written notes for *My First Summer in the Sierra* in 1869, describing his miraculous few months following sheep to the highest meadows of the Sierra. He rewrote and added to the book before its publication in 1911. Whether or not Muir remembered meeting Austin at the Hittels, he evidently responded to her oblique criticism in *The Flock.* Much later, Austin would respond to Muir in *Earth Horizon,* where she derides false "Naturists" and their untrue autobiographies, with Muir and his stance on land use clearly in mind: "All the public expects of practicing Naturists is the appearance, the habits, the incidents of the wild; when the Naturist reports upon himself, it is mistaken for poetizing."[63] Her problems with the "truth" of autobiography aside, Austin offers an alternative to Muir's philosophy based on her experience of the land, from the Mojave Desert to the southern edge of the San Joaquin to the eastern wall of the mountains Muir baptized as "the Range of Light."

The Flock and *My First Summer in the Sierra* intimately reflect their authors, and they overlap. Here two of America's most eloquent advocates for conservation and future planning write with a shared respect for their subjects and a profound but contrary purpose.[64] Both books can be seen as oracular meditations, at once personal and political. Both invite readers to see and hear, almost to experience, the writer's own relationship with the staggering beauty of the land. And both deal with sheep.

As Austin's title announces, *The Flock* centers on sheep, the men who herd them, and the economic and ecological implications of the trade. It begins with a historical sketch of sheepherding from the early days of Spanish exploration to contemporary times, when Austin offers her account of what has been, what is, and what should be in the tending and grazing of flocks. Muir treks into the Sierras because a friendly sheep owner offers him a shepherd's sinecure: traveling with the flock and its real shepherd, complete with board and all the room of the mountains themselves. To the extent Austin honors and likes the shepherds she has observed, Muir finds his shepherd verging on the subhuman. The man learns nothing, seems at times insane from lack of company, eats like an animal, washes less than an animal, and has no interest in the sacred land he sees only as grass.

The two books resist definition, except that Muir's personal account of religious awakening implies what Austin deplored, the egotistical confessional qualities of earlier spiritual autobiographies. No less spiritual in its own way, *The Flock* avoids personal religious effusions, if not those about the natural world. Instead, like *The Land of Little Rain*, it deals with the lives of others, and in this book, too, those lives are solitary and hard counterparts to the "hard places" themselves. Austin presents the shepherds' journeys in a cyclical, almost mythical, world, in which she talks of astrological signs, earthly seasons, and remote ancient practices. Personal at times, distant at others, Austin the witness recounts stories told to her by French, Basque, Scottish, German, and Italian shepherds who drive their (or their employers') flocks across tracts of desert and mountain to the upper Tuolumne and other meadows of the High Sierra that are Muir's own destination.

Whereas Muir dismisses the sheep as "hoofed locusts" scouring the ground and eating everything in front of their noses, Austin considers the animals and the industry they represent benign. No less than Muir, she loves the land the sheep tread, and she may be the more consistent. Hers is a carefully hewn book, and Muir's an ever-rising account of physical climbing and spiritual rapture. Though quite different from a writer like William Wordsworth, Austin works in the same tradition and for a comparable end. In "Michael," Wordsworth tells the story of an old shepherd in whom he finds the strengths and values of Old Testament prophecy for a modern world. Sheep matter to him as they matter in the Bible, in which "the Lord is my shepherd," and the Patriarchs and Christ guide their flocks. Like Wordsworth a century earlier, Austin creates a new pastoral, which honors the ordinary man and woman, including the socially outcast. Her shepherds are anything but stinking idiots or cowards unworthy of respect. Many are foreign and therefore not fluent in their adopted language, but most, she believes, are bred to be storytellers. She speaks to a human dignity that is inclusive and forgiving. Pleading for better treatment of the independent shepherds he called "statesmen," Wordsworth sent a copy of his poem to Charles James Fox, Britain's foreign secretary; democrat as she was, Austin sent hers to the American public.

Muir writes in a contrary tradition, the transcendental and middle-class tradition of Henry David Thoreau, for whom a rural retreat enabled spiritual awakening on the shore of Walden Pond, though balanced by visits home. Muir in his quest goes farther and higher. Like Thoreau and Austin, he has an uncanny eye for natural detail, whether the angle of a shadow, the flight of a bird, or the soldierly discipline of ants. When, in *My First Summer* or his later writings about the Sierras and the Sierra Club, Muir thinks of the wilderness he has so intrepidly walked and climbed—hanging over Yosemite Falls or helpless *once* on a mountain wall—he urges the protection of land for those who appreciate the glory of God in the sublimity of the mountains. The long European and American passage, aesthetic and physical, toward venerating that sublimity comes to its climax in Muir's writing—as in Ansel Adams's photography. Adams, indeed, revered Muir, as he did Austin, with whom he collaborated and whose *Land of Little Rain* he edited with a selection of his own photographs. He recognized Austin's singular grasp of the landscape and its people and saw a kinship between his work and hers, perhaps, too, between Austin's and Muir's. Adams singled out *The Land of Little Rain,* and it would have been that book rather than *The Flock* that came closest to Muir, not because her vision of the land had changed in principle, but because the later book emphasizes ecological and aesthetic issues a little less and human needs more.

Unlike Muir, who farmed the San Joaquin as if farming were unconnected to the mountains and deserts nearby, Austin did not argue for national parks and preserved land; instead she wanted intelligent land use based on unbiased policies. She understood, for example, that the alpine meadows Muir wanted to hold pristine were not natural to the Sierras. Indian fires and the grazing of sheep had created those mountain meadows and flowerbeds and kept them intact, as well as protecting the sugar pines and other trees that have since become so vulnerable to fire.[65] There may be no right or wrong side in the virtual debate between Muir and Austin, and Muir clearly won in terms of public opinion and the establishment of the national parks that have become essential to Americans' sense of their country. Austin openly spoke about bad shepherding that could and sometimes did ruin grassland. She remained no less committed to the livelihood of ordinary people and a fuller use of natural resources for what she saw as equally natural purposes.

As Austin learned from her brief mentorship with William James, *natural* may not necessarily mean what Muir and the Sierra Club have argued; the term must be defined in part by human practices. Austin's whole historical argument comes to this: after thousands of years, sheep and their cropped pastures are more natural than national parks "protected" from cleansing fires and benevolent grazing. Given the intervening history of Yosemite National Park's commercialism, she might have asked whether humans or sheep have the better record. But this, of course, simplifies the issues. Who would have managed the growing numbers, the hundred thousands of sheep in those mountains? Who would have parceled out the ranges? And if the sheep were welcome, why not strip mining? The cutting of the sequoias? The diversion of rivers? Muir may have better understood the situation: the need for protection in a region, regardless of competing values, where population has long outstripped a will to conserve—if only in Austin's sense of the word. But however persuasive Muir's arguments, Austin would not have given an inch. "I know something of what went on in Muir," she writes in her autobiography, still distrusting the man and his ideas.[66]

With the success of books like *The Land of Little Rain* and *The Flock,* Austin felt herself to be hitting her stride as a writer. Specifically, she thought she could negotiate a living wage with her publisher, Houghton Mifflin. "It isn't a question of loyalty any more, it isn't even a question of what will be best in ten years, it is just a question of paying my board here and now. I think I have it in me to do bigger novels than anybody in the west is doing," she wrote in June 1907, "but I can not do them and work at other things for a living. There are publishers willing to back me for the effort if only they can have book as well as serial rights, and unless you can manage some way to make some money for me, I shall have to close with them."[67]

"There is little to be said beyond what we have already written to Mrs. Austin," her editor W. S. Booth advised his colleagues. "She evidently needs a lesson, and also an impresario as a publisher, who will 'finance' her and 'promote' her—I should let her go and get her experience: in a friendly & polite letter." Her suggestion that they bring out a limited edition of her desert books—*The Land of Little Rain, The Flock,* and *Lost Borders*—earned two exclamation marks from Booth.[68] Not for the last time did she misread her publishers and overestimate her literary coin.

Anyone meeting Mary Austin during her Carmel time would have had to look closely to find the young woman whose awkward earnestness touched General Beale's heart nearly twenty years before. Beale had been dead more than a decade and so too a part of his young friend, whose endearing hesitancy had turned, after years of personal and professional struggles, toward obstinacy. Maybe with Charles Lummis rather than William James as her model, she had developed a persona that made an easy target for critics and reporters looking for copy. Elizabeth "Elsie" Sergeant, a friend and professional writer, thought her at once misunderstood and immature. "Naively dislocated and frustrated as a human being," she "had no gift, such as Amy Lowell had, for exploiting her own idiosyncrasies, and never ceased to suffer the curse of the outsider."[69] Not to mention that she lacked Lowell's wealth.

For all the ambrosial talk and companionship of Carmel, Austin felt herself an outsider there too, and so did nearly everyone: it was the curse of the artist—or a fact of life. Carmel had offered an Arcadian interlude, but life, in the guise of death, now paid a call. Although her health had never been good—she took stimulants for her heart, at times every half hour, and endured chronic pain in her left arm—Austin had learned to live with illness. Disappointments and frustrations, clashes with publishers, and lack of money: these worries paled in the summer of 1907. Thirty-nine years old, she was diagnosed with terminal breast cancer, which a second doctor confirmed. Accepting that her death was imminent, she bade goodbye to friends in Carmel and set off, as she and everyone else expected, to end her life quietly and cheaply in Rome.

five

IN ITALY AND ENGLAND

1907–1910

If I die here
In a strange land,
If I die
In a land not my own,
Nevertheless, the thunder
The rolling thunder
Will take me home.

MARY AUSTIN
Children Sing in the Far West, 1913

EXPECTING TO DIE BUT READY to fight for her life in the fall of 1907, Mary Austin prepared for her voyage to Europe by tying up loose ends at home. She stopped first in Los Angeles to visit her brother Jim and his new fiancée, though mainly to see the other Mary, Jim's troubled daughter, "a cross" for her to leave behind and someone for whom she had begun to feel responsible.[1] From Southern California she took the train to New York City where, for reasons of money and ego, she made arrangements to speak with her editors at Houghton Mifflin. Confident that her presence would sway them, she got a surprising snub. They offered no reassurance about her new book, *Lost Borders,* or the proposed *Santa Lucia,* and refused the advance she needed for travel. Caught off guard, she turned to Harper & Brothers, who promptly gave her a generous contract for *Lost Borders* and took first refusal on *Santa Lucia.*

There were understandable reasons for Harper's welcome. Austin had published with the rival *Atlantic Monthly,* which issued parts of *The Land of Little Rain.* Bliss Perry, *The Atlantic*'s editor, thought highly of her work, but so did Perry's friend, the scholarly editor at Harper's, Henry Mills

Alden. Alden had an eye for talent and no doubt wanted Austin's books as well as magazine pieces for *Harper's Monthly*. A spiritual man who looked rather like a Scottish minister and shared Austin's interest in religion and the afterlife, he was known to lull his guests to sleep as he discoursed on metaphysics. Having lost a beloved wife after painful and futile operations for breast cancer, he would have been sympathetic to someone who merely hinted at similar distress. Skilled at smoothing ruffled feathers, Alden made converts of notorious eccentrics, including Lafcadio Hearn, the man who wrote luminously about Japan and offended even his staunchest supporters. Austin, for her part, wanted a decent return for her work and a sympathetic editor who prized her. Alden assured her that she belonged "to the first rank of American writers," on a par with and maybe outshining Edith Wharton.[2]

Apart from Harper's, an unsolicited bonus came as an invitation from the New York theater impresario, David Belasco, who offered to produce one of Austin's plays in his own Stuyvesant Theatre. A star maker and playwright, Belasco wrote a script that Puccini adapted for *Madame Butterfly* and successfully collaborated with entrepreneurs of the American theater such as James A. Herne and Henry C. DeMille, whose son Cecil (producer of such films as *The Greatest Show on Earth* and *The Ten Commandments*) he mentored. Austin crossed her fingers and sent Belasco a script based on *Isidro,* aware that his name on any project promised lavish sets and standing-room-only audiences. To her Stanford University friend, Vernon Kellogg, she wrote, "My business has occupied so much of my time that I have seen very little of New York but what I have seen is very fascinating."[3] She would see much more of the city in years to come; at the moment, it seemed grimly ironic that fame in New York or anywhere else promised to be posthumous. Her business taken care of, she followed Kellogg's fiancée Charlotte Hoffmann, who had sailed in late May or early June for Italy. Austin planned to travel with the couple and witness their wedding.

She could not have found more supportive or like-minded friends: Charlotte, a large and prepossessing woman, resembled a Wagnerian heroine and acted in amateur theatricals, especially Carmel's. Vernon, an eminent entomologist and geneticist, got along with international colleagues in various disciplines as well as with the bohemians at Coppa's restaurant. A founder of the National Research Council, he wanted science to improve people's lives. During the First World War, the Kelloggs would serve their country in Belgium, where Vernon spearheaded American relief efforts; they both reported on the war for *The Atlantic Monthly.*

Austin's more or less casual letter to Kellogg indicates her public way of dealing, or rather not dealing, with her illness. She hoped for a quiet exit, complained little, and, though in great pain, said that her worst fear lay in finding the right place to die. She had not wished to impose on the Sterlings, or worse, follow the example of Nora May French, who committed suicide less than two weeks after Austin left Carmel and whose ashes a stricken George Sterling scattered at Point Lobos.[4] Longing to see Rome, Austin decided that she had money enough to end her life there and to sail in the meantime first-class. On the voyage to Genoa, by way of the Azores and Gibraltar, she serendipitously met Prince Cagiati, a papal representative who sympathized with her desire to learn about early Christian prayer, which she hoped might help her to die comfortably or—that remote and seductive fantasy—to prevail over her illness. Willing herself into resignation, she still worried about a false optimism of the sort that had driven the young and terminally ill John Keats to the ancient city almost a century before. At the same time, she would not give in, not surrender. If the inevitable happened, she would have resisted to the end—and would have found a way to die with grace.

When, in later years, she remembered her resolution to fight and make the most of a short life, Austin framed the experience of her journey in epic terms. She saw herself threatened in the face of seductive European traditions, as if the experience of Europe might divide her from the vitality of American art or steal her hard-won identity.[5] She soon discovered that the art she saw in Italy reinforced her convictions, for she took the "old masters" to be mavericks, artists who saw the world with a clarity and fearlessness resembling her own. In large part, Austin approached and understood Italy through its painters. The account of her struggle with death she called *Christ in Italy: Being the Adventures of a Maverick among Masterpieces* (1912). While giving no false deference to anything she considered unworthy, she accepted those masterpieces as a new standard. She would take home an original Della Robbia and lithographs of prized paintings—coal to Newcastle, perhaps, for a writer who would collaborate with Ansel Adams and befriend painters like Marsden Hartley.

Looking back on these troubled times, Austin speaks in antitheses, as if describing a religious battle of the soul and self. She characterizes her illness as something lurking between death and continued life, and at the same time entwined with the old masters' paintings. Despite her rejection of Christianity, *Christ in Italy* grows into a meditation on Christ the person, who belies the sallow, pathetic portrayals by many of the old masters and emerges, like her, a fighter who will not "go gently into that good night."[6] Austin, who professed to have seen a vision of Christ in the American desert, acknowledges his presence among the shrubberies of Italian gardens and the provocative spaces of Medieval and Renaissance art. Without explanation or by-your-leave, she reports what she encounters, the living Christ or, as she calls him elsewhere, "the *man* Jesus" entering her life.

Christ in Italy offers limited details about the trips she took, the places she lived, or her meetings with Italians, excepting men and women of the church and the long-dead artists who guided her. One section of her book, titled "Love and the Young Lady," she devotes wholly to an afternoon in Rome's Borghesi Palace, when "the pictures hung in a heavy drowse; they nodded; suddenly as if the hot Roman afternoon had weighed them past the breaking point of tension, they snapped wide awake."[7] Almost in hiding, she overhears a conversation between the two women in Titian's painting known as *Sacred and Profane Love*.

As with the Christ encounters, Austin tells an extraordinary story with a certain nonchalance. She looks from a dark recess at the painting, which depicts on the right side a magnificent and nearly nude woman, Venus, standing and holding a lamp above her head. On the left side sits another woman, richly dressed—perhaps a middle-class bride—with Cupid lounging behind her. The two women resemble each other and may be intended as the same person in full garb and seminude. One interpretation of the painting holds that the women represent Venus at the extremes of love, the first sacred, the other earthly or profane.[8] Austin describes Venus responding to the young woman's questions as if to a novice or supplicant ignorant in love's ways: " 'Titian painted you,' she said, 'and you have the failings of your time. It comes of thinking too much about your souls. No man ever loved a woman because she deserved it. You are worth exactly as much love as you can create.' "[9]

The conversation goes on until "the guard's feet scraped at the door. Love took up the Lamp of Life and her station at the fountain. The young lady fell a dreaming again and I crept up under the picture." Seductive as this is (including the narrator *creeping* to the painting), she goes further, directly addressing "the Lady with the Lamp." Once more the painted figure offers a disquisition on love and its necessary guiles, though now to a less patient audience. "Tell me why it is," Austin asks, "women can not give love, and laugh, and think no more about it, as men do?" "Because," replies the Lady, "love means laughter to men, laughter and delight, but to a woman it has always meant pain and the giving of life." Unlike the innocent who spoke before, Austin has a few things to tell her tutor about the ways of men and the afflictions of women. "Titian painted *you*," she says, quoting the Lady's words against her, "and you have the limitations of your time. . . . But I knew, in fact, that we had come to the end of Titian's age; we would have to do our own answering."[10] An active amateur artist and drawn to various arts, Austin plays with illusions, creating a fantasy beyond the painting in her own and her reader's imagination. This is a witty tour de force and her homage paid to a work she admired. She chose well. Titian's painting, restored for the reopening of the gallery in the 1990s, remains the pride of the Borghesi Palace—though perhaps not because Austin conversed with Venus there a century ago.

Someone picking up *Christ in Italy* might think its author an eccentric dreamer, or better, an enthusiastic scholar, a student-connoisseur of John Ruskin. In this respect Austin had rivals. Edith Wharton could, as Austin almost certainly could not, distinguish the misidentified paintings of lesser-known Italian painters. William Dean Howells protested his ignorance of art and knew Venetian painting intimately by the time he ended his four-year consulship in Venice. Little as Howells's *Tuscan Cities* says about specific paintings, his knowledge of them informs his several books about Italy. And of course there were the Vernon Lees and Bernard Berensons, along with a host of informed artists, from the illustrator Joseph Pennell to John Singer Sargent, every one of whom had more knowledge, if not necessarily more insight, than Austin about the centuries of Italian painting. What distinguishes Austin is her unpredictable perspective—whether on art, natural splendors, or the way people take their boiled eggs, all driven at this time by her increasingly sad sense of what she had missed. "I take even my sin experiencingly," she would write. "We have a price to pay for the purchase of intelligence."[11]

Austin's Italian journey served as both her forty days in the wilderness and her seemingly final holiday. Along with her religious searching and her near or imagined encounters with Christ, she traveled in Europe on the American equivalent of the "grand tour," one of thousands admiring the duomo by Giotto, its doors by Ghiberti and Pisano, the sites, the ruins, the art, from Roman times through the *Risorgimento*. She made the obligatory pilgrimages, pressing flowers, for example, from the graves of Keats and Shelley. Yet on the whole she did not think the tour "grand" at all, partly because of bad health and depression, partly because she felt out of her element. She met her share of like-minded people, and in Rome she reconnected with an acquaintance from her days at El Alisal, the poet Grace Ellery Channing.

Channing and her husband, the painter Charles Walter Stetson, had lived abroad since 1901. Deaf and ill, he would die in Rome the summer after Austin returned to the United States. Surviving her husband by more than a quarter century, Channing, like Vernon and Charlotte Kellogg, reported from the front lines during the First World War. Excepting Channing and her husband, the Kelloggs, and one or two others, Austin remained scornful of fellow travelers and, at times, cantankerous about Italy itself. As she wrote later from Lausanne, Switzerland, to Eve Lummis, Italy appeared to her "squalid, swarming with beggars, and misborn, overworked women and malnutritioned children." She could only afford third-rate *pensiones,* full of "broken down school teachers and unsuccessful artists," bitter women, undesirable, and "people who had gotten into trouble at home, or were so disagreeable nobody would live with them."[12]

With the Kelloggs, Austin explored Tuscany, beginning in Fiesole with the "Etruscan places," as D. H. Lawrence called them, atop the hills near Florence, where Charlotte and Vernon held their wedding service. After the wedding in late April 1908, the Kelloggs, intent on their honeymoon, arranged for Austin to visit the south of Italy with a new acquaintance, Edna MacDuffie, "a charming and interesting young woman" from Berkeley. They traveled as far as Pompeii and Herculaneum before turning north toward Rome. On the return from her southern journey, Austin noticed an improvement in her health. "By the time we reached the Cathedral of Siena," she writes in *Earth Horizon,* "the pain had receded. At Venice and Roncegno it disappeared. So we came up through Italy and lost it altogether." Her brief account omits the many setbacks recounted in letters, which spell out a list of new and continuing infirmities: rheumatism, neuralgia, and neuritis in Florence; various afflictions in Siena; partial loss of the use of her left arm during spa treatments at Roncegno, in the Tyrol. Yet she did slowly recuperate. Friends at Lake Como commented that she wore no sling for her arm and, unaware of changes to that point, she realized that her cancer symptoms or the cancer itself had disappeared. In her own words, she "had evaded it." A hundred years later, no one can say definitively whether Austin had been misdiagnosed (again, her symptoms conformed to those of angina) or made some sort of miraculous recovery. *Earth Horizon,* in which she compresses the eve of her departure for Italy and Ruth's institutionalization—"She had put her daughter in a private institution, being too ill herself to take care of her"—suggests one underlying root of her illnesses.[13]

Austin liked to attribute her cure to prayer. Through Prince Cagiati, her fellow traveler to Genoa, she had met Cardinal Merry del Val, who in turn introduced her to Mother Veronica, the Irish woman in charge of the Blue Nuns, an order dedicated to nursing and famous for their blue habits. The gracious Veronica proved the single most important person in her recovery. "It was Mother Veronica who taught me what to do about my pain . . . how to leave it behind me."[14] From her, Austin claimed to have learned the art of *useful* prayer, a process of entering another state of mind in which suffering diminishes and the mind grasps the reality of God or Christ's presence while putting aside the slightest chance of recuperation. She found kinship between ancient Christian prayer and forms of American Indian worship, believing that for all their apparent differences, the mode of prayer she learned from Mother Veronica (and an unnamed priest to whom Veronica introduced her) worked in ways analogous to the rituals of the Native men and women who taught her on General Beale's ranch and in the campoodies of the high desert near Lone Pine and Independence.

The woman who befriended and supported outcasts at home chose some strikingly different associates in Italy. Prince Cagiati and Cardinal del Val were high-ranking supporters and diplomatic representatives of an autocratic pope, Pius X, who had risen to the papacy in 1903. Known as an unbending opponent of Catholic liberals, Pius arranged for priests and others to spy on their peers and defrocked or excommunicated those he deemed insufficiently in step.[15] (The career of the converted Irishman and outspoken "liberal," George Tyrrell, is a case in point; fully aware of the risks he took, Tyrrell was silenced and all but excommunicated shortly before his early death.) Elevated by Pius X to cardinal and then, while still in his thirties, to papal secretary of state, Merry del Val won the disfavor of many priests and took blame for increased bitterness between France and Rome.[16] Both he and Prince Cagiati worked as trusted agents of the pope and spokesmen for his doctrines.

Austin assumed the cardinal admired her for the accounts she wrote of Carmel's Mission San Carlos Borromeo, which he had read.[17] He would have taken interest in anything related to Carlo Borromeo, once archbishop of Milan and a favorite Italian saint. But though a Spaniard born in London and at home across Europe, the cardinal had strong interests in the Americas for personal and professional reasons, including the pope's determination to strengthen and broaden the American church. Given the circumstances, Merry del Val and Prince Cagiati may have viewed Austin as a prize convert and potential advocate. It seems odd that she made these friendships and immersed herself in Catholicism at a time when she had rejected all Christianity other than her own. Whether she flirted with Catholicism or felt flattered by the attention of church dignitaries, she had to know that her Roman friends represented the reactionary side of the Catholic Church. She may, of course, have been flattered or intrigued by the irony of her maverick self at home with those who thought so differently.

Austin never hesitated to seek out people if she found them interesting or attractive—as she did the cardinal and Prince Cagiati, or before them, William James, whose hotel room door she had knocked at years before. One day in Florence she caught "a glimpse of a slender woman walking; a slender woman with suave motions incredibly beautiful," whom she followed, lost, and found again, along the Via Tornabuoni. The woman turned out to be Isadora Duncan, and what caught Austin's eye was the elegant movement of the dancer who, she said, strove to embody "the freedom of women."[18] To quote another admirer, Duncan seemed to tell "the air the very things we long to hear."[19] Austin agreed, though she thought that Duncan's Grecian-inspired costumes (they resembled her own in Carmel) were better suited for a cook than for the mother of modern dance. Through a mutual friend, Edward Gordon Craig, Austin and Duncan eventually met and found that they had more in common than their attraction to Craig. They talked together "of love and its checks and losses," profane love, that is, a topic both held dear.[20]

Austin most likely knew Craig through Arnold Genthe, who befriended and photographed legions of American and English theater people and gladly provided introductions. Craig had recently published his manifesto, *The Art of the Theatre* (1904) and produced *The Vikings* and *Much Ado about Nothing* for his actress-mother, Ellen Terry. A multitalented man—artist, author, actor, director—Craig called for minimalist theater effects and for directors to have absolute control over productions. He showed open disdain for the kind of lavish sets David Belasco favored as well as for egotistical actors, who included Ellen Terry. A flamboyantly handsome man, with long hair flowing back from a high brow and a winged mouth, Craig, rather like George Sterling, had scores of women—Austin called them "prairie dogs"—yearning for his affection. Chief among them was Duncan, the mother of their two-year-old daughter, Deirdre.[21]

Austin enjoyed her discussions with Craig and disagreed with him about the merits of realistic theater he debunked—though both appreciated the power of ancient Greek theater and wanted more poetic or uncluttered and evocative sets. Duncan had written that Craig's vision for modern theater promised a new and harmonious world for playwrights. Austin partly agreed. Her later judgment, however, was that Craig stood for tradition in the theater, she for upheaval. In fact, Craig stands with Bertolt Brecht and few others as a driving force in twentieth-century theater. Much as she may have learned from him, Austin would not pursue her friendship with Craig when they were both in London.[22] In later encounters, Duncan snubbed or chose to ignore her.

In the early spring of 1909, Austin, accompanied by Edna McDuffie and another acquaintance, left Italy for London by way of Paris, where her escorts "went into a school" and she "into a *pension.*" Just as she had met Craig in Florence, she now met James Wilkinson, another young man "part French, part English, who proved companionable."[23] Her Parisian interlude might have been another woman's Roman spring, a time for love and renewal, and with a man of the theater. She and Wilkinson, who went on to be a successful set designer, acted in a student performance of *Macbeth,* attended exhibitions (Cezanne's paintings "sang" to her), the ballet and plays, including the anti-Semitic *Israel.*[24] Wilkinson remembered Austin as "indignant" at people, "looking down on them [Jews] just as America does on negroes."[25] But in her autobiography Austin has little to say about Paris, where she suffered another bout of illness and spent much of her days confined to her *pension.* She also fretted about putting money aside for Ruth, whom she assumed would outlive her. Hoping to save fifteen thousand dollars in income-bearing property, she had managed only five.[26]

Though marred by pain and eye troubles, Austin's months in Paris offered, as her letters to Grace Ellery Channing show, a time for reassessment. These letters are among her most intimate, both because she trusted Channing and because her restored health in Italy now seemed as doubtful as her original death sentence. Channing had qualities that made her an ideal correspondent quite apart from being a poet of some standing. Not unlike the descendants of many famous men, she began her career by editing the memoirs of her grandfather, William Ellery Channing, founder of the American Unitarian Church. In addition to sharing Austin's spiritual curiosity, she too had a troubled family history. Her brother suffered from mental illness and alcoholism and spent time in sanatoriums.

Whatever problems Channing faced, she enjoyed easy economic circumstances that Austin could only envy. "When I say that I have nothing, I expect to be literally accepted," Austin wrote at her most discouraged. Too often her problems had come down simply to money, with a little more of which over and above expenses she "could still make good." Catching herself, she acknowledged that money accounted for only part of her discouragement: "I have not love which you have found to stay your heart upon, nor children, nor a home, nor health, nor money to make good these things, nor [with the exception of Eve Lummis] old friends, nor a long contact with the environment which must make the background of my work, nor any memories of time when these things were."[27]

Austin had sent Channing a copy of *Santa Lucia,* a frank study of marriage, asking her to remember that its author was not yet forty, "Thackeray's proper age for a first novel."[28] (She was now forty-one.) "Do you wonder," she asked Channing, who had reservations about the book, "that it was not greater?" Austin had always been "poor and sick, much of the time grieved and made ashamed," in short a victim of society's false teachings about women, their natures and place. "Well do you wonder?" she repeated, now referring to Ruth, "when the material for it was drawn either from my early memories or from slight observation made in half yearly visits of a few days each to [San] Jose where I go on the saddest errand in the world—Oh, much sadder than to visit a grave!" She described her years with Wallace trying "to make a wet string stand on end, and when I finally made up my mind to the hopelessness of that, I found I had lost the chance of the one thing that would have made my best possible."[29] She poured out to Channing her deep resentment of the desert years when books were at a premium and conversations with educated people a rare pleasure, years that taught her why people fail and that made her fail for remaining in exile.

Channing responded with sympathy and invitations to Rome and Capri, where she and her husband intended to summer. Mostly she commiserated as her friend waited for the strength to go on, to somehow "make good." Austin confessed to having "wild impulses to cry out, to appeal to somebody, to snatch somehow the thing" she needed to succeed. Brushing aside Channing's suggestion that she should just do her best, she admitted to heartbreak: "Having once or twice touched a very high mark, I am pained and humiliated to have ever ever again fallen below it."[30]

> The truth is that I have come to realize during the last three years that I am never to be a great artist—never rise to the full development of my natural gift. I shall be a tolerably successful writer, though I confess I have at present very little appetite for it, but I took the wrong turn of the road years ago and can not now retrace my steps. I wanted to ask you, and yet hesitated, if you had come to that place, or if you still felt the way open and the largest possibility still before you.
>
> It is not my years nor my health that convince me, but the certainty which I can no longer avoid, that no woman can become a really great

artist and remain such as you and I. At least no one ever has, and it is too late to think even of anything else. This is very bitter to know, that one is defeated by what one believes to be best in one's self. I should not like to live a life which I could not recommend to anyone else, and yet to live rightly and fail is a very hard matter. The worst of it is that I can not accept the situation and think no more of it. . . . I write and write as so many women do, and wonder how many others know the truth, how many grope unknowing, how many hope without knowing. Mrs. Wharton who knows turns her knowledge into service, whether she will find a way out interests me to see.[31]

Austin most likely refers to Wharton's hodgepodge of a novel, *The Fruit of a Tree* (1907), which seemed a falling off after the critical and popular success of *The House of Mirth* (1905). Wharton did of course go on to prove the exception by supporting herself in grand style at home and abroad and winning the Pulitzer Prize for *The Age of Innocence* (1920). But even she suffered the defeat Austin so eloquently expresses. Austin speaks for the countless women writers—the likes of Constance Fenimore Woolson—forced to swallow compromises that made their dinners possible, and more generally for women artists floundering in the marketplace.

Not surprisingly, Austin found her "way out" by writing. As she confessed to Channing, she fed pages of a new novel (begun in conversations with George Sterling) to a typist. James Wilkinson perhaps reminded her of Sterling and of the days spent together in Carmel. Published in England under the pseudonym Gordon Stairs in 1910, *Outland* would be yet another book different from anything else she wrote. A love story and a fantasy, it tells how Mona and her unlover-like lover Herman stumble upon the magical Outlanders and become involved in their feud with the Far-Folk. In the process, Mona and Herman discover much about themselves and each other. Outland resembles an idealized Carmel, a place where people strive for the common good, where the tribe feasts on fish and abalone, and where a Far-Folk hostage named Ravenutzi proves as fatally charismatic to women as Sterling or Jack London. "With a shout the Outliers stripped and cut the molten water with their shining bodies; laughed and plunged and rose again, laughing and blowing the spray as long as the moon lasted. They were at it again with the earliest light, and I should have known they were gathering sea food. . . . When the tide allowed, they gathered fish and abalones, which the women carried to some secret place among the pines to cure and dry."[32] Austin's English typist, assuming

Outland to be a socialist tract—it has qualities reminiscent of William Morris's didactic romances—wanted to have a hand in something big and offered to type the manuscript free of charge.

In its portrayal of human relations, *Outland* might be read as a happier version of *Santa Lucia* (1908), the book Channing gently criticized. A realistic novel set in a college town like Palo Alto, *Santa Lucia* anticipated Sinclair Lewis's *Main Street,* while the fantastical *Outland* belongs to the utopian-dystopian tradition Edward Bellamy spawned with *Looking Backward* (1888). Each of Austin's novels deals with obsessive love and adulterous betrayals that end violently, a wife in *Santa Lucia,* for example, killing herself with cyanide, and Ravenutzi's wife murdering his lover in *Outland.* Austin nevertheless contrives in both books unpredictably happy marriages. William, the doctor's daughter in *Santa Lucia,* marries a man who honors her parents and promises to continue the spirit of her father's work; in *Outland,* Mona and Herman come together with new understanding. "How shall we ever find the trail to that country again?" Mona asks. "The trail is here," Herman tells her, pointing at his breast.[33] For their service to the Outlanders, Mona and Herman are spared drinking from the cup of forgetfulness. They take their memory of Outland to a better future, one in which love and friendship and the virtues of community continue. *Santa Lucia* closes with a woman waiting for her husband to return home. They have managed to salvage their nearly bankrupt marriage, and as she looks toward the far hills she understands at last her husband's "wish to be one with the current interest of his time, as the relish for life, the undaunted male attitude which begot great achievement on the West."[34] If these books seem Western for more reasons than their settings, it would be for this kind of statement and for Austin's insistence on the possibility of new beginnings. Despite living abroad or struggling to escape the label of provincialism, she found her topics and her settings in the American West.

The writing of these novels hints at Austin's own wandering in the woods. Like the "Outliers" who discover Outland, she opened herself to new forms and possible failure. In her novels, Eden—be it Outland or the town of Santa Lucia—exists through the spirit of fellowship she had sought in Carmel and in the intimacy she found with people as unlike and geographically separated as George Sterling and Grace Ellery Channing. Her wandering, her bad health, and the need to work rarely allowed the luxury of lasting relationships, which, with the leisure to write, meant to Austin a contented life. Much as she complained, however, and she complained voluminously to Channing, she made the most of what she had. "Happy," she has a character say in *Santa Lucia,* "happy—I don't know that it is so necessary to be happy. I would rather be doing something."[35]

———————•◦•———————

Austin, the Western writer, went abroad in December 1907 and arrived in London in April 1909. She educated herself in Europe, above all studying Italian, French, and English societies as she had studied American Indian, Mexican, and urban societies at home. She would see herself as a shaper of her own country in years to come, often by drawing parallels with foreign lands. Yet her long stay—until September 1910—gets short shrift in *Earth Horizon,* which follows chronology in the loosest ways and moves through three years in as many pages. About her writing, her thinking, her activities abroad as anything more than meetings with literati or dignitaries, Austin speaks circumspectly, as if she avoids exploring that phase of her life.

Of the many cities she visited in Europe, she felt happiest in London, where, if not escaping to country byways or tripping to the Continent for a week, she made a second home. In 1910, she might have sat in a London cinema to watch the first Hollywood film, D. W. Griffiths's *In Old California,* a romantic drama about life under Spanish rule, not unlike her own *Isidro,* from which it could well have been purloined. She might have made her way to the new Selfridges department store and doubtless did go to the Victoria and Albert Museum, which opened the previous year. She had come to London to take advantage of the arts and to meet people, especially writers she thought mattered.

Before her arrival, Austin had begun a correspondence with the English novelist H. G. Wells, who invited her to his self-built Spade House near Folkestone, Kent. An earlier visitor, William Dean Howells, much impressed with the house and its view of the English Channel, described his host as "a little cockney man, but of a brave spirit, who is socialistic in his expectations of the future, and boldly owns to having been a dry goods clerk in his past."[36] Austin had much in common with the iconoclastic Englishman, who considered himself a feminist and shared her impatience with institutions such as marriage and formal religions. Both reveled in speculative science, and both wrote tributes to the other. In *The Mind of the Race,* published under the pseudonym Reginald Bliss, Wells predicted that the work of Mary Austin "would live when many of the more portentous reputations of her day would have served their purpose and become no more than fading names."[37] If he meant that Austin enjoyed no immediate reputation, Austin returned his backhanded compliment. Writing "An Appreciation of H. G. Wells" for the *American Magazine* (1911), she praised him as a citizen of the world whose understanding of people matched that of Charles Dickens, and then offered her tit for tat. Wells's female characters, she said, "might have known the novelist better than he knew them."[38]

How Wells found time for building houses and making new friends is anyone's guess. He wrote like a dervish, in 1908 alone publishing his social creed, *First and Last Things: A Confession of Faith and a Rule of Life,* as well as *The War in the Air* and *New Worlds for Old,* a book of essays that brought him fame as a voice for social justice. *New Worlds for Old* divided him from what he thought to be the impractical Fabian socialists led by Beatrice and Sidney Webb. The following year he published *Tono-Bungay* and *Ann Veronica,* the story of a suffragist who lives openly with her lover.[39] According to Austin, who could speak to him more freely than to any man she had known, his mind at this time "began to itch for the world horizons that have since engaged his attention."[40] Wells helped draft, for example, the United Nations Charter.

In the few years before Austin met Wells, he had sought out a wide range of people, among them the novelists Henry James and Joseph Conrad and, at Cambridge, the radical economist and Bloomsbury figure, John Maynard Keynes. Now he entertained the American woman whose newly published *Lost Borders* (1909) he read and admired, particularly her story of unbending independence, "The Walking Woman." Mutual respect, shared politics, and probably curiosity worked to bring Austin and Wells together. Austin took in stride the unconventional arrangements of Wells's household, though she recollected them in her autobiography to Wells's detriment. "I have just advised my wife," she quoted Wells as saying, "that a friend of mine is about to have a child by me." "Well, we must be kind to her," the patient Jane Wells supposedly replied. In December 1909, Amber Reeves, the twenty-one-year-old daughter of a Fabian couple, gave birth to Wells's baby. Almost twenty years later, Wells would angrily contest Austin's report of their conversation, responding to her account in *Earth Horizon* as if to a personal betrayal.[41] Whether or not she recollected public gossip as private knowledge, Austin remembered vividly the dinner Wells arranged with Duffield, his American publisher, who had expressed interest in her play *The Arrow Maker.* The evening was a triumph, featuring Austin resplendent in yellow satin and the witty Catholic writer G. K. Chesterton in high form as he recited William Morris's poem "Democracy." The Bernard Shaws sent their regrets. The next day, Wells and Austin walked for miles over the heath as, according to her, he poured out his feelings to a ready listener.

Austin's London hosts, Lou and Herbert Hoover, had not approved her visit to the notorious Wells, who stood for much of what they deplored. Despite their reservations, the Hoovers were a cosmopolitan pair, she the first woman to graduate in geology from Stanford University, he a member of Stanford's earliest class, in 1891. At Stanford, the Hoovers met people like David Starr Jordan and Vernon Kellogg, with whom they kept in touch. They also associated with people Austin had not encountered, people of great wealth in the fields of engineering, multinational banking, and mining, though she did know something about the working and the dangers of the silver and gold mines in the West. (The year 1910 was a particularly deadly one for miners in Great Britain: 344 coal miners died at Hulton, Lancashire, and nearly 140 at Wellington Pit in Whitehaven.)

Herbert Hoover, a self-made millionaire, jumped from office clerk to gold miner (at twenty cents an hour for ten hours a day) to engineer to partner in the international mining conglomerate of Bewick, Moreing. He would go on to serve his country as its thirty-first president—and be blamed for the Great Depression. His rise from rags to riches began in Oregon, where he had been sent to work as an office boy and driver for his uncle, a physician. While still a young man, he made surveys of natural resources in Arkansas and after college won a world-wide reputation for mining know-how and administrative genius. During the seven years before Austin's arrival in London, Hoover, accompanied by his wife and young children, attended to mining business in Canada, New Zealand, the United States, Germany, Egypt, Burma, France, South Africa, and above all Australia, where his company ran vast projects. The Hoovers witnessed China's Boxer Rebellion, in 1900. Retiring from Bewick, Moreing in 1908, Hoover started his own consulting firm and worked, with Lou, on an English translation of the sixteenth-century mining text *De Re Metallica* (1914). They settled in London, comfortably wealthy and eager to spend more time in both England and the United States.

Hoover welcomed Austin as his wife's friend and as a gifted writer, apart from their having acquaintances in common and sharing a love for California's mountains. As with the Kelloggs in Florence, Austin could not have found more generous friends than the couple at the Red House on Horton Street. First acquaintances, then friends, supporters, and finally patrons, the Hoovers not only provided Austin with a monthly stipend in coming years, they sent her large sums in emergencies.

Austin remembered that she toured "a great deal with the Hoovers; weekends and excursions; we went to Stonehenge by night to see the comet [Halley's]; to Dover and Stratford-on-Avon, to Bath and the Cathedral towns. Mr. Hoover was always in a hurry; many times, Lou and I would gladly have lingered, but sight-seeing bored him; he wanted to get on."[42] Hoover's limited patience makes it all the more unusual that he drove Austin to Kent to visit Joseph Conrad, the novelist about whom he was as indifferent or uninformed as most English men and women of the day. Chauffeured by the future president himself, Austin visited Conrad in his country retreat in Postling, not far from Wells's home in Folkestone. Austin had sent a greeting card with a copy of *Lost Borders* and in turn received an invitation to Capel House. The meeting that resulted lasted the entire afternoon, while Hoover waited in the nearby lane. An impressive looking and tailored man on the order of a military general, he marched up and down to stretch his legs, counting the hours.

The time with Conrad deeply impressed Austin, who considered herself one of his first discoverers. She describes their talk as her sorting out her own ideas about romance and realism, which, she acknowledged, Conrad did not quite catch. "How, indeed, was one to explain . . . that there was as yet no realism in American fiction that was not simply the obverse of the romanticism of men and women about each other as male and female." Not appreciating Austin's attempts to distinguish between American romance and realism, or the fictional treatment of women and men, Conrad simply waved the topic away. "I think I did not get far in explaining all this to Joseph Conrad," she recalls. But similarly, how was *she* to understand her impression "of being shown in the core of a tropic hurricane, the missing fragment by which the pattern of human society had been, once for all, rendered intelligible"?[43]

She found in Conrad a man with a similar appetite for the ineffable. Conrad not only spoke of the sea as driving his thinking and the moods of his writing, but as a force that made "a kind of peace around him."[44] Conrad told his guest that she wrote better than any woman he knew, in all likelihood praise without irony from a man who cared about quality of writing. They knew some of each other's books and, for Austin, Conrad—especially the Conrad of *Typhoon* and *Heart of Darkness*—had set a standard for the new century. It makes sense that she would applaud a man who, like herself, depicted single and singular characters in a world largely unknown to his readers.

Both authors wrote tales about people confounded by wilderness, whether ocean expanses and Congo jungles or, in Austin's case, the borderless lands of the West and Southwest with their seemingly infinite vistas. Austin recognized that her desert approximated his oceans. Her descriptions in *Lost Borders* echo Conrad's sense of men tested beyond their capacities. Speaking of Mr. Wills's pursuit of mining riches in *Lost Borders,* Austin says: "Of all the ways in the West for a man to go to pieces this is the most insidious. Out there beyond the towns the long Wilderness lies brooding, imperturbable; she puts out to adventurous minds glittering fragments of fortune and romance."[45] Conrad wrote relatively little about women, especially in the works that Austin then knew, and his novels may seem distant from her own interests, but among other qualities Austin appreciated his understanding of men's worlds as separate from women's. She acknowledged "the impersonal quality of man in adventure with the elements which I thought women had yet to learn."[46]

Her sympathies went out to the man whose "face looks out, lean, harassed, touched with the illimitable melancholy of the sea," and she would, in a sense, continue their conversation in a 1923 essay titled "Joseph Conrad Tells What Women Don't Know about Men." On this first visit she passed the time "explaining" herself to Conrad as they "sat at the upper window of the low old Kentish farmhouse . . . and Herbert Hoover . . . passed and repassed along the hedged lane."[47] Austin took away with her a rose Conrad kissed and held out to her on parting. On a later trip to England, she would gather and press flowers from his house and from Thomas Hardy's birthplace.

Generous as they were, it was not unusual for the Hoovers to entertain writers, artists, and intellectuals, not to mention stray mining people from China and the newly designated dominion of South Africa who found themselves in London. With Lou Hoover, Austin navigated the British Museum, took tea with friends, and came to feel at home in the city of parks and gardens. Lou affectionately called her Pomona, after the goddess of gardens and orchards. Considering the number of people Austin met from California, she might have been living in Pomona—or Carmel-by-the-Thames—but either through the Hoovers or on her own, she fulfilled her wish to learn about English men and women. "I met the less-known writers, Hilaire Belloc [an antifeminist, journalist-friend of both Wells and Shaw] who was a guest with me at the Women's Lyceum Club, [and] William Butler Yeats: I asked Yeats what he thought of American poets. 'American poets?' he said, 'I never read them.' I lunched with [the novelist] Mrs. Humphrey Ward. She asked for my impressions of England. I said that the standard of the working-class home was not so high as in America. 'Home!' she said; 'Americans have no homes; they are all divorced.'" She goes on to quote the indomitable Mrs. Ward on Henry James, whom Ward faulted, not for homelessness, but for his failure to seek advice. "I could have told him," Mrs. Ward announced, "how to be successful."[48]

Austin chanced upon James at the theater and found—as had the Southern writer Ellen Glasgow—the once aspiring playwright "so deaf that I doubt if he understood to whom he was being introduced, but he understood that I esteemed it a privilege." She assumed that, deaf or not, "his intention towards me was positive." In their "few minutes of exchanges," she came to a realization. "It was characteristic of all the English people I met [James evidently included] that they seemed uninterested; at least they were not interested and curious about me as I was about them."[49] If James meant to keep his distance, that put no brake on Austin's seeking out other writers and artists at teas and lectures at the Lyceum Club, where she met, for example, the novelist May Sinclair. Sinclair shared Austin's political views and emphasized in her writings troubled mother-daughter relationships. At gatherings of the Fabian Society, Austin encountered George Bernard Shaw, the absent guest at the Wells' dinner. She saw him often and "occasionally fell afoul of him, getting angry when he wittily evaded the point as he so often did."[50] Austin approved the Fabians' approach to social reform through education and debate, though she had reservations. "Even when they have turned the shooting parks of the gentry into gardens for the poor, they will be far short of the problem of unemployment."[51] She celebrated with the Fabians after the 1910 general elections, which brought the liberals into power and allowed Lloyd George to introduce his "People's Budget." That same year Leo Tolstoy, the hero of democratic socialists, died at eighty-two.

If Austin's accounts of her English stay read like a quick overview of months not years, her correspondence gives a fuller sense of what she enjoyed: riding, for example, on the upper decks of omnibuses to get the best view for a penny a mile, or attending meetings of the Anthropological Society, or matinees of *Hamlet* and Henrik Ibsen's *An Enemy of the People*. She missed the Wagner cycle at the Grand Opera House, interrupted by the death of King Edward, and she missed the funeral procession because a four-guinea seat along the route exceeded her budget.

Among the bits and pieces about trips and meetings, theater and processions, chance acquaintances and visits to museums, one encounter stands out. Austin already knew the suffragist and, at thirty-two, former professor of history, Anne Henrietta Martin. They met again in London, thanks to Lou Hoover, who had been friends with Martin since their Stanford days. Martin, the daughter of a Populist politician from Empire, Nevada, was a lifelong feminist and, for Austin, the most influential person in her London circle. Austin and Martin, who later settled in Carmel, found kinship as like-minded suffragists. Long-faced with doleful eyes, Martin was a determined woman; she would lead the successful Nevada campaign for women's voting rights. In 1910, she began her training with the Pankhursts and other British radicals at a time when women faced jail sentences for suffragist protests and often starved themselves until force-fed by jailors. Austin describes Martin's first arrest:

> We walked in the processions and Anne got herself mixed up with them on various occasions, when Herbert had to rescue her. Herbert was annoyed because he thought American women ought to keep out of England's racket. On one occasion Anne succeeded in getting arrested. She had tried beating up a policeman who told her that she would have to hit harder than that if she wanted attention. He took her by the arm and twisted it in the iron railing over Westminster Bridge. "Hang on that long enough," he said, "and I'll arrest you for obstructing traffic." So she hung on and finally was arrested. Herbert went down and bailed her out. Not long after that she went home and mixed with the pickets there, to his great relief.[52]

Hoover's memory of this episode differed only slightly. Martin, he wrote, "got herself a banner; bought a hammer; smashed a plate glass window on sacred Bond Street; was arrested and then hit the policeman with the hammer"—a "Number One crime in England." To him, the women's suffrage movement in England consisted of a thousand such "publicity outrages." Not sharing his wife's view, he had already summed up Martin as "an inoffensive pedantic nonentity." After standing bail, he faced an angry outburst for denying her martyrdom, even if it meant "sitting on a bench alongside drunks. Finally the British Suffragettes persuaded her to go home and reform her own country."[53]

When she came to write about Martin's clash with the law, Austin used it to set up an episode of her own. After dining one evening at the Hoovers' house, she borrowed a raincoat from a servant to protect her evening dress. "At the tube station a group of policemen were coming off duty in high spirits, and one of them caught my arm and said, 'Come on my girl, and give us a kiss.'" As if on stage, she let the raincoat fall open to disclose her evening dress and asked what the man had in mind. He said that his "blood was up" because of "a scrimmage with suffragists." Austin writes, "I lost all taste for suffragist scrimmages after that."[54] In fact, it would be many years before the movement or the scrimmages bored her. At the time she thought it odd that "with all this fuss about women's suffrage, so much of the work in politics is done" by English women.[55] In June 1910, she marched with Martin in a suffrage parade and felt part of a great historic event. Their friendship had continued despite an early misunderstanding. For a few months in late summer and into October 1909, the two shared an apartment in Bramley—in the Surrey countryside, near Guildford—collaborating on feminist projects. Austin moved there to save money—her pocketbook "looked as if an elephant had stepped on it"—and also to escape the city heat (which followed her to Surrey). She needed privacy to work on parts of *Christ in Italy,* called at this time "A Soul in Italy."[56] Martin deserted her, as Austin understood it, to escape the tumult of their slum neighborhood for the comfort of a rich friend's country estate.

Important as they were, the Hoovers did not account for all Austin's introductions to people in London and, as with Wells, did not always appreciate the company she kept. They may or may not have met Jimmy Hopper, one of the many Americans with whom Austin reconnected. Hopper, still close to those at Carmel, promptly informed George Sterling that Austin led him to believe she had seduced a cardinal or was carrying on with either a matinee idol or the prime minister. Interestingly enough, Austin had asked Grace Channing's help in retrieving a stray letter from Cardinal Merry del Val, which he considered an indiscretion. (The mysterious letter, its contents unknown, finally surfaced). To Channing she confided what she only hinted to Hopper. "I have made many profitable acquaintances, and feel not quite so much a stranger in the big world . . . and, this is very absurd, and there is nothing to come of it but such comfort to my vanity as such an incident provides but someone has been good enough . . . or mad enough . . . to love me, and so contribute to that sense of being important which is so necessary to an artist."[57] She comes no closer to identifying the mysterious "someone."

George Sterling also corresponded with Austin, who tried and failed to find him an English publisher. "Dear woman!" he wrote. "It was good no end of you to try to sell my poems. But I don't remember actually asking you to do so. So far as *I'm* concerned, I try to express only beauty, beauty unattainable and unimaginable, and in art your words 'efficiency' and 'achievement' are meaningless to me, except insomuch as they apply to such success as I may have in glimpsing that beauty—call it sterile if you will. Of course I may be suffering from incurable immaturity, and I cheerfully confess I'm leagues less human than you—and Wells, and Browning."[58] He assured her, as if it mattered, that Ambrose Bierce agreed with him entirely. After Bierce, a despiser of Walt Whitman's verse, called Sterling America's greatest poet, fans flocked to Carmel eager for souvenirs. Not finding the desired painted plates or key chains shaped like lighthouses, they supposedly took wood chips from his chopping block. Gertrude Atherton, who testified to Sterling's sense of humor and self-deprecation, was "willing to wager his mind rippled with laughter as he stood before the architrave of the 1915 Panama-Pacific Exposition and read those deeply carved lines of poetry with the names SHAKESPEARE, MILTON, STERLING."[59] By now, Austin had begun to see California as a provincial backwater, overly eager to tout its own artists.

On her return visit to England in 1921, she would renew her acquaintance with Wells, Sinclair, and Shaw. For readers of *The Bookman,* she recounted an address she made to the Fabians at King's Hall in London, which she called "My Fabian Summer." She did not, like William Butler Yeats, brush Shaw off as a smiling sewing machine but laughed at his "habit of kicking up the cloven hoofs of his mind in a manner so engaging that you forgave him for having kicked dust in proportion as he found himself unable to meet your thrust."[60] The implication that she *would* have won the argument is characteristic. She enjoyed jousting, or to continue her metaphor, dancing a foxtrot with Shaw, along with Sidney and Beatrice Webb and others she encountered at the Summer School. The annual event, held in Prior's Field, Surrey, allowed Austin and other Americans to test English and Irish counterparts in debate, on matters of sex and politics, and to join in entertainment, including long walks "in lovely Surrey byways, much tennis, folk dancing in the gymnasium, and jazz in the evening." Fridays, the participants put on revues and "burlesqued one another."[61]

That same summer, at Canterbury Cathedral, Austin would come across another acquaintance from Carmel and New York, Sinclair Lewis, whose infatuation with English authors led him to name his son after H. G. Wells. She remembered Lewis telling her that his new book had sold three hundred thousand copies. She trumped his boast with a hidden ace: "What else could I do but produce as my own counter-irritant, that I was on terms with

G. B. S. which permitted me to take promising young American authors to tea without waiting to be invited."[62] By the time she recalled their meeting for *Earth Horizon* (1932), she was probably envious of his enormous sales, never mind his 1930 Nobel Prize for literature. But that is a later story. Apart from her 1921 voyage to England, where she reconnected with Joseph Conrad and got to know Rebecca West—a woman she pitied for her tempestuous relationship with H. G. Wells—Austin continued to visit Carmel.

———————————•◦•———————————

In *Lost Borders,* the book Austin published in 1909 (the same year Gertrude Stein published *Three Lives*) Austin again hearkens back to her years in the desert regions of California. The frontispiece conveys that sense of nostalgia for home: a man and a woman stand between two horses on a grassy plain; the caption reads, "He said, 'I have missed you so.'" A sequel to *The Land of Little Rain, Lost Borders* opens with a comparable panorama of lands between Death Valley and the eastern wall of the Sierra Nevada, with "The Land" as seen by the Paiute nations breaking westward though the mountains and down the "saw-cut canyons" of the Kern and Kings rivers to the eastern foothills of the San Joaquin. "Every story of the country is colored by the fashion of life there," Austin writes, "breaking up in the swift, passionate intervals between long, dun stretches, like the land that out of hot sinks of desolation heaves up great bulks of granite ranges with opal shadows playing in their shining, snow-pile curves."[63] Like the earlier book, *Lost Borders* offers a series of stories—about the desert and equally about the men and women struggling for survival in that inhospitable environment.

"First and last," she warns in one of her most quoted passages,

> accept no man's statement that he knows the Country of Lost Borders.
> . . . If the desert were a woman, I know well what she would be: deep-breasted, broad in the hips, tawny, with tawny hair, great masses of it lying smooth along her perfect curves, full lipped like a sphinx but not heavy-lidded like one, eyes sane and steady as the polished jewel of her skies, such a countenance as should make men serve without desiring her, such a largeness to her mind as should make their sins of no account, passionate, but not necessitous, patient—and you could not move her, no, not if you had all the earth to give, so much as one tawny hair's-breadth beyond her own desires.[64]

The passage may be the most "passionate" that Austin wrote and, as it comments on herself as a woman and a writer, one of the most revealing.

Lost Borders contains a number of Austin's finest stories, including sardonic accounts of men's obsessions. "The Woman at the Eighteen-Mile," its subjects love, skulduggery, and storytelling itself, offers a series of overlapping and digressing narratives that grow in the consciousness of the storyteller and speak to Austin's writing process. Her narrator follows the scent of a murder and mystery, which reveals itself in fits and flashes until she hears it whole from the woman who may or may not be at its heart. Through lies and interrupted stories, Austin probes the manner and motives of any narrator who promises, like her own, not to tell the stories that they tell.

The volume closes with H. G. Wells's favorite and Austin's most anthologized story, "The Walking Woman," whose maverick protagonist sheds with her name "all sense of society-made values" and accrues, in the process, what the narrator desires: meaningful work, love, and a child. "It was the naked thing the Walking Woman grasped, not dressed and tricked out, for instance, by prejudices in favor of certain occupations; and love, man love, taken as it came, not picked over and rejected if it carried no obligation of permanency; and a child; any way you get it. . . . To work and to love and to bear children. *That* sounds easy enough. But the way we live establishes so many things of much more importance."[65] The story, like others before it, mimics a series of Chinese boxes. The narrator hears about the Walking Woman first at Tremblor, then again in the Carrisal and at Adobe Station; she glimpses her at the Eighteen-Mile House and finally corners her at Warm Spring. In retrospect, she wonders who surprised whom, for in "some flash of forward vision" the Walking Woman reaches out to comfort her, as if she sees all the narrator will miss in the "unimpassioned years" ahead.[66] The story might be read as a response to Henry James's "The Jolly Corner" (1908), in which the repatriated main character both tracks and flees the ghost of the man he might have become had he remained in the United States.

The title *Lost Borders* says as much about the author as about its subject. Austin knew "the Country of Lost Borders" probably as well as anyone; the title serves as a metaphor for her own drifting in the emotional desert between Europe and America, the hard purgatory in which she made her peace with life and death and the person she had become. When she returned to the United States in 1910, it was not to Inyo County or Carmel, but to New York City. She came home to write plays, to join the American suffragist movement, and to lecture about the broader America from which she had absented herself for the past three years. She did not stop writing novels after *Santa Lucia;* nor did she entirely give up the kind of work that had brought her fame. *California, the Land of the Sun* (1914) would be as enthusiastic about landscape as either *The Land of Little Rain* or *Lost Borders.* She had, however, changed course, crossed her own borders, moved at least temporarily from West to East, and expanded the range of her writing and of her experiences.

Almost immediately, she would begin her arduous career of lecturing, a lucrative source of income for many writers and for Austin a means also to broadcast her positions. On one lecture trip to San Diego, soon after her arrival in New York and before stopping briefly in Carmel, a Mrs. Snyder called at her hotel:

> "You don't know me," she said. "Would it help if I told you I am Mary Patchen?"
> "You were a friend of my father."
> "Ah, I was much more than a friend."[67]

Austin recalled books her father owned, with her guest's name inside, and the half-secret story of their youthful romance. George Hunter, then sporting a faultlessly combed pompadour, had made himself welcome at the Patchen house, where he talked about Keats and Shelley, or Mrs. Browning and John Ruskin, with his friend Charles Patchen and Charles's younger sister Mary, a handsome young woman with gray-blue eyes who taught in the public schools. "She was taller than George and perhaps a year or two older, but it was said to be delightful to those who knew them to hear the young couple discuss, as they often did at her brother's house, the literature and aesthetics of the day."[68] They read the new *Atlantic Monthly* aloud and courted at the Lyceum lectures.

The Lyceum figures badly in their story, for there Mary met a lecturer named Hutchinson, who slandered his rival and won the girl. Within weeks of their marriage, Charles learned that there was another Mrs. Hutchinson raising two children in New York. Indignant townspeople nearly lynched the offender, until Mary's brother convinced them to let the law and Mrs. Hutchinson deal with the bigamist. (In one version of the story, Hutchinson went to jail; in another he joined the army.)[69] Mary went into seclusion, to be comforted not by George Hunter but by a Mr. Snyder, a teacher from the State College at Urbana summoned to complete her school term.

Should someone think Mary Patchen possessed a fickle heart, she had come to tell the other Mary that she always loved George Hunter. The summer before Mary Hunter's birth, she had visited the Hunters to find, it seems, only a pregnant Susanna. Somehow she knew that Susanna did not want this child, and it grieved her "because she wanted nothing so much as a child herself; and George Hunter's child." "This should be your child," she thought to herself, and imagined the baby fulfilling her father's untapped gifts.[70] When the child was born and named Mary, she took it for an auspicious sign.

Whether she had been George Hunter's lover or constant admirer, Mary Patchen Snyder had in a sense devoted her life to the memory of George and to his daughter's career. She had read and preserved every book and essay by Austin, loving especially her writings about the American West. No one could have been more different from Susanna, who attributed Austin's work to Jim and claimed that she did not understand her daughter's stories. Mary Patchen praised her as if they had remained close, as if she had been the mother Austin longed for and never found. She had brought a spray of grass and flowers gathered from George's grave. Deeply affected by Mary Patchen's reappearance, Austin felt again the presence of her father. "He moved beside us there in the room like a living presence, a loved and reciprocal presence. She made him to live again for me; I saw him, felt him, breathed him in."[71] Mary Patchen stepped into Austin's life like the Venus in Titian's *Sacred and Profane Love,* who had experienced and understood the multiple ways of loving.

When Austin asked whether she might be of help, Mary Patchen assured her that she wanted nothing. She was married to a man who "understood how she felt; who knew how she felt about me; she had no wish to intrude upon my life. If I would make a point of sending her any little thing of mine, which she might otherwise miss, she would be grateful. And if I would think of her as being interested in me; if I would think more intimately of him through her; if I would feel more warmly; if I would never forget the reality of her experience . . . I felt I never would. I never have." Austin calls the encounter "the most real experience I had, a healing and reassuring experience."[72] It was the kind of personal, almost beatific encounter she and William James had discussed more than a decade before. Austin speculated about the possibility of her father's loving the woman more than he loved Susanna, but it seemed finally not to matter. She had been drawn closer to a stranger than she could have imagined, and the intimacy, the unconditional love, gave profound satisfaction. Though she never saw Mary Patchen again, she did not forget her. She was grateful to have been included, however slightly, in the love that her father and this woman shared.

The meeting with Mary Patchen seems a fitting coda to Austin's sojourn in Europe, from which she returned in better health and ready to work. "I have however gotten rid of the desert at last," she wrote to Grace Channing, "and have established my right to write of other things."[73] She corrected an interviewer who described her as Mary Austin of Carmel: call her, she said, Mary Austin of the world. To quote Henry James on his return to the United States: "Europe had been romantic years before, because she was different from America; wherefore America would now be romantic because she was different from Europe."[74]

six

NEW YORK

1911–1914

If I were to stay here now it would be because I am afraid to go home again—and I am not—I feel it necessary to insist that I am not afraid. I must go back and look America between the eyes.

MARY AUSTIN TO GRACE ELLERY CHANNING

12 March [1909]

MARY AUSTIN RETURNED TO THE UNITED STATES with the bitter realization that if she had not failed by her own measure, neither had she succeeded. Despite every effort, none of her books had found their way to the best-seller list or to book clubs, which sold in the hundred thousands. *Isidro* led all her books with 11,700 printed copies. Her stories brought in about two hundred dollars each, the going rate, but small reward for long labor.[1] Then there was, as she put it, "the difficulty that my books were always of the West, which was little known" and "never known as 'Westerns.'" To people who wanted another incarnation of *The Land of Little Rain,* she explained: "I had used up all I had in the first one. I should have had to find another country like that, and pay out ten thousand dollars to live in it ten or twelve years. I wrote what I lived, what I had observed and understood. Then I stopped."[2]

Though topics of her past and future work contradict this statement, during her three years abroad Austin had come to think herself a changed person and, in turn, another kind of writer. Not only had she faced death and lived to tell about it, she had come to understand the extent of her ambition, which demanded a wider range of books—and residence in New York. The capital of American publishing at least since the 1890s, the city offered libraries and museums, lunches with editors, and the proximity of writers and other artists she cared about. Yet during the fourteen years she

119

made New York her home, she was often elsewhere, taking long vacations in Carmel, for example, where she directed her plays at the Forest Theater. However much Carmel still attracted her, after the years in Rome and London, it evoked bittersweet memories of lost opportunities and dead friends. In the early months back, she retreated to a rural part of Long Island, both to escape the intensity of the city and to renew her energies. Before finally pulling up stakes in New York City, she would spend increasing amounts of time in Santa Fe, New Mexico—drawn to those Western interests she hoped, on returning from England, to put aside.

Austin made as little of her arrival in New York as about her leaving in 1907, when she had negotiated contracts with Harper & Brothers and embarked on the uncertain journey to Rome. About the ship she returned on, or fellow passengers she met, or who if anyone waited at the dock, she evidently left no record. She had gone to Europe buoyed by literary promise and facing what she believed to be inevitable death—and she went first-class. In a sense she came back "steerage." Without much money and intent on renewing her career, she disembarked almost like an immigrant from the old world: optimistic and determined, but unsure about where to live, let alone where she might sleep her first night. Even for the one night, she could not afford expensive lodgings or consider a luxury hotel like New York's Ritz-Carlton on Central Park. That landmark opened its doors for business in December 1910, three months after her homecoming.

In the years she had been away, New York had changed as radically as the circumstances of her life. She landed in a city fraught with ethnic tensions and violence. Through the summer of 1910, New York endured race riots, a strike by sixty thousand garment workers (their second strike that year), the attempted assassination of New York's mayor (about to embark on *his* journey to Europe), and the massing of more immigrants, more people, than at any time before or after in the city's history. Forty percent of Manhattan's 2,300,000 inhabitants had originated in foreign countries.[3] Immigrants of another kind came from the American South, black Americans whose numbers swelled the population of New York and other northern cities. The NAACP began its long life in 1909, and in the year of Austin's return W. E. B. Du Bois launched *The Crisis,* an influential African American voice for politics and literature.

Noisy, dirty, under construction, often dangerous, New York also allowed a protective anonymity that Austin turned to her advantage. She would live in diverse New Yorks, one represented by the National Arts Club, another by Greenwich Village, and still another by the city's ethnic pocket-neighborhoods, especially on the Lower East Side. Once more, though not the first to do so, she made a point of searching out what others ignored. Before the turn of the century, Theodore Roosevelt had accompanied the reformer Jacob Riis on sociological explorations of immigrant neighborhoods; and novelists such as Stephen Crane, William Dean Howells, and Theodore Dreiser studied the ways and warrens of the city for their fiction. Austin attended her first Jewish wedding and toured an area on the west side of Manhattan known as San Juan Hill, where African American residents must have viewed her with curiosity. Frightened by the experience, she called those she saw "primitive" and, using language she avoided for American Indians, spoke of "something animal in the carriage, smooth, as though they walked on cushiony paws."[4] Ashamed of her reaction, she tried to persuade herself not to notice skin color, at least in negative ways. The first African Americans she dined with were James Weldon Johnson and his wife, Grace. When Johnson passed her bread, she noted how black his hand looked against the white plate and thought, "I am eating dinner with a black man!" She felt she should be astonished, until an inner voice said, "Well, I don't see it," meaning his color, and looking again she decided that she did not see it.[5] In the 1920s, Austin would admire the art and dance of the Harlem Renaissance and insist on its centrality to American life. She met Paul Robeson and W. E. B. Du Bois, whom she honored, along with much of intellectual New York—as they dined on broiled half chicken, Virginia ham, peas and potatoes, chiffonade salad, and savarin ice cream—in celebration of Du Bois's return from his special ambassadorship to Liberia in 1923.

With her usual disregard for conventions, Austin took short-term jobs, typing or peddling—shoelaces, pencils, and flowers—to earn money, but no less, she said, to learn how immigrants and the home-grown poor paid their way.[6] She ate at a place on the West Side below Forty-Second Street, catering to railroad workers, and rented rooms in the Chelsea district from a woman whose husband earned his living selling phony alibis. For a time she was courted by a man from Chicago who made the concrete foundations for skyscrapers. Her days were full of contrasts: a socialist meeting in the afternoon, for instance, followed by a ball where she danced until midnight with a college professor and a stagehand from the Century Theater. After writing in the morning, she might volunteer at the Milk Distribution Center or the Bowery's Gospel Mission and attend a lecture in the evening. She excited little attention. The Byzantine customs of immigrants, whom she watched gathering dandelion greens near Grant's tomb or leaving a synagogue on Morningside Drive, inured city dwellers to the unfamiliar. Middle-class women like Austin routinely toured the missions, tubercular clinics, and tenements near the East River. After befriending the indefatigable journalist-reformer Ida Tarbell, famous for her exposé of the Standard Oil Company, Austin herself spent time with dockworkers and "undercover" city detectives inquiring into commercial sabotage.

Living a divided if not at times clandestine life, she continued to write and to lecture. New York city provided her main but not her only forum, as her meeting in San Diego with Mary Patchen Snyder suggests. From podiums across the country, she tackled issues of "the woman question," modern drama, regional writing, American poetry, along with Indian arts, education, and politics, all of which fed her growing reputation as an expert on contemporary life. She speculated about the cultural impact of movies, predicting the public's readiness to detect and forgive silent and celluloid illusion as "the idiom of the screen becomes more familiar."[7] In the hope that the new genre of what she called "photodrama" would accelerate "the rate at which a great literary artist might become known and enjoyed during his life," she tried to sell the rights to *Isidro* for three thousand dollars.[8] Indeed, she tried to sell one after another of her writings to companies in the new industry and did manage to sell options. Hollywood showed most interest in *Isidro* and a murder story called "Blue Moon." There was a brief flutter about *The Flock,* revamped as a cinematic epic featuring a young shepherd with his faithful dog braving windstorms, thirst, coyotes, snakes, and loneliness, until he rescues and wins the heart of a beautiful girl.

Her ambitions shifting, Austin wanted to address a larger America in any available way. Those who heard the lectures commented on her "assumption of grandeur," as well as her flare for the theatrical, which had its humorous side. When demonstrating what she believed to be the inherent rhythm of the Gettysburg Address, she would lift and lower her arms as if to the beat of a woodsman's ax.[9]

Austin targeted her articles (they appeared in *The Nation* and *Harper's,* for instance) to enlighten an already educated audience. Sometimes ironical, always forceful, she provided a historical context for her arguments and appealed to her reader's intellect. Writing to the hospitalized Charles Lummis in 1924, she urged him to "apply your intelligence to the problem of making your work support you by bringing it as far as possible into alignment with the immediate magazine demand. I do that, just making a living and no more, not always writing what I would prefer to write, but never being driven to write anything I don't believe, or in a fashion less than good, though not always my best."[10] Her patronizing tone notwithstanding, Austin knew firsthand about the struggles of writers. How many, for example, considered themselves successful? Or could count on a regular income from writing? Sherwood Anderson sold real estate, and Edgar Lee Masters practiced law. The unlucky ones like Stephen Crane suffered from chronic ill health and, in Crane's case, died young.

———————————•◦•———————————

During her second winter in New York, short of money and homesick for California, Mary Austin wandered the streets in search of inspiration. The wind whipping through drab, concrete-tunneled streets made her yearn once more for the shimmering blue-green water at Carmel, which she dreamed about at night. She craved "beauty and color" so much that she stood in front of florists' windows until her toes froze. In the silk departments of stores like Macy's and the new Gimbel's, she spent hours imagining the clothes and curtains she could not afford to make or hope to buy. Then she found the goldfish. "It was in the window of a Japanese art shop," she remembered. "There was a large hand molded bowl of glass. Not quite crystalline but with an iridescence running like fire just under the surface. It stood on a graceful teakwood base, and inside the bowl the gold fish flashed in and out of streamers of green water grass. On the surface floated a water hyacinth with an orchid tinted blossom lifted above the green translucent bud. In and out the goldfish dove and darted."[11] Austin visited the goldfish every day, weighing the cost of such beauty while reminding herself that thirty-five dollars might as well have been a thousand. One day, the goldfish vanished from the window.

As with goldfish, so with men, particularly one elusive man she had known for several years and come to love. Austin first met Lincoln Steffens in either San Francisco or Carmel, when he visited their mutual friend, George Sterling. At that time, as if caught in Sterling's long shadow, the delicate-looking man with round, wire-rimmed glasses, cropped mustache, and Mephistophelean beard made little impression on her. Yet by all accounts, Steffens was charismatic, and Austin came to think him more than that. She had written about the power of a similar man in her short story "The Fakir" (1909), who had a "Look," which bound women to him. Austin thought Steffens "a great man, a great reformer, and [her highest praise] a Jesus type."[12] The muckraking author of *The Shame of the Cities*

(1904) and *The Struggle for Self-Government* (1906), editor of *McClure's* and, with Ida Tarbell and Ray Stannard Baker, of the radical *American Magazine,* Steffens had a knack for drawing people out. Teddy Roosevelt felt comfortable pacing off the evening's meal in his company, and so did dissimilar people like the newspaper king William Randolph Hearst and the anarchist Emma Goldman, a propagandist for joys of the flesh. Best remembered today for his 1921 comment about Russia—"I have seen the future, and it works"—Steffens impressed contemporaries by exposing corrupt police and politicians in major American cities: Chicago, Minneapolis, Pittsburg, St. Louis, Philadelphia, and New York.

In 1910, the year Steffens and Austin reconnected, Steffens reported on the Mexican Revolution, sympathizing with the rebels. That same year he tended and watched his wife Josephine succumb to the ravages of what was then called Bright's disease, a generic name for acute kidney failure. On Christmas Day, he informed one of his sisters that he was seeing much of Mary Austin, "an odd but interesting woman."[13] Josephine Bontecou Steffens died not long after, on 11 January 1911. Four months later, Steffens wrote to dismiss Austin's notion that he "nourished" his widower's sorrow and to warn her, because he hated to write them, not to expect letters.[14] This was a tangled one:

> I have left a deep sympathy for the feeling you express, and I wish you to
> know that I shall read all that you care to write, especially in that mood,
> with more understanding than may appear. For I think I can understand.
> I certainly want to understand. I'd rather a thousand times understand
> than be understood. . . . My whole training has been to understand; to get
> things that are outside myself. We are opposites in this respect. But I must
> say to you sincerely, and earnestly, that if you wish to put yourself down
> on paper you may do so with me and be sure, oh, absolutely sure, that you
> would be read as I would be read—with the wish only to understand."[15]

He signed himself, "yours, warmly," and she responded by offering to serve with tenderness and understanding. A photograph from this time shows her looking frail and vulnerable, her eyes averted from the camera.

Austin and Steffens might have seemed an unlikely couple—though hardly "opposites." The trumpeter of radical causes, Steffens came from a wealthy Sacramento family, attended the University of California at Berkeley, and studied abroad, where he secretly married the older and unconventional

Mary at 13

Mary Hunter at thirteen years old (1881). She felt the pressure of "all the knowledge in the world, pulsing just out of reach." Courtesy of the Huntington Library, San Marino, CA.

Captain George Hunter (n.d.), "a man to whom it was a pleasure to listen." Courtesy of the Huntington Library, San Marino, CA.

James, Mary, Susanna, and young George Hunter (1880). Her family felt Mary had "to have something different from the rest of the family." Courtesy of the Huntington Library, San Marino, CA.

Mary Hunter (c. 1896). "Her hats were always marvels of feminine intricacy, dash of line, and swift surprises of color." Courtesy of the Huntington Library, San Marino, CA.

Top: General Edward Fitzgerald Beale (n.d.), described by some as "a sparkling combination of scholar, gentleman and Indian fighter." Library of Congress.

Bottom: The shepherd Little Pete (n.d.), whom Austin wrote about in many of her early books, notably *The Flock* (1906). Courtesy of the Huntington Library, San Marino, CA.

E. W. Baker, *at marriage* Photo.

Wallace Stafford and Mary Austin's wedding photograph (1891). "My family thought I was doing well to marry . . . I wasn't particularly pretty or rich." Courtesy of the Huntington Library, San Marino, CA.

Top: Austin's daughter Ruth in her stroller (n.d.). Austin dreamed of giving birth to the smartest daughter in the world. Courtesy of the Huntington Library, San Marino, CA.

Bottom: Austin, about the time of her move to the Owens Valley (c. 1900–02). Courtesy of the Huntington Library, San Marino, CA.

about 1900 – 1902
RAMSDELL

William James (n.d.), an important influence in Austin's life. Library of Congress.

Sincerely Yours,
Chas. F. Lummis

Charles Lummis with his son, Jordon, whom he called "Quimu" (n.d.). Courtesy
of the Huntington Library, San Marino, CA.

Top: Four friends at Carmel: George Sterling, Mary Austin, Jack London, and James Hopper, photographed by Arnold Genthe (n.d.). Courtesy of the Huntington Library, San Marino, CA.

Bottom: Austin directing *Fire* at the Forest Theater in Carmel (c. 1913). Henry Mead Williams Local History Department, Harrison Memorial Library, Carmel, CA.

The publisher Henry Holt with Charlotte and Vernon Kellogg (n.d.). Austin attended the Kelloggs' wedding in Fiesole, Italy. Courtesy of the Huntington Library, San Marino, CA.

Top: Grace Ellery Channing with her uncle, William Douglas O'Connor, one of Walt Whitman's staunchest supporters, in Pasadena, California (1887). Library of Congress.

Bottom: Lou and Herbert Hoover (*left*) around the time Austin would have met them (c. 1909). Austin called Hoover "Chief." Herbert Hoover Presidential Library.

The suffragette Anne Martin (c. 1920). According to Herbert Hoover, "the British Suffragettes persuaded her to go home and reform her own country." Library of Congress.

H. G. Wells (1905). Austin could speak to him more freely than to any man she had known. Library of Congress.

Joseph Conrad at Capel House in Postling, England (1917). Austin thought that Conrad set a standard for fiction of the twentieth century.

Witter Bynner, Ernest Thompson Seton, and Arthur Davison Ficke at the Palace of the Governors, Santa Fe (1928). Courtesy of the Huntington Library, San Marino, CA.

Willa Cather (1915). She claimed that writing a biography of
Austin might tempt her. Library of Congress.

LINCOLN STEFFENS

Lincoln Steffens (n.d.). "I count it the greatest event of the past year," Austin told him, "not to have produced a play at the New Theatre, but to have met someone who makes dreams possible again." Library of Congress.

Mabel Dodge and future husband Tony Lujan in Taos, New Mexico (c. 1920).
Dodge was Austin's friend, rival, and patron. Courtesy of the Huntington Library,
San Marino, CA.

Ansel and Virginia Adams (1928). Albert Bender told Austin that the Adamses needed "food every hour in large quantities, and if you have no mortgage on your house now, you will have at the time of their departure." University of Arizona.

Top: Austin's library at Casa Querida, her house in Santa Fe, New Mexico (n.d.). Willa Cather wrote part of *Death Comes for the Archbishop* in Austin's library. Courtesy of the Huntington Library, San Marino, CA.

Bottom: Austin with Daniel Trembly MacDougal, of "the cactus country," near Tucson, Arizona. Courtesy of the Huntington Library, San Marino, CA.

Bill "Bojangles" Robinson (n.d.), featured in Austin's book *Everyman's Genius* (1925). Courtesy of the Huntington Library, San Marino, CA.

Chief Standing Bear (c. 1919). "We seize upon everything from your [Austin's] pen regarding the native American." Library of Congress.

The artist Frank Applegate in Santa Fe, New Mexico (n.d.). He was closer to Austin than her own brothers. Courtesy of the Huntington Library, San Marino, CA.

Mary Austin as the goddess of plenty. Courtesy of the
Huntington Library, San Marino, CA.

Josephine Bontecou. Having taken courses in medicine and psychology at Leipzig, Josephine, who resembled Austin in build and character, might have been her older sister. An aspiring writer, Josephine had called on Austin shortly after the publication of *The Land of Little Rain,* wanting to know how she managed to write and remain married. Steffens appreciated his wife's independence of mind, her advanced views, and her ambition: "she will have a life," he said, "and a life's work of her own."[16] Early in their relationship the Steffenses, like the Austins, realized that their relationship lacked whatever ingredient makes for a close marriage. Their failure to have children rankled, and both mistakenly assumed the problem his. But though they led largely separate lives, Josephine's death shattered Steffens. Friends had not predicted the depth of his remorse or how much he would miss her. They may or may not have been surprised by his attraction to Austin; her attraction to the man with a luminous mind and a sudden, enveloping smile they took for granted.

Austin and Steffens shared what Goethe had called "elective affinities." Theirs included a stubborn willingness to defend unpopular positions, curiosity about science (the publisher Henry Holt asked her for a textbook about animals), a penchant for psychology (Jean-Martin Charcot had dazzled Steffens in Paris), writing of all kinds (he too wrote novels), and food. While food—"thin bread and butter, ripe olives, and cheese beaten to a paste with oil and paprika," to give a menu from *No. 26 Jayne Street* (1920)—touches every relationship, for Steffens and Austin it was fundamental. Austin talked about food—its social ramifications and her personal recipes—for hours on end. Events often take place in her novels "over baked potatoes and buttermilk."[17] Steffens, in honor of Mark Twain, ate at one sitting green-turtle soup, Kennebec salmon, terrapin, and canvasback duck.[18] The two food-loving lovers talked in out-of-the-way restaurants, enjoying their wine and favorite dishes and sharing culinary lore. Before or after dinner they might indulge a second love, theater, which New York offered with a diversity matching its ethnic populations.

To Austin, theater involved more than entertainment; it offered a grand new medium and yet grander personal opportunities. Beginning with *The Arrow Maker,* her 1911 play, she intended nothing less than to reform the American theater; at the time, she made her ambition seem subordinate to her lover. As her guest, Steffens attended the opening night of *The Arrow Maker* at the New Theatre. "I count it the greatest event of the past year," Austin told him, "not to have produced a play at the New Theatre, but to have met someone who makes dreams possible again."[19] To celebrate, she stayed at the Algonquin that night.

She liked to be with men who did great things, and Steffens, who presented himself as the conscience of America, had earned a national voice and could make or break politicians. "In the flush of their discovery of each other," Austin would write, "they had told themselves that they were so eminently what man and woman should be to one another: he the discoverer, the prophet of social evolution [the man with the muckrake], and she the matrix, the eternal female through whom it passed into living shapes of human conduct."[20] Steffens claimed to prefer unsentimental, intellectual women; and Austin, who had no problem believing him, said that she required a man with as much work to do as herself and who to the world seemed "rather more important." Although she had long heard rumors about his courting more than one woman at a time, indeed bragging about his conquests, she claimed to prefer an unfaithful man to a stingy husband—a bit of short-lived bravado she would come to regret.[21]

Several months after settling in New York, Austin began a diary. "I have opened this account at the instance of my friend Lincoln Steffens to prove to him that I can not write a book about the city as interesting as the Land of Little Rain. Steffy is saturated with the city. He can look at his watch any time of day and tell you what is going on in any part of it at that particular hour, and he can't understand that it will take me more years to learn my way about in it than were necessary to know the trails from Mohave to Lone Pine."[22] She did not dissuade herself from trying, however, and for the purpose took a furnished apartment decorated with garishly sentimental paintings on Riverside Drive, not far from Columbia University. She covered with a sheet a troubling portrait of a child that hung in her study and, seated at her typewriter, concentrated on blocking out house noises—the dumbwaiter going up and down, a woman singing, and the hiss and clank of steam radiators. Despite her protestations and with Steffens her model, she studied the city as she had the San Joaquin Valley or the high desert. In this she again followed John Van Dyke, who had written a 1909 book, *The "New" New York* (*new* was the word of the day). She made notes about neighborhood children dressed in ready-made clothing, which she saw as a sign of neglect: no mother, aunt, or grandmother had lovingly labored over their garments. And she managed to carp about the infestation of nursery maids and perambulators in the parks.

Her journal for Steffens is more self-conscious than the one she kept at the Rancho El Tejon. In her later musings she figures as a witness and a character, someone who compares her own inexpensive hat to costlier models, or watches her reflection in store windows, or, once, visits domestic court to give advice to a judge. In the court case, the pretty, well-dressed wife demanded more financial support from her husband, who claimed that she ran around with other men. The judge thought she didn't look the type. Austin, the self-designated professional, drew on the eugenic wisdom of the time and disagreed: "Her upper lip is too short. Ask her what she paid for her hat." The wife flushed, and her "boy husband cut in, 'You know where you got your coat, too.'"[23] Case dismissed.

Among Austin's papers is an undated draft of a letter that she very likely wrote to Steffens. With no one else did she feel, or claim to feel, submissive or frightened by love. Addressed to "Dear," it makes its forlorn plea through a labyrinth of crossed-out lines:

> I have got up in the night to write this to you, what because of your dominating personality I find it impossible to say when I am with you.
>
> It is strange that the thing which makes it right for us to be together, I mean the complete and voluntary submission of my mind to yours should also be the means of preventing my saying to you that perhaps it is a mistake for us to be together at all. At least I want to try to find out if it is a mistake for I am frightened and perplexed.
>
> I shall have to go back to the first time we met three or is it four years ago, because though I had not the smallest inkling of what you have since told me of your feeling for me, the habit of deferring to you I had already somehow fixed my mind on. . . .
>
> You must understand in all these three or four years since first we met, without ever guessing at what you have since told me of your feeling for me I have somehow [been] looking forward to meeting you again and resting my mind worn out with perplexity.[24]

Austin wrote the letter on a scrap of paper, the reverse side of which tells the story of a king in love with a commoner he cannot marry.

Her letter seems at once to reinforce and contradict biographies of Steffens that depict the harried lover dodging into entryways and decamping for Mexico to escape her frantic attachment. Another story circulated at the time about John Reed reporting on Pancho Villa to get breathing room from Mabel Dodge, a friend of Steffens who would soon begin holding court at 23 Fifth Avenue in New York. Marty Martinez's young wife, Elsie, perceptive commentator on the Carmel group, saw the Austin-Steffens affair from another vantage, no doubt because she herself "dodged bullets." ("Marty," she said, "should have been married to some nice little Indian girl who would spend her time looking down at her feet. I liked to look around and be admired.")[25] Elsie remembered Steffens dogging Austin's footsteps:

> He'd asked her to marry him. Finally, they got to the point where Mary decided they might marry. "Well," she said, "the only thing, Lincoln, is I must go back to New York [from Carmel] to finish my book." So they both went back to New York. She returned to her apartment and he to his apartment. They decided that they'd spend some time together and see if they could really make a success of marriage. He told us that he was certain Mary was cautious. Mary would say, "I can't see you until four o'clock this afternoon. My work's going well." Or, "I can't see you at all until this evening because my work's going very well."

So at Austin's suggestion, they lived separately. When she felt ready and decided to surprise him with an apartment that suited both, she found him there with another woman, his old sweetheart, Gussie. That, according to Elsie, "finished up the romance with Mary."[26]

Though probably unaware of Gussie Burgess before their awkward meeting, Austin must have chosen to forget Steffens's well-known amorous proclivities. He had, in this case, become involved with Josephine while engaged to Gussie. Shortly after Josephine's death, he had run into Gussie again, now Gussie Burgess Nobbes and conveniently separated from Mr. Nobbes. Steffens thought in terms of transitions rather than transgressions and, as a readily indiscreet raconteur, told a good story about the awkward meeting between Gussie and Mary. And so did the jilted novelist, who wrote *No. 26 Jayne Street,* originally named "The Muckraker," with its Steffens–like protagonist—said to write far less well than he talked.[27] Austin's insistence that it takes (or should take) two to end a relationship would inform her disquisition on marriage, *Love and the Soul Maker,* her 1915 play titled *The Vacuum* (posthumously produced in 1935), as well as *No. 26 Jayne Street,* which cribs from the author's own letters to Steffens.[28]

By an odd twist, in June 1911, the month she discovered his disloyalty, *American Magazine* carried Steffens's fulsome tribute to Austin. In her books, he wrote, readers would find "knowledge and religion, nature and human nature; they contain all the plain facts of the desert, but so understood—with such sympathy and such comprehension—that they are life and the poetry of life anywhere."[29] This was no consolation to the spurned lover. The end of her affair with Steffens proved to be "one of those soul scarifying things that happen so unexpectedly that they unseat the inmost self." Needing a listener, Austin wrote obliquely to the sympathetic Lou Hoover: "I shall not tell you what it is . . . I dare say I shall get over it in time . . . but just now I am feeling not only the blow but that kind of resentment one sometimes has against the whole world for allowing such things to be. . . . It is nice of you to let me write, it is the only vent to my feelings I have. I can't cry very much on account of my eyes . . . I can't even kick the cat!"[30] A month later, she spoke of having lost "the chief thing which has made life at all possible. . . . It was a terrible trial to me when I had to go away and leave my child among others of her kind and know that I was never to have her again, but that had been slow in coming and I was prepared, but this thing has fallen out of a clear sky and leaves no hope behind."[31] Mabel Dodge, another confidante who saw a pattern in Steffens's relationships with women (he liked to "dazzle their minds and then dance off"), may have best understood Austin's situation. She needed, Dodge said, "to have him come back to her, and let *her* be the one to withdraw. It appeared to be not so much a wound to the heart as to her sense of power."[32]

Whatever the diagnosis, Mary Austin did not take jilting lightly. "The real trouble," she told Steffens, "is your utter lack of honesty with me. . . . If you had said to me in the beginning, 'I do not love you, but I wish to do you no harm; I am in your hands,' I would have been bound to give you up by the logic of the situation and that without complaint."[33] Humiliated and enraged, she refused to break off the relationship on his terms. "You have been loved by one of the most notable women of your time," she told him. "You treated me as if I were a dog." And in the same letter: "I think you ought to remember that I still love you, that I must by my code always love you."[34] No matter how unwilling and unfaithful, she insisted, he would be hers until she freed him. Austin, who threatened to make their relationship public and expected compensation for lost work and suffering, wanted more than an apology; she wanted and demanded his company. "I asked you to come back and reestablish your relation to me so that it would be broken off in a manner that would not quite ruin me, but because to do that meant some weeks more control for you, you preferred to ruin me."[35]

Steffens called her hysterical but, hoping to calm her down, or giving in to blackmail, he occasionally visited. No concession satisfied her. "You say in your letter that you have an inkling of some need in me which you could supply. . . . *All this a damned rot* [her emphasis]. The need I had was for decent treatment and not to be turned out like a courtesan to make room for another one. The need I had was to be saved from expensive illness and loss of work. The need I had was not to be ruined and abandoned."[36] Urging that he take responsibility for his behavior, she made clear how close they had been: "Try and remember that when a woman has accustomed herself to think of a man in the most intimate relation in the world, she can not all in a moment get over being moved by him, and often when we were together last winter, I had to sustain my anger against you because my whole soul and body cried out to you for the love that you had taught me. If you had had the sense to know that, with a kind word, a kiss, you could have won my consent to anything in the world."[37] At the time of these letters, Steffens likely did hide in doorways or wish to be in Mexico.

The two worked hard to avoid each other. Steffens could look out his second-floor window at 42 Washington Square South and see where Austin resided. At the expiration of her lease in October 1912, she moved out of sight but remained just as unrelenting. From California, she asked for the return of letters, which led to further recriminations and the threat of lawyers. "If this keeps up much longer," she told him, "you will have ruined my work to the extent that you will owe me a lifetime of reparation. . . . [It] is dying—dying—bleeding to death."[38] Worry and work brought on something the doctors called "congestion of the brain."[39] When her condition grew dangerous, her brother George came to take care of her.[40] She preferred death, "were it not for the necessity of living and trying to do something" for her child.[41]

The Austin-Steffens-Gussie story had more than one coda. No more faithful to Gussie than to Austin, Steffens began a relationship with Ella Winter, a much younger woman who eventually became his wife and bore him a son. Four month's before the boy's birth, Gussie—whose on-again, off-again relationship with Steffens lasted more than thirteen years—wrote to Steffens's sister: "He has deceived and *lied* to me, time and again. It sounds awful, but that is what shocks me most of all. . . . If I had a character like M.A., it would be different. How can L. write so well and stoop so low?"[42] Austin gives a tacit answer to Gussie in *A Woman of Genius:* "It was all a part of that revelation which sears the path of the gifted woman as with a flame, that no matter what her value to society, no man will spare her anything except as she pleases him."[43] The same could also be said of the next generation of women, including Steffens's wife Ella, who left him for a time because, as Mabel Dodge told Austin, he was "an old man."[44]

Austin responded to Dodge's gossip with a lengthy letter. As to Steffens being an old man, she had little sympathy with his wife on that score. "She knew his age when she married him" and—"a bit of an exhibitionist"—gave newspapers interviews saying how desirable it was to marry a man whose character was already formed. As to cruelty, however, Austin had no doubt. His first wife had "more than hinted that he was jealous of her literary qualifications" and had to "watch him with other women. And I didn't believe any of it," she told Dodge. "I was very young then, and didn't know what I now am convinced of; that when a man's wife tells you anything about him, it may not be strictly true as to the personal application, but it is pretty certain to be true to his general character." The curious thing about Steffens for her was that "he came nearer than any man living to making the great sociological discovery of his generation, and missed it by just those limitations which he exhibits in his personal behavior." Limitations, she concluded, which he shared with many of his contemporaries.[45]

In *Love and the Soul Maker* (1914), a Socratic dialogue between two women, Austin undercuts her earlier views of love and creativity. The narrator concludes, like Jack London and George Sterling—and Sigmund Freud in "Creative Writers and Day Dreaming" (1908)—that books and plays and music grow from a redirection of sexual energy. "I go so far, indeed," she says, "as to wonder if . . . the base of all religion—is not the root and stock of sex, and love and art sprung out of it, a red rose and a white, on either side."[46] She sent a copy of her book to H. G. Wells, who was enmeshed once again in domestic drama. She decided he needed the same kind of talking to she had given herself in her most desperate, despairing moments with Lincoln Steffens.

One benefit of Austin's relationship with Steffens—with whom she somehow renewed cordial relations—was the introduction to Mabel Dodge, the widowed, recently divorced, free-thinking, and almost regal woman who conducted her latter-day salon in Greenwich Village. Dodge had tired of a dolce vita existence in Europe and chose New York with the express idea of surrounding herself with talented people. She rented an apartment on the corner of Ninth and Fifth Avenue and decorated it in white: white walls and white woodwork along with a white bearskin rug. Had she lived in ancient Greece, she would have been, by Steffen's account, a *hetaira*. It amused her to think that in the apartment below hers lived a symbol of the old order, General Daniel Sickels, a man who had served at Gettysburg and been acquitted thirty years before of murdering his wife's lover.[47]

At Mabel Dodge's, all talk was liberal and the talk about sex paramount. On one boisterous evening, Steffens secretly recorded a discussion about "sex antagonism," led by Hutchins Hapgood, the journalist who antagonized respectable New Yorkers for his perverse interest in cubist art, the Industrial Workers of the World, and the turkey trot. A drunken Hapgood pontificated about "free love" and, as only that womanizer could, about man's deep, primordial pain, until Steffens interrupted and the recording machine (probably a Dictaphone), as though reeling from the task of making sense, broke down. Appropriately, the letters exchanged by Hapgood's long-suffering wife, Neith, and Mabel Dodge wail about male infidelity, the costs of open marriages, and a double standard. "As to your famous question," Neith wrote, " 'Why do we want men to be monogamous?' I should respond: Do we? So long as they won't be, why should we want them to be? Why want anybody to be what they are not? Perhaps we like the excitement of catching them in flagrante delicto—and their excuses are so amusing! An absolutely faithful man, but what's the use of discussing him—he's a mythical creature."[48] To the chagrin of his wife, Hapgood argued that "modern marriage" made victims of men like himself who feared rivals stealing their "property." When that happened, "no matter what his advanced ideas were, his deeply complex, instinctive and traditional, nature often suffered, a suffering the woman was relatively spared."[49] Despite Hapgood's stentorian voice, Steffens had the final word: he pronounced the evening and the Dictaphone's experiment "Quite Steinesque."[50] Mabel Dodge liked to refer to her guests as the Dangerous People. For most, "naughty" might have been more accurate. She ambiguously called Hutchins Hapgood "the warmest, most sympathetic hound."[51]

Though open-minded about other people's sexual habits (she once stated that there was nothing better for the soul than healthy sex), Austin spoke circumspectly, or maybe philosophically, about the topic.[52] "Chastity was no longer at the head of the list of desirable behaviors for women," she wrote about her years in New York, where love "was to be taken where it was found. It was . . . the purchase price of political freedom."[53] Affairs, she told a friend, "were engrossing and inspiriting while you are at it, and when it is over leaving you with a few withered remembrances and a strange wonder that you could ever have suffered such an illusion."[54] She herself lost interest in "dangerous" characters, at least the type of middle- or upper-class bohemians who replicated the life she had known in Carmel, growing old too soon or killing themselves by alcoholic self-indulgence. Or for the people Max Eastman called "sentimental rebels," those who sipped champagne as they purported to speak for the downtrodden.

At this time when she sought to avoid writing about the West, Austin began churning out articles on topics of public interest, including but not limited to the sexes. Her papers contain newspaper clippings about the urban poor, juvenile delinquents, grotesque crimes and punishments—the electrocution of men convicted of hacking a woman to death—a pamphlet titled "Marketable Manuscripts, A Booklet for Authors," as well as a hand-drawn map of Greenwich Village factories. Because magazines typically paid women 25 percent less than men for comparable work, her agent advised her to publish serious articles under a man's name. In retrospect, she must have wondered why her role as magazine pundit won no larger audience for her fiction. Edith Wharton presented herself as a grande dame of European culture; and Gertrude Atherton wrote a social history of California as the state's "first daughter"—and a much-abused wife. The selling of her personality did not stop Atherton, and it need not have stopped Austin, from creating a more accessible persona than "America's most intellectual woman." When Austin asked Atherton whether she agreed with that label, Atherton reportedly shot back, "Hell, no, Mary." Austin might have promoted herself more ably with a better sense of humor, like Atherton's, and with a better "image." (William Dean Howells predicted that the "adman" would become the leading artist in the twentieth century.) Though she took an active interest in the distribution and marketing of her books, and later asserted her expertise, Austin also confounded the public, which had come to know her as a "Western writer" and now drowned in her flood of miscellaneous work.

Austin envied those who had the unrestricted time to write that money allows: "It isn't really success in a worldly way which the artist wants," she explained to Mabel Dodge, "but freedom to do his own work in his own fashion. I wonder how many of them ever get that."[55] Unlike Steffens, who casually disposed of art as a border of flowers along the road of civilization, Austin believed it to be the lifeblood of civilization, with an implied if hard to define moral purpose. She might have quoted Henry David Thoreau on the topic: "Do not be too moral," Thoreau advised a friend. "You may cheat yourself out of much life. So aim above morality. Be not simply good; be good for something."[56] Once, when Austin turned to Jimmy Hopper for sympathy about her personal and writing woes, her old friend refused to be drawn in: "You can't make *me* sentimental, Mary Austin; and I know very well that you ain't got no heart—only a typewriter, just like me."[57] Both had good hearts, though Austin could claim the larger typewriter, or the stronger drive to write, which may be what Hopper meant to say. With the force of a machine, she would in her career produce well over two hundred articles, dozens of short stories and poems, additional books of nonfiction, and nine novels.

In her 1912 novel, *A Woman of Genius,* Austin's actress-heroine rises from the depths of despair through work. "Past all loss and forsaking, past loneliness and longing," Olivia Lattimore says about her experience with a man like Lincoln Steffens, "there was something which had stirred in me which would never waken to a lighter occasion; and whether great love like that is the best thing that can happen to us or the most unusual, it placed me forever beyond the reach of futility and cheapness."[58] Olivia's autobiography to some extent parallels and anticipates the out-lines of *Earth Horizon.* The odd child out in her family, a family very much like the Hunters, who made a cult of the oldest son, the dissenting Olivia seems ridiculous to her contemporaries. She marries and bears the child of a decent man reminiscent of Austin's own husband, and after the death of her child deserts her husband for a career on the stage. "I do not know now exactly why I married Tommy, except that marriage seemed a natural sort of experience and I had taken to it as readily as though it had been something to eat, something to nourish and sustain. I hadn't at any rate thought of it as entangling."[59]

"Since when is genius found respectable?" asked Elizabeth Barrett Browning, the nineteenth-century author of the autobiographical *Aurora Leigh.*[60] Equally subversive, Austin's novel about a woman artist calls into question many of the organizing premises of middle-class society. As Olivia announces on the first page, the novel's targeted villain is a town named Taylorville, otherwise Carlinville, Illinois—or Winesburg, Ohio, the fic-tional town Sherwood Anderson wrote into American consciousness. In Taylorville, women like Olivia's childhood friend, Pauline Mills, raise the barriers against genius, requiring every woman to conform to the same soul-killing pattern of respectability that keeps women second-class citizens "under disguising names of womanliness, of tact, of religion even."[61] Olivia's husband conveniently dies after he finds solace with the local seam-stress, who presents a picture of Taylorville itself: perfect when viewed from the front but all askew with crooked stockings, missed buttons, and for-gotten pins when viewed from the back. Olivia is, above all, honest with herself. If polite convention demands that she play the wronged wife or set herself above other players who choose dishonor over starvation, she knows that with a little less talent or another day in subzero Chicago she would make the same decision.

When that day comes, when the bitter and engrossing need for money can no longer be ignored, she has the sense to pray not to an indifferent God but to the great actor Mark Eversley, who sends her to a man called Polotkin. Though decidedly higher on the social ladder and luckier than Theodore Dreiser's Sister Carrie, Olivia avoids starvation and seduction only by chance. Her unlikely guardian angel is a Jewish manager, whose financial backing gives wings to her genius. In this novel, as in Charlotte Perkins Gilman's groundbreaking *Women and Economics,* money is more serious than marriage, more necessary than passion, to the workings of genius. *A Woman of Genius* ends with Olivia married to an old friend and fellow artist. A playwright, he understands something that the great passion of her life—an engineer who demanded that she leave the stage to raise his daughters—did not; he understands the imperatives of genius. "If love does anything for you," Olivia concludes, "it is just to give you the use of yourself."[62]

A Woman of Genius forms part of the late-nineteenth, early twentieth-century debate about the nature of genius. Was it innate? Could it be grafted and nurtured? Long before, Aristotle had concluded that there could be no genius without a mixture of madness; John Dryden, that genius must be born, not taught. In the late 1880s, the topic had the poet Edmund Stedman and his good friend, the novelist-critic William Dean Howells, taking shots at one another in the magazines. Departing from mentors such as Ralph Waldo Emerson and James Russell Lowell, Howells denied the existence of genius as anything but the product of a good brain, luck, and hard work, whereas Stedman saw it as a gift. *A Woman of Genius* (which Austin dedicated to Lou Hoover) both debunks and promotes the notion of genius. "I don't see why it is important that we should know what we are working for," Olivia's future husband, the playwright, tells her: "We might, in our confounded egotism, not approve of it, we might even think we could improve on the pattern. I write plays and you act them and a bee makes honey. I suppose there's a beekeeper about, but that's none of our business." Olivia responds: "Ah, if we could only be sure of that—if He would only make himself manifest; that's what I'm looking for, just a hint of what He's trying to do with us."[63]

Austin's definition of "genius" reflects one of its oldest accepted meanings as a guiding spirit rather than exalted intellectuality or creativity. Somewhere between Howells and Stedman, she might have agreed with Elizabeth Barrett Browning that genius is the power, inseparable from slogging work and patience, to express individuality. Her notion probably comes closest to Simone de Beauvoir's pronouncement that geniuses are never born, they become.

Whether referring to her heroine or herself, Austin called *A Woman of Genius* an autobiography, and certainly Olivia's admission that her husband provided "cover, something to get behind in order to exercise more freely in the things he couldn't understand," has a ring of hard-earned truth.[64] Two years after the publication of *A Woman of Genius,* Wallace Austin sued Mary Hunter Austin for divorce on grounds of willful desertion and abandonment without cause since October 1907. The Austins would remain friends, and neither married again. One needs to "be faithful to one's experiences," Mary had written in "The Woman at the Eighteen-Mile," but experiences are rarely simple, and time and circumstance corrupt all memories. The honesty readers crave in autobiography may be possible only in stories like "The Woman of the Eighteen-Mile" or a novel like *A Woman of Genius,* in which Olivia measures the distance between herself and her husband by his taste in wallpaper.[65]

As Austin well knew, the most mundane differences make couples incompatible—and also connected. She echoes Olivia when she writes: "On the whole, what I regret is not the lack of a satisfying marriage, but the loss out of my life of the traditional protection, the certification of lady hood. I have never been taken care of; and considering what that has meant to women in general, I feel a loss in the quality of charm and graciousness which I am unable to rationalize. The experience of being competent to myself has been immensely worth while to me. . . . But without the experience of being take care of . . . I feel always a little at a loss."[66] In the divorce settlement, Austin received exclusive title to all earnings from her writing, property she had purchased, and one hundred shares of stock from Wallace's employer, American Trona Corporation. Retaining whatever remained of their joint assets, Wallace made Ruth the beneficiary of a two-thousand-dollar life insurance policy.

—•◦•—

Austin tackled, in both a novel like *No. 26 Jayne Street* and her journalism, a range of social and intellectual causes that occupied New York and the nation, or *The Nation,* the proud weekly that epitomized the city's liberal aspirations and carried many of Austin's essays. She had come to New York to write for the theater—with an eye on the movies and money for Ruth's future—hoping to gain instant fame and authority. But instead of contemporary life or the social inequities she addressed in the pages of *The Nation,* she had chosen a topic that branded her yet again a "Westerner." *The Arrow Maker,* as the title suggests, hearkened back to Indians, which for Austin still meant the Indians of California. Quite apart from her commitment to the urban world around her, or her conversations with masters of the theater like Edward Gordon Craig, this was a time when a *new* American theater, a theater rejecting nineteenth-century models, became possible.

Innovators like James A. Herne had long argued for theater that reflected the tenor and diversity of American life.[67] Herne followed his own precepts with *Margaret Fleming,* the story of a woman who adopts her husband's bastard child. Influenced by Henrik Ibsen's *A Doll's House,* American playwrights began to focus on contemporary issues, particularly "the woman question," and to create what Craig abhorred, a realistic theater. *Realism* is always a vexed term, defined largely, as Flannery O'Connor would say, by an individual writer's imagination. Eugene O'Neill, living in New York in the same years as Austin, would begin his version of Ibsen and European-American realism in 1920, with *Beyond the Horizon.* Austin saw "realism" through several lenses. In her own life, she made a distinction between the prosaic facts of existence on the one hand, and "Reality," life's profoundest truths, on the other. In her fiction, she often associated "realism" with the "ironic," as in a little play titled "The Realist" (for the Forest Theater at Carmel) in which a hero named Gerald Sterling gets his come-uppance from a woman he thinks of little account.[68] She would return to this plot in her novella *The Cactus Thorn.*

Austin had been proud of her acting since she first dressed up as an Irish widow and begged door to door in Carlinville. Neighbors gave her bread, cast-off clothing, and money, until Susanna forced her humiliated daughter to return the items and confess her masquerade. Encouraged by her father's penchant for acting, Austin wrote plays as a young girl—and continued in Lone Pine. There she had at least enough popularity to enlist a crew and actors, including her own husband as Shylock, and to start a theater. Some townspeople mistook the theater for (and would have preferred) another saloon. Her papers include watercolors of sets in Lone Pine as well as later manuscripts of unpublished plays, notably "The Coyote Doctor" (1906) and "Island of Desire" (1912), a comedy in four acts that satirizes the Carmel colony. The title refers to an island sanatorium for the insane, run along socialist free-love principles, where the inmates live by laws of their "own being."[69] Chaos reigns until the director is unmasked as another patient.

Believing in folk theater, Austin would promote plays written, acted, and produced by members of a community, after the model of Dublin's Abbey Theatre or New York's Yiddish theater.[70] Since the middle of the previous century, theater in the United States had moved toward representations of "the folk," otherwise ordinary people, but in practice dodgy characters on the edges of society. For Austin, folk theater came to mean theater that originated from people (or peoples) in intimate relationship with their environment. Being a decade or more ahead of her time, she said, accounted for the public indifference to her work. Never mind that such claims are often sops to the ego or cold comfort, she had a point. American theater enjoyed a renaissance (or actual birth) in places far from New York and Chicago as communities like Carmel formed their own theaters in protest against worn-out plots and melodrama. In small town and rural theaters, plays enjoyed the same grassroots interest as the contemporary Arts and Crafts movement or the new cinemas. Two years into the century, San Francisco's Bohemian Club began a tradition of staging plays in "The Grove," a magnificent redwood forest in Monte Rio. Austin's *The Arrow Maker* had two predecessors in Charles Kellogg Field's *The Man in the Forest,* based on an Indian tale, and Donald MacLaren's 1906 hit *The Redskin.* New York's Neighborhood Playhouse, founded in 1915 by Austin's friends, Alice and Irene Lewisohn, grew out of dramatic readings held at the Henry Street settlement. The next year, a group including George Cook, Susan Glaspell, John Reed, the Hapgoods, and Eugene O'Neill came together on Cape Cod and founded the Provincetown Players. In the 1920s respect grew for "folk drama" produced in "little theaters" across the country: community centers, church basements, school auditoriums, and private homes.[71]

Austin's dedicated her first contribution to folk drama, *The Arrow Maker,* to Herbert Hoover. The play opened at New York's New Theatre, Sixtieth Street and Central Park West, on 27 February 1911, under the aegis of Winthrop Ames and George Foster Platt. It had for its backers men with names like Vanderbilt, Huntington, Morgan, and Astor. Conceived as a national theater with a stock company along the lines of the Comédie Française, the New Theatre seated over two thousand people and boasted a revolving stage with other state-of-the-art equipment. Additional amenities included a restaurant, tea room, and (for men only) smoking room and bar. Paintings from W. K. Vanderbilt's private collection hung in the gold-and-marble entrance. As Austin would learn, however, money lavished on plush boxes for the founders should have been spent on acoustics and flexible seating, or several smaller theaters, to make theatergoing more intimate.

In its beginnings, production of *The Arrow Maker* went well. The company gave Austin a studio; and theater publicity touted her as a foremost authority on Indians of the Southwest, though she graciously conceded that honor to her old mentor Charles Lummis. From the start, Ames enthusiastically embraced *The Arrow Maker*. Tempers rose when the producer, George Foster Platt, lobbied for revisions that Austin dismissed as sentimental and melodramatic, at best "a poetized Fennimore [sic] Cooper version of my Indians."[72] Then Ames, siding with his producer, ran amuck, as she complained, "mutilating" or "New-Theatreizing" her play and pounding it like a beefsteak into something quite different. In Italy Austin had admired and made marginal notes in her copy of Edward Gordon Craig's *The Art of the Theatre* (he called it *The Art of the Theatre Tomorrow*). She rejected his vision of the stage director, who, having mastered the use of line, color, actions, words, and rhythms, no longer needs the assistance of the playwright. To Austin's annoyance, Ames's method imitated Craig's theory. Ames demanded absolute control that she thought belonged in the hands of the author.[73]

With her livelihood and reputation riding on this play, Austin had expected to be involved in all aspects of the production. She also assumed, like other critics of the New Theatre who objected to the gilt and founders' boxes, that it would be a democratic institution. She should, and in fact did, know better. Olivia explains it this way in *A Woman of Genius:* theater rests, not on a "community of art," but on "box-office returns."[74] Facing possible bankruptcy, Ames could not afford idealistic theories.[75]

Austin's experience with the New Theatre illustrated William Dean Howells's comment that what the American public wants is tragedy with a happy ending. *The Arrow Maker* had, unfortunately, two endings. The published version follows not Austin's script but Ames's production, in which the Chisera's magic elevates her faithless lover, Simwa, into a chief. Simwa, marrying Bright Water, bitterly denounces the tradition that forbids the Chisera what every woman in the tribe takes for granted: companionship, love, and children. Her power spent, the tribe falls victim to famine and war with the Tecuyas until Bright Water pleads with her to dance for the women and children. As the Chisera dances her power builds. The curtain falls as she leads the warriors into battle "with the assurance of victory before them."[76] Austin had wanted to end with the death of the Chisera and the probable extinction of her tribe. Ames rejected the idea outright.

Most critics, scoffing at the play's lack of verisimilitude, saw it as a pretentious costume drama. One quipped that Austin's "Anglo-American Indians" must have spent leisure hours in their childhood reading Edgar Allan Poe's *Eleanora* and Dr. Johnson's *Rasselas;* another, in *Theatre Magazine,* that "there is little or no skill of the playwright in it."[77] Although a program note to *The Arrow Maker* testified to the authenticity of all songs, chants, costumes, and props, scrupulously duplicated from recordings and objects housed at the Smithsonian, a reviewer for the *New York Times* cared more about originality than authenticity. "Tribal customs, Indian costumes, ceremonial dances [taught by Chief Red Eagle, a half-Paiute Winnebago] were interwoven in a love story that was basically universal and as old as Adam."[78]

Devoted as he was to his theater, Ames failed to keep it going. Four hundred thousand dollars in debt (now the equivalent of millions), the New Theatre closed its doors after the second season. Austin, later blaming the play for ending her stage career and the theater for ruining her play, wrote an article for *American Magazine* in which she compared the New Theatre to a soap factory staffed by incompetents. Of Ames in particular, she wrote that "the first Director of The New Theatre was a man of gifts and ideals, but he labored under two insuperable disadvantages: he was born rich and he was born in Boston."[79] The article horrified Austin's agent, who considered cutting her loose.

In 1914, produced by the Western Drama Society and with Austin's imposing friend Charlotte Kellogg as the Chisera, *The Arrow Maker* had a successful revival at the Forest Theater, where the setting matched the subject: a sloping hillside that curved like an amphitheater among giant pines, which gave the impression of a proscenium arch. Without glitz or gilt, Carmel's theatergoers found their seats with candlelight lanterns called "bugs," fashioned from tin cans punched with holes. Idyllic as the setting was, that production too had its squabbling. Long before opening night, the actors and crew took to calling Austin, with her outfits and trailing braids, "Sitting Bull."[80] A kinder George Sterling drew the line at "Coyote-Woman." Among community theaters and schools, *The Arrow Maker* became a popular choice, and Austin usually waived the fifteen dollars she asked as royalty.

She followed *The Arrow Maker* with another play for the Forest Theater. In July 1913, she proudly attended the premier of *Fire,* with Herbert Heron playing Evind, a man who steals fire for his adopted tribe and in turn receives suspicion and threats of death. After he escapes with his wife and coyote sidekick, the tribe belatedly recognizes him as a god.[81] *Fire* also played in Palm Springs (5 and 6 November 1921), as the playbill reads, when "the sun nears the rim of the San Jacinto Mountains, at the entrance to Tahquitz Canyon." Austin believed that art must originate from the people, but as H. L. Mencken would famously quip, "There was no underestimating the taste of the American public"—or the contradictory impulses of artists themselves, who wanted to change the focus of the American theater while coveting large audiences and financial success. Austin would have only one other run in New York. The Children's Theater in 1916 produced *Merry Christmas, Daddy,* the story of a Scrooge-like father learning about Christmas customs around the world and deciding—much to his daughter's delight—to celebrate the holiday at home.[82]

The debacle of *The Arrow Maker*'s eight-night New York run proved a bitter disappointment with lasting repercussions. Already defensive, Austin targeted the prejudice of Eastern critics, particularly Jewish critics, who to her mind monopolized the arts. In a 1920 review of Waldo Frank's *Our America* ("New York Dictator of American Criticism"), she faulted Frank for not recognizing regional contributions to a national literature. Ironically, both Austin and Frank saw a possible alternative in Mexican and Indian traditions—Frank would say a doomed alternative—to modern materialism; and both saw "America" as a work in process. Austin, who acknowledged the contributions of Jews to science, economics, and publishing, questioned their "preponderance . . . among our critical writers": "Can the Jew," she asks, "with his profound complex of election, his need of sensuous satisfaction qualifying his every expression of personal life, and his short pendulum-swing between mystical orthodoxy and a sterile ethical culture—can he become the commentator, the arbiter, of American art and American thinking?"[83] She then listed Frank's chosen arbiters by name: "Stieglitz, Stein, Ornstein, Rosenfeld, Oppenheim, Mencken, Little, Hackett, and Brooks." Ludwig Lewisohn, an author and prominent Zionist, took Austin privately to task for her slighting remarks—on letterhead from *The Nation,* which he edited in the 1920s before joining the faculty of the new Brandeis University.[84] The African American writer Jean Toomer attacked her publicly: "Desiring the inevitable amalgamation and consequent cultural unity, Miss Austin's article has given new cause for old race consciousness. Aiming at a community of cultured differences, she serves the cause of disunion."[85]

Austin wrote at a time of heightened anti-Semitism and, as Toomer knew, escalation of Ku Klux Klan terrorism. In 1921 the U.S. Congress would pass an immigration restriction act aimed primarily at Jews. Austin, delighted to have caused a stir, saw nothing vicious in her comments. She cavalierly dismissed suggestions of prejudice and looked forward to continuing the debate about race and ethnicity with correspondents like Lewisohn. Frank thought she resented not being among the spiritual pioneers he discussed in *Our America,* and she did object to Amy Lowell being singled out as an early practitioner of free verse when as early as 1911 her free-verse play, *The Arrow Maker,* had opened on Broadway. She made no mention of its fortunes.

Anyone trying to come to terms with Austin's attitude toward Jews faces irresolvable contradictions. If her prejudice fed on what she saw as the slighting of her work and the work of Western artists generally, it also took another form. In her autobiography, she writes that "sometimes I think if I had the wit to look for a Jew for a partner, I might have found both love and opportunity. Only the Jews are warm enough to tolerate art as a shareholder."[86] At least one friend thought she had a chance with Abraham Hilkowich, a doctor who invited her to accompany him to Jerusalem and write about his establishing a national medical system. "I am missing him more than I thought I would," Austin said of Hilkowich, "and I may go out there for a visit myself next year."[87] Another friend had told her that she should marry Hilkowich, but Austin was not persuaded. This friend's notion of a good husband was, Austin said, "any man with money he doesn't have to earn, and nothing more important to do than hold the hoop for his wife to jump through."[88] When he married, Austin wished Hilkowich a happy life. In 1934, the novelist and war correspondent Dorothy Canfield, aware of Austin's books on Jesus and obviously thinking her ecumenical in outlook, would ask her to serve on a women's advisory committee for the National Conference of Jews and Christians.

———————————————— •·◆·• ————————————————

In 1914, Austin wrote Lou Hoover: "I have lost the fame, or at least I have so near lost it that it is all over but the mourning and I suppose before long the world will know I have lost it. And I lost it by just such silliness as not wanting to break promises or to hurt other people more than they have hurt me, and I wish to goodness I hadn't been brought up a Christian."[89] If Austin had overextended herself, the main culprit was, as always, money. In need of money, she agreed to write a series of articles for *Harper's Weekly,* which D. Appleton and Company contracted to publish as *Love and the Soul Maker* (1914). She also completed for fall publication *California, the Land of the Sun,* approached Harper's about the book that would become *The Ford* (1917), and began a biography of Christ to be called *The Man Jesus* (1915). As might be expected, *The Man Jesus* features the robust figure of *Christ in Italy,* while its trajectory, again somewhat autobiographical, resembles that of *A Woman of Genius.* Austin begins her book with its expected ending, Christ's painful return from the dead: "The misery of his world rose up against him, assailed him through his great gift of compassion, threatened to engulf him; but always we see him striking clear of it, committing himself to the Word with such confidence as a bird commits itself to the air or a great fish to the deep."[90] If Austin's range of interests becomes apparent in *The Man Jesus,* so does her floundering. Bitterly disappointed about the sales of *A Woman of Genius,* she followed it with *The Lovely Lady* (1913), a book its diametric opposite, and even less profitable. The story of a man who has lived his life by the ideals he sees embodied in "Woman," the idealized lovely lady of the title, it seemed to critics a relative failure—and not redeemed by some exceptional lyrical passages.

As usual Austin had yet another project in the works, *The Trail Book* (1918), written for her niece, Mary, and children who had little knowledge of the West and its native peoples. Van Wyck Brooks described her going at night to the Museum of Natural History to do research for this book, in which a boy and girl discover that the stuffed animals and the waxed Indian come alive at night and with them a mythological world as vivid as Ovid's *Metamorphoses.* Austin fell "into a trance," Brooks wrote, "that placed her in a mystic communion with the Great Spirit and the soul of the dead. And once, by daylight, to the alarm of the guard who supposed for a moment that she had designs on the collection, she took several relics from a case that had been opened for her and placing them in her bosom fell into a state of silent ecstasy. Great was the guard's relief when, after a few minutes, she returned the relics to the case and explained that she had been in communion with the gods of the red men."[91]

The grueling regimen Austin set for herself in the next few years intensified her bad health, especially problems with her heart. Her inability to sleep sapped her energies and, as she acknowledged, made her cross. Unenthusiastic reviews and shrinking sales did nothing to help. She fretted that her books seemed to go out of print almost as soon as they appeared. In an attempt to resume her relationship with Houghton Mifflin, Austin explained to the editors that she intended to produce a book or a play every year: "There is no question in my mind that I am to succeed with drama on a very high level. As to fiction, I am artist enough to know that the only good fiction is pure creation, and that problems except as they are eternal problems of living, have no place in it."[92] The next year she lobbied Ferris Greenslet directly: "Once for all let us agree that the chances of your making money out of it [her work] are small. I don't know why since I get quite smashing reviews and there is not an English critic and few English writers who have not agreed in print that my work is easily the most distinguished in America. Add to that that I am one of the . . . most interviewed women in America, and say if you can why I am one of the poorest paid."[93] Greenslet did not bite. All that his company would gain "would be the privilege of standing over you with a lash, as you phrase it, to persuade you to finish a novel [when] you might or might not be diverted to write a play, conduct a propaganda or what not. If there were a new book actually at hand, finished and ready for press, the situation would be of a different quality, but as it is with so many important affairs pulling you in so many different ways we hesitate to assume the responsibility."[94] Given her widely disparate writing and increasing involvement with causes, notably women's suffrage before the First World War, Greenslet made a shrewd decision and offered sound, if implicit, advice.

To the sympathetic Lou Hoover, Austin expressed a wish to go back to London "to meet men like George Moore and Conrad and Galsworthy and get forgiven for being respectable." Of her career, she said:

It just [has not] worked at all. I have been the best and the biggest thing I knew how to be and said damn the consequences, but it is I that am damned. I am losing, I have all but lost my creative faculty, by starving it in the interest of something that I believed to be right, and I thought if I could go over to England there are others who have fought this out and not lost, that they could somehow help me to hold on to what is leaving me so rapidly. There's nobody here in America can help me."[95]

Despite her pessimism, Austin already found herself in a ready-made community of female peers no less peculiar or (to borrow her own word) "queer" than herself and equally caught up in women's issues.[96]

seven

THE VILLAGE

1914–1920

Such people as you and I and Hoover—artists and engineers must get
into the game. People with creative vision, with creative capacity,
must have more power in the processes of government.

MARY AUSTIN TO H. G. WELLS

1917

LIKE MOST WRITERS, AUSTIN DEPOSITED papers of all varieties into a kind
of savings account—in her case, notebooks and diaries—for future projects. In the New York diary she kept for Lincoln Steffens, she introduced
a document written for her by Joseph Boardman Jr. of the Boardman
Detective Bureau, located at 104 East Twentieth Street, on the edge of
Greenwich Village. In her autobiography, Austin mentions her own brief
stint in a detective agency, possibly Boardman's, and she may have used the
connection for a new if risky kind of research. Austin either hired or cajoled
Boardman to gather information about her radical friends and acquaintances in the Village. At the time, she had begun research on a work in
progress that became *No. 26 Jayne Street,* a novel like Henry James's *The
Princess Casamassima,* which takes an ironic look at anarchists and their
supporters.

The question arises: what could have persuaded her to employ a private
detective, even one she trusted, without weighing the possible consequences? In a different frame of mind she had threatened to use a detective
to hound Lincoln Steffens when he withheld his address. The actual hiring
of someone to spy and report on associates was another matter; it implied
a breach of trust and privacy she would have been hard-pressed to defend.
From a purely self-protective point of view, she risked the discovery of ille-
galities or other embarrassments best left alone. Many Greenwich Villagers

already found themselves under scrutiny by the government, not to mention at odds with the values of Austin's friends the Hoovers.

In fact, Herbert Hoover offers a possible clue to Austin's intentions. If he asked for information about Village life, Austin may have jumped at the idea of espionage as an irresistible and harmless lark. She knew how much Hoover interested himself in dissidents and their activities from the days he had disparaged Anne Martin's efforts in support of women's rights. Martin appeared laughable in comparison to the petite, Madonna-like Emma Goldman, whom Hoover called one of the most dangerous women in the United States. Though it seems unlikely that a strong advocate of free speech like Hoover would have requested information garnered by a private detective and passed on through a second party, he could have justified the exchange as keeping abreast of public opinion. Supposing on the other hand that Hoover had nothing to do with Boardman's undercover work, Austin may have used the connection to repay her patron as best she could.

Whatever Austin instructed Boardman to find, it was not treasonable. His accounts of people reflect an amused affection and suggest Austin's own likes and dislikes among the inhabitants of Greenwich Village in the years before the United States entered World War I. Boardman described Hutchins Hapgood, whom he cornered simply by showing up at the anarchists' local "headquarters," as looking "for all the world like a Harvard man, short, rather stocky, well dressed, blue-eyed, a mighty pleasant fellow. He smelt a ratty odor of newspaper notoriety about me, and led the conversation assiduously afield into the general or philosophical fields of Anarchism." Hapgood gave him a list of books to read on the topic. "Emma Goldman's apartment at 210 East 13th Street," Boardman reported, "is the great social gathering-place for Anarchists in their lighter moments. Among the tribe it is the common phrase to say 'going around to two-ten,' assuming that there is only one two-ten, as there is only one Vatican. It is a small apartment on the top floor of a walk-up flat house, scrupulously clean, very simply and even poorly furnished. (Here I quote Henrietta Rodman.) Emma keeps no servant, does her own housework and does it mighty well, is a splendid cook and always has a push of hangers-on, cheap Anarchists, down-and-outs of every description, who batten on her good-nature. [She] is of course tremendously magnetic and tremendously tender-hearted." Boardman signed his report to Austin "your faithful, if rather Romantic Servant."[1]

In these years, a detective like Boardman might have filed a similar report on Mary Austin. Forty-six-years old in 1914, she too was a splendid cook and meticulous housekeeper, albeit now with the help of a housemaid. A handsome woman, by Boardman's and his fellow detective's reckoning, she appeared more shy than self-possessed and drawn to what she believed the right causes, if not always to the right people. The maverick, or proud solitary, had become a joiner of organizations, and possibly a mole. A member of the Liberal Club, dedicated to questions of labor and education, and the Twilight Club, with its "poet's code of ethics," she worked with passionate intensity for women's enfranchisement, and though she slighted in retrospect both the cause and her suffragist-friend, Anne Martin, much of her time went to advancing the goals of the National Woman's Party and the Woman's Peace Party.[2]

Austin, who disliked "isms"—meaning loose ill-defined catchalls—worked for feminist causes but not for *feminism* as she saw it develop. She disagreed with those who believed women to be smarter or morally superior to men. Nor did she think that their full enfranchisement guaranteed a better world. She held that women should have equal privileges with men and that they would make the same muck of them. A 1927 article published in *The Nation* best summarizes her position: "Too much has been made of the long rankling injustice of woman's position in the nineteenth century and earlier. Too little of that injustice was intended as such or can be historically traced to male initiative, to have become legitimately the source of widespread resentment. What every honest feminist now knows is that they simply seized upon existing injustices, sought them out, and flourished them as so many excuses for entitling them to what they so ardently wanted, a working partnership in social affairs."[3] A full partnership cannot be realized, she argued, until women have control of their own bodies, but her readers must accept that the result of self-control (and equal partnership) will be fewer, and probably not better, babies. According to Austin, women have no greater insight into men than men have into women: "there are springs of activity in men that women know very little about, that they haven't respected as they should, and that they must try to understand before trying to make over a society that is composed, fifty percent, of men."[4]

Still very much interested in men, abstractly and personally, Austin in middle age disdained charm as though it were unfair play in love or politics. She thought it possible that her early life had made her, as she put it, "stiff to know." "It is also true," she disingenuously told Mabel Dodge, "that I have a deep seated resistance to being personally liked. Nothing stiffens me quite so much as being called charming. . . . Three times a week for the whole of my life somebody has told me, as you do, that I could charm people if I would simply be 'myself,' which simply means to be one of my-selves which the other person likes. . . . Perhaps my resistance to being liked comes from my experiences of finding that the person who likes me always tries to make me stay in the preferred mode of life."[5] The "personal," what her new friend Willa Cather described as the power to suggest something lovelier than one's self, won friends but not necessarily arguments.[6] The Boardman episode aside, Austin tried to put principles above the personal, and following her own prescription made an effort to see the relationship with Lincoln Steffens more philosophically—in other words, as one of those "tragic necessities" of human life.[7] Friends remember her achieving a new dignity. At five foot five, she "stood tall with the upward inclination of her head," as though gazing beyond you. Her voice, which seemed to "rise from some stored well of spiritual energy," suggested "a life remote from the common run of things." Above all, it communicated "intelligence."[8]

"I am without fear," Austin once told Steffens, with the bravado or blind-ness of a Brontë heroine.[9] She meant that she had the courage to know and, knowing, the responsibility to speak, whether or not people called her a Cassandra or—often enough—merely a nuisance. "She herself prefers less to be judged by any of her numerous books," Carl Van Doren would write in *Contemporary American Novelists* (1922), "than to be regarded as a figure laboring somewhat anonymously toward the development of a national culture founded at all points on national realities."[10] Van Doren's admira-tion for Austin leads him to see her much as she saw herself through these New York years: courageous, ambitious, but floundering between the tal-ented writer and the universal expert.

Her early life in Carlinville had shaped her perspective more than she ac-knowledged. Like the Wisconsin writer Zona Gale, who reimagined her hometown of Portage, Washington, as "Friendship Village"—a name that captures the widespread utopian impulse in the early decades of the twen-tieth century—Austin had sought her equivalent of Friendship Village first at El Alisal, Charles Lummis's sylvan retreat in Los Angeles; then in Carmel with George Sterling. Greenwich Village offered instead the energy and di-versity of a sophisticated urban community. Henry James knew the district—roughly bounded by Fourteenth Street on the north, Houston Street on the south, Broadway on the east, and the Hudson River on the west—as Washington Square writ large, or simply *writ,* as the setting of his novel *Washington Square.* In James's youth, it remained an enclave of New York's oldest families, their customs and idiosyncrasies preserved behind impenetrable brownstone fronts. By 1880, the year James's novel appeared, families like his had been supplanted by immigrants, who appreciated the neighborhood's architecture, tree-lined streets, and tucked-away parks. Around 1910, the year Austin returned from Europe, the Village began to attract such artists and intellectuals as gathered in Munich's Schwabing, London's Soho, or the Left Bank of Paris.

To many of its habitants, Greenwich Village offered, as the poet Floyd Dell put it, a "moral health resort where people came to solve some of their life problems."[11] He might have had Austin in mind, or Mabel Dodge, who chased, to use her own word, the newest "It"—an ever-elusive quality of self and life—through sex or psychoanalysis. Above all, life in the Village meant meeting and accepting people of differing professions, persuasions, sexual orientations, politics, and ambitions; and Austin found these in spades at Mabel Dodge's evenings.[12]

Austin's new (and not so new) acquaintances, some of them subject to arrest or desiring it, seemed unlikely revolutionaries, especially the middle-class figures brought up in middle- or upper-class circumstances. The architects of the Armory Show, Arthur B. Davies and Walt Kuhn, were respectively fifty-one and thirty-three in 1913; John Sloan, of the Ashcan school of painters and illustrator for *The Masses,* past forty; and Lincoln Steffens, who grew up in a mansion that would later house California's governors, three years shy of fifty. The exception, Dodge's current lover, John Reed, who turned twenty-six in 1913, was nonetheless born to money (he remembered deer feeding on exotic trees at his grandparents' estate). At the beginning of his career and fresh from the success of his play to benefit striking silk workers—*The Pageant of the Paterson Strike,* staged at Madison Square Garden—Reed abandoned playwriting to follow the Russian Revolution of 1917. He befriended Vladimir Ilyich Lenin and, before his early death, published *Ten Days That Shook the World* (1920). Buried with other Bolshevik champions alongside the Kremlin wall, Reed remained to his American friends, in Van Wyck Brooks's words, "the wonder boy of Greenwich Village."[13]

Austin's circle widened to include like-minded women of her day, from Elizabeth Gurley Flynn, an admirer of *A Woman of Genius,* to Margaret Sanger, who during a visit to England contrived affairs with both H. G. Wells and her fellow proponent of sexual education, Havelock Ellis. Austin admired the intrepid Sanger as a woman of "great strength and power." Through her friend Charlotte Perkins Gilman, Austin also met Herbert Hoover's "dangerous" Emma Goldman, the woman Mabel Dodge credited with establishing love as a serious undertaking. Reed, Flynn, Sanger, Goldman: the names highlight Austin's radicalization. Sentenced to a year in the penitentiary at Blackwell's Island for urging the poor to take their daily bread by force, and again for distributing birth-control pamphlets, Goldman was finally deported to Russia for organizing the No-Conscription League in protest against the First World War. Flynn proved equally daring. Theodore Dreiser described her—an organizer for the Industrial Workers of the World and a founding member of the American Civil Liberties Union—as an East Side Joan of Arc. When Flynn, a "flaming torch; pretty and serious in an Irish way," served time in Leavenworth, Austin pledged help for her children.[14] Austin honored the willingness of these women to sacrifice for what they believed. Of Goldman, she wrote that "she knew where she was going and who was going with her. I couldn't go along with her; for Emma, modern history began with Marx; modern literature began with the revolt of Labor; archaeology had not begun at all, and she thought I just didn't know; but nevertheless, I liked her." Goldman, ethical by Austin's reckoning, lived by her principles and allowed no "schism between life profession and life practice," a quality Austin found distinctly lacking in Lincoln Steffens.[15]

Her relationship with Goldman suggests why few of the people Austin met in the Village mention her in their memoirs. She became part of many groups and central to none. Among her new acquaintances, she felt especially drawn to the New York high-school teacher Henrietta Rodman. Rodman, who affected the dress of a medieval page, had a flare for the theatrical, which Austin shared. A leader in the birth-control and school-reform movements and the guiding spirit of the Liberal Club, Rodman lost her teaching job, according to Austin, for enlightening her students about the nature of George Eliot's relationship with her common-law husband, George Lewes. Secretly married, Rodman lobbied for the rights of married women, including the right to teach. Rumors flew about the ménage à trois she and her husband and his former wife maintained in their Bank Street apartment. Seeing herself as a social engineer—and dismissed as "a Candide in petticoats and sandals"—Rodman argued for apartment houses to be equipped with basement kitchens to serve all residents, and for rooftop classrooms staffed by teachers trained in the Montessori method.[16] Among her schemes, she designed a Futuristic Baby-Raising Plan to free women for their professions, which made her an easy target in the press. "You put the baby and the breakfast dishes on the dumbwaiter," one critic wrote, "and send them down to the kitchen-nursery-kindergarten-laundry to be cared for until needed."[17] Although Austin herself poked fun at Rodman's "Better Babies" in *No. 26 Jayne Street,* she would put such theories to use during the coming war when organizing communal kitchens across the country.

Thanks to Anne Martin, whose work took her frequently to New York City—and whom Austin nominated for membership in the Cosmopolitan Club—Austin knew and sometimes collaborated with the formidable Alice Paul, a woman with the reputation and influence of a latter-day Frances Willard, Susanna Hunter's idol so long before. A banker's daughter, Paul graduated from Swarthmore with a degree in biology at sixteen and traveled to England at twenty-one, where she connected with Emmeline Pankhurst, the guiding force (with her daughters) of the British women's suffrage movement. After participating in hunger strikes and serving three terms in jail, Paul returned to the United States to organize what to that time—3 March 1913—proved the largest demonstration in the nation's history. Austin, then director of publicity and a lecturer for the National American Woman Suffrage Association, helped to assemble the flamboyant procession.[18] Leaders from each represented state rode on horseback behind flag-and-banner carriers dressed in gold-trimmed purple capes with white stoles. About eight thousand women marched with them in white suffragist costumes. Some rode floats—including a lavishly decorated replica of the Liberty Bell—down Pennsylvania Avenue from the Capitol to the White House. Police stood by as hecklers in a crowd of nearly a half a million pelted the protestors with whatever came to hand. It took six hours for the women, drawn from all classes and walks of life, to reach the steps of the Capitol. In 1916, the year Paul became director of the National Woman's Party, Austin planned the party's pageant, staged on the east steps of the Capitol where members of the House and Senate received suffrage envoys from the West.[19] Paul and Austin traveled together on several speaking tours. While Austin claimed that she could not keep up with the much younger woman, she made an impression on the movement's leaders. Inez Haynes Irwin, fiction editor for *The Masses* and the future biographer of Alice Paul, would write to Austin, "You certainly ought to come onto the editorial board of EQUAL RIGHTS—the organ of the National Woman's Party, for you belong there if any woman does."[20]

So, much of Austin's time in New York centered on public events, mainly in Greenwich Village, where the worlds of art and politics came together. She enjoyed the company of Fola La Follette, whose father, "Fighting" Bob, sought political reform as a founder of the Progressive movement. Thanks to the Stage Women's Division of Suffrage, she met the actor Mrs. Fiske (Augusta Davey, otherwise "Minnie Maddern"), celebrated for her role as Nora in Henrik Ibsen's *A Doll's House;* and Rachel Crothers, who, apart from casting, producing, and directing about one Broadway play a year, founded the Stage Women's Relief Fund. Austin also befriended two famous Russians of the day, Alla Nazimova, the actress who shot to fame with the antiwar film *War Brides,* and Anna Pavlova, the classical ballerina who had a passion for ethnic dances. Theatrical on and off the stage, Pavlova admired Austin as an expert on American Indian dance; each time they met, she would kiss the older women's hands before plunking down at her feet for a good chat. (Not so Isadora Duncan, who once again snubbed her.) Austin enjoyed meeting these women of the arts *and,* as she phrased it, taking their measure—with or without the help of Detective Boardman.

Joining Dorothy Canfield, Fannie Hurst, and Kathleen Norris, in 1917 Austin contributed to *The Sturdy Oak: A Composite Novel of American Politics by Fourteen American Authors,* the profits of which went to the women's suffrage movement. Even as Austin repeated Susanna Hunter's pattern of service, participating in organizations and public events, she saw in her own writing a reflection of earlier pioneers. She began to reread novels from the 1880s and 1890s—Mary Augusta Ward's *Robert Elsmere* and Sarah Grande's *The Heavenly Twins*—as prophetic books, and she found it odd that the radical young women she met failed to realize how much they profited from women writers and activists in earlier generations.

Austin's varied, probably too varied, activities came hitched together in New York's bustle of reformers and movements. It was not unusual to see organizers of a socialist rally one night hosting English royalty the next. Austin preferred to meet her favorite nonconformists, insiders or outsiders, artists or revolutionaries, at the National Arts Club, the former mansion of New York's governor, Samuel Tilden, who had won the popular vote but lost the presidency to Rutherford B. Hayes. An elegant example of period Gothic, with elaborate carvings and a glass-domed library, the mansion was expanded in 1906 with a thirteen-story annex for artist studios and studies. When not keeping her own apartment in New York, Austin made her home at the club. She became such a regular that the chairman of the Restaurant Committee wrote her a poem:

> "Owed to Mary" poem 19 June 1916
> O, Mary thou art just and wise
>   On many topics (one is pies)

So listen to our tale of woe
  Before to other joints you go.

A cook we had of high degree
  Who could elucidate pastry
In many forms, cross-stitch, cross-bar
  But he went where the money are!
. . . .

But if our patriot hearts know well
  That cooks come high and money's—hell!
O, Mary be right on the spot
  And in the pie-line show what's what![21]

Apart from rallies and meetings or evenings at the club, Austin frequented publishers' galas, like Harper & Brothers' seventy-fifth birthday party for William Dean Howells, held at Sherry's restaurant in 1912. That evening she sat between the respected journalist William Allen White and his forgotten colleague Paxton Hibben, an actor who entertained the company by impersonating Howells's best-known character, Silas Lapham. These occasions made Howells unusually confiding. Avuncular in his later years, he warned Austin against the risks of isolation, saying "he had suffered from that very thing, that he had kept too close, narrowed his scope."[22] If Austin at that time suffered from isolation, it must have been the loneliness of crowds. She had in fact taken a very different trajectory, and so had Howells himself. "Literature," he told his well-wishers, "which was once limited to the cloister, the school, has become more and more of the forum and the market-place. But it is actuated now by as high and noble motives as ever it was in the history of the world."[23] He meant both to congratulate and inspire. In the audience sat a cross-section of American authors, including Willa Cather, Emily Post, Zane Grey, Ida Tarbell, Hutchins Hapgood, and Austin herself, who William Allen White would say "was vainer than a wilderness of gargantuan peacocks," but that he loved her "tough-fibered brain."[24]

Seven years after the Harper's dinner, Austin would write to Hapgood, then mourning the death of his daughter, that her own burden of sorrow had kept her from knowing him and his friends better during the Village years:

I saw many of you interested as I was in the work of social regeneration, but I also saw you either kept by happy accident from the things I knew, or putting sorrow from you under various names of freedom as though sorrow also were not part of the break of life. I have been thinking of late that the failure of those who know social problems, who see social needs and the remedy, to save the world . . . is very largely their failure to digest sorrow and pain and loss and sacrifice. They have been fed too much on pleasant meat.[25]

Despite the emphasis on her own distress, she speaks shrewdly about her circle of friends—and unwittingly about herself. She, too, had failed "to digest sorrow and pain and loss and sacrifice," and who has not? She may have eaten less of the pleasant meat. Despite the implied scolding, Hapgood valued her letter and kept it. He knew that she alluded to Ruth, the daughter she could hardly bear to visit and whose life she lamented every day. That sorrow put her failed relationships with men and her stuttering career in perspective.

Mabel Dodge's portrait of Austin—sitting with lips thrust out, alone when in company, and her now "gray hair coiled high, portentous in prairie-colored satin"—captures the paradox of vulnerability and affectation that confounded so many of Austin's contemporaries. She described herself during these years as "not very generous":

I sincerely submitted myself to be taught [she told Dodge], I faithfully went to all their gathering, read what they wrote, and came to realize very slowly that their economics were inadequate—not even they deny that now—their science antiquated . . . I suppose I was not very gracious after making this discovery. I felt imposed upon. I thought that they had no right to offer me stale ideas and call them advanced, I was honestly puzzled and disappointed.

Then for that 'deep rich life' which you thought they had, I did not find either rich or deep. . . . And I thought in comparison with what I had been having, in the Fabian Society in London for instance, that the New York life was thin, decadent in spots, shallow, uninformed, almost wholly unillumined. What passed for illumination was quite evidently a repercussion of the sex life which was lived almost wholly in what you call 'feeling' instead of wisdom. I found it full of falsities and contradictions and shocking violations of the code they were prescribing for other people in economics and politics.[26]

Whatever recognition she came to in later years, the pattern of her "New York life" continued on a different tangent. Needing people and a cause, she would put her conflicting passions for belonging and independence into new service, when the so-called Great War crippled Europe in 1914 and she joined forces with her friend and patron, Herbert Hoover.

———————————— ◆•◆ ————————————

Before and during the war, Austin took on two assignments, both of which she owed to the Hoovers. In January 1913, President Taft and Congress commissioned Hoover to promote the Panama-Pacific International Exposition in San Francisco, celebrating the opening of the Panama Canal and the four hundreth anniversary of Balboa's discovery of the Pacific Ocean. Hoover enlisted Austin as a publicist for the exposition, "the state's first major communal expression, [which] showed," as she wrote, "a taste for pageantry, festival, and secular liturgy."[27] On opening day, 20 February 1915, Governor Hiram Johnson and San Francisco Mayor James Rolph led 150,000 people into the grounds. Organizers of the exposition meant to promote and in turn define California by representing its history and achievement. A statue paid tribute to the state's "pioneer mothers." Mrs. Patty Reed Lewis, the last survivor of the ill-fated Donner Party, spoke about the horrors and braveries of the 1846 winter; William Keith had an entire room set aside for his Californian landscapes; and Mary Austin attended the world-premier performance of her play *Fire,* which she had written expressly for the occasion.[28] The exposition, built on land previously under San Francisco Bay, featured the diesel engine—noisy successor to the Paris Exposition's dynamo—as a symbol of the city's phoenixlike rise from the ashes of 1906.

For a writer committed to a world beyond California, the exposition served as a welcome homecoming and reminder of what she had yet to do. Austin wrote, and published in England, *California, the Land of the Sun,* which appeared in the fall of 1914, after the first German advances of World War I had stalled and the trenches already stretched from the French coast to the Swiss border. Austin's book, as if from another world, featured a stunning design with mounted illustrations of paintings—they resemble upscale picture-postcards—by the artist Sutton Palmer. An American edition of the book, published thirteen years later, bore the subtitle *The Lands of the Sun.* Both titles hearken back to Austin's first book, *The Land of Little Rain* (and Charles Lummis's magazine, *Land of Sunshine*), and her time in the region where "twenty-five years of cultivation have served to shift the lines of greenness but not greatly to modify the desert key." As she tells her readers, "One must learn to think of the land in terms of human achievement." Following the stream of life-giving water along an "empire belt" to places in the Central Valley—Bakersfield, abloom in roses, Fresno, where raisins and other fruit abound, and Madera, overflowing with port wine and sherry—she recapitulates the desert struggle to survive. "Wherever along the belt the rivers fail, the pumps take up their work; strenuous little Davids contending against the Goliaths of drought." Everywhere she sees signs of the victors. "Much of the history of that country is written in the names"; Spanish locutions give way to Americanisms, to be overlaid by the -villes and -tons of French and Anglo-Saxon derivation, "Coulterville, Farmington, Turlock."[29] For Austin, California remained a paradoxical land of dispossessed people and miraculous advances. Just as she pleaded the commercial rights of shepherds in *The Flock,* she advocates here for the reclamation projects and water usage that she elsewhere resisted. *California, the Land of the Sun* brings Austin close to the positions of John Muir, who wanted his mountain water untouched *and* available to the valley farmers in the flatlands below.

Dividing California into geographical regions, which largely determine the content of her chapters ("Mothering Mountains," "The Twin Valleys"), Austin begins *California* with a mythical tale of the region's creation once told to her by the Shoshone medicine man, Winnenáp. A lyrical tribute to the beauty of her adopted land, and also a strong advertisement for tourism, the book recounts a history of occupation, from Spanish missionaries to agribusiness farmers. "I do not think even—because I make a practice of thinking as little as possible of a matter so discreditable to us as our Indian policy—of the procession of the evicted *Palatingwas,* even though the whole region of Warner's ranch is still full of the shame of it and the rending cry."[30] To readers aghast at war in Europe, such passages from *California, the Land of the Sun*—"a land rife with the naked struggle of great pagan forces"—verged on parable. "The struggle of men with men," Austin writes, again touching on her country's policy toward Indians, "is at best a sick and squalid affair for one of the parties; but men contriving against the gods for the possession of the earth is your true epic."[31]

World War I turned Austin into a propagandist, and not her alone. Gertrude Stein, Mary Roberts Rinehart, and Gertrude Atherton among many writers used their talents in support of American intervention or to raise money for relief efforts. The war elevated Herbert Hoover—as director of the Food Relief Campaign—into the world's chief purveyor of food to war-ravaged countries. This remarkable effort, more than any other single factor, would propel Hoover into the White House. (A 1920 *New York Times* poll already touted him as one of the greatest living Americans.) Appointed U.S. food administrator in 1917, Hoover made every effort to supply American and Allied forces. His program, officially known as "American conservation," came to be called "Hooverization." Everywhere one looked, posters encouraged people to "Drink less sweetened beverages" or "Sow the seeds of Victory! Plant & Raise your own Vegetables," on the assumption that "Food will win the war." Meatless Mondays and Wheatless Wednesdays, inviting ordinary Americans to feel part of the military effort, became commonplace, and on their heels new slogans addressed the rebuilding of Europe as the war dragged on to its end. Women proved essential to the success of these "campaigns," which aimed to reduce domestic consumption by at least 10 percent and achieved a surprising 15 percent.

Recognized for her public work and her writings about the war, Austin found herself invited to sail on Henry Ford's peace ship, *Oskar II,* which embarked in early December 1915, carrying emissaries of peace to Europe. She declined the invitation. "Deeply sympathize with Mr. Ford's ideal of permanent peace," she wired. "I regret that I have neither the knowledge of conditions nor capacity which would justify interference with the European situation."[32] Quite apart from her commitment to programs at home, she made a wise decision. If he could make automobiles, Ford announced to reporters, he could talk world leaders out of war. The expedition—to many critics a collection of fools, knaves, and crackpots and dubbed "The Floating Chautauqua"—ended ingloriously after three weeks when Ford jumped ship in Oslo.

The next summer, under the auspices of the Authors Association for Social Relief, Austin ran free lunchrooms in public schools for more than a thousand children of railway strikers. On the side, she fed the Hoovers gossip about Woodrow Wilson's "little affairs with the ladies" and the machinations of the Republican National Committee.[33] With women as his special audience and with Mary Austin a growing irritant, Hoover offered her a post that may have been designed to keep her at arm's length. She had insisted on helping in a meaningful, high-level administrative position and expected Hoover—who enlisted Vernon Kellogg to lead humanitarian efforts in Belgium and northern France—to be supportive. He had other plans. "You can render the best service," he told her, "by being our general advisor on psychological propaganda. Your knowledge of the country will, if you can travel about, bring to us . . . just the information that is most desirable." A position so amorphous amounted to no job at all—or one better suited for a trained informant—and while the work invited her observations and came with an expense account, it took her as far as possible from those corridors of power she longed to frequent.[34]

Undeterred, she managed to make the best of her opportunity. Beginning to address Hoover as "My dear Chief," she crisscrossed the country in an effort to win support for the food program without having her lectures credited to the U.S. Food Administration. In years when the word *propaganda* assumed its modern connotations, Austin described her lecturing as "constructive propaganda." She wrote an exemplary propagandistic piece, with a title evoking Soviet Russia, called "The Potato Patriot," which Universal Films bought in 1917. The movie focused on a French immigrant to the United States who soldiers on the home front by planting a victory garden on his roof. In a scene to test the imagination, the film cuts from gardening to Herbert Hoover making a speech, then to Europe's devastated farmlands where hungry Belgians eat American canned goods. Irritated when Universal altered the already improbable script, Austin refused to have her name associated with the film.

In every available forum, Austin pushed for cooperative enterprises such as community gardens, storehouses, and markets, and grew so tired of communal kitchens that she stopped talking about them—except to her boss, calling his attention to the need for centralized cooking to preserve food and as a way to address the labor crisis. Now a representative of organized labor (she served on the Publicity Board of the Women's Trade Union League), she warned Hoover that in order to win the war "changes in methods of feeding the working classes must not seem to come as a necessity of famine or the result of inadequate wages." To appease labor leaders, she urged adopting their vocabulary. Necessary adjustments might be called "Social Experiments, Constructive Experiments, or any other of the phrases so dear to labor in America."[35]

Though their friendship managed to limp along, the Hoover-Austin partnership did not. Austin demanded that Hoover broaden his efforts from food to matters of women and child labor. Fixed on tons and kilograms, he wanted none of her meddling. "I have set up the principle," he told her, "of taking no interest in any matter except food." He scoffed at her raising "spiritual" aspects of conservation.[36] What Austin, in such innovations as communal kitchens, saw as a way of changing family structure and responsibilities, Hoover the engineer dismissed as social engineering. His opinions seem to have meant little to Austin, who more than matched him in peremptory tone. In July 1918 when the fate of the war hung in balance and Hoover's job proved especially hectic, Austin wrote this: "What the women want, *what your whole movement needs* [her emphasis] is the sense of social directions. That's what I'm doing with it. *If I can't do it with your approval*," she pronounced, "I'm going to do it anyway."[37]

Two months later, she offered an olive branch to "the Chief" through his wife, who had donated two hundred dollars in Austin's name to the Women's War Hospital. At first Austin wondered whether she herself had written a check she could not afford. When Lou explained the situation, Austin replied in a way to justify any or all of Hoover's reservations about her state of mind:

> As I have had a great deal of trouble with the phenomenon known as double personality, I was afraid it might be something of that kind. I hadn't caught it signing any checks, but it had got hold of both my letters and my literary work at times, and I was uneasy until I had your letter. . . . I had to have expert help before I could get the upper hand again, and of course, one never knows when a thing like that happens. Now I am quite myself again. . . . I have been feeling that the Chief has behaved very badly to me, and that in ignoring it, I have behaved rather well. There were certain things I had to give him, and my country, which no other woman in America could give. . . . Thank Heaven the Chief is big enough to admit a mistake when he has made it, and I notice he always takes the suggestions I make nowadays.[38]

Austin's reference to "double personality" or "double conscience"—it went by several names—suggests her own periods of confusion or changes in character, a condition some psychiatrists diagnosed as a symptom of hysteria and treatable through hypnosis. The term *double personality* also served as a popular equivalent for moral equivocation. In 1906, for example, William James observed that on the subject of "war" civilized man had developed a sort of double personality. Austin may have used the phrase in that sense. She may also have confided her worries about "double personality" to Lincoln Steffens, who in turn used it against her. Toward the end of her life she would be diagnosed with hardening of the arteries, the early and intermittent signs of which might have begun ten or more years before. From this distance in time no one can assess Austin's mental health, especially since she believed meditation, prayer, and writing itself to be altered states of being and recorded her experiences of them for those interested in psychical research.

Without mentioning the bout of poor health, Lou responded frankly to Austin's letter. With similar frankness Austin insisted that Lou teach her husband how to handle women, a service she called "the sole prerogative of a woman who loves him." Women who were feminine and agreeable, she said, were likely to be third-rate and "big ones" rarely tactful.[39] Lou Hoover's response to the politics of the National American Woman Suffrage Association should have warned Austin about the need for restraint. Referring to the senatorial election of 1918, Lou wrote: "I have always felt so strongly that the human question was so much more important than either the man one or the woman one, that I never can feel I can play the 'Progress of Woman' against the 'Abstract Right for Humanity!'"[40] Though at other times she could agree with Lou, Austin joined now with Anne Martin against Herbert Hoover's appointment of "wrong" women to key positions in Washington. Probably remembering her arrest in London and the trouble she caused him, Hoover wrote of Martin: "Her notions seem to have been along the line of women of political rather [than] expert knowledge, and my administration was not built upon that basis. I have no regrets for the selection of Miss Gertrude Lane, Miss Sarah Field Splint, and Miss Martha Van Rensselaer [all of whom Austin and Martin dismissed as "society women"], in charge of this most important division of the Administration. . . . I do have a distinct feeling of pain at personal attack from those who have accepted my hospitality over so many years."[41] Whether or not Austin felt the intended sting, she continued to tangle with Hoover about other government appointments or trends in policy, and of course she never got the call for higher appointments.

The First World War presented both personal and professional problems for authors like Austin. Unlike Edith Wharton or Dorothy Canfield, who nursed blinded soldiers in France, or May Sinclair—Austin interviewed her for the *Ladies Home Journal* in 1921—Austin did not report from the front, or for that matter go near it. Upton Sinclair, for example, served with an ambulance corps and published *A Journal of Impressions in Belgium* (1915). Her friend Vernon Kellogg wrote *The Food Problem* (1917) with Alonzo E. Taylor, based on Vernon and Charlotte's war years. In *Fighting France: From Dunkerque to Belfort* (1915), Wharton shows the horror of war by juxtaposing images of disemboweled corpses and the sacred objects of everyday life, such as plaster saints and photographs of loved ones. If Austin had not read Wharton's writing about the war, she knew about her relief efforts in France, especially on behalf of orphaned children.

Among her contemporary rivals, Austin had most praise and most criticism for Wharton. She made clear that no one could touch Wharton in style or penetration of character, but Wharton's war books evidently left her unmoved or irritated. In her lecture, "American Literature as an Expression of American Experience," Austin writes, "You would never discover from the novels of Edith Wharton that a world war and several European revolutions and wireless and radio and flying machines had all happened during the span of her literary career."[42] This misrepresentation aside, Austin shared Wharton's understanding that the war demanded not merely new fiction, but entirely new patterns of existence.

Living in Paris as Belgian refugees flooded the streets, Wharton had become, against temperamental and artistic inclinations, another voice demanding American intervention in the war. Her experiences forced her to conclude that the novel as she and others had known and practiced it was dead. Before the war, she reflected, "you could write fiction without indicating the period, the present being assumed. The war has put an end to that for a long time, and everything will soon have to be timed with reference to it. In other words, the historical novel with all its vices will be the only possible form of fiction."[43] Wharton accepted fate by writing *The Age of Innocence* (1920), a novel set in the 1870s. Austin took a similar tack. Apart from *No. 26 Jayne Street* (1920) and "The Ex-Serviceman's Story," an unpublished short story in which the spirit of an immobilized sergeant leads his men to safety, she wrote *The Ford* (1917), a historical novel of her own.

Although *The Ford* looks back to the moves and countermoves of a provincial conflict—the fight for the Owens Valley water—its real target emerges as the ubiquitous presence of big business, which Austin condemns as America's destructive shadow government. Radical in spirit, her book speaks to the collapse of cultural values, if not of civilization. In Austin's critique, politicians follow capitalism as children followed the Pied Piper, with the result, as she puts it, that "capitalism in the end would have them." The tragedy in this novel lies with the "System," any system, which rests on ignorance of "that strange, ineradicable quality of men called righteousness."[44] According to Austin, the world changed sometime around 1910—the year Virginia Woolf called a turning point in human nature—when the public discovered the unhealthy relation of politics and big business, and when "the money boss had made his way to the centers of power."[45] In *The Octopus,* Frank Norris despised railroad moguls; in *The Ford,* Austin shows a grudging respect for her financier, Old Man Rickerts. Long ago and with Herbert Hoover's collaboration, Austin had made a mining engineer the flawed protagonist of a play, and Rickerts, a politician in his own right, represents another side of her mixed feelings for Hoover. "The greatest common factor of the Tierra Longans," she writes, "was their general inability to rise to the Old Man's measure; they were inferior stuff of the same pattern." Their only chance of defeating the Old Man or selling to him at a fair price depends upon something they cannot do: stick together. "It was as simple as that," she concludes. "Too simple by half."[46]

The month before the United States entered World War I, in April 1917, Austin published an article in the *New York Times* titled "Germany's Mexican Intrigue—What It Means," in which she argued that an agreement between Germany and Mexico served the interests of Japan and denied the United States a potential ally. "Mexico was our job by every right and obligation to understand and sustain through her most trying period [of revolution]. If our idea of peace is anything more than a womanish avoidance of war, if our neutrality was anything larger than a mere Chinese Wall drawn about our own security, we might have bound Mexico to us past even Germany's power to alienate."[47] She urged politicians to rethink their assumptions and study the effects of hunger, homelessness, low wages, and despair on world affairs.[48] Later, she would take the U.S. government to task for allowing the exploitation of Mexico's oil reserves while asserting "that the majority of the Mexican people really want political and industrial conditions like ours and won't be happy until we go in and cram them down their throats."[49]

She was more prophetic than consistent. Much as she deplored American power and blindness, Austin felt obliged to explain to H. G. Wells her compatriots' foot-dragging about the war as an outgrowth of their historic character:

> I am particularly anxious that you shouldn't miss knowing our Pacifism isn't just the love of comfort, nor yet the spectacle of waste and loss which this war has shown us.
>
> It goes deeper than that:—it comes to a profound distrust of fighting as a *means for getting something done* [her emphasis]. War, in the vernacular, "doesn't get us anywhere"; and the profound, the controlling American impulse is to "get somewhere." I believe in Europe you call it "materialism." Really it is our idealism and it is the inner meaning of phrases not always the happiest I'll admit—which puzzle Europeans, "too proud to fight" "Peace without Victory."[50]

In *The Young Woman Citizen* (1918), a book commissioned by the YWCA, Austin repeats her belief that "we must look even more closely at the principle of nationality than we have yet done if we are to find any ground of decision in regard to the expansion of populous nations, for I do not think that we can find it in democracy. Germany may become a democracy; but if her people continue to resist the modifications of environment in favor of a Teutonic ideal of life, she would be quite as much a menace to the world." Without a kaiser, she writes (not many years before Hitler's rise to power), we could not see Germans, with their "unregenerate" desire to Germanize the world, "going into any country in large numbers without knowing it would mean death to whatever contribution to civilization we have a right to expect from that soil." At the same time, she predicts an expansion of Japanese power. "If we do not wish to make Japan our enemy, we must not decide against her on account of her form of government. There are some very significant differences between imperialism in Europe and in Japan," she writes, describing the emperor as "a symbol of the secret flame that lights the soul" of his country. "He is more like what the Ark of the Covenant was to the Hebrews. He is the sign of sovereignty, very much as the King of England is, but in a more intimate and mystic way." As for Africa, "Let us waste no more time deciding who is to have Africa, but determine once of all that Africa is to have herself." Austin felt it imperative for the United States to establish workable relationships with the world, rather than impose a system of political, social, and economic reforms that "had been worked out as an expression" of our national temperament.[51] Austin's argument assails mindless and arrogant aggression that too often results in wars and revolution.

After the United States entered the war and American soldiers began to die in European trenches (British brass called trench fatalities "wastage"), Austin wrote the novel that epitomizes her thinking about American politics. Given her sociological bent, she assumed international problems to be inextricably linked with national life, itself an outgrowth of the most fundamental relationships between men and women. *No. 26 Jayne Street* focuses on a triangle of lovers. Neith Schuyler is a repatriated American, whose name Austin filched from Hutchins Hapgood's wife, Neith. Having seen the slaughter in Flanders, Neith comes back to discover the lack of concern among her compatriots, including those closest to her: Adam Frear, a moral conservative masquerading as a social activist, and Rose Matlock, his political helpmate and discarded mistress. Both women, having made the mistake of taking Frear at his word, learn that words like *democracy* form no part of his domestic vocabulary. Seeing the justice of Rose's claim on her fiancé's loyalty, if not his affection, Neith ends her engagement. The rejected Frear follows nonfictional men like Lincoln Steffens and

John Reed to Russia, while Rose, determined to live out the terms of their original contract, remains faithful to a lost ideal.

Austin's characters appear to represent a lamed America, the country that, as her letter to H. G. Wells suggests, she nonetheless considered to be the world's best hope. "The whole world is looking to America. . . . It's the whole hope of the world and almost its only faith that there is a point beyond the upsetting of passion and prejudice, by which we *can* act [her emphasis]."[52] Rose and Neith do what they can, yet their efforts amid a world war and a maelstrom of contending causes—from Henrietta Rodman's Better Babies and Voluntary Parenthood to Curing Criminalism—prove no more practical than the men they love and disparage. "Women are more to blame than they think," Neith says, echoing her author. She means that no less than men of their class, women profit from war, in which police can and do torture protesters without recrimination, causes become fashions, young men learn the glories of war from moving pictures, and words lose their meanings. As one intellectual says to Neith, "a bomb is just a sort of medium of expression."[53]

No. 26 Jayne Street may have exorcised the ghost of Lincoln Steffens ("I killed a man this morning," Austin told Mabel Dodge after finishing the novel), but it did nothing to advance her reputation.[54] The book earned so little that she turned for a time away from novel writing. In the year of its publication, Carl Van Doren paid tribute with the ring of a premature eulogy. Austin, he wrote, "wears something like the sybil's robes, and speaks with something like the sybil's strong accent, but the cool hard discipline of the artist or of the exact scholar only occasionally serves her. Much of her significance lies in her promise [Austin was fifty-two]. Faithful to her original vision, she has moved steadily onward, growing, writing no book like its predecessor, applying her wisdom continually to new knowledge, leaving behind her a rich detritus which she will perhaps be willing to consider detritus if it helps to nourish subsequent generations."[55] Wishful as Van Doren's optimism proved, he grasped Austin's motives and weaknesses at a time when war had challenged conventional thinking and belittled human endeavors.

———

In the summer of 1917, Austin went to Byrdcliffe, the Arts and Crafts community in Woodstock, New York, to recuperate after months of lecturing. There she had an extraordinary experience. As she sat mending silk stockings, the room and her immediate surroundings appeared to flash with light. She envisioned a ball of fire arising out of Russia—"an organizing, revivifying light, far reaching activities, a purging of old ideas, new forms, center of civilization, all this far away, years away—ten, twelve, years before it begins to make itself felt. And closer at hand a small man, a dark man with a sword in his hand."[56] The Russian Revolution, which John Reed vividly reported for *The Masses,* occurred that October, and in retrospect Austin—who considered herself something of a gypsy and told fortunes at relief bazaars—identified Joseph Stalin, at her own five foot five, as the small, dark man of the apparition.

In those days, highly intelligent and well-educated people took such experiences seriously, which helps to explain Austin's frank discussion of her mental states. In 1885, William James and G. Stanly Hall, of Harvard and Johns Hopkins, respectively, had helped found the American Society for Psychical Research. Apart from psychologists, members included the dean of Harvard's divinity school, a philosopher, an astronomer, and Henry Holt, friend and publisher of both James and Austin. Holt would introduce Austin to Walter Franklin Prince, principal research officer and editor of publications for the society and a specialist in cases of multiple personality. James had no explanation for the medium named Leonora Piper, who could identify the deceased from locks of hair and wondered "why one person cut the hair from the end, where it was lifeless, instead of nearer the head."[57] Austin had no explanation for her own visions, let alone those of Mrs. Piper, who remained one of the few mediums never discredited. (Piper proved just as clairvoyant when taken to Europe—away, that is, from familiar circumstances.) Fascinated as she was by automatic writing and crystal-ball gazing, Austin granted that her vision of Stalin might have been a piecing together of ragtag ends of conversation and forgotten reading, "the reaction of an over-wearied mind."[58] The strain of her government work and conflicts with the Hoovers, the bloodshed of war, let alone her consistently poor health, cannot have helped. She had also worried for the past year about the precarious health of her brother Jim. Suffering the last two years with a liver ailment, Jim died in the summer of 1917 from a heart attack.

Austin now found herself in the generation next to death. Her brother George, a doctor at the Red Cross Hospital in Los Angeles and the executor of Jim's estate, wrote with details of Jim's funeral and proposed to buy lots in Hollywood Cemetery so that the Hunter siblings could lie together when their time came.[59] Jim left his wife Georgia a one-thousand-dollar insurance policy and for his daughter Mary left $7,000, enough to give her about $350 a year. As Mary's guardian, George encouraged his sister to write to her niece, a request he soon regretted. Her determination to rescue Mary from what she saw as soul-killing circumstances would tear the remaining Hunters apart. In September 1917, Austin went to San Francisco to lecture, with the added inducement of visiting her orphaned and mourning niece. Austin felt deeply about her namesake, seeing her through the lens of her own experience as a gifted young woman struggling to realize her talents. George considered Mary an ordinary scholar at best, whereas Austin saw untapped genius. She could give Mary everything she had not been able to give her daughter.

The family confusions and ill will worsened after 13 November 1918, two days after the armistice ending World War I and the day that Ruth Austin died. At twenty-six, Ruth had been institutionalized fourteen years. George wrote to inform his sister that her death resulted from an acute form of asthma (likely, since asthma recurred in the family, but no more likely than influenza in that pandemic year) and from malnutrition. Although the circumstances of her care remain unclear, the word *malnutrition* must have brought to mind the likelihood of bad treatment and given pause to both George and his sister. Austin went to Santa Clara to arrange for her daughter's cremation.

In 1915, Austin had written an untitled poem that ends:

Oh, child shall we who loved so well
Before you took on shape or breath,
Love less the years you wait for me
Beyond the formlessness of death?[60]

Austin's feelings for her daughter resonate in her fictional treatment of children, particularly in stories such as "The Castro Baby" and "A Case of Conscience" or novels like *A Woman of Genius,* where mothers cannot articulate the depths of love or loss. "The Lame Little Lad," an early story, reads like a fable on the order of D. H. Lawrence's "The Rocking Horse Winner": "Once there was a poor man and his wife who expected to have a large family, but it turned out that they had only one little lame lad. Therefore they loved him with seven times greater love, and great as their love was it was not greater than their grief." A story of a mother's excessive love and the boy's failed operation, it ends with the mother's collapse, and her dream of the good he will do in the world after her death. "The little lame lad is living yet"—but Austin leaves open the question as to whether he is doing the great work she dreamed of.[61] Equally poignant is Austin's article "If I Had a Gifted Daughter," in which she prescribes ways to nurture the young. Not often inclined to sentimentality, she allowed herself more emotion when writing about mothers' fierce ties to their children—and says little (except in *A Woman of Genius*) about a father's. Wallace Austin, who never wanted Ruth in an institution and had listed her as the beneficiary of his life insurance, now made a change in his will so that his wife would inherit.

An eclectic thinker and intellectual magpie, Mary Austin rightly considered herself an anomaly. The work she thought her best, editors rejected, with the result that she often lost confidence about separating the chaff from the wheat. At times she protected herself by dismissing what she held dear. In the early 1920s she told a friend: "I am getting more interest in my poetry than almost any thing I do. This is amusing, because I *know* that my poetry is second rate, and I wish I had the strength of mind not to write any more."[62] Such admissions may have had less to do with how talented she felt than with the vagaries of publishing, and they seem to have had little bearing on her judgment about the work of other writers.

When she left for Europe in 1907, Austin made a promise to herself to help other writers if she were lucky enough to survive. She fulfilled her promise many times over. Anzia Yezierska, an immigrant writer from Russian Poland she met in 1920, probably through Henrietta Rodman, would write of their first meeting: "It only made me hungry for more—And now your letter this morning—Such generous giving overwhelms me—leaves me dumb. I cannot find words to tell you what rushes out of my heart to you except to ask you again, please see me soon—very soon. The longing for friendship—for the stimulus of intellectual association which I had to choke in me—you have roused in me again. I walked away from you weeping."[63] Houghton Mifflin, likely on Austin's recommendation, published Yezierska's short-story collection, *Hungry Hearts* (1920). Despite writing movingly about New York's Jewish ghetto, notably in *Salome of the Tenements* (1922), Yezierska is little known today.

Not so Willa Cather, another friend and writer Austin supported. There is no record of Austin and Cather meeting before Austin wrote *Santa Lucia* (1907), a novel that contains a boyish heroine called William, the name Cather herself preferred as a young girl in Red Cloud, Nebraska. They probably met around 1910, when Austin would have been forty-two, Cather thirty-five. At that time Cather lived with her friend Edith Lewis in a not very comfortable apartment off Washington Square. Cather published her first novel, *Alexander's Bridge,* in 1912, the year she and Lewis moved to Five West Bank Street, a tall brick house built by a wealthy brewer. They occupied a seven-room, multiwindowed apartment facing the street, the three front rooms serving as one large living room, heated by a marble-manteled coal grate. Mahogany furniture, open bookshelves, gas lights, an etching of George Sand by Couture, and copies of Tintorettos and Titians brought home from Italy gave the rooms an old-world feeling. Cather was "at home" Fridays from four to seven.

People characterized Cather's voice as "Western," by which they meant so fresh and breezy that it made friends like the young journalist Elizabeth Shepley Sergeant (she wrote memoirs of both Cather and Austin) think of "crude oil, red earth, elemental strength and resoluteness."[64] Names of Cather's idols—Flaubert, Balzac, Henry James, and Sarah Orne Jewett—ran like musical phrases through her conversation. Guests enjoyed the lilt of her voice and the hominess of her apartment, where the hostess would not allow conversation to "divert one from the quality of food on the plate and the wine in the glass." As for tea, Cather liked hers "hot, Hot, HOT," and so, apparently, did Austin.[65]

According to Lewis, Cather did her best work on Bank Street, where she could see and hear "singers like Cressida Garnett, along with Hungarian violinists and German pianists from Western mining towns."[66] Austin lived not far away, either at the National Arts Club or, in the early 1920s, at Ten Barrow Street. When she first met Cather, she was the more successful writer; Cather, still managing editor at *McClure's,* had yet to publish *O Pioneers!* (1913), the first of her novels to celebrate the American West. Apart from Lincoln Steffens, who had ties to *McClure's* and also probably introduced Cather to Mabel Dodge, the women shared a number of literary friends and acquaintance, Elsie Sergeant among them.

Cather called herself an "admirer" of Austin's work, and Austin returned the compliment. Of *My Ántonia* (1918), she wrote to Ferris Greenslet, the long-suffering editor they then shared at Houghton Mifflin: "Compared to what most American writers are doing, Miss Cather's work touches a high mark indeed. . . . If you can sell books like that to my countrymen, I shall think vastly more of them and their literary taste than I have been thinking of late."[67] Austin asked Greenslet to send her Cather's books, and she more than returned the favor with favorable notices and suggestions for marketing Cather's work, especially to midwesterners: "I think you should be very well to send a copy of *My Ántonia* to The People's Voice, Olivia, Minn., and to The Farmer's Wife at St. Paul with a note saying that I thought they ought to recommend the book to their readers."[68] Welcoming the attention, Cather told Greenslet that should he need copies of her books to send to Austin, she had extras, though—wanting to avoid any suggestion of impropriety—she preferred them sent as if from the press.

The imaginations of the two writers ran along parallel lines, and while neither left a record of their conversations, their books at times interact like dialogue. In 1909, for example, Austin had approached the editor of *Youth Companion* about "a series of tales embodying the experience of a girl settler [who] would supply both your demand for stories of empire building and the need of stories for girls."[69] Cather wrote that story and called it *O Pioneers!* She may also have borrowed the title of Austin's 1908 novel, *Outland* for the surname of Tom Outland, her young westerner in *The Professor's House* (1925). Outland discovers the hidden village of cliff dwellers, a people who lived, like Austin's Outliers, in an Edenic land and violent society. He keeps a diary of his time on the mesa, which ushers his friend, Godfrey St. Peter, a professor of history, outside his humdrum life into an imagined civilization he much prefers. In terms of chronology, Cather's novel of a female artist, *The Song of the Lark* (1915), seems a response to Austin's *A Woman of Genius* (1912). Austin called her friend's book the "best presentation" of a woman artist ever made.[70] The protagonists of both novels experience prejudice and poverty before realizing their gifts—Austin's Olivia Lattimore for acting and Cather's Thea Kronberg for grand opera.

Despite these coincidences, Cather and Austin come closest when the one writes fiction, the other nonfiction. Cather's experiments with form, her layering of parallel scenes and images in *The Professor's House* and *A Lost Lady* (to give just two instances) have their precursor in *The Land of Little Rain* and *California, the Land of the Sun*, which, to borrow from Henry James, "catch the color, the relief, the expression, the surface, the substance of the human spectacle."[71] Of all Cather's novels, Austin singled out *A Lost Lady* (1923)—published the same year that Cather won the Pulitzer Prize for her war novel, *One of Ours*. It had, to her mind, been conceived "Indian fashion" or "in episodes of high significance, so distributed that the blank spaces between are occupied without being filled," very much, in other words, as Austin conceived her own books. Realism meant for both writers an elastic quality of mind, dependent upon what Cather described as "a vague indication of the sympathy and candour with which . . . [the artist] accepts, rather than chooses, his theme."[72] Their realistic methods did not compete with shared interests in Catholic mysticism, history, and exotic cultures, whether the New Mexico pueblos in *The Professor's House* or new-world missionaries in *Isidro*, in which each ascribes, for lack of a better word, a *spiritual* dimension to time and being.

Austin had long nagged Houghton Mifflin to promote her books vigorously in the West. She saw a market in ordinary people like the Sierra Reserve ranger who gathered his men around the campfire to hear her poem, "The Forest Ranger": "His work toward the viewless lines / That guard a thousand years of pines." One of those men wrote for the rangers "as a body" to thank her for expressing their lives in verse.[73] Austin believed, as she said of Cather, that Western writers were born (not always in the West), rather than made, and so in tune to the spirit of their region that every book they wrote, whatever its setting or subject, became a Western book. She spoke more about herself than her friend, who seems in comparison the kind of regional writer Marjorie Kinnan Rawlings called "accidental": one who uses a logical or coherent background for commonly shared feelings or beliefs.[74] If this is a strange claim to make about Cather (in Nebraska it would smack of heresy), the distinction works with Austin, who believed that the land had its own genetic coding, which those sensitive to it absorbed as racial characteristics. Cather's interest lay less in landscape itself than its imaginative projection, the stories and visions it generates. "The history of every country," she writes in *O Pioneers!*, "begins in the heart of a man or a woman."[75] She talks about memory, the basis of novels like *O Pioneers!*, in ways that Austin talks about region: as an inherited "mental complexion left over from the past."[76] In Cather's novels, whether *Death Comes for the Archbishop*, *A Lost Lady*, or *Shadows on the Rock*, the land provides a canvas for human ambitions, be it the building of cathedrals or railroads. In Austin's, the best of ambitions grow from the land itself, which, no matter the human inscription, retains its original character.

As Cather explained years before she wrote her first book, when you come to write, "all that you have been taught leaves you, all that you have stolen lies discovered. You are then a translator, without a lexicon, without notes. . . . You have then to give voice to the hearts of men, and you can do it only so far as you have known them, loved them. It is a solemn and terrible thing to write a novel."[77] Austin felt something of this in the decade following her return to the United States as she continued to write "Western" books—whether set in the West like *The Ford* or Western in outlook,

meaning iconoclastic and democratic, like *California, the Land of the Sun*—
and struggled with her shifting career.

War and the end of war prompted Austin to reassess. "Truly the world is
younger every way than it used to be," she had written in 1916 at forty-eight,
"and I have more beans than I had at twenty."[78] In 1919 she sold her house
in Carmel, receiving after accounts were settled a check for $2,636.16. That
same year, she made a commissioned survey of Taos County, New Mexico,
which opens with the history and customs of Native peoples, and she received mail at the School of American Research in Santa Fe. She had begun
her long leave-taking from New York City.

eight

THE CALL OF THE WEST

1920–1924

The call of the West . . . is never quite silenced in the soul of anyone who has once heard it.

MARY AUSTIN
"Willa Sibert Cather," 1920

ON 8 JANUARY 1922, A cross-section of New York's literati gathered at the National Arts Club to pay tribute to Mary Austin. Nearly twenty years had passed since publication of *The Land of Little Rain,* during which Austin had made herself into a different writer. As the master of ceremonies noted that evening, "Bret Harte continued to write California mining stories long after he had put that state behind him, but Mrs. Austin has made the world her field and has written of human nature as she has found it in various parts of the earth."[1] His point may have been lost on an audience staring at a woman dressed in a designer equivalent of the New Mexican flag, as if stepping out of a Diego Rivera painting. She had ordered the outfit in honor of her beloved West, after "the fashion which refuted that ancient scandal about the Queen of Spain having two legs, without . . . concealing the fact that she was very much a woman." She wore silk the color of an Arizona sunset—rose with a silver sheen to it that "took the light like flame and ran to lilac in the shadows"—and carried a bouquet of sweetheart roses threaded with forget-me-nots. Then there was the fan, which "to be quite Spanish . . . must be lacy and spangly, and stand for vivacity."[2] As a final touch she added a few black plumes.

Her escort for the occasion, a young Chickasaw painter named Overton Colbert, wore quill-embroidered buckskin topped by a headdress made of black and white flamingo feathers. When one guest asked what teeth were used for his necklace, Colbert replied "alligator." "How horrid!" she said, before adding, "I suppose they are the same to you as my pearls." "Not at all," Colbert replied. "Any fool can take a pearl away from an oyster." After formal speeches by three of Austin's staunchest supporters—the critic Carl Van Doren and her publishers Henry Holt and John Farrar—and the reading of her poem "War Thoughts," a young man from the *New Republic* tried to compliment Austin for taking "the horror off middle aged femininity."[3] A friend who looked back on the gala recalled for her "the goshamightly simple direct . . . sense of the full blown woman that makes you stand out . . . as a prophetess . . . a seer . . . a leader."[4] The guest of honor, less effusive, put it this way: "First of all, there was I."[5]

Something of a milestone for Austin, the belated birthday dinner announced the extent of her public recognition as well as critical changes in her life. The evening managed to be both hail and farewell for a writer who had, over the past decade, headquartered in New York and spent increasingly more time in the West, especially in Carmel. By now, however, Carmel had lost most of its original crew and, for her, much of its charm. In *California, the Land of the Sun,* she makes fun of Carmel's views as cheap because they are accessible from every window. Drawn more to the Southwest, she flirted with the possibility of living in Taos or Santa Fe, where a room could be rented for ten dollars a month. The region offered another lure, the proximity of a man she had met as long ago as 1913, who had become the mainstay of her life and work, Daniel Trembly MacDougal. The recipient of her letter about the National Arts Club dinner and a ready correspondent, MacDougal delighted in her wit, her thinking, and her audacity. What other woman would assume the mantle of a Descartes or Luther to pronounce: "there was I"?

A distinguished scientist and professor at the burgeoning University of Arizona, MacDougal made his reputation in botany, specifically as an expert on Monterey pines. One of the first scientists to study chlorophyll, he also experimented with the new dendrograph—developed by the astronomer A. E. Douglass in Flagstaff's Lowell Observatory—equipment for analyzing the characteristics of tree growth with a wider application to historical studies. Among a host of juggled positions, MacDougal served as a founding member of the Ecological Society of America. In 1907, he had organized the Pinacate expedition, which brought him together with the geographer Godfrey Sykes and the zoologist William T. Hornaday (founder of the National Zoo) to explore the lava fields of Mexico. Five years later, he and Sykes teamed up in the Libyan Desert.

Director of the Carnegie Institute's Desert Plant Laboratory in Tucson and its Coastal Laboratory in Carmel, MacDougal went back and forth between the two centers and likely met Austin on one of her visits to Carmel. As a trustee of the Forest Theater, he arranged for the production of Austin's *The Arrow Maker* in 1914. Born in Indiana, he appreciated her Midwestern roots as well as her passion for the environment, psychology, and the workings of American Indian and Mexican societies. Austin wrote this squib about the scientist who wore with aplomb his medley of hats:

> A conversation overheard between McDougal, the Botanist, and McDougall, the Psychologist:
>   Said the Botanist to the Psychologist, "Where do you think self-consciousness might begin in the life of plants?" Said McDougall, the Psychologist, after consideration, "Possibly where there is accommodation between two tropisms."
>   "Then," said MacDougal, the Botanist, "there is self-consciousness in a daffodil."[6]

MacDougal the intellectual matched Austin's interests even more than Lincoln Steffens had, and like Steffens he was unstoppably busy. When not at Carmel or otherwise traveling, MacDougal lived in Tucson (then a town of about twenty thousand inhabitants). He made his larger home the deserts of the American Southwest, which he explored, often alone, on foot or on horseback.

Austin and MacDougal shared a love for desert life and, through years of corresponding, for one another. To MacDougal, Austin shone as a celebrity, an established artist, and a woman whose dedication to the study and conservation of desert lands matched and enhanced his own. In "The Woman at the Eighteen-Mile," Austin imagines a comparable relationship: "He had never known what it meant to have a woman concerned in his work, running neck and neck with it, divining his need, supplementing it not with the merely feminine trick of making him more complacent with himself, but with vital remedies and aids."[7] MacDougal looked to her for help when founding *Science Service,* a journal directed at both scientists and the general public, and he drew on her experience when writing for popular magazines. Their collaborative talk gave each a broader perspective and a more accessible language with which to address the wider readership they both sought.

As an author in and beyond his scientific field, MacDougal understood the pressures of writing. Austin, an amateur scientist with only undergraduate training, talked to him about his work in ways that few of her contemporaries could. She fluctuated between calling herself a creative writer who wrote about science and asserting her authority in scientific matters. Her extensive knowledge of plants did not match that of MacDougal, on whom she depended—and enlisted—when a name or species escaped her. "Does the ironwood have an attractive blossom?" she asked. "What is the bluish-green wood called 'condalia' which Lumholtz mentions as being wood from which bows are made?"[8] He would answer promptly, as if to an equal. For several years, Austin had relied on MacDougal emotionally as well as professionally. She had signed a copy of her book, *The Green Bough* for him in 1913 and would dedicate the book marking her full return to the West, or Southwest, *The Land of Journeys' Ending* (1924) "to Daniel T. MacDougal of the cactus country." Her dedication pays tribute to the man who had brought her back to temporary health and to her writing roots. She understood his help not as simple healing, but as her own resurrection from a flawed life and an unsteady career.

To give just one example of how far she had strayed or lost a sense of pur-pose, Austin amassed the equivalent of several long articles, if not a short book, in correspondence with a "Mr. Schroeder" that lasted from January to December 1919. Schroeder, probably Theodore Schroeder, an ex-lawyer friend of Lincoln Steffens, wrote books and articles with titles ranging from *"Divinity" in the Semen* to *"Obscene" Literature and Constitutional Law,* and *Converting Sex into Religiosity.* Austin berated him (and Steffens by way of Schroeder) in letters as dismissive as any she wrote, on subjects ranging across psychoanalysis, marriage, prayer, and above all sex. The topic of sex teased both, he asking indirect questions, baiting her, and she spouting what sounds like a parody of Sigmund Freud—an expert she calls a distant third to William James and herself: "I think it is only fair to you to say that writing done along the lines of Freudian psychoanalysis as practiced in the United States would command about as much respect from me as a horo-scope cast by an astrologer."[9] Exercised about the "difference between sex and religion," she writes in this way to Schroeder:

> I deprecate your bias toward the theory of religion as a debased and per-verted sex experience [a theory she herself sometimes espoused]. . . . My re-lations with God (or gods) resemble my relationships with my brothers, with my father, with my lover and father of my child, with my mother and sisters. It has features which have their prototypes in all these. It also has features which distinguish it from all these. . . . I am firmly of the opinion

that the failure of modern marriage is very largely due to the woman's attempt to make a husband do duty as God, to make sexual love perform the offices of religion. I believe man's inferior capacity for establishing relations with God is a large factor in his inferior fidelity to sexual relations.[10]

And so on, to a correspondent she disdained, encouraged, argued with, and freely insulted as if she were Louis Agassiz and he Asa Gray in a cockfight about evolution. Such mind-sapping letters squandered time as well as energy. By contrast, she approached MacDougal as a fellow explorer and as a man with whom she could speak openly. His interest in her theories gratified her, all the more so when critics forced her to defend statements about Native Indians, say, or the traits of "genius," or the ubiquities of what she called the "American rhythm," for which tight definitions evaded her.

By the time of the National Arts Club dinner, Austin and MacDougal were—there is no direct evidence—almost certainly lovers. Fifty-seven in 1922, MacDougal remained in a peculiar though stable marriage. His wife, reclusive and, according to gossip, uninterested in sex, features in his letters as a quiet presence who shared his house and opinions. In the eyes of friends, MacDougal's personal qualities made him "impatient of any weakness" and ready to pursue "someone on the outside."[11] His love, or this love, found Austin in the autumn of her life (she turned fifty-four in 1922), making it all the richer, as one of her poems reveals:

Love came to me late.
Passion, whose feet when I kissed them
    blackened my mouth;
    Duty that galled me worst
    where the hurt was sorest.
Then with a sound of wings
    down-edged for silence,
With a stir as of evening primroses blowing
    wide apart among orchard grasses
Secret, contained and aware
    great Love came walking
Came and sat down at the loom
    where I stooped overwearied,
Swift were his hands and light on the shuttle;
And suddenly, as he wrought,
    duty and passion and youth
    came back and served him![12]

Delighted with MacDougal, she liked herself more and was not above a little bragging to Lou Hoover: "It is rather interesting to get better looking as one gets older," to be told that "you are really beautiful and not just interesting looking." Had she ten thousand a year, she quipped, she could pass for a handsome woman—as in some portraits she does.[13] In answer to Mabel Dodge's questions about her beau, she said, "All I can say is that if I had had as much attention when I was in my twenties or thirties as I am having in my fifties, it would have ruined me."[14] Austin kept an undated poem, probably written around this time, titled "On Receiving a Book of Erotic Verse." The topic was on her mind.[15]

MacDougal had helped her recover from the devastating if sometimes farcical break with Steffens, which bled her creativity; he stood by her through later disappointments and disillusion. "How terribly alone we all are!" she confided in him—knowing that he, too, fought episodes of depression. "Outside of you and Mabel [Dodge] I don't know a soul who would treat this crisis [a temporary inability to write] as anything more than a phantom of the literary 'temperament.'"[16] Mabel, her affection for Steffens notwithstanding, had sided with Austin during the breakup and proved an extraordinary friend. At different times she provided a monthly stipend to Austin and free lodging. To Mabel, Austin could speak confidentially about the man she called "my MacDougal."

MacDougal provided stability and devotion. He wrote poems to her, sent Valentines and flowers along with little presents—a wampum necklace and cactus sweetmeats—and passed on the gossip from Carmel. His letters, commenting on national and international affairs, offer detailed responses to almost everything Austin published and to the drafts she did not. He joined her explorations of unconscious memory, her beliefs in what she called "soul-making," indeed everything that engaged her, from Pueblo culture to women's franchise to the ways that people (and peoples) live and die. He listened when she complained about editors rejecting her work on grounds, as she put it, that "advanced ideas among women lessen the consumption of bottled mincemeat, colored insert breakfast food, and full-page flour."[17] Or when one wrote bluntly that "no one in the office seems to be quite sure of what you mean to express in the article, and to be quite frank so far as we are sure we do not find ourselves particularly interested."[18] After praising an essay on the Pacific Northwest, MacDougal mocked an unflattering notice of it in *The Freeman*: "My own viewpoint of life is one of optimism and my tendencies are almost wholly constructive, so I am not at all a fair judge of the value of efficiency or real worth to society of a journal of criticism which stands off, girds and scoffs at the social order. . . . The problem is to find some way of getting moral support to your high daring and achievements which are made in loneliness as must be those of any great artist."[19]

With solid criticism and informed praise, MacDougal coaxed her to be true to her talents, which for both of them came to mean a renewed focus on America's West. In these years, Austin more or less hovered between East and West. Though gradually committing to the topics that would occupy her last decade, she clung to the role of pundit about broader American life. She spoke out on politics, birth control, religion, theater, and Mexico, a subject dear to both Austin and MacDougal, and she wrote more than her share of boilerplate articles for women's journals, some of them redeemed by shrewd commentaries on the implications of women's suffrage. Lack of money drove her to write the lesser journalism, the hack work she scorned and could not put aside. "The only sort of work the public has been willing to take from me is a thin, glittering kind of intellectual essay," she told MacDougal, and "not being able to find any acceptance for the kind of work I want to do, I am getting a hard surface shell."[20]

"Your discussion of the apparent change in attitude of the American Magazine editor tempts me to something pretty close to an I-told-you-so," MacDougal commiserated. "You must surely recall that I have been urging you to stay by your Southwestern work as one of the very few people who have ever really interpreted it. Movie tastes may come and go [they collaborated on several desert scenarios] but I do not believe that interest in any real interpretation of anything so important as the Southwestern atmosphere will ever really go."[21] You belong, he told her, alongside "the shock troops in practical matters and human relations."[22]

That last statement fits the view of Austin held by at least one other friend, who spoke of her preference for impersonal over intimate friendships, audiences over husbands.[23] There were exceptions, in friendships with Eve Lummis or George Sterling, Edward Beale or Mabel Dodge, and late in her life with the painter Frank Applegate, the poet Witter Bynner, or the photographer Ansel Adams, and no clearer exception than her relationship with Daniel MacDougal. Yet while MacDougal's every letter seems to return to the question of when they might meet, there were periods when both he and Austin found themselves too busy. After one visit to New York—and two trans-continental journeys—he offered this laconic apology: "I am sure your disappointment was no greater than my own that we failed to have a visit together. So many personal matters came up, however, that my schedule while I was in the East was not good more than 24 hours ahead."[24] More often than he (and with an echo of the Lincoln Steffens fiasco), Austin chose pressing work over a visit, even from the man who had become a kind of husband-at-a-distance. The missed encounters seem to have had little effect on their intimacy, or their sense of shared purpose, which emerged as Austin's step-by-step move to the Southwest and to the man who embodied it. "Do please make every effort to get here by the middle of April," he wrote early in their friendship. "We could show you desert people and villages as far away as a hundred miles without any difficulty. . . . Now don't be selfish about the matter."[25]

Austin grew fond of MacDougal's daughter, Alice. She pulled strings to get Alice a job with the publishing company of Horace Liveright, which in turn—and perhaps at Alice's nudging—expressed an interest in an American edition of Austin's *Outland*. After Alice's early death, MacDougal and his wife Louise looked after (and finally adopted) Alice's son, Philip—"little Mac" as he called himself, to his grandfather's "big Mac." Austin advised MacDougal about the child and about dealing with Harold Stearns, whom Alice had left before the birth of their child. The soulful-eyed Stearns, who came to embody the hapless, expatriated youth of his generation, used his son to extract money from MacDougal, who despised him for his cavalier treatment of Alice. A charming scoundrel or, to borrow Van Wyck Brooks's description, a literary bum, Stearns was renowned for not picking up the check; he either decamped before it arrived, downing a last brandy, or remembered he had left his wallet in another suit. "There is no possibility of my returning to America for a year or so, perhaps never," he wrote his mother-in-law and ally. "I have no interest there except my own mother, you, and Dr. MacDougal. In time I hope we may be together here. Beside Mary Austin lives in the country and glories in it, which is too much. . . . Philip presumably, is at the dirty and disgusting stage, also the period when one has to treat him most—I will not say carefully, but most considerately. Between two and three is a bad age for anyone, especially for the people who have to look after it."[26] Austin, who reported to MacDougal what she heard of Stearns's affairs from friends, said she would kill the man if she had to deal with him.

Austin's involvement with the MacDougals' custody case and Stearns's resentment illustrates how interwoven her relationship with MacDougal had become by the early 1920s, how much they shared intellectually, and how familiarly they could write to each other. "I have begun several letters to you," she tells him, "but find myself in so many minds at once that nothing I wish to say comes true to intention." She gives an account of her work—"two essays this week, [including] the one asked for by the New Republic for their symposium on the scope and form of the novel." As for her research, which was not going well, she shows frustration. "I have spent two or three of my evenings at the Metropolitan library—surely the most awkwardly arranged institution of its kind in the world." She goes on to share her views of the rhythmic nature of Indian art, an area in which she distances herself from "the academicians"—except that "this time I find them supporting me at every point, having painfully arrived by years of laboratory experiment at what I easily discovered by the happy observation of Indian dance and drum rhythm." (Martha Graham, a future admirer, would have seconded that.) She asks casually for help finding a laboratory *and* any spare scientist to explore "the rhythm of emotional stress," a not uncommon request for research support from friends or lovers.[27] Despite her proposals to work with universities on common projects, or their invitations to her or MacDougal's own PhD and academic appointments, Austin loved to hate what she dismissed as the stale and second-rate thinking of university faculties, particularly in the sciences. To some extent MacDougal agreed with her. He could be scathing about lazy or inept colleagues.

Their correspondence took on a new intimacy in late December 1921. Austin bristles a bit at his request to see her work in progress. "No, I can't send you a draft of my address. There isn't any draft." Then her tone shifts. She begins to flirt—with him and with a new idea. "Making a speech of that kind is very much like love making. It has to be shaped and informed by what is coming from the recipient. I shall have to assume that your experience in love making includes the possibility of things happening all at once and quite differently from what might have been anticipated."[28] Three days later, she admits that "for a long time—more than a year—I have been dissatisfied with the letters I have been writing you. You are the one correspondent I have left, with whom I try to keep up a regular exchange of personal expression. But for some time my letters have not expressed me. I am sure that anyone who happened to read them would find me hard, and wholly engrossed in rather grinding intellectual interests."[29]

At the time of Austin's National Arts Club dinner in early 1922, MacDougal, on his way back to Tucson, wrote daily letters to her from the train. He had spent two months in the East, as much as possible in Austin's company. His letters read like one letter, a long, affectionate account bemoaning his distance from her but filled with vivid description, anecdotes, and humor. "Nearing Kansas City," on 2 January, he speaks of "throwing things out of the car window—going over my feathers like a crow pulling out the odd & old ones and putting the others in order—The perspective becomes clearer hour by hour & the matters in which we are mutually & deeply interested loom up far above anything else of this way too." His thoughts move farther back still. "I'm trying to think what our pioneers thought when they started west. Their urge was probably vague but imperious and not to be denied." He talks about the mixed races he has observed in Chicago and, as he and Austin so often did, reflects on their own conversations about race and racial inheritance. He closes with a glance at the darkening landscape, and a tribute: "Leaden skies and flat lands are good for my soul after the exaltations of the last month."[30]

The next day he tells her about fellow passengers, among them "an old Irish lady [in the] next section [who] lost her rosary & could not say her prayers until it was found"; he listens to schoolboys boasting about girls and sex; and he traces the shifts in landscape passing by his window, as in " 'short grass' country today into the cactus and cedar." They have crossed into New Mexico. He thanks Austin indirectly for the "delicious" autobiography of Benvenuto Cellini she has recommended and, as he looks back through the railroad car, is reminded of his baby grandson. "You see me in the midst of life," he tells her, and closes with his usual refrain: "I hope the next time I see this road you'll be coming this way too."[31] His every letter reverts sooner or later to the West and her place in it: at best to live there, at least to hold as an alternative to New York, and always to sustain her writing.

At times Austin felt that having lost her feeling for art, she must wait at her typewriter each day to write whatever occurred to her. She saw her intelligence playing "the part of Svengali to the unhappy Trilby of my deep self, who may, by this process be made to sing without getting any of the joy or pain of the singer's life."[32] There were none of the inequalities and cruelties of George du Maurier's character in Austin's relationship with MacDougal, only, it would seem, a partnership. Thinking of home, MacDougal himself waxes nostalgic and contradictory. "Several times lately," he admits from his rail car, "I've been a bit discouraged that I feel at home almost anywhere. No place gives me a shock—almost every place shows a glow & radiates understanding—I'm not blasé—that's not it, but I simply like my America & like much of the human part of the race." But then, "I'm glad I'm coming back to Arizona just now—the desert seems to fit the mood—I'll be thinking of your book and your visit." Once again he hints at the failure of her life away from its sources of nourishment—*failure,* as he knew, was a word Austin often associated with herself.[33]

From Tucson, he writes an omnibus letter, following up their recent conversations and laughing about their private jokes. He praises before admonishing her: how can she think that he undervalues her creativity? "I surely know something of the creative mind, but who am I to say that I understand the artistic temperament. No mere scientist would be so rash. However you may depend upon knowing the direction in which you have gone and the level at which you are flying." He repeats her phrase "tinny intellectual" and applies it to philosophers unlike Austin and much like Herbert Spencer (the nineteenth-century British philosopher and man-of-all-fields), and he soothes her about work that will become *The American Rhythm,* insisting that her premise is right, that rhythm underlies the way of the world and the lives of its inhabitants. Without an obvious prompt, except his wish to cheer her, he repeats an anecdote: "Remember the story of my mule driver on a long trip in Sonora [Mexico] who sitting across the campfire at dinner with the bread on my side of the fire would say 'Dr I wish you would make me have another biscuit' when he needed more." That reminds him of another dinner, her celebration at the National Arts Club, which he hopes has gone well. Can they meet soon? Later in the spring, perhaps, when he gets back to New York? "It would be fine indeed if you were ready to start at the time I would be ready to come this way from the Philadelphia session."[34]

In the 1920s, Austin found a main source of income—and main drain of energy—in debilitating lecture tours. Her penchant for lecturing would have tried the strongest of constitutions, which she did not have. Lectures paid her bills and provided an immediate audience at the risk of her health. The thousands of miles she covered exhausted her, and the long absences kept her distant from MacDougal, unless his nonstop schedule took him to New York or her to Arizona at times when the other happened to be at home. What follows is a skeletal, and probably incomplete, list of lecture assignments she accepted between 1922 and 1931. She spoke in Carmel; New York; at the University of California, Berkeley (five times in 1922, and several years in the summer school, on American rhythm and theater); Monterey (on patterns of American literature); Cincinnati (on the poetry of American Indians); Boston (on community culture and psychology); Elizabeth, New Jersey; at Clark University (on spiritualism and death); Fort Worth (on American rhythm); Dallas (on the shape of society); Evanston (on the American novel); San Francisco (on Indian arts); at Mills and Mount Holyoke colleges; in Las Vegas; Wilmington, Delaware (on the psychology of crowds); Mexico City (on cultural relations); Reading, Pennsylvania; Boston again; Jersey City; Sioux City, Iowa; Carlinville, Illinois; at the University of California, Los Angeles (five lectures on American literature); Chicago (on Indians); Boston yet again (on religion); Philadelphia; Seattle; Waterbury, Connecticut; Memphis; at the Denver Writers' Colony; England (at the Fabian Summer School); Providence, Rhode Island (on the American pattern); Kansas City; St. Louis; and Keene, New Hampshire (on social patterns of the American novel). She also lectured in Santa Fe (on colonial arts); and in Taos (on southwestern literature and the common life).

Some lectures, MacDougal and other friends arranged; some came through booking agencies like the L. J. Albert World Celebrities Lecture Bureau, with whom she contracted in 1919. Austin won a reputation as a dramatic and persuasive speaker. Lyman Beecher Stowe, grandson of Harriet Beecher Stowe and Stowe's biographer, paid a glowing tribute, saying that he had lived all his life with a flawed sense of his grandmother until a speech by Austin revealed to him Stowe's place in American history.[35] Carl Van Doren (she could always rely on Van Doren) called Austin a force in American history, adding that no one could appreciate her eminence without hearing her. "She speaks as if she had just come back from the desert with fresh truth." His sense of Austin as "a prophet" comes close to her own estimate, as does his mention of the desert, the American wilderness in which she finds her moral strength.[36] When lecturing, she often felt her audience responding as though one body to her slightest inflection or pause. Van Doren told readers of his *Many Minds* (1924) that Austin was America's great new voice, singular and powerful. She alone seemed able to plumb the past, or frame a future, in the welter of American life. He believed her to be equally at home in New York City or the Mojave Desert, or anywhere on the lecture circuit.

MacDougal may have been shrewder. Excepting those on Western life and literature, Austin's lectures, like her journalism, tended to draw her away from what she saw as more important but also more demanding work. She sought almost any lecture opportunities well into the hard times of the Depression, when fees dwindled along with audiences. Her passion for lecturing and her need to make a living placed her in a venerable tradition of American writers, as Mark Twain, Charlotte Perkins Gilman, George Washington Cable, or any number of eager or reluctant performers might have testified. Like the theater, the lecture circuit could be profitable and grueling. William Dean Howells, suffering from dyspepsia on his Midwestern lecture tour, said that it was "the *kindness* . . . that kills": "I *cannot* refuse people's hospitality, and it is simply disastrous."[37] Twain lost a friend in Cable when the two lectured their way around the country in a special railroad car. Austin's lectures, like the pamphlets and magazine articles she wrote, may have served her in earlier years when she sought to win national or international fame. To MacDougal they seemed a waste of her powers. The sources of her imagination, he told her, lay waiting in her past.

In her piecemeal move toward the Southwest, Austin followed in the footsteps of her friend Mabel Dodge, who had exchanged Greenwich Village for Taos, New Mexico. Dodge made her decision and decamped. For Austin, who went back and forth, the year 1919 was pivotal—not for a final decision, but for a decisive visit. In that year she offered her services to establish a local theater in Santa Fe, or rather jumped at the chance to outshine Carmel's Forest Theater, and committed herself to long visits in the state that calls itself "the Land of Enchantment." She became a recognized face in both Taos and Santa Fe, where she studied with renewed intensity the dances, the poetry, and the habits of American Indians. Her work led to two books published at about the time of her settling in Santa Fe: *The American Rhythm* (1923) and *The Land of Journeys' Ending* (1924).

Long in the making, each of these books required extensive research and close observation, "fieldwork" to the ethnologists, whom she sometimes emulated and sometimes disparaged. Austin anticipated her approach to the two books in her 1921 review of Frank Hamilton Cushing's *Zuni Folk Tales* and *Outlines of the Zuni Creation Myth* for *The Dial*. She begins by quoting a man she would meet a few years later in Taos: "When D. H. Lawrence in a letter addressed to American artists urged upon them as their particular task the completion of the life pattern interrupted in the New World by European conquest, and the search for native sources of inspiration in the poetry and drama and design of Amerind art, he said nothing that had not already been expressed in one way or another by Western artists. Few of them have failed to experience the necessity of nourishing their own product through the top-soil of human experience laid next to the earth by the earliest Americans."[38] And few students of American Indians, she says, can match the method or the personal sacrifice of Cushing. It is "one of the shames of our own culture," she writes, "that so many of these ["Amerind" epic poems and other mythological stories] have been permitted to perish utterly or decay under the complacencies of missionary effort." Like Cushing, she objected strenuously to Native literature being revamped according to the literary or musical forms of another culture:

> In 1889 it was arranged that Frank Hamilton Cushing, whose qualifications for the work amounted to genius, should make an attempt to secure the text of the Zuni epic. There was but one way that this could be accomplished. This was for Cushing to be adopted into the tribe of the Ashwini, assuming its dress and its speech, and work his way through the varying degrees of its tribal mysteries to such priestly eminence as would permit him to hear and learn the sacred tribal chronicle of the New Made, the adventures of the Beloved Twain, and the issuance of the people of Zuni from the four womb-worlds. All this Cushing did with such thoroughness that he never came quite back into the modern American world.[39]

Austin does not mention the work of Henry Schoolcraft, whose life with and studies of Chippewa Indians in the early nineteenth century anticipated Cushing's. She is interested in contemporary work and how it touches on her own nascent relationship with the Pueblo Indians, the Indian nation first sighted by Spanish explorers in 1540 and associated with the golden Seven Cities of Cibola. While Austin never matched Cushing's immersion, she shared his passionate commitment to American Indians who, along with the Spanish explorers and modern immigrants, remained an obsession for the rest of her life. As someone adopted by Paiutes and familiar with Mexican immigrants in California, she needed little to rekindle her own enthusiasm. At the same time, Cushing's example made clear the need to set boundaries by husbanding her energies. Whereas in the high desert of California she had almost lived in the Paiute campoodies, she now worked with—and to some extent like—the academics she criticized. She sought help from institutions, especially the University of New Mexico and a young professor there, Arthur Leon Campa. As in New York, she committed herself to political and organizational causes that would keep her in touch with Santa Fe or Albuquerque or the U.S. Congress more than with the Pueblo communities themselves. She had no choice about the division of her work. Because of her bad health, Austin rarely had the strength for long fieldwork and the journeys it required.

This makes all the more remarkable the twenty-five-hundred-mile trek she made with the painter Gerald Cassidy and his wife Ina in 1923. There was, to be sure, the added incentive of Daniel MacDougal, who accompanied the group as guide and chief cook. For this, Austin's second research trip to the area, MacDougal once again planned the itinerary and attended to the logistics. In his effort to coax Austin to Western places, he convinced her that she needed to win back the audience lost after *The Land of Little Rain*. Several years earlier, he had raised the topic of a joint book about the desert—his bait, which came with a warning. "I am concerned," he had written from Tucson in March 1918, "that you keep in touch with your subject matter."[40]

The expedition began when Austin and the Cassidys left Santa Fe for Tucson. This was not to be Mary Austin on foot (or, as in early California days, on horseback) through the San Joaquin, the Mojave, or the high desert country, where she herself might have been mistaken for the half-crazed but wise wanderer of her story "The Walking Woman." On this journey she traveled with others, and by car. Just as John Van Dyke made some of his observations through the windows of the Santa Fe trains, Austin and her friends relied on the speed and ease of the automobile. Picking up MacDougal in Tucson, they set off on a route enclosed on the east by "the Rio Grande," on the west by "the Rio Colorado," and with no borders except imaginary ones between Utah and Mexico to the north and south.

By 1923 Austin had written parts of what would be revised and gathered up into *The Land of Journeys' Ending*, her name for the southwestern deserts, and for the book she and MacDougal collaborated on. If there were any doubt about the shared work, and the trust it depended on, a July 1920 letter from Austin should set it aside. "I can take from you," she wrote. "I can use your experiences exactly as freely as I use my own."[41] She was speaking about a mutual investment in a project dear to them both. Two years later she told him that the book "must be in a sense a monument to our common delight in the Southwest."[42]

For Austin and the Cassidys, MacDougal proved an unequalled guide to a land he knew intimately. In charge as he liked to be, he chose the campsites and, when they had wiped off road dust in the late afternoons, he grilled the meat for dinner. Austin sat while Gerald Cassidy made watercolor sketches and Ina Cassidy wrote. Hers is the one written account of the adventure, a short memoir titled "I-Mary and Me," which presents a talented and well-matched group, if not the best of friends, sharing respect for the wilderness. Ina alludes to Austin's lecturing her (by this time it had become pure habit) about the places and Indians they came to see first-hand.

"Mary," Ina writes, "is a rich source of information. Whether this role is prompted [by] a spirit of generosity, a desire to share her knowledge, a subconscious prompting of her old 'teacher' habit, or an exposition of egotism, one is never sure. Her friends commend her for it; her enemies condemn." Ina mainly commends. "Our supper is finished. I-Mary and the Doctor [MacDougal] are in deep discussion, Gerald busily sketching in some last color nuances before the light fails; I have cleared away the supper things and tidied the camp ready for the night." In what sounds like a pleasant elder-hostel trip for four, Ina admits to an apprehension about the vast land, and about Austin, whom she watches carefully. "Were I inclined to be superstitious," she says, "I would give myself to fear, for I-Mary is not well, the desiccating heat has been almost too much for her. The desert is no place for illness."[43] Ina Cassidy was right. Austin fell ill soon afterward, in Santa Fe, where ailments and a conviction of failure laid her low. From Tucson, MacDougal would stand by her against the widespread rejection of *The American Rhythm* (1923).

That book and *The Land of Journeys' Ending* stand as a pair of unlike sisters. *The American Rhythm* proposes a theory based on Austin's assessment of American Indian art. She translates patterns of dance, music, and poetry into a bold thesis, that the workings of rhythm define or govern human experience. "The major rhythms of the human organism are given by the blood and the breath," and they are closely related to environmental stimuli, the workings of the subconscious, the "well being" of healthy people, and the workings of memory.[44] "Suggestibility of the human organism in the direction of rhythmic response is so generous," she writes, "that the rhythmic forms to which the environment gives rise, seem to pass through the autonomic system, into and out of the subconscious without our having once become intellectually aware of them. Rhythm, then, in so far as it affects our poetic mode, has nothing to do with our intellectual life. It is located in the dimension of appreciable stress."[45] To confront such a passage is to understand her readers' difficulties, and also to appreciate how much Austin applied her knowledge of multiple fields, including American Indian customs, to what she believed to be a comprehensive theory. The psychoanalytic philosopher Julia Kristeva has received some of the same criticism for a strikingly similar position in our own day, which sees the female body as the source of a kind of prelanguage composed of inherent rhythms and tones.

Memory, for Austin as for a number of writers in the generation before her, serves the needs of survival and art. In *The Green Bough* (1913), a retelling of the resurrection in "the season of the green bough," Christ wakes after "the agony in the garden and the falling away of all human support." He returns through memory to his own humanity: "For more than an hour past he had swung from point to point of consciousness on successive waves of pain; now he was carried almost to the verge of recovery, and now he felt the dragging clutch of the Pit from which hardly he had escaped. By degrees as he was borne toward life . . . and recurrent memory began to play."[46] Austin's thinking about "recurrent memory" echoes in particular the work of Charles Darwin's nemesis, the brilliant Samuel Butler, who in addition to novels as unlike as *The Way of All Flesh* and *Erewhon* published studies of what he called "Unconscious Memory," a way of coping with the world *and* passing on learned characteristics to the next generation. For Butler, human or inherited memory, which extends backward to primeval slime, allows human beings to function efficiently with built-in knowledge. The problem with both Butler's and Austin's theories lies in their hypothetical nature. They leap from premise to conclusion, and they read like personal testimonials, however persuasive and far-reaching their implications. Like Butler's, Austin's ideas seemed idle speculation to some critics, nonsense to others. Yet many of her contemporaries speculated along similar lines. Carl Jung posed a "collective unconscious," with anthropological and psychological applications and on the basis of little more evidence; as did Sigmund Freud, not only with his theories of "philogenetic reference," but in the studies of taboo and in his essay "Civilization and its Discontents." People in diverse fields shared assumptions about what William Butler Yeats called the "spiritus mundi," his version—drawn from a long, esoteric tradition—of collective memory and its recurrent symbols. Austin draws from other sources. Open about her borrowing, she acknowledges such scholars as Alice Fletcher and Frances Densmore, Franz Boas and Alfred Kroeber, along with her favorite, Frank Cushing. "Though they do not always take me so seriously as I take them, it would be unfair not to admit that they always take me good-humoredly."[47] She may have written her book in admirable company; that did not mean she wrote convincingly to a waiting world, which by and large chose not to listen. The anthropologists unanimously dismissed her.

Stoically facing attacks on *The American Rhythm*, Austin told MacDougal that she refused to be cheered up:

> I want nothing less than absolute sincerity from my friends now. If I must take failure I will take it straight, and not sweetened with compliments

and consolations. If I have failed it is because I have missed the truth, and after all, I want the truth more than I have ever wanted anything else. If I have been, as most people think, a conceited pompous fool, then I must find it out. I haven't been conceited in the way many people think, of supposing myself better than other people. But I have supposed that some sort of truth is discoverable, and that I had discovered some of it. . . . I don't suppose I will ever know.[48]

In the first six months, sales of *The American Rhythm* hardly paid for page corrections.[49] Austin went to lick her wounds at Mabel Dodge's house in Taos, where Dodge reinforced MacDougal's advice to use the summer for organizing her life and rediscovering her creativity.

Austin's success with *The Land of Journeys' Ending* can be measured through its contrasts with the earlier work. Avoiding the argumentative leaps of *American Rhythm,* it is, without being history, a narrative grounded in history. It blends some of the descriptive strengths and storytelling of *The Land of Little Rain* with a beginning that parallels both *The Flock* and *Isidro.* Like those books, it opens with landscape and moves quickly back to Spanish explorers, in this case the fearless Cabeza de Vaca and the later Francisco Vásquez de Coronado in the southwestern region. The book seems both piecemeal and continuous, switching from distant times to present conditions, from appeals to the reader to reflections on the sprawling desert that Austin knows with the uncanny sharpness of a scientist and the sensibility of a poet. Her two faces (or ways of thinking) might suggest the collaboration of Austin and MacDougal, whom readers glimpse as characters. "Ever since Mac, to whom this book is dedicated, told me that a lichen is the perfect cooperation of two living and unlike plant organisms, grown into one the better to compass the rock's devouring, I have been afraid of lichens."[50] There seems no fear in the book itself, a labor of love and, as the dedication to MacDougal suggests, an expression of love, which brings to a culmination Austin's thinking about the West.

While close kin to *The Land of Little Rain, The Land of Journeys' Ending* is, as one recent commentator suggests, less "the result of a long, day-to-day engagement" with the landscape than "the result of an even grander impulse and a grandiose sensibility." In the later book Austin addresses "the large patterns and pulses of the Land which, in the immensity of their reality, go unremarked and even unnoticed."[51] A further difference in *The Land of Journeys' Ending* is the relative absence of people—the shepherds, the wanderers, the characters—who inhabit *The Land of Little Rain.* Austin speaks

of Indian tribes and Spanish settlements across the land, but without speci-
ficity, which makes them seem less like living people than historical figures.
She described *The Land of Journeys' Ending* as having a ritualistic approach,
a weighing of truth over fact. It reads as prophecy, and its claims *are*
"grandiose," but that word scarcely touches Austin's ambition. As the
prophet of the Southwest region, she feels at liberty to speak like an Isaiah
or Amos—at times a Jeremiah—about the spirit of the land and the religious
intensity of the Native peoples who inhabit it.

The off-and-on sense Austin has of personal power cuts two ways. The
trumpet-clear voice she assumes (modulated in any account with asides or
anecdotes or shifts in mood) becomes mannered at times, yet allows her the
power to call her countrymen to account. She decries among others those
blind to the beauty of the land and its spiritual qualities; and those of the
past who "massacred the game and gutted the mines; cast down the shrines,
seeking buried treasure; built nothing, preserved nothing, roared muddily
through the land, and ran out like Western rivers, in the sands of a time that
shows every disposition to forget them."[52]

> For this is what we have done with the heritage of our Ancients. We have
> laid them open to destruction at the hands of those elements in our own
> society who compensate their failure of spiritual power over our civiliza-
> tion, by imposing its drab insignia on the rich fabric of Amerindian cul-
> ture, dimming it as the mud of a black-water tide dims the iridescence of
> sea-shell. Robbed of his lands, wounded in his respect for himself, all the
> most colorful expression of his spiritual experience filched from him in
> the name of education, the great Left Hand of modernism closes over the
> Pueblemo. But if the Holders of the Paths laugh at all, it is at us they are
> laughing. For we cannot put our weight on the Left Hand of God and
> not, ourselves, go down with it.[53]

The other "cut" of her rhetoric is more insidious. Like Charles Lummis
or John Van Dyke in the early years of the twentieth century, and Edward
Abbey and Leslie Marmon Silko toward its end, Austin takes the southwestern landscape as personal territory. Genuine, heartfelt, and informed
as her passion for the land and its original people was, it came with a competitive edge. Who saw the landscape best? Who loved or understood
American Indians most? In *The Land of Journeys' Ending*, she writes of El
Morro, the Spanish name for the national monument called Inscription
Rock: "You, of a hundred years from now, if when you visit the Rock, you

see the cupped silken wings of the argemone burst and float apart when there is no wind; or if, when all around is still, a sudden stir in the short-leaved pines, or fresh eagle feather blown upon the shrine, that will be I, making known in such fashion as I may the land's undying quality."[54] The unspoken question might be why so much talent needs to be squandered on issues of what might now be called intellectual property, as if lovers of the West each made his or her claim on the land. In Austin's case, claiming meant reclaiming—though seldom reclamation. Lummis, who thought he had said everything before Austin, began to think around the time of *Land of Journeys' Ending* that someone so possessive, so intent on having been the first, needed a comeuppance.[55] Lummis was sure *he* owned the Southwest, having, after all, named it.

The expedition with MacDougal and the Cassidys that made *The Land of Journeys' Ending* possible fulfilled a long-planned hope. It took Austin back, as MacDougal intended, to the desert lands she had first encountered, intimately and viscerally, twenty and more years before. She came home, however, disappointed with her career, often with her life, and in precarious health. Through the 1920s until her death in 1934, almost no letter to Austin from any correspondent omits to mention her state of health. MacDougal, for example, refers to three separate episodes of the flu she suffered in the spring of 1920 (still a time of rampant influenza after World War I), and she seems to have been susceptible to a host of opportunistic ailments. Her books about dying and resurrection reflect personal burdens, indeed the patterns of her life, and they bear on her personal relationships. Sickness and restored health might be called *her* personal rhythm, the "LUB-dub, LUB-dub" beat of the heart she describes in *The American Rhythm* and sees underlying all natural process—uniting the seasons of the year, the drum beats of ancient peoples, and the stressed-unstressed trochaic foot in poetry. Every trip to the Southwest, whether to Tucson, Taos, Santa Fe, or remote Indian settlements (quite apart from the visits to California) seemed a promise of improved spirits with a healthier climate and restored imagination.

Putting together her autobiography, *Earth Horizon,* in the late 1920s, Austin recalled the effect of Indian art on her life: "I had worked to have Indian Art called 'ours,' to have it accepted as an item of the beloved environment; now I was to see it become the weft of a community of feeling which made the Indian one with us." The original manuscript also included another paragraph, this one designed to set up a discussion of her mysticism that essentially talked about going home. Before publication, she deleted the passage, perhaps as too personal.

> I knew, too that I would have to go back to the West; I had been there too long to let it go. It had for me a kind of reality that no other section of the country had. When I had gone east that first time in 1907 I had entered into a strange experience; I had looked out of the car window and seen Indians walking in the woods. Not as an illusion, a hallucination. I saw them walking in their local dress and accouterments, slipping stilly among the trees and by the water courses, but they were not in the landscape, they were in my mind and were projected like figures upon the screen with the effect of reality. Little shivers went up and down my back at the sight of them. I saw them in the woods, trooping across the plains, everywhere it was natural for them to be; sometimes in the middle of streets the background faded and the original scene returned, but always in my mind. I carried them with me. And the desire to realize them factually worked in me like a spell. I had to go back to New Mexico where this could happen.[56]

The passage expresses much of her homesick longing for the region. But it omits strong personal incentives, above all those two imploring friends, Daniel MacDougal of the cactus country and Mabel Dodge, who sought in Taos her own Arcadia and, having never found it, wanted Austin and other friends nearby. In the years before her own move, Austin spent a few weeks each winter in Dodge's house. "I am determined to get back to my original ideal of having this place [in Taos] a creative center," Mabel had written her, "not just a place for people to retreat into—as to go to sleep in—or to barge in for just a good time. I want people to use it freely but for creative purposes. 'This means you!'"[57]

———— ·•·•· ————

At first sight, Mabel Dodge thought Santa Fe the strangest American town she had ever seen. "There were wood-carts drawn by burros, with the short lengths of piñonwood made into square piles and set in sort of high cages, and these were led by dark Mexicans." Among them, silk-scarfed Americans dressed in riding clothes and sporting wide-brimmed hats loitered outside the shops. Except in the circus, this was the first time she saw Indians: "They had black, glossy hair, worn in a Dutch cut with brilliant, folded silk fillets tied around their bangs. With their straight features, medieval-looking blouses and all the rest, they were just like Maxfield Parrish illustrations." She didn't like the town—it was one of those places where everyone knew everyone else—but she loved the land, the desert rolling toward the blue-black mountains, and she wanted to know the Indians. "No one can know an Indian except an Indian," one of the local shopkeepers told her.[58] Those familiar with Mabel Dodge and her endless, restless searching—"her inability [to quote Hutchins Hapgood] to let go of anything even for a moment casually within her domain"—could have predicted her response.[59] She set off the next day for the less trodden Taos and more of "It."

On 22 June 1918, Dodge obtained the deed to a small adobe house on twelve acres. Work began immediately on additional stories, three in all, and a solarium with views in every direction, especially of the Sacred Mountain (Pueblo Peak or, commonly, Taos Mountain), a source of creative energy for many; a gateway to heaven for others. Dodge furnished her pueblo-style house with objects representing different parts of her life: Louis XVI sofas and tapestries, Chinese Buddhas, Mexican chairs, and Navajo rugs. In the process of housekeeping, she would shed her third husband, the painter Maurice Sterne, and acquire a fourth, Antonio "Tony" Lujan (which she would spell *Luhan*), the handsome, self-possessed Tiwa Indian who introduced her to the life of the pueblo.

If, as Henry James wrote, America had turned "romantic," the shift reflected neither the "what" nor the "where" he imagined. He would certainly not have appreciated the romance that others found in the dry and "undeveloped" Southwest, where even statehood came hard: Arizona and New Mexico did not win acceptance until 1912. But for Mabel Dodge Luhan and those who came before and after her—for the artists and intellectuals seeking spiritual sanctuary from the city and from the increasing commercialization of American society—New Mexico beckoned with its own romance. Taos and Santa Fe emerged as artist colonies well before Woodstock, MacDowell, or Provincetown, and they lasted longer, roughly to the beginning of the Second World War. And no wonder, with such land around them. "This is the provocative landscape that stirs the emotions," Mabel Dodge Luhan wrote. "Tender and strong, sometimes darkening dramatically, the half-circle of mountains surrounds the somnolent desert and embraces the oasis that is named Taos." To the north the Sangre de Cristo Mountains meet the Rockies, to the west mesas and desert stretch toward the horizon. D. H. Lawrence in his early enthusiasm gave this advice: "Go to Taos Pueblo on some brilliant snowy morning, and see the white figures on the roof: or come riding through at dusk on some windy evening, when the black skirts of the women blow around the wide white boots, and you feel the old, old root of human consciousness still reaching down to depths we know nothing of."[60]

A painter himself, Lawrence saw the landscape with a painter's eye, and so did a long string of artists led by the English-born Thomas Moran, who brought his glorious Western paintings to Americans in the 1870s. From early Spanish times, Santa Fe flourished as a three-way crossroads where travelers heading west refitted for the journey on to California, or turned south for Mexico. Around 1890, the Santa Fe Railroad began its transcontinental service and, though Albuquerque got the main line and Santa Fe settled for a branch line, Santa Fe flourished as a center for "lungers," archeologists, and tourists and became a magnet for writers and painters. Travelers to New Mexico admired E. Irving Couse's paintings of Pueblo Indians and their lands, which were commissioned by the railroad and became popular advertisements on its calendars.[61] Austin speaks about "the attraction New Mexico has for types as diverse as Dr. Jung, of psychoanalytic fame, Willa Cather, Sinclair Lewis, Agnes de Mille, Sidney Howard and more poets and painters than have elsewhere set their faces in any other common direction." For these men and women, she writes, the appeal of the region lay first in "new color relations," but also in "a more robust sense of form, new rhythms in verse, new approaches to the story."[62]

She might have added that the painters came before the writers, and that by the time Mabel Dodge moved to Taos, both communities were a mix of artists who made Taos and Santa Fe at least their summer homes. Many of America's most respected painters—Marsden Hartley, John Sloan, George Bellows, Edward Hopper, Andrew Dasburg, and Georgia O'Keeffe—found their subject matter complete with a new palette in the southwestern desert. Robert Henri, a leader in the Ashcan school, contrived a parallel realism for the Southwest as he had done for Monhegan Island and the Maine coast. Master painters such as Rockwell Kent came to New Mexico to paint the dramatic landscape, in a light "that never was on sea or land." Some American painters, like Moran, had found their light and plein air in the same years that Caillebotte, Cezanne, Renoir, and Monet found theirs (Moran himself learned from the Englishman J. M. W. Turner's revolutionary art). Others painted in the same era as the "California impressionists," who basked in the light of Southern California. Austin saw some of their paintings at the 1913 Panama-Pacific International Exposition.

The rise of Santa Fe and Taos as artist colonies began in earnest through the 1890s, when Joseph Henry Sharp and other summer residents, including Oscar E. Berninghaus, Bert Greer Phillips, Ernest Blumenschein, E. Irving Couse and their colleagues, made reputations as Taos's "eight painters," Los Ochos Pintores. Several won international reputations and sizable incomes, Couse, for example, averaging about twenty thousand dollars a year from his paintings. By the summer of 1915, a hundred artists were at work in or near Taos, home to the newly founded Taos Society of Artists.

Santa Fe's colony developed later, thanks to Carlos Vierra (another tuberculosis patient at Sunmount Sanatorium, founded in 1902) and Kenneth M. Chapman. John Sloan, a friend of Austin's in New York, became the acknowledged leader of the Santa Fe group, which rivaled that of Taos years before Austin came to live there. Mabel Dodge Luhan, in *Taos and Its Artists,* gives an affectionate account of the many artists she knew personally and respected for catching the terror as well as the beauty of the high valley she loved.

Residents of Taos and Santa Fe differed from artistic counterparts in experimental communities like Ascona, not only because they came early and stayed longer or because of their shared response to contemporary art, but because their sense of belonging cut across social barriers to include Indians, Spanish Americans, a few French, and fairly recent Mexican immigrants along with white Americans. Mabel Dodge Luhan's desire to know an "Indian" might have been inseparable from her desire to know herself at a time when psychoanalysis had become for many a necessity, and world-weary Anglos, "the hollow men" and women of T. S. Eliot's poem, associated "primitive" peoples with feeling, with *Life*. Although Luhan had dabbled in Eastern religions before she witnessed a Pueblo dance at the Santo Domingo pueblo, the experience affected her like no other. "For the first time in my life," she wrote, "I heard the voice of the One coming from the Many . . . when all of a sudden I was brought up against the Tribe. . . . Where virtue lay in wholeness instead of in dismemberment."[63] Perhaps the main ideal in Taos and Santa Fe came down to what might be called an appreciation of ecological history. This is what Mabel tried to define when she spoke of "the sense of an illimitable past [in these places] . . . , an archaic past, still alive and ruling the ether."[64] She had in mind the civilization of the Anasazi, forerunners of the Pueblo Indians, whose kinship with the land she and her friend Austin believed they understood and unquestionably revered.

Mabel Luhan had popularized Greenwich Village, but not with the intensity she popularized the Southwest. Even when married to Tony Lujan,

Mabel knew Indians in her own, inflated way, and some of what she knew she learned from Austin's lectures in New York. The young Mabel had seen her first Indians through the eyes of Maxfield Parrish, or the medium of his illustrations, and the images stuck. (In her wake, a writer for the *New York Times* called Taos "the garden of Allah in the New World; an oasis of twentieth-century culture in a vast desert of primitive nature.")[65]

If the primary appeal of New Mexico came from the light and the land, another came from a sense of isolation more imagined than real. Joseph Foster, who wrote *D. H. Lawrence in Taos,* prided himself on living a separate and independent life in Taos with his wife Margaret. He looked back on the first years in this way: "We lived alone—Margaret and I. It was frontier life—austere, frightening. The hardships of winter unbearable. But our lives were dominated by the beauty around us. The sky was so vast, the mountains so everlasting. And Margaret the heroine of it all. . . . Our small adobe house was lost in the sage."[66] Foster and those around him were drawn to the solitude of that scarcely populated region. Amy Lowell said to D. H. Lawrence, "In New Mexico you are almost as far away as in Australia." Lawrence soon felt to be "far away" in Taos. He was definitely not alone, and neither were the Fosters.[67] Tony and Mabel would ride over to see them. The Fosters spent time with visitors like Lawrence, who became their friend, before Lawrence's angry departure to brave a winter in the mountains with two Scandinavians. The Fosters knew artists and writers, people similar to themselves and, however separate their private lives seemed, they shared the companionship and the ideals of a colony.

The advantages of the New Mexico colonies did not mean for Mabel, or Austin, an escape from problems. Apart from a new wave of ill health, disappointment with *The American Rhythm,* and the unavoidable headache of moving a household, Austin separated from Daniel MacDougal around the time of her arrival in Santa Fe. Looking back on the situation, in a 1929 letter to Eve Lummis, she wrote that she "and Dr. MacDougal used to be very good friends. For twenty years he was the closest man friend I had." The relationship ended, she remembered, four years earlier (it was more like five), when she suffered a severe, painful, and protracted illness that required major surgery and lasted for the better part of two years. She said that MacDougal was vexed because she could not answer his letters; she had not heard from him since. "The whole experience seems to have left me feeling for the first time in life a little less interested in living than I was before." No one, she told Lummis, seemed to care or take an interest in alleviating her situation, MacDougal included.[68]

Her account might have surprised MacDougal, who wholeheartedly sympathized with her and wrote more than once to say so, though when her letters stopped altogether he did not visit or, beyond a few attempts, keep on writing. Was the relationship already in trouble? Had he determined to distance himself from her and saw this as an opportunity? More likely he was hurt by the lack of any response from Austin, who could easily have dictated a note to a friend or secretary. Always affectionately solicitous, MacDougal begged her for letters, thanked her profusely on the rare occasions she did write, and pleaded that he could not understand her silence. "Nothing is quite so important," he told her, "as taking care of what you have, and of yourself as in trust for the rest of the world."[69] Finally, there were no gestures from either one.

In the years to come, Austin shifted her male relationships to the next generation, to younger married men like Ansel Adams and Frank Applegate, or gay men like Spud Johnson and Witter Bynner, with whom she shared professional interests. Apparently she did not see MacDougal through the last nine years of her life. She had written to him in 1923, devastated by the withering critical response to *The American Rhythm* and anticipating their breakup: "Try to think of me as if you had heard that I had been widowed, or robbed of an only child."[70] She had suffered the breakup of a marriage and the loss of an only child as well as the end of her affair with MacDougal, but she had also kept death at bay.

nine

SANTA FE

1924–1929

How are you anyway—outside of Indians?

HERBERT HOOVER TO MARY AUSTIN

30 January 1923

ON THE PENITENTE TRAIL BEHIND Mabel Dodge Luhan's house, Mary Austin had experienced another vision, this one announcing New Mexico as her future home. Still at the time a resident of New York, she may well have chosen Santa Fe because of that vision, or because Taos seemed too small for both Mabel Luhan and herself. Then, too, she had helped to launch Santa Fe's first civic theater and felt more connected to the larger and historically rich city, which touted itself as the oldest capital in the United States. Not only the state capital but Spain's governing town in that region for 150 years before the Mexican-American War, Santa Fe offered an ideal community for someone drawn to antiquity and determined to address the plight of American Indians. Austin had turned thirty-seven when she moved to Carmel; arriving in Santa Fe in 1924, she was a more brittle but scarcely less active woman of fifty-six.

She remained something of a vagabond, making trips to New York and hanging on to the diminishing lecture circuit, but Santa Fe became the anchor in her life, her home in a way that Independence, Rome, London, New York, even Carmel never matched. She felt to be fully at home when, in 1925, she moved into Casa Querida, her "Beloved House," a low-roofed adobe structure on sloping Camino del Monte Sol. Casa Querida faced—and still faces, in its latest incarnation as an art gallery—the Sangre de Cristo Mountains, with Mount Picacho rising in the east.

Like Mabel Dodge Luhan, Austin filled her house with objects emblematic of her life. The library, which had an attached vault for manuscripts, contained a picture of her distant ancestor, Louis Daguerre; an autographed photograph of Charles Lummis, who had stopped in Santa Fe on his 1884 walk to the West; a photograph of her Carmel house; flowers gathered during her time in Italy from the graves of Keats and Shelley; and a more recent acquisition, a sketch of Frieda and D. H. Lawrence. In every room, there were signs of her abiding interest in other cultures, a Cristophero Santo carving in the living room (a gift from her new friend and neighbor, Frank Applegate), Pueblo pottery, a Navajo blanket, and a modern Spanish colonial mat. In years to come she would decorate her walls with art by local artists, including Applegate, Will Shuster (another neighbor), her fellow traveler Gerald Cassidy (famous for portraits of Pueblo Indians as well as New Mexican landscapes), and visiting friends like Ansel Adams.

For the design of her expansive and airy house, Austin had a wealth of choices. She selected John Meem, a local architect responsible for creating what art historians have referred to as the "historical fantasy" of Santa Fe. In the decade when John D. Rockefeller Jr. funded the construction of over three hundred buildings at Williamsburg, Virginia, Santa Fe designers and architects like Meem and his counterparts across the country looked to the past for models.[1]

Austin's more obvious choice of architect might have been William Penhallow Henderson, who popularized the eclectic combination of Pueblo, Andalusian, and Mexican designs that characterize the Santa Fe style. Henderson taught at the Chicago Academy of Fine Arts until 1916, when he settled in Santa Fe with his wife, the poet Alice Corbin Henderson. A polymath versatile as a painter and designer of furniture, Henderson excelled as an architect, creating, for example, the Museum of Navajo Ceremonial Art. The Hendersons had gone to Santa Fe to treat Alice's tuberculosis in the Sunmount Sanatorium; they stayed in a community that supported their work. Like other idealists, they found in the town a model for a new society, but they nevertheless clashed with Austin's group of friends, who had a different outlook, if not different politics. For all his talents, Henderson seemed to Austin a type of self-promoter she could not stomach.

With Alice, then associate editor for *Poetry Magazine,* Austin remained on uneasy terms. The two had clashed in 1920 when Austin accused Alice of editorial bias. "You certainly understand me very little if you think it would even occur to me to intentionally hold back a ms. of yours for any reason," Alice wrote, "and least of all in favor of my own work. It had never occurred to me that there was any connection or conflict between my work and yours, and if there had been, I hold that good work can only help good work, and the more of it the better. As a matter of fact, I have always done more to advance the work of others than to push my own, about which I entertain no false idea of superiority." She probably intended to stop here but grew too irritated: "If this claim to priority in free verse is your object in publishing, you can perfectly well let your publishers make it for you. On the score of drama, you may be accounted a, or the, pioneer so far as I know, even though your form is not quite perfectly achieved. . . . As far as priority in free verse is concerned—apart from drama, Stephen Crane and Walt Whitman anteceded the 'movement' in this country; and I think the subject of form alone is rather sterile anyhow. . . . With best wishes, and deeply regretting your misunderstanding of me."[2]

Austin, who tended to forgive misunderstandings, seems not to have forgiven this one. Newspapers at the time urged responses from well-known people who had been slighted or corrected in their pages, and the resulting letters fueled more disagreements and sold more papers. Given the opportunity in 1922, Austin sent a sharp rebuttal of Alice's comments to the *Chicago Daily News,* defending her use of the term *Amerindian*—about which she herself had doubts:

> I neither invented the term nor am I exclusively user of it. Perhaps this is the place to clear up a certain misunderstanding which our too easy journalistic habit of attributing authority has created about my relation to things Amerindian. I am not an authority on any phase of Indian life. I have made use of what I have learned from my study of the American Indian in certain other fields in which I also have some reason to speak if not with authority, at least more freely than other American writers. Outside of these special subjects—poetic rhythm is one of them—I leave the questions of terms to authoritative workers in that field. And Mrs. Henderson is not one of them.[3]

Actually Alice *was* one of them. She too labored for Indian rights and Indian arts, publishing on these topics and helping to bring about organizations that would further the cause. She had become one of many in Santa Fe addressing the same issues, each with his or her conviction as to who knew best. No wonder Austin refused to give her the last word, *Amerindian* or any other.

Clashes with the Hendersons and other like-minded rivals, the remoteness of Santa Fe and its high altitude, which meant air too thin for someone with a heart condition, seemed minor drawbacks. Austin had found a beautiful place to write and display her Indian and Spanish treasures and—what she liked most—the right house in which to entertain her guests.

—·◆·—

Austin brought to Casa Querida her dead daughter's ashes and, soon after, her surrogate daughter, the nineteen-year-old Mary Hunter. Calling the girl "the one disturbing element in my life," she thought that Mary could get a "real" education in Santa Fe, by which she meant experiences to foster her artistic and moral development.[4] The two had corresponded for years, and in 1918 Austin dedicated *The Trail Book*—it offered tales told by a mastodon, a coyote, a puma, and a mound builder—"To Mary, my niece in the hope that she may find through the trails of her own country the road to wonderland." She had defended Mary against real and imaginary dragons: a prosaic stepmother; an unsupportive administrator at Wellesley College, who recommended that Mary take a leave of absence for reasons of health and immaturity; and George Hunter, the uncle-doctor. Austin considered her brother incompetent for not recognizing the young woman's thyroid condition, from which she and Mary both suffered.

A battle with George over Mary's education had dragged on for a number of years. In 1922, George wrote about their niece—whose father had wanted her to study at least a year at a women's college in the East—that she "was about to take her affairs in her own hands" and enter Wellesley. "Mary is a fine girl," he said, "and I have no fear for her. She has some faults and deficiencies some of which she will outgrow and some are temperamental and constitutional. She has never revealed any brilliancy in any of her schoolwork and is decidedly intellectually lazy but she has the very essential quality that enables her quickly to 'catch on' and if she finds her bent during the next few years will I believe make good."[5] Hearing echoes of what she herself put up with as a young woman, Austin acted accordingly. She had, after their brother Jim's death, stopped talking to George and accused him of stealing family papers and relics. Now, though she wanted to adopt Mary and needed her brother's support, she made a frontal assault. Because George opposed her adoption plan (as did Mary's stepmother and Mary herself), he was, Austin told him, a petty tyrant and a hindrance to the girl's upbringing; in short, an enemy: "I shall do what I can to rescue Mary as she wants to be rescued."[6]

At one point Austin considered running away with her niece. "This is the first time in my life that I have rebelled against God," she told Mabel Dodge Luhan. "Even my child I gave up, and the only man I ever loved without feeling embittered."[7] She believed she had a right to the love and company of her niece, so near to her in kin and so alike in temperament, and she did persuade Mary to live with her for a time. In the ongoing family feud, Mary felt mauled between the two sides and ready to run away herself. By all accounts, Mary turned out a charming woman who treated her aunt with kindness. Claiming independence, however, proved a trial for her and for Austin, who had not lived with another person for years and sometimes considered Mary another project. She liked to say that a pretty niece was an expensive luxury and spoke openly to friends about the young woman's failings: a tendency toward secrecy—otherwise an understandable need for privacy—and her avoidance of responsibility, of which Mary carried more than she could bear.

Austin's health had worsened the summer before she moved into Casa Querida. Needing an unspecified abdominal operation, she tried self-administered infrared ray treatment at home, and when that failed asked her physician to summon the very man she berated. George agreed to care for her, but, explaining that he could not leave his other patients, urged her to come and stay with him. Austin refused, citing her work and the expenses incurred building her new house. About her time in hospital, the summer of 1926, she wrote a disjunctive and revealing fragment of a poem:

Now I know that life
Is much more important than I had imagined.
. . . because it cost so much,
Wherein we are admitted to secret sharing
Of God's incompetence, His last, least perfected adventure.[8]

Worn out by nursing her aunt for five months and by the family squabbles, Mary Hunter escaped in 1928 to Chicago. She had tried teaching in Los Carillos and Santa Cruz, California, and now, without family interference, intended to pursue her love of the theater. For a time her aunt lost touch with her except through the offices of well-meaning friends such as her publisher Henry Holt, the Henry Canbys (he a critic and Austin's literary executive), and Anna de Mille (daughter of the economist Henry

George and mother of the choreographer Agnes de Mille), who gave this advice: "Now about Mary. stop worrying. LET GO. She is in some little theatre movement & is directing as well as attending most of the business end. . . . She is finding herself. . . . If she falls it is her own problem. Let go. We must learn to do it with our children. I am writing to you—but talking to myself!!!"[9]

If Austin's illnesses played a part in ending her relationship with Daniel MacDougal, they defeated her niece and tested friendships with the people she met in Taos and Santa Fe. The woman who wrote vituperative letters to her brother and threatened him with legal action appeared at other times strangely subdued. As early as 1922, Fanny Bandelier, the widow of Fred Hodge's colleague Arthur Bandelier (an archeologist known for his 1890 novel, *The Delight Makers,* about the early inhabitants of the pueblos), found Austin "more and more sad and queer . . . she seems to put a damper on all social gatherings. . . . While she was there [visiting in Santa Fe], dear woman as she is, we all had to behave and talk sense, which is *so* difficult for me."[10] Bandelier's flirtatious exchanges with Charles Lummis, the recipient of this letter, offered up her friend as a chronically ill tyrant with an unparalleled ego. This was at most a small part of Austin's story. She managed a busy life in Santa Fe as she had in New York, and she now renewed herself with a broad range of friends, finding the sense of community she had never found in Greenwich Village.

Like other more or less utopian colonies, Santa Fe and Taos had their share of eccentric personalities given to political divisions and squabbling. Austin herself refused to see people in the morning, which she reserved for writing. When disturbed, she appeared to look through her unfortunate visitor as if he or she were elsewhere, which she wished them to be. Mabel Dodge Luhan outdid her. Mabel once invited a correspondent named Dorothy Hoskins to Taos and, after the woman had driven across country on bad roads swamped by torrential rains, entirely ignored her. She finally sent a note to Hoskins, explaining her behavior as one of those unpredictable "chemical" aversions. Hoskins took her revenge with notes for a scathing memoir of "Mabel in Taos" (1932). In a shrewd but more generous account of Mabel, Hutchins Hapgood spoke of her "terrific but formless needs, her occasional sharp unkindness, her extraordinary and otherwise incomprehensible jealousy," not to mention her tenacity and "eager love."[11] He could have used the same words to describe his friend and Mabel's, Mary Austin.

Although the two perceived "divas," the one of Taos, the other of Santa Fe, bickered about what they considered the other's presumption, their friendship lasted until Austin's death. Their correspondence is frank, sometimes too frank, as when Austin told Mabel that friends thought Tony "a joke—a good natured and occasionally ribald joke . . . [and] have resented my being used 'as a nursemaid to Mabel's husband'"; or when Mabel, accusing Austin of playing unbidden hostess at her house in Taos, commiserated with Mary Hunter about her suffocating aunt.[12] This last comment drew blood. "You wrote maliciously to discredit the only person on whom Mary has to depend for help. You made it plain to the most ordinary intelligence that nothing mattered to you, nothing impinged upon your consciousness but the satisfaction of your own rage, your blind, fatuous self interestedness. . . . You can't be friends with me on the assumption that you are one of the gods."[13] Mabel apologized, and Austin gladly forgave, attributing her friend's behavior to too much psychoanalysis. The relationship, however complicated for both women by Mabel's patronage and by their misconceptions of self—quite apart from the intangibles of sex, womanhood, art, and friendship—gave each a sense of the other's worth and her own legitimacy. For Austin that meant being "understood"; for Mabel, having someone take her seriously.

The circles at Taos and Santa Fe grew and shrank again, especially with the invasion of summer visitors but also as the residents came and left. Elsie Sergeant lived for a while at Tesuque—long enough to have a falling out with close friends over the allocation of Indian lands.[14] To Sergeant and others, who wanted to preserve the integrity of the region, sometimes at the cost of ghettoizing the Pueblos, New Mexico seemed a place "where time has so largely stood still."[15] In her collection of New Mexican poetry, *The Turquoise Trail* (the title refers to the trail taken by northern Indians on their way to barter macaw feathers for stones), Alice Corbin Henderson includes among her southwestern poets the Nebraskan Willa Cather; the Englishmen John Galsworthy and D. H. Lawrence; the son of Ukrainian immigrants, Yvor Winters; the Chicagoan Carl Sandburg; and the Illinois "sucker," Vachel Lindsay. Austin protested that "many of the poets included had no right to be named as New Mexican. They have merely passed through . . . we have no poets here now who have any more claim to be called New Mexican than Witter Bynner and myself."[16] Austin had also been included, along with Luhan and Henderson, and with no more claim than any other latecomer.

Bynner, a friend of the Hendersons, more or less disliked Austin until she wooed him with pickled peaches and praised his translations of Chinese verse. She soon became his "angel of the hill," and he "Hal," the name he preferred to Witter.[17] Photographs of Bynner invariably show him in casual dress with a scarf tied jauntily around his neck. A man of endless good humor and ribald wit, he lived for literature and, a counterpart to George Sterling at Carmel, enjoyed the pleasures and parties as Santa Fe's "high panjandrum." One observer wrote that "he told stories, made puns, drank and smoked constantly, did monologues, played old tunes on the piano, imitated his mother . . . or a toothless old aunt."[18] His affection notwithstanding, Bynner declared Austin "mad," "like one of the old De La Guerras, all wrapped up in a shawl and an Indian tea cozy. . . . She is coming for tea this afternoon with Mabel Edith Dale Dodge Luhan."[19] Conservative in his poetic tastes, if not his politics, he called Austin's thesis in *The American Rhythm*—that Indians sang in exactly the forms that became native to Spoon River, the Land of Little Rain, and Cornhusker country—hare-brained, and let her know he preferred Austin the artist to Austin the scientist.[20] Much of the time, Bynner could be found with a tall whiskey and lime juice in hand, nibbling caviar on stale crackers. The Lawrences thought him compatible, and much to Mabel Dodge Luhan's chagrin, invited him and not her on their 1923 excursion to Chapala, Mexico. In one of her legendary jealous rants, Mabel accused Bynner, who figures as a character in Lawrence's *The Plumed Serpent* (1926), of bringing homosexuality to New Mexico. He retaliated with *Cake,* a farce that mocks Mabel as a dilettante trying to ward off boredom with everything from sex to religion—and, finally, cake. Mabel missed the opening performance, but enjoyed the play.

Bynner's literary friendships spanned the better part of a century, from the idols of his youth (George Meredith, Mark Twain, and Henry James, whom he escorted through New York streets), to young poets of the 1960s. In 1916 he and Arthur Davison Ficke staged one of the great literary spoofs, the Spectra Hoax, which burlesqued Imagist poets like Amy Lowell and Ezra Pound and laughed at poetic manifestos. Under the names Anne Knish (Ficke) and Emanuel Morgan (Bynner), the two published a volume of poetry illustrating the "Spectrist" creed that "apparently unrelated impressions reflecting through a theme or idea may be artfully enough selected or directly enough recorded, without the conventional mental or verbal bridges, to reproduce, in the reader's mind, their effect on the mind of the poet."[21] The creed should have alerted anyone to the joke, but many took it seriously, probably because it sounded like the Imagists' actual pronouncements.

Bynner's partner and secretary, Willard "Spud" Johnson, described as having gentle eyes and an English accent, had once made a pilgrimage to

Los Angeles to see Charles Lummis, who disappointed him—more poseur than pioneer, he quipped. A founder with Bynner of the literary magazine *Laughing Horse*, Johnson asked Austin's advice about marketing and content. Both men called her Aunt Mary, and all three worked to bring artists and academics to Santa Fe and to Taos, where Mabel Dodge Luhan, lying on a couch lit by the falling afternoon light in a room scented by peonies, enjoyed her role as hostess. Johnson, who to Bynner's chagrin deserted him to become Mabel's secretary, a.k.a. publicity agent, bridged what might have seemed competing groups, the Austin-Luhan faction and the circle around the Martha and Elizabeth White sisters at El Delirio (The Madness), which included Bynner and the Hendersons.

The Whites, whose father owned the *Chicago Tribune* and the *New York Evening Post*, had money to spend. After serving as nurses abroad during the First World War, they settled in Santa Fe and soon became known for raising Irish wolfhounds, giving elaborate costume parties, and taking up the cause of Pueblo Indian rights and arts. In this they sought the help of Austin's friend, Fred Hodge, whom they had known in New York when he was associated with Columbia University's Bureau of American Ethnology. Austin brought her modest treasures from New York, while the Whites had the entire living room of their New York apartment dismantled and reconstructed. It included a full-length portrait of Martha dressed like an Amazon queen. At Elizabeth's death in 1972, El Delirio—designed by William Penhallow Henderson—became the School of American Research.

Despite Austin's protestations that there was no "Santa Fe school," she, like the White sisters, Mabel Dodge Luhan, and Alice Corbin Henderson, promoted the idea. It remained a loose idea, encompassing cowboy songs, Spanish folksongs, nativity plays, Penitente hymns sung during Lent, Indian songs, and books such as Henderson's *The Turquoise Trail* and Austin's *The American Rhythm*. "Here in New Mexico is the bridge between America-Hispana and the other dominant political entities of the new world," Austin would write. "New Mexico stands at the focal point of cultural integration."[22] She hardly sent a letter in later years without inviting her correspondent to come to Santa Fe. Willa Cather, Sinclair Lewis, and Vachel Lindsay (whose wife's mother attended Blackburn College with Austin) took her at her word. An unabashed booster, she did everything she could to promote a southwestern literature, from sending editors the names of promising authors to giving radio reviews. When asked, with Mrs. Calvin Coolidge, to submit her favorite recipe to the *New York Telegram*, Austin sent "New Mexican Enchiladas." She had no success luring Edna

Ferber or claiming her for the region. The Michigan-born Texan wanted none of it: "I am afraid you are giving me a little undeserved credit when you say that I am interested in the Southwest, and know that region. I really know absolutely nothing of the Southwest, and have never traveled in it except to go to Oklahoma, briefly. And Oklahoma I hate and loathe, stern and stem, people and habits, towns and country, up and down, forever and ever."[23]

Austin's public relations cum chamber-of-commerce promotions included local civic projects and paralleled her scientific studies. On her first trip to New Mexico in 1918, she had surveyed, with Mabel Dodge—Tony Lujan drove them in a wagon—the Spanish-speaking population of Taos County. In 1925, Austin served on the Council of the Institute of Social and Religious Research for the Survey of Race Relations at Stanford as well as on the Spanish-speaking Communities for the Carnegie Americanization Study, where she pushed for an extended survey along the entire Southwest border. The next year, invited by Walter Prince, the doctor studying automatic writing, she participated in a symposium on psychic research at Clark University.

The editors of the symposium's published proceedings, *The Case for and Against Psychical Belief* (1927), divided the topic into five sections: Part I: Convinced of the Multiplicity of Pyschical Phenomena, Part II: Convinced of the Rarity of Genuine Psychic Phenomena, Part III: Unconvinced As Yet, and Part IV: Antagonistic to the Claim That Such Phenomena Occur. Austin's essay, "A Subjective Study of Death," can be found in the first section, with pieces by Sir Oliver Lodge, Sir Arthur Conan Doyle, Frederick Bligh Bond, L. R. G. Crandon, and Margaret Deland. Harry Houdini appears posthumously, having died just before the conference started. Houdini's wife did everything imaginable to resurrect him—or induce him to escape his fate—despite his being "antagonistic to the claim" of psychic phenomena. In 1926 Austin also went to Yale, where drama students produced Spanish plays she had adapted from those presented at Santa Fe. (According to one coed, some of the men objected to her large stipend.)[24] Had there been a forum like *Booknotes* or a Discovery Channel, Austin would have been invited to expound on everything from how to speak with God to the *real* characteristics of American Indians.

For years, she had warded off critics challenging her supremacy in a host of fields. In 1922, she and Fannie Hurst, the author of *The Imitation of Life*, quarreled about what constituted a genuine "folk play." Austin gave her imprimatur to "Abie's Irish Rose," an immensely popular play that Hurst called a travesty. On the other hand, and in that same year, an apologetic Amy Lowell begged Austin's forgiveness: "I see perfectly what you mean by my giving an entirely wrong interpretation to the basket dance, in that little group of Indian poems which came out in 'The Dial' some years ago." All she knew, Lowell admitted, came from books, in one of which she found a minute description of women throwing baskets at the men who pursued them, splashed them with mud, and threw them down. "I took it," she wrote to Austin "as fecundity symbolized by human intercourse. I can see perfectly that this was not exactly what the Indians intended, but I am still a little in doubt as to what throwing the women down and spattering them with mud can have meant if not this. Perhaps you can elucidate the mystery."[25] Austin had described Lowell to Daniel MacDougal in 1922: "Imagine a middle aged woman, abnormally stout of body, with a shrewd, 'clever,' kindly face, plainly dressed, without the slightest suggestion of feminine allurement, a thin lipped New England mouth coarsened by the smoking of large black cigars, and a manner which varied from the assurance of the cultivated woman of the world to that of the 'hearty' wife of a small town hotel keeper! I was wearing an apple green satin slip with frosty beads and my lace mantilla, and I declare I felt like a scarlet lady!"[26] (MacDougal had written Austin about Amy's brother, Percival Lowell, the author of books about the Far East and Mars and builder of the Lowell Observatory, who had wanted to become one of the first two senators from Arizona.)

Austin had an easy time dismissing the insistent Amy Lowell, who meekly accepted correction; but not Willa Cather, a writer she truly admired and judged herself against. By the time Cather came to Taos to visit Mabel Dodge Luhan in 1926, she had surpassed Austin in public recognition, winning the Pulitzer Prize three years earlier for her war-time novel, *One of Ours*. That did not stop Ferris Greenslet from twisting Cather's arm to write a biography of Amy Lowell. "I would be as likely to undertake a history of the Chinese Empire!" an almost desperate Cather wrote Austin. "I wouldn't do it for the whole amount of the Lowell Estate, simply because that sort of writing is an agony to me."[27] Cather claimed that writing a biography of *Austin* might tempt her, though not enough to break her resolution.

Differences between the two arose over time and largely from contending versions of Western history, as if—and both knew better—there could be one version. Yet they managed to remain friends and supporters. Austin, who had no qualms about puffery, had presented Cather in "Willa Sibert Cather" as Emerson's answer to the bards of England. Cather's vision of the

West is all her own, she wrote, and "our own to the extent that it is utterly trustworthy and American."[28] Cather depicted a West in which issues had public implications but were fought between individuals or within the self, as *The Professor's House* (1925) suggests. Austin emphasized the public, the social patterns that shape people and their environment. If Cather tended to build her novels, as with *The Professor's House*, by creating parallel worlds that seem to erase differences of time and culture, Austin leaned toward ironic encounters between or within cultures and wanted to deny European sources for American inventiveness in the arts.

When Cather visited Taos in 1926, she was more concerned with housing than with issues of culture. Invited by Mabel Dodge Luhan to stay with her, she found the Luhan household in shambles and Tony the sickest he had ever been. She decided instead on the La Fonda Hotel, until Austin, awaiting an operation in Missouri, offered her house. Cather, always sensitive about space, went to see Casa Querida before accepting: she had to feel she could write there. Austin's "fine, big" library appealed to her, and Cather claimed it each morning. Sitting in a cozy blue-plush chair, with her writing pad on her knee, she enjoyed the breeze through the window and could see the girl who watered Austin's flowers arrive punctually each morning. Calling Casa Querida a satisfying sort of house, Cather imagined in its library the last days of Jean Marie LaTour, the protagonist of *Death Comes for the Archbishop* (1927). She inscribed Austin's copy of the novel: "For Mary Austin in whose lovely study I wrote the last chapters of this book. She will be my sternest critic—and she has a right to be. I will always take a calling-down from my betters."[29]

Polite sentiment notwithstanding, Cather set limits. Austin had first criticized her, in an otherwise flattering essay, by questioning Cather's courage to present stories as she saw them. She then told Ferris Greenslet, who might have passed on her criticism, that Cather "does not know the country [in *The Professor's House*] as well as I do, and so failed to graft her story on to the living tree of New Mexico. The best she could do was to split her story wide open in the middle and insert a green bough of New Mexico in such a fashion that I suppose nobody but myself really knew what she was trying to do."[30] Annoyed by this or similar statements, Cather later insisted that she had written just a few letters in Austin's library.

The rift between the two did not last. They still corresponded, notably after the death of Cather's mother when Cather said she might be well enough, in time, to revisit Santa Fe. Nevertheless, and despite Cather being one of the few people to whom she bowed, Austin pursued her role as Cather's "harshest critic" with an odd censure of *Death Comes for the Archbishop:*

> Miss Cather used my house to write in, but she did not tell me what she was doing. When it was finished, I was very distressed to find that she had given her allegiance to the French blood of the Archbishop; she had sympathized with his desire to build a French cathedral in a Spanish town. It was a calamity to the local culture. We have never got over it. It dropped the local plays almost out of use, and many far-derived Spanish customs. It was in the rebuilding of that shattered culture that the Society for the Revival of Spanish Arts (so dear to its president's heart) was concerned.[31]

The mix of fiction and life here, not to mention the idealization of the conquistadors, the subject of Godfrey St. Peter's eight-volume history in *The Professor's House,* shows Austin's passionate commitment to Spanish colonial traditions—and her lifelong readiness to criticize friends, publicly or privately, for a principle. She remains silent in this passage from *Earth Horizon* about the two women's mutual respect, for example the influence her *Woman of Genius* might have had on Cather's *Song of the Lark,* a book that, for Austin, could not be praised too highly.

Austin dealt once again with the question of genius in her 1925 book *Everyman's Genius,* originally a series of articles published in *The Bookman,* which she intended as a kind of self-help guide. For the project, she interviewed friends and acquaintances from widely diverse fields by asking them to fill out a questionnaire. She thought that she could identify writing talent with the answers to four questions:

1. Why do you wish to write?
2. What have you read?
3. What are your favorite studies?
4. What are your reactions to your environment?[32]

Contributors to *Everyman's Genius* include Fannie Hurst, who wished to remain anonymous; Marianne Moore, winner of the Dial Award for poetry in 1924; Wilfred Lewis, an inventor and efficiency expert; and Bill "Bojangles" Robinson, a buck-and-wing dancer in (Benjamin F.) Keith's Vaudeville. Democratic in principle, the book puts forth the idea that ordinary people, through an understanding of their own strengths and practices, can realize their genius. Austin's assurance that genius could be acquired—and existed among shepherds, blacksmiths, and cooks—not only won her followers, it made a frontal assault on lingering nineteenth-century notions about brain size or the shape of skulls determining intelligence.[33] That said, *Everyman's Genius* also reads like a book at war with itself, largely because Austin frames the appealing testimony of her contributors with what she would elsewhere have dismissed as "academic" commentary. To give one example: Bill Robinson writes that he "can't say exactly how the dances come into my head. It's not anything that happens to me that makes them come. They just sort of spring up. Sometimes in dreams. I dream that I am dancing for the king or some big person in some foreign country, and when I wake up I try to remember what I danced, and I work out the taps." The footnote to this passage reads, "Folklorists tell us that the original of the Buck and Wing was a religious invocation for the increase of spiritual power. It is possible that in this dream origin we have a reversion to racial sources slumbering at the bottom of the deep-self."[34] Her language confuses the issues and, more importantly, undercuts Robinson's personal authority, which Austin seeks to honor.

To the extent that *Everyman's Genius* relies on the eugenicist vocabulary of Austin's day, it plays Mr. Hyde to the Dr. Jekyll of nearly all her other books, which present race as the interplay of social constructions, personal choices, and tribal identification. In the story "White Wisdom," for example, Dan Kearny grows up thinking his paternal legacy Irish, his maternal Ute. He dreams of bringing the knowledge of his father's people to those of his mother, until, rejected by a white woman, he remakes himself as Ute, using his "white wisdom" to defend his tribe against the federal government. The irony lies in Kearny's ignorance that he has no "Indian blood." In 1925, Austin won the O. Henry Prize (that year's "best story") and received a hundred dollars for "Papago Wedding," a story about a custody battle between a white man named Schuler, who wants to marry a white woman, and Susie, the Papago mother of his five children. When the judge asks Susie if she has anything to say about why her children should not remain with their father, she responds: "What for you giff them to Schuler? . . . Shuler's not the father of them. Thees children all got different fathers. . . . You tell Schuler if he wants people to think hees the father of these children he better giff me the writing." Susie finally marries Schuler, which in her children's eyes means that she must now wear a hat as a sign of her respectability. "Go, children, and ask your father," she tells them. "But it is not known to the Papagos what happened after that."[35] The O'Henry Prize Committee thought the story represented "genetic American form," comparable in its ironies to a work like Charles Chesnutt's stories collected in *The Conjure Woman* (1899), which similarly confronts stereotypes about race.[36] Stories such as "Papago Wedding" and "White Wisdom," and studies such as *Everyman's Genius,* suggest the complexities in Austin's radically varied kinds of writing, quite apart from the woman herself.

Granting the difficulty of coming to some "truth" about another person's motives and behavior, D. H. Lawrence had a good time trying. In a lighthearted and unfinished play called "Altitude," he captures the fun and fellowship that drew Austin to Santa Fe—before, that is, he objected to the suffocating atmosphere of Mabel's compound and set off to the mountains, "blanket-wrapped / Round the ash-white hearth of the desert," as he writes in "Men in New Mexico" (1928).

Spud Johnson published Lawrence's comedy in his magazine *Laughing Horse* (1938) with Frieda Lawrence's blessing and a tongue-in-cheek disclaimer that "although it is obvious that, contrary to custom, none of the characters are fictitious, it should be clearly understood that the 'Mary' of the play is by no means Mary Austin; that 'Mabel' is certainly not the author of Lorenzo in Taos . . . and that Lujan is not the patronymic of 'Tony.'" Mary is "a woman With Ideas, who can also cook"; Mabel, "a determined lady who always knows what she wants—and gets it"; Tony, "an American Indian philosopher"; and Spud a pseudo-intellectual.

MARY: Brains and dreams won't start a stove. Hands, muscles, and common-sense must be ready for any emergency, in the new mystic we are bringing into the world. . . . Mabel, you may trust many things to me, the least of them being the coffee. Won't you all sit down and discuss the situation, while I solve it? . . . Will one of our young Intellectuals go to the well for water?

MABEL: [to Indian] Fetch a pail of water, Joe. [Joe goes out with pail.]

MARY: Don't you notice, the moment an Indian comes into the landscape, how all you white people seem so meaningless, so ephemeral? . . .

MABEL: [snorts] It is extraordinary! It's because the Indians have life. They have life, where we have nerves. Haven't you noticed, Mary, at an Indian dance, when the Indians all sit banked up on one side, and the white people on the other, how all the life is on the Indian side, and the white people seem so dead? The Indians are like glowing coals, and the white people are like ashes. . . .

MARY: There is something which combines the red and the white, the Indian and the American, and is greater than either.

In the interim Mabel and Mary squabble over the cooking of bacon, with Mary declaring: "I am officiating at this altar." Someone asks 'Oh, what about Professor Mack [Daniel T. MacDougal]. Is he still desiccating in the Arizona desert, studying the habits and misbehaviours of the Cactus?" Mabel announces that he is expected soon, and another character asks: "Don't you feel awfully bucked, Mary?"

> MARY: Professor Mack and I have had a perfect correspondence all our lives. This is the first time we shall have slept under the same roof.[37]

Lawrence would not be the only writer to poke fun at Austin. Intentionally and not, she herself led the way. Louis Adamic, a Slovenian immigrant whom she introduced to H. L. Mencken and supported for a Guggenheim Fellowship, thought her crazy when she sent him a fetish to release his "subconscious forces" and called her passion for Indians mere "crackpot" (she still claimed "Indian blood—a little, not too far back").[38] Adamic found her "a curiously magnificent woman—at once a mystic and a realist, intuitive and intellectually keen, calmly strong." When he heard of her death it came as a blow. "My feeling for her had been one of affection, but also more than that—of deep respect."[39] Adamic and Lawrence capture the absurdity, but also the camaraderie that Austin (whom friends called both respectfully and jokingly "Chisera") found in New Mexico, where her ashes, and Lawrence's, would finally rest.

When Austin left the Owens Valley in 1905, she knew that its water would be taken and that she could do no more to stop the inevitable. "I never went back to Inyo," she wrote in *Earth Horizon*. She had done what she could, "And that was too little."[40] In 1927, she made amends by taking up the cause of water rights in a different cause and from another perspective. The fundamental issues remained the same. "Touch water [in the West]," as John Gunther wrote, "and you touch everything"; it is blood, life, the chief occupation.[41] Austin, appointed by New Mexico's governor to the Colorado River Commission, attended the Seven States Conference and reported on it for *The Nation*. Wyoming, Utah, Colorado, Nevada, New Mexico, Arizona, and California had agreed to negotiate conversion of "the rampageous Rio Colorado into irrigation ditches and hydroelectric power." Austin's allegiance belonged now to New Mexico. From the beginning, she believed that California held itself aloof from nearby, relatively undeveloped states that were "anxious to restrain development rather than to hurry it." The history of the Owens Valley seemed to be repeating itself across the entire Southwest as California, fueled by its "outrun" resources and "characteristic expansion," pushed its claims on the Colorado.[42] The population of Los Angeles had grown to six hundred thousand by 1920, and the old nemesis of the Owens Valley, William Mulholland, lobbied for a dam on the Colorado to meet the city's needs for water and electricity.

Though in Austin's estimation California had the least right to the Colorado's waters because it contributed "no flow," the state intended to grab more than its share. "It is always a little difficult to deal with Southern California as one deals with other localities," she writes. "In Southern California boosting has become a religious duty; and the divine right of that section to all it can get, by any method whatever, is unquestioned." She also raised the specter of international rights, since landowners in Mexico stood to have their water "impounded." It further troubled her that her state, the size of France, with an immensely "varied climate, topography, mineral wealth, and crop possibilities," would not have an opportunity to develop a marked regional culture: "This adventure of the Southwest can never happen again," she wrote. "Southern California will continue for a time her phenomenal material expansion. She will produce more of the same thing in the same limited district of the identical limited type of what goes by the name of 'prosperity.'"[43] As Austin first illustrated in *The Land of Little Rain*, water patterns do not simply influence, they determine individual fortunes and national life. More recent books support her position: Philip L. Fradkin's *A River No More: The Colorado River and the West;* Marc Reisner's *Cadillac Desert;* Donald Worster's *River of Empire: Water, Aridity, and the Growth of the American West;* and Wallace Stegner's brilliant lectures, published as *The American West as Living Space*. Of course the prophetic John Wesley Powell had seen the future as clearly as anyone in his 1878 *Report on the Lands of the Arid Region*.

Believing herself prophetic, Austin once again proved to be so. She predicted the interstate lawsuits that would have repercussions for the entire economy of the United States and that would damage the Indian tribes excluded from negotiations. Although the Colorado River Commission had endorsed a 1922 provision, which Herbert Hoover called the "wild Indian article"—that nothing in the agreement should "be construed as affecting the obligations" of the government to Indian tribes—water went to those with political clout. Hoover's response seemed to Austin his typical blindness to fundamental issues. Today dams and aqueducts prevent water from flowing to the Gulf of California, and some scientists question whether the reconfigured Colorado should be called a "river" at all.[44]

Austin encouraged Louis Adamic to write an exposé about the proposed Boulder Dam and salvage the negotiations. Walter Lippmann, then at the *New York World,* scoffed at the idea. Lippmann, one of "the smoothest" men Adamic had met, said that the Colorado controversies were "too old and too locally western"; he wanted no more articles on that subject. When Adamic reported his interview to Austin, she felt " 'disappointed and disgusted.' She was bitter, not particularly about Lippmann, whom she tried to interest in Adamic's career, but generally about these 'New York editors, most of whom are more in Europe than in America . . . most of whom have not been west of Hoboken since they came to New York from Kokomo, Indiana, or Peoria, Illinois . . . and to many of whom the American West is as remote as Ethiopia.'" She thought the press biased or simply not interested enough to form an intelligent opinion. Adamic sided with Austin, whom he called "deeply interested in the West . . . [and] its perennial and epic water problem."[45] His book devotes an entire chapter to this woman he believed to be an eccentric but vital ally in the fight for water rights.

Austin may have been reacting to the Colorado River controversy when she wrote her preface to the American edition of *California: The Lands of the Sun* (originally subtitled *The Land of the Sun*). Ferris Greenslet asked if she would consider cutting the following:

(1) "Southern California north to Carmel Bay is forever so changed from what it was to something hardly worth describing outside a realtor's circular."

(2) "If I had guessed how early the beauty of Southern California was to be torn to tatters to make a trippers' holiday."

(3) "Too much of what I described has utterly vanished, too much has utterly changed, so blatant and bristling with triumph from the unresisting beauty of the wild."

When he suggested that the comments seemed "a little like inviting guests to dinner and then criticizing their clothes as they arrive," Austin knew he was right.[46]

In 1931, the year after Sinclair Lewis became the first American to win a Nobel Prize for literature, Austin wrote to her friend from Carmel days about the possibility of their collaborating on a great American novel. The two had kept periodically in touch, exchanging news and taking stock of one another's books. In 1920, they had an affable dust-up over Lewis's female protagonist in *Main Street*. "Mary Austin," he responded at the time, "you of all living writers ought not, like our friend Mrs. Dawson of the Globe, to suppose that because I like Carol and am sorry for her, I intend to present her as a model, a standard. . . . And you know darn well that if Carol had a Mary Austin, she'd be less desolatingly lonely in Gopher Prairie, she'd turn less queer and frightened. . . . If I didn't love Main Street would I write of it so hotly? Could I write of it so ragingly?"[47] He told her to reread a chapter.

Austin explained that the benefits of collaboration had occurred to her long ago, when writing *The Ford* (1917). She "realized that every little while my material disappeared into the intricacies of male life beyond my capacity to follow it." Since she faced the likelihood of Western water's requiring three books, she needed Lewis's help. The first she could write herself:

> Its dramatic climax would be the wresting of the first irrigation system from the Indian by the Whites. A middle phase might deal with the struggle between the ranch lands and the towns. The third—and this is where your genius would be triumphant, would illustrate the turning of the indivisible utility of the acequia madre with the equally indivisible utility of Power.
>
> I know everything that needs to be known: How the Indians learned irrigation and taught it to the whites; how the cities 'framed' the farmers and stole the river for the use of the realtors . . . I know all about the corruption both commercial and political that goes to that business. I lived through the Owens River theft and know why the Watterson brothers still languish in jail. . . . In twenty more years it will be impossible for anybody to know it as directly and completely, and in two or three hundred years more such a book as you could write will be pertinent and readable.
>
> Dear friend, don't turn this aside because of a traditional objection to collaborating with a woman. I know I'm feminine, damnably feminine, and not ashamed of it, but I'm not ladylike. You can count on my behaving like a gentleman.[48]

Midwesterners like Lewis could probably recall patches of drought and tales of rainmakers firing at clouds, but his interests lay far from the Colorado River. He would not be persuaded.

In a sense, Austin's life had come full circle, if not back to the Land of Little Rain, then to a parallel desert in the Land of Journeys' Ending. As she neared her sixtieth year, she began corresponding with lost friends and relatives with an eye toward her autobiography and maybe a family history. She filled notebooks with details about Carlinville, including the occasion in 1887 when Clara Louise Kellogg gave a concert under the town's first electric lights. She read letters her father wrote from the front in 1862— "John W. Hopper here fell dead at my feet, shot through the breast by a 6 pound cannon ball. Charles Huffman had his right foot shot off. Delevan Daniels, again wounded, also lost his right foot"—and constructed a chronology that included Jim's first prize for oratory and Susanna's presiding over the Woman's Christian Temperance Union. Whether or not she sought to recover a sense of family or felt prompted, because of disagreements with George, to leave her own record, Austin reached out to people like her Aunt Effie, who commiserated with her about her upbringing and passed on news of old acquaintances. Jimmie Foster, who died of tuberculosis of the spine, confided in Mr. Stoddard that he still cherished fond memories of Austin. "Uncle Alex and I knew of the misunderstanding between you and your mother, and Jim's dominance," Effie wrote, "but what could we do! Just love you all the more."[49] Austin sent her money, partly for a new artificial eye, partly to make her aunt feel less dependent on her children, who struggled during the Depression. Austin too felt its pinch in reduced lecture fees and the shortage of paper facing publishers.

With Mary Hunter in Chicago, Austin lived alone in her new house but communed with members of her family. In the summer of 1929, researching *Earth Horizon,* she returned to the town she had left forty-one years before, where she lectured to curious citizens and recited Indian verse. The visit might be seen as triumphal. The "queer" young woman, with her odd passions for books and butterflies, had found her fortune in the West. Hailed as Carlinville's most famous daughter, she might have wondered if anyone had read her description of Taylorville in *A Woman of Genius.* This was not, however, a time for settling old scores. If she had reached the age for looking backward, when others became professional memorializers of dead friends and deader times, she could still look forward, as John Milton writes in "Lycidas," "to fresh woods and pastures new."

ten

INDIAN DETOURS AND
SPANISH ARTS

From Santa Fe to San Francisco, Mary Austin is the high priestess of
those who love the Indian even though they know him.

Los Angeles Times, 1 November 1933

FOUR YEARS AFTER MOVING TO Santa Fe, Mary Austin wrote an article
called "Indian Detour," describing the detour as a back route through Indian territory and a state of mind. She invited readers to join her. We ask a
similar indulgence for our own detour, if not into cactus country, then into
the shifting landscape of Austin's mind, on topics that had long engaged her
and became, after her move to Santa Fe, near obsessions. With good reason
had Herbert Hoover asked how she was, outside of Indians, and he might
have added Spanish descendents and Mexican immigrants.

Austin had taken her detour into desert wilderness with Daniel
MacDougal and the Cassidys the year before she moved to Santa Fe. Her
essay suggests a new way of life, which meant less travel and more organizing and politicking in the town itself for Spanish and Indian causes. If she
wrote "Indian Detour" for those passing through the region, she also wrote
indirectly on behalf of the Santa Fe Railroad and its subsidiary, the Harvey
Company, which spawned the idea of a tourist route through Indian country in the first place. The detour, not a single route so much as a variety of
entertainments, included a stay in the Harvey Company's new hotel and
automobile side trips for passengers with the time and inclination. Each
chauffeured car came with a trained "Courier Girl," at once a guide to "the
beckoning, footloose distances of New Mexico" and a view herself.[1] "Off
the Beaten Path" (another name for the excursions) reached destinations as

far away as the Petrified Forest and the Grand Canyon, together with visits along dusty roads to Pueblo, Zuni, Navajo, and other Indian settlements, ancient and new. Austin described one detour in this way:

> It takes off from the continental lines at Las Vegas in New Mexico, and goes on past the blooming meadows, past Starvation Rock, past the ruins of old Pecos, past little Spanish-speaking towns that have not changed much since the road through them was the Santa Fe trail, with great ox teams lumbering down to the Fonda, where the first stage of the present Detour comes to rest. Here the Indian interest begins. It alters north toward Taos, toward the little towns of the Sangre de Cristo, towns with names such as you would expect of mountains that call themselves Blood of Christ. . . . Here where within the fifty mile circuit of Santa Fe there are more ruined cities than can be found in Europe . . . here, against a past in which every driven spade turns up another thousand years, the strain of the great American future is sensibly relaxed. . . . As far as the insistent pressure of white life permits him, the Pueblo Indian is leading the good life, the life of complete adaptation between his spiritual perception and his natural environment. It is the dignity, the courage and the profound spiritual integrity which the Indian opposes to the pressure, continuously brought to bear upon him to abandon this good life for a shallow imitation of lower middle-class American ways, that first of all excite the interest of the artist group [in Santa Fe].[2]

Curious here is Austin's picture of the Pueblo Indians "leading the good life," which she elsewhere contradicts. And while she praises the "profound spiritual integrity" of the Indians and, later, of the land itself, her aim is clearly to entice travelers, any and all travelers, to the region. (In her lecture "The Wonders of the Pueblo," she presented the Pueblos as "one of the few remaining great American adventures. Every year thousands of automobile parties visit them with interest and delight.")[3] Alluding to Sinclair Lewis's *Babbitt* in this essay, she says that even the uninformed, and thick-headed find themselves moved by the vast, dry land and the ancient civilizations it fostered. Austin accepted the Babbitts as she had the California shepherds, and like the Santa Fe Railroad executives she had commercial designs of her own. She once offered her advertising services to the railroad. A disappointing "no thank you" enclosed a coupon for free travel. She also welcomed any publicity the company could give her; they obliged with a 1928 booklet titled *They Know New Mexico: Intimate Sketches by Western Writers,* which featured Austin and her off-and-on-again friend, Alice Corbin Henderson.

Scattering tourists across the desert may well have been desirable, though likely not to John Muir and definitely not to John Van Dyke, who had written: "The deserts should never be reclaimed. They are the breathing spaces of the West and should be preserved forever."[4] Austin's positions echoed her mix of ecology and human needs in *The Land of Little Rain* and restated her stronger views in *The Flock*, which values the uses of the wilderness almost as much as the wilderness itself. She wanted the land to be worked protectively, by locals, visitors, miners, shepherds, and railroads alike, while giving priority to the Native populations. These desert lands stretching through New Mexico, Arizona, California, Nevada, and Utah evoked her sometimes shifting but inclusive understanding of the West, particularly issues of water rights, land use, and Spanish and Indian civilizations.

It would take a small book to summarize Austin's writing about Indians, which falls into several categories. She wrote dozens of articles that hypothesized about Indian arts, religion, and psychology, for instance, and the centrality of Indian customs to "American" life. She propagandized for various causes, including the sovereignty of the Pueblos and the value of Indian crafts. She lectured for the American Indian Defense Association, as to the public generally. And she wrote a stream of letters to those newspapers and politicians—from Herbert Hoover to Ray Lyman Wilbur and Harold Ickes, secretaries of the interior—inclined to give a friendly hearing. As she told Fred Hodge, then excavating at Hawikuh near Zuni, Indians had become her bread and butter.[5] Magazine editors not only identified her with Indians, they generally paid more for her Indian material than for other subjects. As early as 1922, *McCall's* commissioned her to write three Indian stories, each at $750.

In the Owens Valley, Austin had taken sides in the seemingly endless strife between whites and Indians. The magic she originally found in California's high desert and later in New Mexico could not be separated from its Native peoples, whose fight for dignity and self-government she accepted as her own. Some might say that she needed a public outlet for her "sacred rage"; others that her change from entertaining readers to educating them resulted in dissipated energies. It is of course impossible to speak confidently about another person's imagination, or about the twists and turns of a career, when issues of health, place, people, and money daily intrude. Then, too, as Eudora Welty writes, "the events in our lives happen in a sequence in time, but in their significance to ourselves they find their own order."[6] This was true of Austin, whose identification with the Southwest and incremental move to Santa Fe had some of the fervor of a prodigal daughter's return. Much of that return can be linked to her passionate caring for the well-being of American Indians.

Austin's 1918 appointment to the School of American Research in Native American Literature and her article "Aboriginal Literature" for the *Cambridge History of American Literature* (1921) had assured her reputation as an expert, though the long-suffering Fred Hodge complained that she sponged material from him. Charles Lummis raged after reading a version of her talk called "Culture and Primitive Arts of the Southwest": "If she knows anything about the Indians—though God knows she has had plenty of opportunity—everything she has ever written has carefully disguised the fact. Mary is a brilliant lady; above all, she has the misfortune of Doubling for the Almighty. . . . I get sorrier every day that I didn't review, as requested, her last book on New Mexico [*The Land of Journeys' Ending*]. That would have settled Mary's hash, and sent her to the retirement which she would really grace."[7]

In the 1920s, when Mabel Dodge and Tony Lujan held court in Taos, Austin asserted herself in Santa Fe. She continued to censure missionaries and government officials intent on suppressing indigenous religious practices, especially the dancing that both groups damned as "obscene." Once more she objected to teachers forcing students to sing Christian hymns rather than their own songs, and across the board she protested the inadequate education of children and the lack of services and health care available in the Pueblo communities. To give just one example of the health problems, Mabel contracted syphilis from her husband, Tony.[8] In 1922, Austin and Mabel joined forces against the notorious Bursum Bill. If passed by Congress, the bill promised to undo federal treaties across the nation by legitimizing non-Indian titles to Indian land. Largely owing to the efforts of people like Mabel and Austin, the Bursum Bill roused concerned citizens across the country. Among others, women's clubs, the American Ethnological Society, and the Campfire Girls and Boy Scouts joined in opposing the bill's passage. Carl Sandburg, Zane Grey, Vachel Lindsay, and Edgar Lee Masters signed a national petition against it. Austin's friend Elsie Sergeant wrote a critique of the bill for *The Nation,* and Austin herself (who shepherded Indian delegates through New York clubs, drawing rooms, and the gallery of the stock exchange, where they stood and sang the Morning Song) wrote another for the *New Republic.*

In their campaign, Mabel Dodge Luhan and Austin looked for guidance from the social reformer John Collier, a man who later directed the Indian Bureau. The two had worked to entice Collier to New Mexico and succeeded in 1920. Collier had been in charge of the People's Institute at Cooper Union, an organization dedicated to the principles of socialist thinkers such as William Morris and Lester Ward. Cooper Union's mission allowed Collier to pursue his efforts to help immigrant communities. After visiting Taos, he turned to Indian affairs. Mabel, in a shrewd portrait, described Collier as "a small, blond Southerner, intense, preoccupied, and always looking wind-blown on the quietest day." And, with application to herself, "Because he could not seem to love his own kind of people, and as he was full of a re-former's enthusiasm for humanity, he turned to other races and worked for them."[9] Among the Pueblo Indians, Collier discovered a way of life anti-thetical to the industrialized world, to its uprooting and dispersal of families and embrace of the mass produced. Within two years of his arrival in New Mexico, he accepted a position as a research agent for the Indian Welfare Committee, which charged him to investigate social and economic condi-tions among the Pueblos. By a Supreme Court decision of 1913, American In-dians suddenly found themselves wards of the government, as if children and to be treated as such. Collier saw a miserable people not only sick from poverty but subsisting on bone-dry land. With Austin's help he determined to right some of those wrongs.

The fight against the Bursum Bill gave both Collier and Austin a brief na-tional stage. Mabel Dodge Luhan, who at Austin's urging had married Tony to forestall enemies publicizing their affair, kept a lower, though still active profile.[10] While Collier lobbied politicians, Austin lectured. In January 1923, addressing members of the National Popular Government League, she called the destruction of Pueblo life "as deliberate as it is iniquitous." An Indian's annual per capita income at Taos was thirty-nine dollars; at San Ildefonso, fourteen. "Pueblo Indians face starvation; their lands have been infringed upon and their waters stolen by squatters." She explained that land titles conferred by the Bursum Bill would be illegitimate: first, because Indian land was held communally and private sales had been made tem-porarily, and out of sympathy, to whites; second, because such titles would be irrelevant "because no title given by an Indian is valid." Indians, who cannot plead their cases in court, obviously cannot evict; they can only sub-mit complaints "and wait patiently." Long upset about the government's Indian policy, she did not contain her sarcasm:

> Not a day's journey from these Pueblos there is an immense tract of land
> set apart forever as a national monument, never to be farmed or grazed
> upon, nor mined nor timbered, and in other parts of the Southwest other

similar tracts. Why? Because they contain the ruined dwellings of the ancestors of these Pueblonos. Because our ethnologists have told us that these ruins are of great scholarly value to us. Oh, I have no doubt that this is what we will do with the ruins of San Ildefonso, of Taos, of Zuni and Acoma, once we have successfully ruined them. I have no doubt that Secretary Fall will cheerfully draft a bill to preserve these ruins to New Mexico, and that we will put a fence around them and charge tourists a fee to come and see how completely our politicians can pick the heart out of our national assets. This is the sort of thing that brings our culture into contempt with the nations of the earth.[11]

When Austin turned for support to her old friends the Hoovers, Lou responded that on this issue, as on women's rights, she and Austin disagreed. "I feel certain the bill can be so amended as to give their rights to those few hundred settlers who have held their lands for many generations from the Indians—and yet not make possible any further alienations of the Indian property." The intention of the Bursum Bill, Lou insisted, was not to disperse Indian holdings, but "to give legal recognition of title to descendants of old Mexican settlers who had gotten land by intermarriage or from Indians." She saw the problem as "only a few hundred of old-time settlers against the 19,000 Indians holding the community lands."[12] Undeterred, Austin wrote to Hoover himself. Having opened her husband's mail in his absence, an irritated Lou snapped back, "I here announce firmly that I am not going to bother him by bringing such a lot of silly nonsense to his attention. Regarding Indians, they are not connected with his work in any way. I have heard him say a number of times that he could not be a constant messenger to the Secretary of the Interior, who is exceedingly approachable on the subject." In her letter, Austin had accused Hoover of telling the citizens of Phoenix that she was "not reliably informed on the Indian question—or on any other." Lou denied this categorically. "I happened to hear him recommend you amongst a number of other people to the Secretary of the Interior as being likely material to sit on a once proposed Indian Advisory Commission. . . . Well, don't spend so much time or energy or vital force over the Indians, or any other subject, and become so obsessed with it that you lose your sanity or sense of values, or that better sense of humor!"[13]

On 5 November 1922, Pueblo leaders convened the first All-Pueblo Council since 1680 to draft an appeal against the Bursum Bill. The Senate killed the bill in January 1923 only to have it resurrected, with modifications, as the Lenroot Bill one month later. The new bill, which the New

Mexico Association supported and Collier's American Indian Defense Association opposed, further split the Santa Fe–Taos community into factions, each claiming to speak for the Pueblos and thereby the right to influence, or determine, government policy. The division would deepen with the Indian Defense Association's proposed Indian Arts and Crafts Bill (1927). Members of the Indian Arts Fund felt pushed aside, and though Austin chose not to chastise Collier publicly—many saw him to be empire building—she did not hold back in private. In 1931, artists in Santa Fe would hang an effigy of "Demijohn" Collier. Hal Bynner quipped: "Love for the Indians is my boast, yet I love John Collier the most—Amen."[14]

Mabel Dodge Luhan wrote to Austin about a plan more ambitious than Collier's political reforms. "We want interest and appreciation of the Indian life and culture to become a part of our conscious racial mind," she wrote to the already converted Austin. "We want *as a nation* to value the indian as we value our selves. We want to *consciously* love the wholeness and harmony of indian life, and to *consciously* protect it. This publicity is invaluable. That it began in politics does not prevent its being channeled into aesthetics. Please get busy and write—write. *No one* but Alice Corbin and Bynner is writing in Santa Fe."[15] Austin did write, advising "apostles of a new social order" to eschew "the cafes of Prague or the cellars of Leningrad." Come to New Mexico, she urged, and discover "the most interesting possibility of social evolution that the world scene at present affords."[16]

To get a sense of where Austin stood and what she opposed, consider a statement issued by Indian Commissioner Charles Burke in 1923 addressed "TO ALL INDIANS":

> Now, what I want you to think about very seriously is that you must first of all try to make your own living . . . I do not want to deprive you of decent amusements or occasional feast days, but you should not do evil or foolish things or take so much time for these occasions. No good comes from your 'giveaway' custom at dances and it should be stopped. It is not right to torture your bodies or to handle poisonous snakes in your ceremonies. . . . Something must be done to stop the neglect of stock, crops, gardens, and home interests caused by these dances or by celebrations, pow-wows, and gatherings of any kind that take time of the Indians for many days.[17]

Six years later, Austin wrote an article for *The Forum* implicitly responding to Burke's assumptions. "Why Americanize the Indian?" she asked, and offered an alternative:

Restore the Indian family. Wherever possible, restore Indian village life and encourage adequate sanitation and the coordinated education of parents and children. Establish normal schools for the few Indians who wish to serve as teachers or skilled craftsmen among their own people. Open all the doors to civilized opportunity, just as we have to all other racial elements according to their capacity; but neither nag nor compel them to enter. Restore the Indian's freedom of religious observance. Encourage native crafts without being too censorious of the God who has endowed these people with peculiar gifts of their own which they can contribute to our culture.[18]

If Burke's paternalistic letter damns itself, Austin's article proves more slippery. Few would disagree about restoring families and communities, educating parents and children, or respecting religious freedom. Such goals were and are apple pie. The problem lay partly with the conditions of Pueblo life and partly with the word *restore,* which implied a single preceding state, a usable model.

If Austin's prescriptions appear to treat *culture* as a static entity, she more commonly spoke about *cultures* changing over time, indeed had made that argument when defending sheepherding in the high desert. She made it again when she spoke of Santa Fe as a laboratory of democracy and cultural integration, by which she meant not assimilation, but coexistence and interaction, both harbingers of change. Abstractions are one thing, however, and lived situations another. What, after all, should be or should have been done about the dilapidated state of the Taos pueblo, the subject of one of her books? How does a historic place (or society) retain its identity without the risk of continued destitution or becoming a Disneyland theme park, even a colonial Williamsburg, created for tourists and advertised as the world's largest living museum? Today, visitors can tour Taos pueblo for a fee and gamble in a small casino on its outskirts.

Mabel Dodge Luhan recalled her third husband, Maurice Sterne, asking whether she wanted an object in life. "Save the Indians, their art-culture," he told her, "reveal it to the world."[19] A similar effort was taking place in Harlem, spearheaded by Mabel's friend, Carl Van Vechten, the white author of the controversial novel *Nigger Heaven* (1926), which W. E. B. Du Bois dismissed as "an affront to the hospitality of blacks and the intelligence of whites."[20] Harlem—a name on everyone's tongue—provided an exciting model for those interested in Native arts. Austin, who knew both James Weldon Johnson and Du Bois, especially for his support of women's rights, admired the poetry of Countee Cullen and Jean Toomer (whom Mabel also subsidized and tried to seduce). Austin followed the careers of African American artists and acknowledged, while lecturing at Yale University, a spiritual debt to their music and to translations of aboriginal folktales into contemporary art. Her library contained a copy of Langston Hughes's essay "The Negro Artist and the Racial Mountain." Yet for all her interest in Harlem, dance, and folklore, African American experience seemed at best secondary to her own experience among the Indians.

Crediting Native artists as the most "authentically" American, Austin argued that the "Amerind tale-maker sees his world as honestly as any young novelist writing from Main Street or Spoon River or West Twenty-third Street. He sees man a lonely adventurer into the playground of powers vast and inexplicable, but for the most part friendly. . . . It . . . is not the Amerind tales that are childish, but those American tales which insist on depicting a world in which nothing is mysterious or unexplained, and nothing happens which is not immediately obvious."[21] One problem for patrons such as Carl Van Vechten and Mabel Dodge Luhan or interpreters like Austin lay in the responsibilities of the translator to reproduce or imitate original material without *appropriating* it.[22] Van Vechten himself warned that white artists would poach whatever material black artists—not to say any minority artists—ignored or rejected. He himself poached with the best.

Austin and other supporters of the Pueblos walked a fine moral line. Naive, quixotic, at times self-serving, they offered themselves as the initiated, if not the chosen, guardians. As president of the Indian Arts Fund, which marketed among other things "authentic" Navajo blankets and jewelry, Austin and her organization found people in the community who still practiced and could teach arts otherwise dying out, including embroidery, beadwork, and weaving. She would argue for a museum "of Indian arts for Indians" (a phrase that, again, can be read generously or not), which she saw as a lending institution for religious objects and a sacred space for rituals.[23] For Austin, arts and economics went hand in hand. A really fine Navajo blanket takes two years to make, she wrote: "What the American friends of the Amerind have to realize and put into effect is, that the economic law of art-craft is not toward quantity consumption, but preferred consumption. If a Navajo came into Santa Fe to-day with a blanket really worth $600 to $800, he wouldn't be allowed to get out of town with it."[24] Despite some differences, she supported Elizabeth White's ventures. White, on the board of the Indian Arts Fund, opened an arts and crafts shop on Madison Avenue in 1922 to sell goods from Guatemala; in 1931 it became the Gallery of American Indian Art. In Santa Fe that same year, the Laboratory of Anthropology opened to the public, having already incorporated organizations such as the Historical Society of New Mexico, the Indian Arts Fund, and the Society for the Revival of Spanish Colonial Arts. John D. Rockefeller Jr. subsidized the project. In addition to the School of American Research, White gave land for the Wheelwright Museum and the Laboratory of Anthropology.

"The country," Mabel Dodge Luhan said, "has seemed to *go indian* [her emphasis]."[25] She perhaps referred to the opening of the Museum of the American Indian in New York City, which brought to public attention issues of patronage and paternalism in the revival and transformation of American Indian arts. Austin herself understood the extent to which Indian artifacts, whose sacred functions were often lost on tourists and collectors, had become part of the marketplace. At the 1927 Indian Fair during the Santa Fe's fiesta, organizers first asked artists to sign their work, a practice that went against the spirit or traditions of their culture. But what exactly were those traditions? And who defined them? Excavation of Puye in 1907 and the Frijoles Canyon in 1909 had revealed prehistoric pottery, the designs of which were claimed by contemporary artisans. Since white patrons preferred the ancestral work to the modern, the marketplace made craftspeople richer to the detriment of the newer, independent traditions they had established.

Leslie Marmon Silko describes people who think they know "more about Indians than the Indians know" as white shamans: "It has happened with Indian graphic art and painting. The people who buy the paintings tell the Indian artist, 'Don't do that, that's abstract—Indians ought to only do realistic sorts of paintings,' and 'Oh, don't paint that, that's a picture of a drunken man passed out on the street of Gallup. That won't sell in our gallery, you know.' In other words, white patrons have very much controlled and molded it [Indian art]."[26] Already in 1927, Chief Standing Bear wrote in his preface to *My People, the Sioux:* "White men who have tried to write stories about the Indian have either foisted on the public some bloodcurdling, impossible 'thriller,' or, if they have been in sympathy with the Indian, have written from knowledge which was not accurate and reliable. No one is able to understand the Indian race like an Indian."[27] Silko and Chief Standing Bear raise a troublesome issue of authenticity. How, for example, would we read Austin's "Indian books" if we did not know her race—assuming *race* to be the appropriate word? For that matter how would we read Leslie Silko's?

Austin wrote in an era no less obsessed with questions of race than our own—though maybe with less hypocrisy. Around the time she went to the Rancho El Tejon as a young immigrant, Theodore Roosevelt said: "I don't go so far as to think that the only good Indians are the dead Indians, but I believe nine out of every ten are, and I shouldn't inquire too closely into the case of the tenth. The most vicious cowboy has more moral principle than the average Indian."[28] In the 1920s, Jim Crow laws applied to American Indians as to American blacks. Austin, who supported the production of Eugene O'Neill's *All God's Chillun Got Wings* (postponed because of the interracial marriage between actors Paul Robeson and Mary Blair), entered the national discussion about race with every piece she wrote on American Indians.

Joking or not, Mabel Dodge Luhan suggested that if Austin genuinely wanted to know Indians she should marry one, to which Austin replied that you couldn't know an Indian without knowing the group. Yet how does one know the group? Though she had spent time in the campoodies of California, she spent less time in the pueblos, and she could not claim to have lived with her subjects, as did ethnologists from Henry Schoolcraft to Frank Cushing—or Franz Boas, who, early in his career in Baffin Land, announced that he was now an Eskimo. Once anointed, however, Austin had no inclination to throw off the mantle—nor much tolerance for doubters. After Boas criticized a review she had written of Ruth Leah Bunzel's *The Pueblo Potter* (1929), she complained that "Dr. Boas is not the only one of his tribe who takes for granted that because I put the results of my study in literary language rather than in the jargon of the —ists, that therefore he is justified of an unsupported attack on my integrity as a scholar and writer."[29] Here of course she avoids the real issue—articulated in her writings on Cushing—about the necessity of some kind of immersion. And like Boas with the Eskimos, she did make oblique remarks about being—or wishing to be—part Indian.

Despite her amateur status, Austin was not an "Indian socialite," to borrow a phrase from the naturalist Ernest Thompson Seton. She believed that she found in ancient civilizations what Willa Cather and Edith Wharton found in France: a source of reverence, continuity, and tradition. Austin traveled to Mexico, seeking, as she always did, a culture tied to the land. At home in the politically minded Santa Fe, she and fellow residents—in tandem with archeologists—occupied themselves not simply with matters of race, rights, and economies, but with the broad questions of culture—that inescapable but "deeply compromised idea," as James Clifford has called it.[30] Culture might mean the best of France or any country in Europe or North America. It might mean the desire to see in Native peoples alternative origins for the nation, and when not origins, ethics and principles. The painter John Sloan, for instance, thought it his duty to spread "the consciousness of Indian art in America" because it "affords [a] means by which American artists and patrons of art can contribute to the culture of their own continent, to enrich the product and keep it American."[31] Like Sloan, Austin faced the unavoidable conundrum of definition and boundaries in which culture—always for her an amorphous entity—reflected shifting historical qualities that she ascribed or chose to see in Native peoples.

On the topic of culture, Austin offered her observations and intuitions in language not necessarily "literary" and sometimes masked as scientific, which editors asked her to make more accessible to ordinary readers. Austin saw her purpose from contradictory perspectives. The woman who took notes on Aztecs—as on the clothing of religious orders, Jewish rituals, dances performed at various pueblos, psychic phenomena, the lives of saints, and the habits of ghosts—strongly opposed the Chautauqua organization establishing a school in Santa Fe. Chautauqua programs, sponsored by women's clubs across the country, aimed to bring "culture" to rural areas. The issue became which culture? To Austin, Chautauqua symbolized canned or diluted European culture, what Sinclair Lewis in *Main Street* dismissed as "wind and chaff . . . and the laughter of yokels."[32] An affront to the cultures she had worked so hard to revive, Chautauqua seemed to threaten the ethos of Santa Fe. It never occurred to her that she had partly her own advertising to blame.

Nevertheless—as the earlier *Science Service* project suggests—Austin sought to bring methods of scientific inquiry to the reading public and, until she died, continued her efforts on behalf of what she considered neglected cultures. She offered advice to the educable Franklin D. Roosevelt, built a museum collection, created a curriculum for Indian arts and literature, and worked on a Social and Economic Constitution of the New Mexico Pueblo. A 1933 newspaper headline described her as "Mary Austin Little Mother to 350,000 Indians."[33] Delighting in such descriptions, Carl Van Vechten satirized her in *Spider Boy* (1928) as Marna Frost, who "stood nearly six feet tall [much taller than Austin herself] and was built proportionately. Her massive ankles were set on pedestal-like feet. Her face, clean-cut beneath piles of coarse red hair, streaked with iron-grey, resembled the face of a horse, her great Roman nose ploughing down between her furrowed cheeks. Rugged was the adjective that would have adequately described this woman of fifty, but from coast to coast in the homes of representatives and senators she was known as the Little Mother of the Indian. Usually a profanely abusive epithet preceded the diminutive adjective."[34]

Among Austin's collected correspondence is a letter countering this image. Sotero Ortiz wrote that his people had not forgotten her efforts on their behalf: "Oh no! Indeed not, we always think of our Friends those who are working with dealing and Pueblo land legislation, we accordingly authorize The American Indian Defense Association, The Indian Welfare Committee of the General Federation of Women's Club, and by their attorneys to take such steps as may be necessary and possible, to protect the rights of the various Pueblos."[35]

In 1930, Chief Standing Bear, who only three years before had pronounced that "*no one* is able to understand the Indian race like an Indian," sent Austin his book, *My People, the Sioux,* with this tribute: "I am doing this in an effort to show you my appreciation for the wonderful work you are doing in writing of the American Indian drama. For some time my niece, Warcaziwin, and myself have read your writings with more and more delight till now we seize upon everything from your pen regarding the native American."[36] His next letter requested that they exchange photographs.

Standing Bear recognized a kindred spirit in Austin, partly because her assumptions about race reflected his own. While she recognized distinctions among tribes, Austin tended to speculate about a generic "Indian," impelled by what she, and like-minded supporters, would have considered an enlightened attitude about race.[37] "By race," she writes in *Everyman's Genius,* "we do not mean what the anthropologists mean—if in the absence of any clear definition they know what they mean. We mean by race the social solidarity expressing the general sum of man's ancestral experience." A race is a "group having a common blood stream and a common societal relation, subject to a common environment for a period sufficient to produce reactions characteristic of that shared experience."[38] Her definition of *race* does not greatly differ from her definitions of *folk* or *regionalism*, except for the addition of "a common blood stream"; all three come into being and evolve in relationship to the environment. The editor of *The New Negro* (1925), Alain Locke, would echo Austin's theories when he described race operating as a tradition that changes through social interaction. At the same time she lectured about the beauty, the deeply spiritual nature of African American traditions, from which America must learn.[39]

Intolerance, Austin argues, results from interpreting "democracy as an obligation to be alike. It is only in such acceptance [of difference] . . . that we can reenter our early American dream of a unified people, made so by the uninhibited opportunity of becoming."[40] This statement is vintage Austin to the extent that it both signals and disclaims racial difference. Typically she writes that "Indian poetry is the key to Indian Design, perhaps to all art among peoples everywhere. . . . Poetry for primitive man is a thing done, precisely as a decoration on a water-jar is done: the abstraction of a human experience sketched upon the audience with the poet's self as the tool."[41] The description romanticizes her subject by assuming all Native Americans to be artists. At the same time, it makes an overly large claim for national, if not international, indebtedness to Indian culture. The editor of *The Atlantic Monthly* told her frankly that no one would accept the sentiments she attributed to "primitive" peoples: "a reader unfamiliar with records of this kind would not believe that the rude original could have been intended to convey ideas so expressive of civilized instincts." In a word, they were "incredible."[42]

Incredible or not, Austin's approach to abstract and representational projections in Native art agreed with progressive ethnology of the time, as did their applications to spiritual or psychological states. If they were incredible, how much did they differ from those of Carl Jung, who visited Taos in 1925? In *Man and His Symbols,* published the same year, Jung wrote:

> It is the role of religious symbols to give a meaning to the life of man. The Pueblo Indians believe that they are the sons of Father Sun, and this belief endows their life with a perspective (and a goal) that goes far beyond their limited existence. It gives them ample space for the unfolding of personality and permits them a full life as complete persons. Their plight is infinitely more satisfactory than that of a man in our own civilization who knows that he is (and will remain) nothing more than an underdog with no inner meaning to his life."[43]

Not only did Jung escape the kind of criticism leveled against Austin, his book of course had a profound influence on twentieth-century thought. Yet for all the attractiveness of his theories, he was far less intimate with Pueblo Indians than Austin, less knowledgeable, and perhaps the more "incredible." To a large extent, as neither would admit, the wishful comments of both Jung and Austin speak more to the era's spiritual vacuum after World War I than to any intrinsic qualities of American Indians.

D. H. Lawrence—whose own flight to Taos and to the waiting (but disappointed) arms of Mabel Dodge Luhan ended in frustration—spoke of

Western America as the one hope, the antithesis of a dead England or a puerile Australia, with India and other countries scarcely worth his attention. Desperately ill when he arrived in Taos, Lawrence felt no better there than elsewhere, and he found the land at once magnificent and horrible, empty space filled by mute and unredeemable Indians who defied him with silence. In a letter to Austin, Mabel described Lawrence as being "completely disconcerted by the Indians! He got all his ideas about them from reading Fennimore [*sic*] Cooper one winter. He says it's all wrong! He is quite put out about it! It's all a lie. That's what it is! Just a wish fulfillment! The Indians are evil. They are witchlike. They are full of hate. They are in opposition. . . . My dear! It is D. H. who is evil at times, witchlike & full of hate! As for opposition!!! He dies of Opposition. He can't be in the room with Indians."[44]

Finishing *Studies in Classic American Literature* (1923) at Taos and hating the women in his life he could not live without, Lawrence wrote: "White Americans do try hard to intellectualize themselves. Especially white women Americans. And the latest stunt is this 'savage stunt.'"[45] He expressed his disillusion in three short lines:

You and I, you pale-face
Pale-face you and I
Don't get on.[46]

Lawrence provides a cautionary tale about claiming what cannot be claimed, or expecting what cannot or should not be expected, above all about believing that anyone can hold the defining keys to lands or people.

Austin gleefully recalled playing Lady Macbeth, her hair streaming nearly to her knees as she clasped a carving knife between her breasts. She had more than a little of the actor in her and, to the chagrin of some, the temperament of a great leading lady. (She once asked Mabel Dodge Luhan to send her a Roman wreath to wear on "Empire Day.") A poet who met her at a literary tea in the 1920s remembered how she arrived, as if to say, "Let the festivities begin." She had secured her hair, roped like a French twist high in the back, with a great tortoise-shell comb and wore "a stunning costume of black lace and red."[47] Had Mabel been there, she would have laughed to see her friend's costume signaling her current passion for things Spanish, which in Santa Fe usually meant Spanish by way of Mexico.[48]

Austin's enthusiasm for what she called Spanish colonial arts went hand in hand with a study of regional cultures and the Pueblo Indians, and again, in these interests she was very much of her time. Ernest Hemingway, who found meaning in life through the rituals of bullfighting, once described his idea of heaven to F. Scott Fitzgerald as a big bull ring—and he the permanent possessor of two *barrera* seats. Edward MacDowell, George Gershwin, and Aaron Copeland incorporated folk themes into classical compositions; Julia Peterkin won a Pulitzer Prize for a novel written in Gullah dialect; and Diego Rivera and Frida Kahlo found international acclaim for folk-inspired narrative paintings, whether political, like many of Rivera's, or deeply personal and autobiographical, like Kahlo's. Between the two world wars, the interest in so-called primitive cultures extended far enough south for people to talk about a Mexican craze. Pundits such as Stuart Chase spoke glowingly of the "two Americas," the United States and Mexico.[49]

"Can this possibly be North America?" John Gunther asked in 1947 about New Mexico, where "ninety-eight per cent of the population spoke Spanish" and "no word of English might be heard from one year to the next."[50] Austin might have said the same about Lone Pine, which in her time there had been two-thirds Mexican. While learning Spanish, she explored the neighborhood around Señora Romero's house and cooked Mexican dinners that people remembered thirty years later. Books like *Isidro* suggest how much Austin cared and wrote about Spanish mores in California. Her professional study of Spanish arts began in earnest when, years later, she met a young man at the University of New Mexico named Arthur Campa. The son of a Mexican-born American missionary, Campa was born in Guaymas, Mexico, but was raised in Albuquerque after his father, a commissioned lieutenant, died in the Mexican Revolution of 1910.

Having learned of Campa's work collecting folk songs and plays, Austin initiated the relationship in 1929. Over the years, she watched this diffident young man become a husband, father, and expert in a field he largely defined with his monumental survey of the region, *Hispanic Culture in the Southwest* (1979). At first, she thought him a translator for her own work and general errand boy who could do preliminary research or price Dictaphones. When Campa's senior professor disabused her, she quickly realized they could work together. "If you tell me the sort of material that you want," he wrote, "we can begin trading any time."[51] Campa treated Mary Austin with respect. Knowing that her health made it difficult for her to travel, he arranged for practicing artists to visit her in Santa Fe and offered to record songs for her in the southern part of the state. She returned his courtesy by encouraging him to take graduate courses toward a doctorate at Columbia University, where he studied lyric folk poetry and theater, subjects that she could have imagined specializing in herself. She hoped, for example, to build—with money from Alice Lewisohn, of the Neighborhood Playhouse—a movable stage along the lines of the traditional "Corrales" or street theaters (or medieval English theaters), where the religious and secular dramas Campa discovered could be performed. (The Huntington Library in San Marino, California, contains a wealth of plays and poems he and Austin collected.) Dedicated to training people in the puppet theater, Campa asked Austin to intercede on his behalf with Senator Bronson M. Cutting, the publisher of the *Santa Fe New Mexican* and *El Nuevo Mexicano,* the foremost Spanish-language newspaper. Cutting supported many of Campa's projects, as he supported New Mexican folk art in general. Austin liked Cutting, first because he enjoyed her cooking, and second because he talked openly about affairs in Washington, which made her feel like a political insider. In a businesslike letter in which she urged him to run for president, she added this playful PS: "I think you should know, being as you are a shy man, that I have changed my style of hair-dressing. Where I used to have a thousand pins to keep up my wealth of gorgeous locks, I now have only one pin which can easily be drawn by that brave who deserves the fair."[52]

There was apparently no flirtation between Campa and Austin, as their slightly formal, always courteous and professional correspondence makes clear. The situation suited both: Campa had the academic credentials in languages, music, and anthropology, and Austin complementary qualities, including her reputation and connections to people like Cutting. "If I am not going to continue this work in your cooperation," Campa wrote in 1931, "I do not propose to remain in it. I feel that you have done already so much work that it is a waste of time to begin anew with one [a fellow colleague at the University of New Mexico] who has done no work whatsoever in research."[53] Austin had documented the commingling of Mexican and Indian traditions for her 1919 survey of Taos, a comprehensive field of study Campa wanted to pursue. "I have found that the chants sung in New Mexico called *alabados* are the same thing sung in Spain," he wrote. "Some of the old folk-songs which I thought were the product of Indian influence are nothing more than Spanish folksongs. . . . We shall speak about that later."[54] During one summer, Campa traveled nearly seven thousand miles—alone—around New Mexico. A man like Daniel MacDougal of seemingly inexhaustible energy, he lobbied businesses for money to fund fiestas, wrote for the *New Mexico Folklore Society,* negotiated with authors and publishers for rights to songs and plays, and pushed to add Spanish folk arts to the New Mexican school curriculum, which Austin, who recommended experiential learning, bilingual teachers, *and* good ventilation, vigorously seconded. Recounting his activities does not do Campa justice. A warm, dignified man, he mentored a generation of modern Mexican American scholars, first in New Mexico and later in Colorado.

The collaboration with Campa reflects a pattern in these years, as Austin sought creative partnerships for fellowship assuredly, but also because her energy diminished at a time of widening interests and demands. The Society for the Revival of Spanish Colonial Arts (later incorporated as the Spanish Colonial Arts Society) is a case in point.[55] What began as an interest became an institution. Not surprisingly, the society's mission recalls that of the Indian Arts Fund: "to preserve to New Mexico many of its ancient arts and crafts and also to provide the means by which the native Spanish speaking population can utilize its spare hours in gainful employment." To spur the revival of traditional crafts, the society sent instructors to schools and communities and offered prizes for new work that most conformed to old models. It sponsored fiestas and theatricals designed to foster racial harmony and restore to the Spanish people opportunities that "we Americans," Austin wrote, "stupidly destroyed."[56] Austin, who saw few of the arts practiced when she first visited New Mexico—Campa reported that weaving had disappeared from the southern part of the region—lived to see Chimayó and Santa Fe become centers of weaving, as members of the society expanded a market for Spanish folk art by means of individual dealers and extensive advertising.

In Frank Applegate, a painter who also did ceramics and printmaking, Austin had a companion and colleague as committed to Indian and Spanish colonial arts as Arthur Campa and herself. This relationship differed dramatically from the other. A friend described the Midwestern Applegate as having "a large, solid, simplicity about him," which may well be accurate, though in some pictures he resembles a healthy Sherlock Holmes.[57] Applegate and his wife, Alta, were ready for any adventure. They first came to Santa Fe for a vacation, and camped out in the Cassidys' orchard, when the town had dirt roads and the houses no street numbers. After a week, they decided to stay in the Southwest. For five months in 1923 they lived on a Hopi reservation, where he studied and taught methods of pottery making; two years later, they returned for a month to the reservation, accompanied by the artists Andrew Dasburg and Jozef Bákos. During these visits Applegate gathered material that would become *Indian Stories from the Pueblos* (1929) and *Native Tales of New Mexico* (1932), illustrated with his own watercolors.

Soon after settling in Santa Fe, Applegate began his study of adobe building for the house he and Alta would pack with Spanish American antiques, handcrafted chairs and cabinets, rugs, tapestries, and hammered tin. Austin thought that local craftsmen preferred to sell their goods to Applegate because he appreciated both their artistry and humanity. His career later took another turn when he packed in ceramics for woodcarving and painting. Applegate's friendship with Austin began with his showing her how to restore a carved figure of Our Lady of Innocence thick with garish house paint. She consulted him when building her house and, though he objected to John Meem's design, he contributed some of its hand-hewn beams and corbels.

Applegate's efforts paralleled Austin's throughout the brief years of a close friendship. In 1924 they had been among the first members of the Indian Pottery Fund, also called the Pueblo Pottery Fund, organized to acquire the best examples of Indian art and keep them in the area. When Applegate took over as vice chairman and curator and Austin as chairman of the Spanish Colonial Arts Society, the two managed to preserve the "Lourdes of America," El Santuario de Chimayó, entrusted since 1929 to the archdiocese of Santa Fe. Their efforts led to a triumphant rebirth for the tiny church that still draws thousands of believers and secular tourists. According to legend, a priest had asked the people of the upper Santa Cruz, after the 1837 Chimayó rebellion, to build a chapel on a specific spot. They refused and the priest disappeared, whereupon a foot appeared on the spot, protruding from a cottonwood, the eventual site of El Santuario de Chimayó. The reported miracle did not end there, however. The church contained a carved wooden image of the Christ child, whose feet the parishioners shod with children's shoes. Every day the statue required a new pair, so worn were they from his nightly round of blessings.

Not everything worked out to Austin and Applegate's satisfaction. In 1930, with their prodding, the Spanish Colonial Arts Society opened a shop in the Sena Plaza, which sold only Spanish revival items: furniture, chests, rugs, blankets, carvings, ornamental tin and iron, painted glass, embroideries, and toys. Brimming with goods, the building looked like an overfilled house, with a kiva fireplace and small bedroom, decorated with weavings, *bultos* (hand-carved wooden statues of saints), and *retablos* (religious paintings on wood). The shop, in addition to serving local artists, shipped goods through mail order and to galleries like the Indian Trading Post in Chicago. But because its wares were less popular with tourists than Indian souvenirs, the shop relied on mail-order demand, which involved costly shipping and breakage. Austin's protestations notwithstanding, customers also complained about the quality of goods. The doors closed in October 1933.

To longtime residents of Santa Fe, the efforts of the two friends sometimes seemed unwarranted interference bordering on a sanctimonious "takeover" of the town. Their patronage certainly had unforeseen ironies. Applegate introduced Austin, for example, to the artist José Dolores Lopez, a member of the Penitente *morada*. With their encouragement, Lopez decreased his production of art to concentrate on chip carving and items suited for ubiquitous, middle-class homes: lazy Susans, record racks, and unpainted Catholic saints. Austin herself, who advocated "high end" craftsmanship, hired him to make screen doors.

Austin and Applegate's business arrangements with the Pueblo, Spanish, and Mexican craftsmen resembled those of the White sisters, who devoted their efforts to good causes with similarly mixed results. In Santa Fe, dubbed the "City of ladies," power came as elsewhere from money, whether railroad and newspaper fortunes in the Whites' case or smaller inheritances as with someone like Elsie Sergeant, a fellow graduate of Bryn Mawr College and close friend of the Whites until they fought about Indian politics. The "City of ladies" moniker reflects the large number of mostly single, often well-to-do women who exercised their freedom in Santa Fe and used their wealth or brains to make shoppers out of tourists and producers or dealers out of Native peoples.[58] By and large these women shared aims and strategies, despite divisions brought on by the Bursum Bill and other political issues. Their activities went beyond local charities or the founding of institutions to a kind of collective vision of Santa Fe as the flagship community and the Southwest as the future of a misguided America, which for many in New Mexico included Mexico itself.

There were no easy answers to any questions about culture, and no reliable guides. When Austin lived in Santa Fe she had access to the best ethnologists and archeologists available. For probably good reason she doubted their wisdom, not simply because she begrudged their authority or doubted their science, but because they themselves differed about the issues they chewed and could not digest. This would be true of Franz Boas's star student, Edward Sapir, who sought to separate class from culture. Or, again,

Carl Jung, whose speculations must have seemed empty to those grounded in the local lore and having extensive personal connection with the Pueblo Indians. Pundits like Stuart Chase, who in *Men and Machines* (1929) compared the lives of a Park Avenue banker, a Samoan, and a clerk from White Plains, New York, came through the region claiming authority on far too little knowledge. Austin struggled with her own biases, sometimes by damning those of her opponents. Despite her criticism of the anthropologists—or rivalry with them—her activities also pulled together the best of current anthropological work, which she presented in articles and books as a tacit complement to her own. Austin might be seen in these matters as the engine driving the machine, and few at the time would have disagreed about the importance of her efforts.

In yet another of her stories that reads like a parable, "Blue Roses," Austin tells of rival Spanish traditions in which two women retain their identities as they form a joint identity. Assunta Martinez makes fantastic feather roses dyed blue according "to a recipe which she had from her mother's mother, who had it from hers, straight down the Thalascan line"; and Doña Josefa De Vargas—"alas for the decay of the Arts!"—makes realistic-looking roses from tissue paper bought from a mail-order catalog.[59] After Doña Josefa's grandson dies in the final days of the First World War, the women make their own truce, which reflects the integrity of separate traditions and the necessity of change. Each will pass on her art to someone in the younger generation; together they plan a memorial wreath of red, white, and blue roses that patriotically threads their arts. Austin wanted this kind of forgiving generosity among races and individuals. "Blue Roses" suggests that her missing questions or downright contradictions reflect the hope of something better in a world given to misunderstandings, strife, and bigotry. As she wrote to Daniel MacDougal about *The American Rhythm:* "What I am really interested in isn't the theory of rhythm, but being able to experience rhythm in all its varieties. I like to dive into a rhythmic stream like a fish into the gulf current and go where it takes me. . . . Best of all I like to flash into the life rhythm of some other human being, and find myself suddenly knowing all about what it was, is now and will be. Then I like to repeat some of these experiences by writing books or poems about them."[60]

eleven

LAST YEARS

1929–1934

I don't like to HAVE TO be nice, it is more enjoyable when it is
spontaneous.

MARY AUSTIN TO FLORENCE HOOVER (A BOOKING AGENT)
6 May 1932

ALBERT BENDER, THE AFFABLE, GNOMELIKE chairman of the California
Book Club, sent Austin this advice about Virginia and Ansel Adams in
1929: "There is only one thing about which you should not be unaware,"
Bender told her, "and that is their appetite. Please do not let them go hungry. They need food every hour in large quantities, and if you have no mortgage on your house now, you will have at the time of their departure. If the
circulatory system permits, I think a special pipe should connect with
Ansel's room, through which a cup of coffee could be furnished to him at
any hour of the day or night."[1] Austin already had some idea of Ansel's appetite, if not Virginia's. When Bender determined that " 'the greatest writer
in the West' should collaborate with 'the greatest photographer' of his acquaintance," he had escorted Adams to Taos and Santa Fe in 1927—the year
of Adams's first commercially signed photograph.[2] On that visit Austin
served them a mountain of homemade doughnuts.

The Adamses visited this time as newlyweds, having married just the
year before after a shaky courtship. A tall, long-nosed, balding man, with
a ready smile that endeared him to women, Adams had his career all before him, although—trained as a pianist—he still wavered between music
and photography. Virginia, an avid gardener, would study voice, raise two
sons, and manage the family studio at Yosemite, which she transformed
with Navajo rugs, classical music, art books, and one of her husband's

folding photographic screens. In spare moments she worked to arrange lectures for Austin that would pay for her return visits to California.

Austin and Adams had taken to each other immediately, in part because she delighted in his calling himself a pagan, and also because they both loved Albert Bender, a man of great tact and generosity. Bender had sent Austin money when it seemed that she might require a second abdominal surgery to correct the first. She refused his offer, then relented. She needed the rest it could provide, though she feared she might not be able to pay him back.[3] He preferred not to have it repaid. Now, as Virginia listened, her husband and hostess boiled over with plans: first, a book on Spanish colonial arts, with Austin and Applegate collaborating on the text; second, the book that would become *Taos Pueblo* (1930). Over the next few years, Austin and Adams would contemplate a joint book on Yosemite, with her foreword; another on little Spanish towns of New Mexico; and yet another on *santos*, the wooden religious figures that were Frank Applegate's passion because they personified human hopes and prayers.[4]

The collaboration with Adams had its problems. With lectures at Yale and in New York, and the demands of both her novel *Starry Adventure* and her autobiography, Austin found little time to devote to a new project. *Taos Pueblo*, which they began first, stalled as Adams worked on photographs for Applegate and struggled to please Austin with dust-jacket portraits for *Earth Horizon*.[5] When Austin looked at his photographs of her, she did not know how to respond—or, rather, she did. "I dare say you can take away that dreadful smirk, and the drawn look about the mouth, but the carriage of the head, with the face thrust down and forward, and the slumped shoulders are not only not characteristic of me, but contradict the effect it is still necessary for me to make on my public. A photo for publicity must be something other than a likeness; it must convey something of the personal drive, the energetic index, the impact of the whole personality as it affects the public." Punctured vanity aside, she still managed to end her letter on a friendlier note: "But wait until I get home and show these to several of my friends."[6]

The correspondence is a tribute to Adams's good nature, and to his and Virginia's affection for Austin, despite the times when she scolded him or threatened to withdraw from further collaboration. An episode with Yale University Press proved a major test. In principle, Yale agreed to publish her collaborative book with Applegate on Spanish arts, tentatively called *Spanish Colonial Arts in America*, for which Adams had taken photographs in the spring of 1929 when he and Virginia occupied Austin's guest apartment.

Austin made decisions about the illustrations because Applegate felt over his head. With Applegate sidelined, Adams began dealing directly with the Yale editor. Austin interpreted his initiative as unprofessional meddling. "No publisher cares to do business on any proposition in which there is a division of labor," she scolded. Besides, he had incontinently revealed "the whole story about the Taos book and a second book with Applegate." (The Depression, not Adams, led the press to renege on its agreement.) They could not proceed if anything of the sort happened again: "You must realize that the illustrator is always a secondary consideration with the publisher. The contract is made with the author, and then it is up to the author to use such influence as he may have to persuade the publisher to agree to a certain type and treatment of illustration. Until that time the intrusion of the illustrator between the publisher and the author is in nearly every case absolutely fatal, besides in the case being a great discourtesy both to myself and Mr. Applegate."[7] Making sure he understood, she followed up with a telegram: "DON'T SEND ANYTHING TO YALE OR WRITE TO THEM—MARY AUSTIN."[8] After several more exchanges, the intervention of the editor and Applegate, and a gift from Adams, the tempest subsided, with Austin sending a thank-you note for "the only Indian portrait I ever had which I would feel willing to put up in my house."[9]

Adams, who had come to the Southwest seeking reputation and fortune, handled every bit of the production and marketing for *Taos Pueblo*. The book sold entirely by subscription, and the one complimentary copy that Adams sent to Fred Hodge at Austin's insistence cost *him* forty dollars and his time. Austin, who received a hundred dollars up front and over five hundred in all, promised to autograph copies. Adams's pricing of the book staggered her: "Two hundred and fifty copies at fifty dollars a copy seems to me beyond belief, and a hundred copies at seventy-five dollars a copy leaves me gasping. You will have to make your own decisions. I am quite sure to be satisfied with whatever you decide." The book sold for seventy-five dollars. She sent her love, to be followed by another shipment of blue cornmeal.[10] On receiving the finished book, Austin wrote: "I agree with you that it is a superb piece of workmanship. I think, however, that we can do a little better next time by getting together on the subject before we begin. I think I should see your photographs before writing the text, so that between us, nothing should be left out. I would like the book to have an equal value for its content and its quality as a piece of book making."[11]

Despite being warned by the Indians about the devils he might let loose, Adams had taken pictures for *Taos Pueblo* during a sandstorm; within hours he was bent double from appendicitis. Back in San Francisco, he worked in a makeshift darkroom in his parents' basement, using an old eight-by-ten-inch view camera as an enlarger. His light source was the sun, "captured via a hole punched through the wall, with an aluminum reflector positioned outside to direct the sunshine through a diffusing screen and into the enlarger."[12] Adams made 1,296 prints for the book. Albert Bender bought ten copies. Austin had worried that their subjects, wooed by movie directors like Robert Flaherty of *Nanook of the North* fame, would associate photographs with film rights and demand prohibitive fees.[13] Tony Lujan—his photograph ranks among Adams's most striking images—negotiated for Adams to have unlimited access to the Pueblo for a fee of twenty-five dollars and a copy of the book. At Austin's suggestion, Adams dedicated *Taos Pueblo,* his first book, "To Our Friends at Taos Pueblo To Whose Interested & Intelligent Cooperation Is Owed The Historic and Human Authenticity of This Book." In spirit, however, he dedicated the book to Albert Bender, whose support had made it possible.

Taos Pueblo contains only twelve black-and-white photographs in Adams's developing style of high, chiaroscuro contrasts. Although the quality of the photographs may be uneven, the book is, as Adams called it, "gorgeous"—over a foot in width and seventeen inches in length and printed on coated rag paper that has a warm, earthy tone. Due to Depression shortages, he insured the specially made paper for a thousand dollars. Adams spoke of Austin's writing as the dominant feature of the book, and to the extent that her text precedes his photographs and ushers readers into the subject he may have been right. She begins familiarly by placing the reader in the landscape and emphasizing the flow of water:

> Pueblo Mountain stands up over Taos pueblo and Taos water comes down between the two house-heaps, North house and South house [the subject of Adams's photographs], with a braided motion, swift and clear and flowing. As you look at it from the south entrance to the valley, Pueblo Mountain, bare topped above, and below shaggy with pine, has the crouched look of a sleeping animal, the great bull buffalo, turning his head away and hunching his shoulders.[14]

Once again, Austin circles to the present by way of history and myth:

> Should you happen upon the pueblo in the one hour of evening bustle, when the men are coming in from the field, young people lingering on the

bridge between the house-heaps, the *pregonero* draped and authoritative as any Roman senator announcing the day's news and advices of the day to come, from North house or South house—Hlauuma, Hlaukwima—you become aware of something subtly excluding in the unfamiliar speech rhythms, the alien tonality, and the utter want of revealing response in the listening citizens. . . . Everywhere peace, impenetrable timelessness of peace, as though the pueblo and all it contains were shut in a glassy fourth dimension, near and at the same time inaccessibly remote.[15]

Capturing, as Adams believed, the essence of his photographs, Austin describes the movements in Taos ceremonies and outsiders' perception of them, which she calls "the White man's favorite myths about Indians." She has in mind, for example, those of buried treasure and secret, sexual rites. At the same time she perpetuates a myth of her own, that the Pueblos will remain what they have always been: "Tap-rooted, the charm of Taos should endure for another hundred years, even against the modern obsession for destructive change."[16]

Plans for a smaller edition of *Taos Pueblo* and a series of books in the same vein ended abruptly when Frank Applegate died from heart failure on 13 February 1931. He had come home from a rehearsal of *The Monkey's Paw* (his first acting role had been in Hal Bynner's *Cake*) and fallen asleep in his chair beside the fire. Austin spoke of a premonition that something catastrophic would interrupt their work: "So I insisted on Frank's committing [to paper] all that he had learned about the technique of the Spanish arts. I did not imagine that anything would happen to Frank, who was apparently so hale and strong; I thought it much more likely that it would happen to me." When she said her annual goodbye for her "usual trip East," she teased him about kissing her good-bye, "thinking it would be a comfort to him to recall it if anything did happen."[17]

"I am overwhelmed with grief," she wrote to Adams from New York, where she had gone to lecture.[18] Another friend described visiting her and never seeing "such desolation, such a lack of all that human contacts give us. The house seemed to extend on into no place, but cried out. Mary sat in the midst of it a monument crumbling, and trembling, stuttering and were it another I'd have said on the verge of tears. But Mary's tears have come so much oftener from hard anger . . . that it would be difficult for her to weep. . . . She's afraid, and that is the desperate sadness of her state."[19] Somehow Austin found the strength to reach out to the Applegate's daughter, Betty:

All the way down from New York I would look out of the car window and see interesting things and realize that the reason why they gave me pain was that I knew I couldn't go back and talk them over with your father as I have done so many years. . . . I know how it was with me when I lost my father, although I was younger than you are. It was many years before I lost the need of talking things over with him. And then I only lost it because I got to the place where I realized that a sympathetic Father is so rare a gift that one must keep on being thankful for it, for him, even after he has gone away. . . . That is the only way you can keep the sense of how wise and sane and tender he was, how understanding, always with you, by being thankful for it, by realizing it more and more, now that you are without it, how much it meant. . . . Grief is hard to bear sometimes, so hard that many people make the mistake of trying to forget it, put it out of their minds and hearts. But it is really the only thing that keeps the heart sensitive to the realization of the indestructible quality of love and understanding. You must not let your sorrow make you bitter and insensitive. Let it keep you warm . . . to the things that distinguished your father from other men, his wonderful kindness, his unfailing sense of justice, his sympathy for men different from himself.[20]

Austin credited the Applegates, her neighbors on Camino del Monte Sol, with keeping her alive after her abdominal operation in 1926. Indeed, she thought of the Applegates as her family in Santa Fe, including no one else except her niece. "Frank was more to me than either of my brothers had ever been," she wrote (echoing Tennyson's *In Memoriam*) in an excised passage of her autobiography.[21] Applegate looked after her house and garden when she lectured, paid her taxes when she forgot, worked to have her assessment lowered, acted as her rental agent for an apartment attached to her house, arranged to sell her Model T Ford, and lived as she did for their common interests. Frank's wife, Alta, who reminded Austin of her long-dead sister Jennie, described Austin herself as sweet, kind, generous, and sympathetic, obviously appreciating a side of her that many did not. Betty, chauffeuring Austin in the summers, became a surrogate sister to Mary Hunter.

There are always ironies when it comes to families. Applegate seemed to Austin like a brother; to his own daughter he was distant and unsupportive. According to a cousin, Betty "never had a kind word for her father." In an "unsettled" family, Applegate's constant organizing, theater work, research and writing, not to mention painting—and he was a talented painter—may have put a barrier between father and daughter.[22]

Despite her hard-won wisdom, Austin found it impossible to follow her own advice to Betty about death and sorrow. The director of *The Monkey's Paw,* Philip Stevenson, tried to console the consoler, reminding Austin how Applegate would talk of her "with great affection, and with regret that you should have been ill in New York. He said he hoped you would be able to give up lecturing and come back to Santa Fe where you had been so well, especially lately. He looked forward to your return. . . . In short, he was entirely and typically himself—concerned for those he cared about, ambitious, energetic, helpful and thoughtful."[23] Austin asked if Applegate's ashes might be saved until she died so that they could be mixed together and scattered. (She would make the same request to Hal Bynner, who helped her weather the dark months after Applegate's death.) Alta gently rejected the plan. Austin perhaps had in mind the Hopi tradition of laying their dead children in "rock crevices with a guide-string pointing the way to the pueblo, so that they may find their way home to wait till their mothers are ready to hold out a hand to them on the way to the under-world. Would it not make death less terrifying to feel, the next moment after, a small familiar hand slipped into yours?"[24]

Acting as Applegate's literary executor, Austin intended to finish their project on Spanish arts as well as two incomplete manuscripts, one a collection of stories, the other a book on architecture. This was more than homage or a labor of love. To some extent she saw these books as her creation, because she thought she had taught her friend how to write. "I try not to impose upon him any bias for a more formal method of expression," she had told another writer, the poet Arthur Davison Ficke (of the Spectra Hoax). "The only thing I am afraid of is that he will have too much success just at the start, which will check his development."[25] Austin asked Adams, who was to provide 130 photographs for the projects, if he could send her an informal shot of Applegate. Alta promised to help with the illustrations and indexes.[26]

Austin lost in Applegate someone who shared her politics and her artistic values. He helped in the fight against Chautauqua and for the Spanish Colonial Arts Society, and he spoke against the erection of "The Pioneer Woman," a monument of "indifferent" or "sentimental" character that failed to honor the real, the Spanish pioneers. Applegate jokingly offered ten dollars toward a fund to keep the statue out of town. Above all they shared a common predilection for spiritual belief or aspiration.[27] Open like Austin to the unconventional, Applegate had flirted with the theories of the charismatic psychologist-philosopher Alfred R. Orage. An editor of

The New Age until 1923, Orage retired to raise funds for the mystic George Gurdjieff's institute in New York. Already in those days Santa Fe attracted people whose religious passions ran over into new fads of "awareness," which might be confused with crystals or peyote. Hal Bynner mocked any kind of spiritualism but particularly despised Orage, whom he called a "highly polished and first-class con man" specializing in incontrovertible jargon. Applegate, more a spiritual dabbler, fell for the con artist while Austin, like Bynner, did not. Bynner scoffed at Orage the man and at his "New Age" message. He described one evening when Orage "mentioned that literature is only important in so far as the writer succeeds in conveying what he wants to the group he intends to reach." Bynner remembered that "Mary Austin challenged Orage repeatedly but without too much heat [because of Applegate's feelings], saying that once upon a time she had easily reached a large *Ladies Home Journal* audience, but that now only dire need of the 1,200 dollars she had received for a recent article had led her to return to that large audience. She said that she would rather not debauch herself by writing for such audiences. She would sell her body but that she wouldn't get as much for it. We all agreed."[28]

In the late 1920s, Austin's circle of literary friends and acquaintance widened. She reached out to writers like Floyd Dell, a radical journalist associated with *The Masses* who had asked her to recommend American books for Russians and whose pamphlet on marriage she applauded; also to Vachel Lindsay, another midwesterner famous for mystical visions and his "Higher Vaudeville" recitations of poems. Lindsay, who visited her in 1929, took his own life two years later by drinking Lysol. She had also come to know Ernest Thompson Seton—a brother-in-law of the San Francisco lawyer and Carmel founder Frank Powers—who created Seton Village, a community just six miles from Santa Fe dedicated to training Boy Scouts, Campfire Girls, and members of his own organization, the Woodcraft League.

Others reached out to her, and no one responded to letters more generously than Austin, who wrote to almost any stranger and to anyone in distress. She gave advice, counseled, and did what she could to console or thank total strangers, many of whom insisted that she had changed, if not saved, their lives. The Russian immigrant author of *The Promised Land* (1912), Mary Antin, wrote to say: "It is almost like talking to myself to talk to you, because I have so long taken you into my inmost confidence, referring my great problems to you, inwardly; especially my professional problems on their spiritual side." She wished to address her directly "instead of mentally asking myself what would Mary Austin think."[29] Antin confided in Austin about the collapse of her marriage, which she blamed on the war (her husband was German), and her health. For the past nine years, Antin told her, she had fought off madness through the power of prayer.

None of these friendships approached the intimacy of Austin's relationship with Applegate, though Hal Bynner, whom she exasperated and amused, helped to fill the void. "I have thought many times that one of the finest gratuities of fate to me is your being here," she told Bynner, "and that we should so genuinely like each other."[30] As for Applegate's death, it was unbearable but not absolute. His spirit would find a way to get through to them to complete his work, she assured Alta and of course herself. In *The Land of Journeys' Ending,* Austin had written that "the dead are spoken of as 'Those who have gone away,' and it is wholly consistent with the notion of the easy flow of life that they may come back again."[31]

The idea of life after death lies at the heart of her book, *Experiences Facing Death* (1931), in which she asserts that there is no such thing as death, that life goes "on and on, untouchably, beyond both hope and fear." "If the dead be truly dead," Winnenáp had once asked her, "why should they still be walking in my heart?"[32] *Experiences Facing Death* is a personal and belligerent book—an "I ain't a arguin' with you, I'm just a tellin' you" kind of book. The copy that Austin wrote for the dust jacket reads: "I don't see why the public should invariably suppose that sexual indiscretions are the only proper material for confessions. Most Americans are more reticent, and possibly more dishonest about their attitude toward death and the hereafter than they are toward any other personal concern." She added: "This is a purely personal document, and the public be damned." Believing that death, like life, needed to be learned, Austin had already damned the publisher's reader who found her manuscript too obtuse: "I am extraordinarily worried by your Reader's Report which you sent me. I have not the least notion what it is about. . . . If however readers are as much confused about the meaning of my book as this one seems to be, I can't advise you to publish it. . . . I think we must have a reading paragraph by paragraph so that I can get some notion of where I have omitted important explanations. I should prefer a reader . . . not wholly unacquainted with recent changes in our concepts of space and time."[33]

The narrative, tracing her thoughts as she lay between intervals of pain, becomes an extended essay on consciousness, its awakening, workings, and mysterious extensions. By offering herself as subject, Austin rules out potential dialogue: she experienced what she experienced and challenges scientists to explain it. She recounts the episode at about age five when she perceived, for a blinding moment of consciousness, a magical unity among the earth, sky, the foxglove at her feet, and herself the child. "God" she came to realize, was "the Universal Consciousness" out of which her "own consciousness stems."[34] The episode she describes is common enough. Ellen Glasgow, after learning of the death of her lover, tried to make herself "part of the grass and the wind and the spirit that moved round them, and in them." Just at the moment of giving up, she had a revelation. The golden August light streamed through her as if she became something outside herself: "Spirit? Matter? Imagination?" It did not matter. The vision sustained her a lifetime.[35] Zora Neale Hurston describes a similar epiphany in *Their Eyes Were Watching God* (1937), as young Janie, on the verge of womanhood, gazes at a pear tree: "The thousand sister-calyxes arch to meet the love embrace and the ecstatic shiver of the tree from root to tiniest branch creaming in every blossom and frothing with delight. So this was a marriage! She had been summoned to behold a revelation."[36]

Austin differs from Glasgow and Hurston by wanting an explanation that bridges faith and reason. She cites mentors as different as William James and Fred Hodge, along with Cardinal Merry del Val, who introduced her to Mother Veronica of the Blue Nuns, who in turn taught her how to pray; even a swami she met in England (but not the mystic Evelyn Underhill, whom she also knew); and Walter Prince, who used her as a medium. In the end, however, she is left with her own experience and its knotted contradictions. "I was a little puzzled by your comment on the Death book," she told Hal Bynner, "and what you meant by putting the character in it in a novel, because I didn't know there were any characters in it. I thought there was only Death and I."[37] There are several ironies here, not least that someone who sought to popularize science disowns it and offers her personal testimony as if preaching from the pulpit.

Austin nevertheless scoffs at table rapping and crystal-ball gazing, albeit she happily experimented with both and wrote a script titled "The Astral Experiences of J. Emory Pottle." If a leading socialist and five-time presidential candidate like Eugene Debs came back, she said, he would neither haunt a house nor answer silly questions in the back parlors of pseudointellectuals. Instead he would exercise his powers to help "the poor, the underprivileged, dumb of mind and yearning of heart."[38] As her reference to Debs suggests, Austin's understanding of religion had a social impetus. She believed religion should help better the world in a large systemic way, and her belief, ironically, leads back to science or at least to the sociology of religion. "Jesus taught that the personal relation of man to God should be reorganized, should be reborn," she wrote in "Do We Need a New Religion?" "But nowhere is there any suggestion of the pattern of social or political reformation which might be expected to follow."[39] She leaves her facing of death in a similarly indefinite or reflective key. "It seems likely now that I shall have from a half-score to a score . . . [of years left] and I am consoled of my secret apprehension of coming to the end of adventures. . . . There will be things yet to be done, and the stuff that we work in will be the utterly familiar and still mysterious and exciting stuff of ourselves."[40]

In her understandable struggle with matters of religion, Austin sounds like a latter-day, more confessional Matthew Arnold, the Victorian critic who, like her, hoped for better social leadership from the church and defined his God in terms of a force not ourselves that somehow makes for righteousness. But Austin goes further, envisioning a god both pantheistic and personal, whom she can summon by prayer. In a 1933 essay, "What Religion Means to Me," Austin writes: "What the Indian believes is very much what I have always believed, that there is a power without us working inwardly to correlate all our experiential activities. That power is friendly and approachable, that it responds to direct efforts at intercourse and can be depended upon in a general way to give us what we ask of it."[41] Faith defies logic, not to mention syntax, and Austin could think of God as a member of her family, someone she knew and liked to talk about. As she explained to one correspondent: "Every day of my life I connect up with God and get charged with creative energy. . . . A woman whose love life had been as unhappy as mine, who had no religion, would have gone mad or committed suicide. I have been very near the last several times. But my religion has kept me occupied. . . . Knowing God is as studious a business as knowing electricity."[42] Mary Antin, who asked her help to become "more effectively alive," and Charles Battell Loomis, an English writer considering suicide, were just two of a number of correspondents for whom Austin served as a kind of lay minister or spiritual adviser.[43] Austin also addressed Unitarian ministers at their Middle States Conference and published in journals like *Religion Today.* One of her most popular lectures bore the title "The Meaning of the Southwest, and Modern Mysticism." After Vachel Lindsay died in 1929, his wife wrote Austin as if she were speaking to herself, trying to sort out the circumstances that defeated her husband and her own coping: "I am almost afraid to think of him very much, lest it trouble his sleep—as one fears to look at a sleeping child, whatever love may desire, for fear there may be an awakening in darkness, with a cry before the full hour of morning. And yet, how think of anything else?"[44]

Austin had long been seen as someone willing to say what other people did not dare. In 1922, for instance, Frank Gelett Burgess asked her to speak at the Authors' League Fellowship about censorship in response to John S. Summer of the Society for the Suppression of Vice: "I know this is not great pleasure I am offering you, but I am in hopes that you may conceive it in some sense a pious duty toward Literature, or even toward Liberty in general."[45] In 1930, Ezra Pound wrote with uncharacteristic deference, asking whether she thought it "possible for someone like yourself, who has the ear of the public," to criticize Columbia University president Dr. Nicholas Murray Butler's oversight of the Carnegie Peace Foundation.[46] Austin became a recognized force in an extraordinary number of fields. With an honorary degree from Mills College in 1929; an invitation from the Mexican government to address the Conference on Cultural Relations in Mexico City; her election to the Literary Council of the Author's League of America, which included F. Scott Fitzgerald, George Gershwin, Ernest Hemingway, Rockwell Kent, Eugene O'Neill, Carl Sandburg, and Owen Wister; and to a council that encompassed the American Game Protection Association, the American Society of Landscape Architects, the Camp Fire Club of America, and the National Council of Parks—all begging her services— it is no wonder that she believed what her editors proclaimed: that Mary Austin was the most intellectual woman in America, or, as she informed her brother's attorney, among the top nine in the world.

When, several months after Applegate's death, Austin held a writing class at her house, the community rallied around her. One woman who participated, Henriette Harris, described "a circle around the library, fire crackling—no, there was no fire, come to think of it, but it was warm." About thirty people came, Hal Bynner arriving last. Bynner took a seat where Austin always sat, on a bench by the window, then, as Harris remembered, "by some queer freak of nature, she almost wept! Wasn't that insane?" Harris wondered whether she actually liked Austin more than she disliked her. That evening especially, Austin treated them as if they were fifth-graders, and when no one gave satisfactory answers "she proceeded to lay down the law! It was like old times." Austin did not disappoint her. "If I were to write an article for the *Saturday Evening Post*," she announced, the editor "would pick it up with a pair of tongs with his nose in the air (demonstrating) and give it to the office boy to return. . . . Because they know anything I might write for them is so far above the audience of their magazine. Because they are afraid that I might use words beyond the comprehension of their audience. . . . But some day I'll fool them and write under an assumed name." The woman felt relieved: "Mary Austin hadn't changed."[47]

• ◆ •

In the year *Experiences Facing Death* appeared, Austin published her last novel, *Starry Adventure* (1931), a work based on her "experience" of the Southwest. She dedicated it to her doctor and friend, Joseph E. Foster (not D. H. Lawrence's friend Joseph Foster), "to whose care and skill I owe the fortunate issue of my own New Mexican Adventure." The novel opens with the young Gard Sitwell experiencing a vision of God in the thunderous sky as "sword-like beams of light" flash like "the sword of the Lord and of Gideon."[48] Gard grows to maturity, aware of his difference, the "Something" that comes from within that brings together broken bottle shards, a blue penstemon flower, and a bee in a blue-and-lilac cup. This is the "starry adventure": the feeling that something must happen to him, "something sort of splendid and—different."[49] He calls this presence, "It," the word Austin borrowed from Mabel Dodge Luhan, whom in this book she satirizes as Eudora Ballintin, the vamp completing Gard's worldly education before he returns to his wife, Jane.

Austin's account of Santa Fe in *Starry Adventure* undercuts the advertising copy she wrote for the railroad in articles like "Indian Detour." In this novel Santa Fe resembles an exotic Carlinville. Newcomers, including Jane's parents, the oil-rich Hetheringtons, ignore the Spanish settlers except as they enhance a colonial fantasy and draw both color and class lines, which separate "their sort" from those manifestly not. Unlike the "Carlinvillains," the Hetheringtons read Freud and D. H. Lawrence and collect Fenwick Marsden's paintings (Austin considered Marsden Hartley a friend; he referred to her as the "Third Layer Woman"), take their entertainment at the pueblos, and supervise the so-called restoration of local churches. Gard is not necessarily better than these people, he simply has a different understanding of the finite-infiniteness of his surroundings, which makes him feel part of some greater pattern. He finds *his* pattern in life with Jane. Together they will restore his parents' house and raise children, and he will write the book Frank Applegate meant to write, a history of the house. *Starry Adventure,* the real protagonist of which might be the land itself working through Gard, pulls together much of Austin's thinking about the relationship between human beings and their environment.

After returning from a trip to the High Sierra, Ansel Adams wrote to congratulate Austin on *Starry Adventure:* "I think it magnificent—one of the greatest things I have ever read. . . . I, too, saw God—in the ocean and the dunes. What you have done with those difficult and evasive perceptions is nothing short of a miracle."[50] She passed his comments on to her publisher for publicity and began thinking of another southwestern novel. Not all her friends shared Adams's enthusiasm. To Carey McWilliams, the lawyer and historian who would go on to edit *The Nation,* she wrote:

> Don't imagine that you have to pretend to like my novel. . . . I may not know how to write, nor how to delineate character, nor even how to tell a story, the one thing I am sure of about myself is that I know the relation of letters and landscape, of life and its environment. No doubt the great literary genius of life and landscape will come after me, when the sense of man as inextricably a part of his background has become part of our social consciousness. I think it possible it will come in time for you to say, she was the first to whom it was clear, even if she did not have the gift of making it clear to others."[51]

Austin's work on *Starry Adventures* overlapped with research for her autobiography, which she first and aptly titled "The Good Fight." The renamed *Earth Horizon* came hard, with much at stake. As she told Arthur Davidson Ficke: "I have always thought of my life as being ahead of me, and now suddenly to be called upon to consider it as lying mostly behind, I was more than a little disturbed. And besides, I haven't lived as a lady should who expected to write an autobiography."[52] He thought she meant romantic indiscretions. That wasn't her point. She assured him that she had enjoyed her share of male attention. "Even more than my share, when you consider that I was never good-looking and spent thirty-five years of my life under circumstances in which I could scarcely expect to meet men who would interest me personally." In absolute reversal of nearly everything she said about Wallace or Lincoln Steffens or Daniel MacDougal, she continued: "As a matter of fact, I married the only man who ever did, and by the time I began to get about in the world, most of the men I might have been interested in were already appropriated."[53] When Austin said she hadn't lived as a lady, she meant that she had lived according to her own pattern and done her work as she saw fit.

Because she had not kept the writing of her autobiography secret, the literary world, aware that she rarely censored herself, twittered with expectation. Isabel Patterson, a leading critic of the time, proclaimed it would rival Benjamin Franklin's autobiography as one of the great American life stories. Austin might have achieved that; some would say she did. But as Austin acknowledged, this book remained unfinished. There were good reasons. Her pain had increased enough for her doctor to prescribe morphine, which conjured large red-and-yellow snakes around her bed.[54]

At the best of times, autobiographies require a long wrestle with the angel, and for a well-known writer the problems intensify: What to include and what to omit? How much to say about living people? Austin knew but could not easily report, for example, that George Sterling's mother took drugs and that his uncle was the town drunkard.[55] On the other hand, why would she want to? Nearer to the bone, how could she deal with her brother George when they were embroiled in bitter argument? After threatening to expose what she believed her brother's failings, she backed off, without, however, sliding safely away from conflict or writing, as some autobiographers protest they do, as if from beyond the grave.

During her work on *Earth Horizon* and *Starry Adventure*, Austin continued with other projects, among them her defense of a book by Andrae Nordskog, through which she relived the fight over the Owens River. Nordskog, an amateur historian, has since been accused of demonizing William Mulholland and other representatives of Los Angeles and confusing a complicated issue.[56] Austin saw him differently. She dashed off a letter to warn Carey McWilliams that politicians and businessmen in Los Angeles would stop at nothing to suppress Nordskog's book, which claimed that they had conspired for profit in the past and meant to once again with the proposed Boulder Dam. Austin tried to interest Louis Adamic in the story and thought Nordskog's life might be in danger, or worse, that he might be paid off. Embattled with one person or another throughout the writing of *Earth Horizon*, she can hardly have been in a state of mind to write the great book she hoped for.

The woman reviled at times for her undue self-confidence does not write confidently in *Earth Horizon*, possibly because she had so much riding on the outcome. Success would have meant more readers, and more readers increased the chances of a collected edition of her books with Harper & Brothers. Austin understood that she had to both disarm and charm her readers, which makes it all the more inexplicable that she wrote much of her autobiography in the third person, referring to herself as "Mary,"

"I-Mary" (her creative self), and "Mary-by-Herself" (her despondent and insubstantial self). Apart from Henry Adams, few writers of autobiography have chosen an impersonal approach, which for Adams underscored the importance of the historian's dispassionate perspective, and for Austin the writer's multiple selves. Adams kept to the third-person narrative, while Austin atomized the autobiographical "I" into an unstable trinity. Her switching in a single paragraph from "I," to "I-Mary," to "Mary-by-Herself" blurs the story and the person telling—without sustaining a sense of distance. Her method undercuts a basic appeal of autobiography, the development of an author-reader intimacy that requires a clear sense of the writer's projected self. Speaking of her father's last days, she conveys the child's horrible confusion at the risk of confusing readers:

> Mary remembers how she tried to cry, as the most natural way of dealing with the sense of stunned alarm . . . for years it gave the child a pained sense of dereliction that just at the last I-Mary came—there was Mary-by-herself apart and aside, seeing her father so frail and wasted in the bed, his hand straying always toward Mother, alternately moistening his parched lips and wiping her own tears—and the look on Susie's face, worn with grief and watching and luminous with love. Then there was I-Mary, and Uncle Otis with his arm around her, and she hiding her face against him lest somebody should see that she had no tears and think she did not care.[57]

Ansel Adams admired the book, as he admired *Starry Adventure,* for its objectivity. The Hoovers found it immensely entertaining. Not so her brother George's wife, who did her best to prevent *Earth Horizon* from being reviewed because it mentioned "a trait of childhood in the Hunter family."[58] She attacked its veracity, claiming, for example, that her sister-in-law had never ridden a horse. More serious objections came from H. G. Wells and Anne Martin, each of whom demanded that the book be suppressed and threatened suits for libel. Wells objected to Austin's statement that he had confided in her about his relationship with Amber Reeves and their illegitimate daughter. "I would be glad if you would convey to Mrs. Austin as clearly as possible," he wrote, "that my objection was neither to frankness nor the reporting of private conversations but to absolute falsehood. The conversation she described could not possibly have occurred because at the time the event upon which she presents me as being so garrulously free had not been foreseen by any human being. She heard it afterwards no doubt in the general swill of scandal." Austin did not argue the point. She had also quoted Wells as saying that he wished he had an American secretary because "here, if I get a young man he climbs on me, and a young woman insists on being seduced." To this he responded, "Only a woman as wrapped up in her own egotism as Mrs. Austin could be blind to the stupid slur this . . . would cast on anyone I may have employed since as a secretary."[59] After she rewrote the offending passages and Wells approved the changes, Austin wrote: "I am greatly relieved to receive your cable, expressing satisfaction with my suggested alterations in the text of *Earth Horizon*. I have been quite ill with distress about it. . . . You have been a sort of pace-maker to pre-thinking Americans, and . . . many incidents in your life are perfectly well known to the American public."[60] She worried that her autobiography had nothing sensational in it when compared to Gertrude Atherton's autobiography or Lincoln Steffens's "best seller," and her decision to include the Wells anecdote may have been prompted by an eye toward sales.[61]

If Wells, whom Austin had long quoted for publicity posters and dust jackets, felt poorly treated for his hospitality those many years ago, Anne Martin felt kicked in the belly. Flabbergasted that a friend would not show her potentially hurtful passages before publication, she complained bitterly: "You say you meant your statement on page 314 'Anne had very little capacity for work' to apply to the month we spent at Bramley. Yet this is an unqualified statement, that in the mind of the reader applies to my character and all the subsequent years of my life. I wish this statement deleted, as damaging to my reputation.'"[62] Martin bristled about Austin's account of her arrest in London: "Herbert went down and bailed her out. Not long after that she went home and mixed with the pickets there, to his great relief."[63] She had never assaulted a policeman, Martin told her; nor had Austin taught her how to lecture. She had worked *with*, not *under* her colleague Alice Paul. And besides, why should she be judged by the standards of professional writing? "This is unfair and unfriendly. It is as if I judged you by the standards of suffrage and feminist executive power and leadership, and in the public prints stated your whole career is a failure. . . . Perhaps my ability to write, as a minor part of my career, would, to a friendly eye, indicate versatility, rather than failure to achieve 'a successful literary career', as you phrase it. . . . I am more and more indignant about this whole matter."[64] In so far as she deserved it, Martin wanted her niece to remember her with pride. Somehow, Austin repaired the rift with Martin; a flurry of letters back and forth ended with a large piece of humble pie. After Austin's death, Martin graciously praised her work for women's suffrage: "Her feminism was active and creative. Her life and work, like that of Jane Addams and Madame Curie and countless lesser women who are going forth into the unknown and are holding their own in fields formerly monopolized by men, validate the rights of women the world over."[65]

Blind as she was to those affronts she gave, Austin recognized worse flaws in her autobiography. She pointed to the imbalance of her story and the rough prose in the final sections. She thought she had captured the earliest years vividly and, suspecting she was too close to the later years to do them justice, considered writing a sequel. Her greatest and acknowledged difficulty came from memory loss, or as she put it, her inability to remember incidents "with any exactness."[66] Because she could not recall certain times, events, or people, she canvassed friends and relatives to help with research for the book. Wallace, for example, solicited information from those they had known in California and from the best of research assistants, Carey McWilliams. McWilliams amassed historical details, provided reference books, collected photographs, and interviewed some of the many men and women Austin had known. To show her appreciation, Austin sent him a turquoise "gambler's stone," which had worked for another good friend, Herbert Hoover.[67]

Despite problems of shifting narrators, blurred chronology, remembered and invented conversations, the settling of scores, and assertions about its author having been "first" in an astonishing number of ventures, *Earth Horizon* ends on a note that may explain why friends such as the Applegates, Hal Bynner, and the Adamses loved Mary Austin. "I have seen that the American achievement is made up of two splendors," she wrote, "the splendor of individual relationships of power, the power to make and do rather than merely to possess, the aristocracy of creativeness; and that other splendor of realizing that in the deepest layers of ourselves we are incurably collective. . . . It is not that we work upon the Cosmos, but it works in us. I suffer because I achieve so little in this relation, and rejoice that I have felt so much. As much as I am able, I celebrate the Earth Horizon"—in the Rain Song of the Sia, the point where earth and sky meet, the source of experience.[68]

Of the many responses Austin received for *Earth Horizon,* two letters stand out. A woman named Mary Bucknam wrote with a business proposition. For a hundred dollars, she offered to correct the book's most egregious errors, which she then listed:

1. a lack of ear for the correct use of prepositions.
2. the frequent use of "the dangling participle."
3. sentence structure that runs off the road and gets struck [*sic*] in deep sand.
4. the frequent use of a singular verb with a compound subject.
5. words incorrectly used, because, I suppose, they sounded vaguely like something that you wanted.
6. constant use of colloquial and provincial vulgarism of speech.
7. and not a few serious lapses of good taste.[69]

Another correspondent asked if she might perform some service for Austin to be paid with a copy of *Earth Horizon,* which exceeded her budget. There is no record of Austin's replies. She earned over five thousand dollars from the book, featured by the Literary Guild, in a market that had fallen 50 or 60 percent. Her editors had expected sales in the upper five figures.

Earth Horizon prompted a letter from Una Jeffers and another from her husband, "Robin," living in Tor House at Carmel. They considered it the best of all her books, and Jeffers intended to read it to their boys once school ended for the summer. Austin sent them an autographed copy and, for good measure, a copy of *Starry Adventure.* Robinson Jeffers, who spent a decade constructing his Hawk Tower from boulders dragged from the shore, felt Austin's presence keenly in Carmel, where he liked to imagine her and another friend, George Sterling, scaling hills or deep in conversation. Sterling had written a book about Jeffers. After Sterling died, already a forgotten poet, Jeffers repaid the tribute:

> And how shall one believe he will not return
> To be our guest in the house, not wander with me
> Again by the Carmel river.[70]

Austin probably met Una—a womanly woman given to braids and loose gowns and domestic discipline—in 1913, when she returned to Carmel to direct *Fire* at the Forrest Theater. She took to both the wife and husband. Like Austin, Jeffers was drawn to science (he studied forestry and science at Occidental College), and Una to cooking and mysticism, the focus of her graduate work. Since their first meeting, the women occasionally corresponded. Austin, who may or may not have known that Jeffers's father had been a Presbyterian professor of the Old Testament, sent them a copy of *A Small Town Man* (1925), her biographical account of Jesus. Austin's friendship with Jeffers grew intimate enough for her to explain in 1929 that she had come to the time of life when sex no longer mattered. Her own personal tragedy had been to love men who did not experience God as she did. Sex was, she said, a projection of the divine. Would poets never cast off its fetters?[71] Jeffers thought not, and life conformed when one of his flirtations resulted in Una's attempted suicide. The Jefferses stayed together, and after Una died in 1950 Jeffers eulogized her in *Hungerfield and Other Poems* (1954), the title poem of which captures a sense of life, and death, he held in common with Austin:

> Here is the poem, dearest: you will never read it nor
> hear it. You were more beautiful
> Than a hawk flying; you were faithful and a lion heart like this
> rough hero Hungerfield. But the ashes have fallen
> And the flame has gone up; nothing human remains. You are earth
> and air; you are in the beauty of the ocean
> And the great streaming triumphs of sundown; you are alive and
> well in the tender young grass rejoicing
> When soft rain falls all night, and little rosy-fleeced clouds float
> on the dawn.—I shall be with you presently.[72]

Austin's friendships with younger people like Jeffers made her feel less like an anachronism. In 1931, the year of *Experiences Facing Death* and *Starry Adventure,* friends had lobbied for her to receive the *Pictorial Review*'s Annual Achievement Award. They noted "her important and constructive work in the field of sociology of the American Indian."[73] Despite recommendations from Fred Hodge and Van Wyck Brooks, she received neither a Guggenheim Fellowship nor the Annual Achievement Award. The Guggenheim Committee, though admiring her application, decided she was too old.

In the 1930s, in addition to Frank Applegate and Vachel Lindsay, Austin lost her brother George. He was shot by a patient, a fifty-nine-year-old "clubwoman" suffering from "delusions of persecution." The woman believed that George, who had gone to her house to treat her, exerted "a strange and evil influence over her life through mental telepathy." A doctor to the end,

George lived long enough to request that the woman be treated rather than punished. She was committed to the California State Hospital for the Insane.[74] In 1917, when George wrote to his sister about a plan to buy burial lots in Hollywood cemetery, he had hoped, despite their long estrangement, that they might all rest together when their work was done. She would not be wooed. As she thought about her own resting place and the company she desired, Austin chose not to be buried with George. She imagined going home to California and the high desert and the shepherds she had befriended as a young woman.

Writing about one's life, as Austin remarked, brings inevitable thoughts not only about ends but about meaning. She wanted her life to count. Cornell University had a special laboratory dedicated to resolving whether differences in the brain signaled differences in human behavior. As early as 1925, Austin began exploring the possibility of donating her brain to Cornell's Brain Collection. In December 1927, she signed the formal papers: "Recognizing the need of studying the brains of educated persons in order to determine their weight, form, and fissural pattern, the correlation with bodily and mental powers and various kinds and degrees, and the influence of sex, age, and inheritance, I Mary Hunter Austin hereby, at my death give and bequeath my brain to Cornell University. . . . I direct my executors to have the same promptly and properly removed, hardened and shipped to the Curator of the Burt G. Wilder Brain Collection."[75] In addition, she was asked to send a photograph with biographical data: a description of her eyes, hair, weight, height, hip, chest, and head circumferences, genealogy, mental traits, and personality. She received, in return, a recipe for preserving her brain in "1 point formalin solution from a drugstore, 5 pts. Water, 4 level tsp. of common salt and a jar or vessel 6 inches in diameter. The fluid must cover the brain which will lie flat within this solution and will not flatten against the jar."[76] James Papez, a doctor at Cornell, explained to what use her donation might be put: "The cortical mechanisms that deal with the higher psychic function of thought and expression are only moderately developed in the general run of individuals. In talented individuals these areas may be highly developed and mature much later. They appear to be the latest acquisitions of the human race and produce the intrapsychic or thinking personality. These are problems to be worked out."[77] No doubt there were, but as Lord Byron said of Coleridge, someone needed to explain the explanation. Austin, however, was not deterred.

More immediately, the University of New Mexico, which considered Austin one of the state's great assets, awarded her an honorary doctorate of letters in June 1933. Two years before, she had turned down a doctorate from Tufts University rather than pay her way there, and she almost missed this hooding because of the difference in daylight savings time between Santa Fe and Albuquerque. The ceremony took place in the campus's original quadrangle under a canopy of cottonwood trees. Walking, as one friend noted, as if cast in bronze, Austin slowly approached the speakers' stand where the president of the university and the governor of New Mexico waited to congratulate her.[78] In her address, she urged the new graduates to nurture their talents.[79] Friends began calling her "Dr. Mary." They might as easily have called her "Sheriff." The notice of her appointment reads: "KNOW ALL MEN BY THESE PRESENTS: THAT I, JESUS M. BACA, SHERIFF OF SANTA FE COUNTY, STATE OF NEW MEXICO, reposing special trust and confidence in Mrs. Mary Austin of Santa Fe N.M. do, hereby commission and appoint said Mary Austin as Special Deputy Sheriff, in and for the County and State aforesaid, for me and in my name to do and perform all acts pertaining to his duty as such Deputy Sheriff."[80]

The honors came at a time of declining health but not declining activity. Austin served as a judge for the American Prix Femina, a literary award selected by an entirely female jury. In 1933, the painter Andrew Dasburg asked her to "please organize protest of writers and painters to Mr John D Rockefeller Jr against possible destruction of Diego Riveras work at Radio City and request that he be allowed to finish it in accordance with Mr Rockefellers previous liberal attitude toward modern painting."[81] Dasburg refers to Rivera's mural of workers at the crossroads of industry and science, commissioned for Rockefeller Center in 1932. In a section of the sixty-three-foot mural depicting a May Day parade, Rivera inserted a portrait of Lenin. Ordered to erase the offending image, he offered a compromise: he would add one of Abraham Lincoln. The managers of the project responded by banning him from the site and hiding the mural behind heavy drapes.

Austin met Rivera in Mexico and admired his work. She and Mabel Dodge Luhan had wanted to commission a mural for the new Laboratory of Anthropology in Santa Fe, but Rivera returned to Mexico in June 1931 before anything could be arranged. On the eve of his departure, he sent, through Ansel Adams, "his most profound personal regards [to Austin]." He had, according to Adams, "spoken of you many times."[82] Austin wrote to the managing agents of Rockefeller Center to register her protest about Rivera's mural. Rallies, protests, and petitions failed to stop its demolition, in February 1934, by workmen wielding sledgehammers and axes. Rivera took his revenge by recreating his mural in the Palace of Fine Arts in Mexico

City and adding a caricature of his former patron, John D. Rockefeller Jr., as a debauched capitalist in a nightclub.

Rivera's celebration of indigenous Mexican culture offered Austin a parallel for much of her own work, including *One-Smoke Stories* (1934), a collection of new and previously published pieces. From the days in the Owens Valley campoodies, she had been interested in stories that last "the space of one smoke . . . each one as deft, as finished in itself as a ceremonial cigarette. . . . And between them, the ingoing and outgoing sense of the universe pulses and spirals with the ascending smoke." For Austin these stories belonged in folk tradition, and she sought to honor them by imitating the original telling: "The essence of all such stories is that they should be located somewhere in the inner sense of the audience, unencumbered by what in our more discursive method is known as background. . . . Just before the end, like the rattle that warns that the story is about to strike, comes the fang of experience, most often in the shape of a wise saying. Then the speaker resumes the soul-consoling smoke, while another takes up the dropped stitch of narrative and weaves it into the pattern of the talk." Austin, who often enclosed sprinkles of sage in letters to friends, ambiguously ends her introduction, "In the words of the sacred formula: I give you to smoke."[83] Whether she meant "I pass you on to the stories" or "we all go up in smoke," she did not say.

In the last year of her life, Mary Austin put on a brave front. Arthur Davison Ficke wrote as Christmas neared in 1933: "Your letter is so cheerful, on its surface, that I wonder about you. Your habitual courage is perhaps invulnerable—yet perhaps you are, at heart, lonely, and would like to have letters, from time to time. Say so, if this is the fact. I shall be very happy to write to you, often, if that meager source of interest would please you."[84] Austin lived another eight months, chipping away at her new novel and other writing projects, as she contemplated additions to her latest book, *Can Prayer Be Answered?* and corresponded with Ernest Powell (of the Powell School of Music) about a lecture tour through Texas. In March 1934, she told Ansel Adams, "I am working on the Public Works of Art Committee, and we are getting along well with it, and have had high praise from Washington for the way we have managed."[85]

Near the end of July, Mary Hunter received a disturbing letter from Austin's lawyer, Francis Wilson. "She has failed entirely and her mind is no longer functioning. Her power of speech is practically gone and she talks only in broken sentences which mean nothing. Her business affairs are an unknown quantity to all of us [there was little or no money in her bank account]. . . . The only thing we can think of to do is to have a conservator appointed and try to impound what estate she has . . . until the inevitable occurs."[86] Ferris Greenslet, Austin's editor at Houghton Mifflin, wrote to Mary in June:

> As you probably know, Mrs. Austin has been extremely ill and at times, due to progressive hardening of the arteries, is not herself mentally. At present she seems to have made rather remarkable and unexpected recovery and we are hesitating to take any definite steps to take over her affairs. . . . Will you please regard this as strictly confidential, as Mrs. Austin is entirely unaware of her mental difficulties and is expecting to correspond with you about a book on Spanish Colonial Arts. I am being advised by her physician and her lawyer, Dr. Joseph Foster and Mr. Francis Wilson, that a conservator should be appointed.[87]

On 9 August, Austin suffered a heart attack. Somehow she managed to attend the Poets' Roundup, an annual event run by Alice Corbin Henderson for the benefit of the Southwest Indian Association. People came to see the poets in Western garb as much as they came to hear their poems. Austin read from *The Children Sing in the Far West*. Four days later, she died, almost a month shy of her sixty-fifth birthday, on 9 September 1934.

Friends gathered at Casa Querida to say their good-byes. Mary Hunter had dressed her aunt in a favorite, brightly colored Spanish shawl. As candles burned, an Episcopal minister said prayers, no doubt unaware that Austin thought it the height of bad manners to pray for someone who didn't explicitly request an intervention. Dana Johnson, editor of the *Santa Fe New Mexican* read Austin's "Going West," and Haniel Long, a local poet, "When I Am Dead":

> I shall take a high road where the flock scent lingers
> In the browsed sage and the blue, bush-lupin fingers,
> I shall find a by-road by the foot changes
> Till I come where the herders' fires
> Blossom in the dusk of the grape colored ranges.
> And I shall sit by the bedding fires
> With the little, long armed men
> Eleheverray and Little Pete and Narcisse Julienne—
> . . . .
> While the dogs edge in to the watching fires
> And darkly the procreant earth suspires.

So it shall be when Balzar the Basque
And the three Manxmen
And Pete Giraud and my happy ghost
Walk with the flocks again.[88]

Hal Bynner served as one of the eight pallbearers who placed her casket in a friend's family vault. A week later people gathered for another memorial service, where Bynner and the scientist-humanist Loren Eiseley read poems written for the occasion. Alta Applegate, who would help Mary Hunter sort through her aunt's clothes, wanted to remember her in a series of outlandish hats. As Austin had written of her heroine in *No. 26 Jayne Street*: "She liked . . . to have people look at her when they talked, and it was only fair that they should have something worth looking at. . . . Her hats were always marvels of feminine intricacy, dash of line, and swift surprises of color."[89]

Among the mourners were some who never met Austin. "This letter," wrote one man,

> is so addressed that I may add this bit of esteem & affection to the sum of tribute due to the memory of a very great woman, probably the most understanding soul of her generation. Out of my deep appreciation for her autobiography I wrote to her. . . . An intermittent correspondence followed which further disclosed her firm deep mind & sympathies. Her last letter of June 4 tells me of wanting to live again, also her liking to stay on here until she could find a 'real companion' to relieve her 'suffering from intellectual loneliness' from which she has now been freed.[90]

He chose not to mention that Austin's picture more than her autobiography prompted him to write at all. "Forgive me dear lady," he had addressed her, "but the primitive quality of you is irresistible."[91]

Austin's body lay "in state" for two years while friends debated whether she preferred burial—neighbors, fearing ghosts and lowered property values, opposed the idea of a burial at Casa Querida—or the eventual choice, cremation. On 13 August 1937, three years to the day after her death, her friends placed Austin's ashes sealed in a "sarcophagus of native stone" in a granite hollow on the summit of Mount Picacho, the grave marked simply by her name etched in concrete.[92]

twelve

THE ACCOUNTING

She was a great woman—also, thank Heavens, a great eccentric.

HENRY S. CANBY

Mary Austin: A Memorial, 1944

ANY PERSON'S DEATH CALLS FOR an accounting, a reading of the will, a sorting out of legacies, an assessment of debits and credits—quite apart from matters of trusts, taxes, and the bureaucracy that turn a once vital person into someone as socially or administratively dead as he or she is dead in body. Biographies as part of that accounting run their own risks, sifting through the detritus and often missing the life itself in the welter of gathered documents and erratic memory.

It might be said that Mary Austin's legacies remain in a kind of probate, awaiting overdue closure in the form of reassessments or reopening of the newspapers. If we turn back to the year 1912 and picture Austin dining at Sherry's restaurant on Park Avenue while listening to President Taft pay tribute to the "Dean of American Letters," William Dean Howells, we might imagine a woman secure in her reputation because of the company she kept. She could look around the room at the writers she knew and respected as original voices, among them Willa Cather, Ida Tarbell, and Hutchins Hapgood. The man they had come to honor had promoted nearly every rising author of his day, including his friends Henry James and Mark Twain. The melted butter flowed as Howells flattered his guests. Hawthorne, Emerson, Whitman, Longfellow, he had known them well. "If we have no single name so sovereign as these names," he told his audience, "let us remember their limitations and consider the potentiality of the artists who now are and are to be."[1] Yet how *has* history dealt with those attending the celebration, including the guest of honor? Shrewd about his own legacy, Howells would have said that Tarbell and Hapgood deserved to be remembered, but that fate or circumstance made the final verdict. Often, as he knew, it takes a single book, an attitude or personality distinct from achievement, or just plain good luck, for an artist to keep his or her reputation. It may be true, as scholars have estimated, that something like 96 percent of the world's art across the centuries has been lost or destroyed; it is also true that many artists are simply forgotten.

Austin, troubled with the disparate quality of her work and low sales of her books, had few illusions about posthumous fame. She had not become the "World writer" she aimed to be or a national writer with a large readership. Instead she found herself both touted and trapped by labels: woman of the desert country, supporter of American Indians, unconventional storyteller, feminist, and conservationist. Willa Cather, who wrote part of *Death Comes for the Archbishop* in Austin's house, has a deserved plaque honoring her and others outside Santa Fe's Palace of the Governors. Austin, who, even discounting her contributions to American fiction, helped to develop the town's theater and museums, along with her countless other activities, has none—at least in Santa Fe. She has a small memorial plaque on her house in Independence, California.

What, then, did Mary Austin leave behind? She made a will in 1926, which in material terms left her house to the Indian Arts Fund, with a stipulation that her niece receive any income from the rental of the apartment.[2] She designated Harry P. Mera, active in the Spanish Colonial Arts Society, and her friend Frank Applegate as executors of her estate. Applegate's death forced her to replace him with Kenneth Chapman, an artist and founding member of the Museum and School of American Research. Henry Seidel Canby agreed to be her literary executor. At Fred Hodge's urging, she donated the San Fernando Indian basket that General Edward Beale had given her nearly forty years before—as well as the bell once used by his "Camel Corps"—to the Southwest Museum, the dream child of Charles Lummis, which Hodge by then directed. The gifts to the Southwest Museum may have been thanks to Hodge for his patient help over the years or a belated peace gesture to Lummis, who had come to dislike the woman he called "Governor."

As we might expect from Austin, there were legacies of different kinds. She left manuscripts that after seventy years still await an editor. She left her brain to Cornell University, with its large collection and prescriptive rules for admission. Generous as she was, she left little money—never enjoying enough to write her books in comfort. When it came to eternity, she wavered between mixing her ashes with those of Frank Applegate or the shepherds of the San Joaquin, and she left no clear instructions. Her remains did not go back to the deserts of California to rest with "Little Pete" and the beloved outsiders who people her early books. They lie instead beneath a stone slab high on Mount Picacho.

The sorting out of her legacy, which in a sense began with Daniel Mac-Dougal's shrewd and affectionate letters, took a formal turn in 1944, ten years after her death. The Indian Arts Club of Santa Fe organized a memorial conference of her friends and colleagues. Excepting Mabel Dodge Luhan, few of those contributors are remembered today, though Henry Canby was a well-known critic at the time, and T. M. Pearce during his tenure at the University of New Mexico worked indefatigably to keep Austin's work before the public. The memorial essays mix nostalgia and affection, annoyance and diplomacy. Canby, for example, struggles with his conscience, praising Austin as "potentially one of the great American women of letters," while fretting about someone who "worked . . . with all her ten fingers in ten different directions" so as to confuse "the mere literary viewer" and, by implication, Canby himself.[3]

Ina Cassidy, who had "memorialized" Austin after the 1923 tour of the southwestern desert with Gerald Cassidy and Daniel MacDougal, begins by describing their first meeting. It took place when both women, escaping a conference, stopped to admire lingerie in a store window. (Austin once said that she would think herself rich if she could sleep in a lace nightgown.) "To know her in all of her aspects," Cassidy writes, "needed years of intimate association. . . . I knew her as an intimate friend and as bitter enemy. Through it all she was ever the grand woman, consistent in her inconsistencies and to me she remained always a stimulating person."[4] Another writer, Elizabeth Willis DeHuff, recollects Austin's "colossal egoism." "Never was I clever enough . . . to manipulate the conversation away from my own short-comings as a writer. One day she said to me, 'Elizabeth, I've been thinking of how I might help you in your writing; but *I'm a born writer* [her emphasis] and I do not know how one could go about learning how to write.'"[5]

What DeHuff sees as hubris, Mabel Dodge Luhan calls "innocence." Her swashbuckling account for the 1944 memorial, "Mary Austin: A Woman," celebrates her friend's energy and gusto. Luhan relishes the idiosyncrasies and takes them as signs of genius. "We do not find any more like her coming along these days," she says. "Who has her zest for life, her competence, and her innocence? . . . Mary was the innocent uninhibited Eve all her life in the garden. She was often ridiculous. She was one of those women whose legs are too short for her top side but she never saw herself whole and did not feel over-balanced." Luhan recalls "a generous woman with big appetites. On a camping trip she would give all her blankets to one more chilly than herself and would rapidly and on the same trip systematically eat a whole crate of peaches, tossing the pits into the road like hail as we sped along."[6] Luhan knew and admired Austin's writing but honors the person, the larger-than-life character she describes as if Austin had stepped out of Rabelais's *Gargantua*.

Carl Van Doren had never been one of her doubters. Unable to attend the Santa Fe memorial, he told Willard Hougland, the organizer, that he stood by his earlier writings on Austin. His was and remains the strongest endorsement of Austin as a modern prophet and, more intriguingly, as the first fully American voice:

> Much of the finest American thought and feeling has been uttered in a dialect which is almost mandarin in its remoteness from the customary speech of the nation; and the vernacular in philosophy, architecture, literature, and the fine arts has busied itself with minor concerns or at least with concerns which have been so little regarded that they have grown up with little discipline or guidance. . . . Between academic odes and Negro folksongs there is a hollow chasm. No small part of the strength of innovators has been spent in trying to bridge this chasm. Yet the best William James, for instance, could do was to shape a more or less coherent logic for the American gospel of workability; the best Walt Whitman could do was to graft the dithyramb upon the stump speech; the best Edward MacDowell could do was to weld Indian themes into a symphony. Somewhere back of these divergences is there not some common ground for the American philosopher or artist to stand on? . . . The work of Mary Austin had been to discover that common ground and to prophesy its uses.[7]

We might ask whether—with or without the comparisons to Whitman or James—Austin was the prophet, the national treasure and writer of a new order that Van Doren believed her to be. But this question, akin to those about beauty and genius, comes down to personal values or accepted pecking orders. We *can* ask about her audience, her reputation, the legatees of her career, or about the books that range from *The Man Jesus* to *Outland* to *California, the Land of the Sun*, and include *The Land of Little Rain, The*

Flock, The Land of Journeys' Ending, The Basket Woman, A Woman of Genius, and *Lost Borders.*

If, as some assume, Austin has been forgotten, why have so many of her books been reprinted or newly printed in recent years? *Cactus Thorn,* a novella, appeared for the first time in 1988; *The Land of Little Rain* has yet to go out of print and has emerged in new guises for over a century. Melody Graulich and others have searched Austin's papers in the Huntington Library in California and found material, stories especially, that should have been published long ago. It may be, too, that more of Austin's books are in print today than during most of her lifetime. Often thought minor (though among her best work), books such as *The Trail Book* and *The Basket Woman* have been reprinted and one of her finest, *The Land of Journeys' Ending,* reappeared with Larry Evers's excellent introduction in 1983. There have been at least three new collections of her writings published in the past half-dozen years. Austin has become a small academic "industry" as much for the currency of her topics as for the quality of the work itself.

Lawrence Clark Powell, an eloquent spokesman for Western life and literature once listed his favorite books about the region's deserts. He began with John Van Dyke (for whose *Desert* he wrote an introduction), suggesting that Van Dyke spawned a string of outstanding works, prominent and second among them, Austin's *Land of Little Rain,* and what he thought the best of all, Joseph Wood Krutch's books on his "desert year" and "man and nature." Although Austin's book ranks high for Powell, he perhaps undervalues its originality and its distinction among the exceptional books he lists. There *is* nothing quite like it, and neither Van Dyke before her nor those who followed achieved the mix of human life and natural landscape as profoundly as Austin. In a 1988 introduction to *The Land of Little Rain,* Edward Abbey—a man alternately hailed as a Western Thoreau and pilloried as a desert anarchist—called American nature writers a "misty-eyed lot." "But, what the hell," he writes of Austin. After a few pages of her "poetical, elliptical, sometimes periphrastical" style, you're hooked. "When Mary Austin looked at the desert . . . she noticed things that most human desert dwellers never see or even know about, such as the efforts of desert birds in the nesting season to keep their eggs . . . coolly spreading their wings to shade the nest from the flare of the sun."[8]

There is little doubt that Austin stretched herself thin, or that she dabbled in areas she pretended to have mastered, or, as MacDougal told her and Austin herself bemoaned, that she spent too many years of her life potboiling in the wrong kitchens. The same might be said of untold twentieth-century writers caught in the squeeze of making a living. Carey McWilliams, who knew Austin and her work as well as anyone, agreed that she sometimes wrote erratically—and told her so. For him the writer and the woman Austin were one. Anyone so daring and so talented was bound to blunder at times—and it did not matter. In his obituary, "Mary Austin," for the *Los Angeles Times,* McWilliams asked readers to "imagine a woman with the emotional background and experience of an American housewife, the stout mental courage of a Huxley, and a streak of ineradicable mysticism, and you have a fair understanding of the incongruous traits that were dominant in Mary Austin." She had, he said, a "heroic mind."[9]

Her good friend Ansel Adams also loved the woman and her work. *Taos Pueblo* is his legacy, and hers. Adams called Austin a "future person—one who will, a century from now, appear as a writer of major stature in the complex matrix of our American culture."[10] Van Doren claimed her as a national figure, and Adams agreed, though for Adams she was a national figure with interests, like his own, focused on the American West. Daniel MacDougal had recognized her "real" work in the 1920s, reminding Austin that her strength lay in her writings about the West. He might have added that being a good *Western* writer meant being an *American* writer, as Mark Twain, Willa Cather, Theodore Dreiser, or William Faulkner are American writers. Faulkner's Mississippi and Austin's West are regional, but hardly parochial.

Ansel Adams captured the spirit of his vast country in photographs of Yosemite's Half Dome and the grandeur of the Cathedral Range. Twenty years after publication of *The Land of Little Rain,* he brought out an edited version of the book, which mimicked the structure of *Taos Pueblo* by having his photographs follow the text. In a note on the land and on his artistic responsibilities, Adams admitted "a certain temerity in attempting an amalgam of Mary Austin's writing and my photographs."

> I am also aware that my friendship with Mary Austin, and my understanding of her character and objectives, have definitely influenced my photographic transcription; I am sure I see the land more clearly because of this relationship. The sharp beauty of The Land of Little Rain is finely etched in the distinguished prose of Mary Austin. Many books and articles have probed the factual aspects of this amazing land, but no writing to my knowledge conveys so much of the spirit of earth and sky, of plants and people, of storm and the desolation of majestic wastes, of tender, intimate beauty, as does The Land of Little Rain.[11]

Adams's tribute to his friend's work equals that of another Western (or adopted Western) photographer, Morley Baer, whose intimate landscapes emerge through a smaller lens but seem equally complementary to Austin's prose. The places she loved, the small places in large areas, these are what Baer made his own, finding in Austin a guide, muse, teacher, and counterpart, though he never met her. "For a photographer to read Mary Austin," he writes, "is to invite an intense and enveloping challenge."

> Her pen all but demands visual accompaniment. The vast scale of her interests in the West is found in its magnificence as well as in its minutiae. Her legacy, however, lies not only in the land but in her preoccupation with its spirit and with how this force re-energizes and fortifies man. . . .
>
> It was in Mary Austin's writing that I first discovered the identification of person and place and how each informs the other. I had never been to the land of lost borders or looked at the sierra from the land of little rain. But I was close. I now began to know them, to believe in them, and to feel their import in an imagery so incessant, so compelling that again I was transported, this time with a precipitous force to go there to photograph.[12]

Baer regards Austin as a writer who looks steadily at the world around her and appreciates qualities that others cannot see or fail to comprehend.

Ansel Adams admired *Earth Horizon, Starry Adventure,* and other books by Austin—along with his favorite, *The Land of Little Rain*—but until recent years few readers apart from Barney Nelson have appreciated a work like *The Flock,* which in some respects reaches farther than *The Land of Little Rain* and, unlike the earlier book, had neither forerunner nor follower. In this idiosyncratic tour de force, Austin blends early Western history with contemporary issues, sketching the evolution of sheepherding in the West and offering a plan for better use of the land. One reader, a man who owned thousands of sheep in widely separated flocks and ran a federal department overseeing the sheep industry, told Austin that her books should be required reading for anyone responsible for the raising and grazing of sheep. A sociologist at the University of Chicago required his students to read *The Flock* as an important document about social organization.[13] The book, written in that "elliptical style" and covering regions and centuries, also gives intimate portraits of the men and women she admired and closely observed.

The Flock, The Land of Little Rain, and *The Land of Journeys' Ending* capture the richness and complexity of the regions they depict, not in the same but in overlapping ways. A stunning trilogy, they offer a wealth of knowledge in an exploratory format, and in their subject matter they anticipate the work of Abbey and Wallace Stegner, along with Aldo Leopold's groundbreaking *Sand County Almanac* (1948). Austin laid a foundation for the fields of ecology and environmental (or ecological) history. When the historian John Opie raises questions about the characteristics of "an ecological thesis of American history," he says it would "incorporate cross-disciplinary methods and resources, beginning with the tools used by ecologists and members of the biological sciences, who point to a far more extensive 'natural history.' Such an ecological approach would also draw to a much greater extent upon contemporary resources available from geography, anthropology, sociology, economics, and other related fields."[14]

Mary Austin thought so too, almost a century before. Without mentioning her, Opie describes something close to the approach she took to the West and Southwest, except that Austin would have added to his list of resources the writers, painters, and musicians she believed no less important. As her relationships with the biologist Daniel MacDougal, a founding member of the Ecological Society of America, and the anthropologist Fred Hodge suggest, instead of dabbling she drew from contemporary experts for studies that cut across disciplines. She saw the desert, the mountains, the great fertile valleys in conjunction with past traditions and future threats, and above all in relation to human beings. Sheepherding had a past in a changing world. Nature could not be seen in terms of simple or unchanging states. The mystery of nature was inseparable from the lives, the histories, of those who inhabited and changed the land.

In 1920 Austin wrote to the publisher Huebsch about a book she had imagined called "Small Town Heroes." She had read half of Sherwood Anderson's novel *Poor White* and wanted someone to know how happy she felt to see so many good books coming out of the Midwest. It made her feel justified for her own effort "and reconciled for not succeeding better. After all it doesn't really matter who does the work, so that it finally gets done."[15] This letter's generosity of spirit reflects Austin's voice in many of her writings, including *The Ford,* the book in which she looks shrewdly at the water issue in the Owens Valley—and by implication the entire West—with a sense of common needs and shared responsibility. Wallace Stegner rightly places Austin in the honored tradition of John Wesley Powell, whose advice to the nation in his 1878 *Report on the Lands of the Arid Region* spelled out the looming issues with precise though unheeded logic. Austin cared about the land and the water, and the people who use or abuse them. It may "not matter," as she wrote, "who does the work," yet she did more than her share, and that too is part of her legacy.

The West she knew differs from the West that Stegner depicts, in *The Big Rock Candy Mountain,* as a "rootlessness that expresses energy and a thirst for the new . . . an aspiration toward freedom and personal fulfillment," which has a way of not panning out.[16] If Stegner sees the region in terms of Henry Adams's dynamo, a forward, ultimately destructive movement, Austin envisions a series of small towns, each a product of topography, of rock and sand and light and color, giving rise to particular customs, patterns of speech, and twists of character. She looks at places like Lone Pine or Independence as a mix of defeat and optimism, shared memory and cultural heritages, which she tries to free from an inhibiting context, the supremacy of the East or of European civilization. For her, the West becomes the West through its particular interchanges, elemental and human; she believes the land itself to be inspirited and inspiriting, a perspective that reflects her faith in a benign higher power. In her books, to borrow William Carlos Williams's definition, "The classic is the local fully realized, words marked by a place."[17]

Because she constantly wrestled with the world and with herself, Austin (as Mabel Dodge Luhan suggested) may not have seen herself whole. But how many of us do? Often blind to others, she could be self-protective, theatrical, at times arrogant, proud of the isolation that allowed her an independent and original voice. The young woman who came to the Rancho El Tejon starved for intellectual companionship could not have imagined herself lecturing Van Wyck Brooks about literary standards or hobnobbing with the Vatican's secretary of state. She treated Herbert Hoover much as she treated Little Pete and the shepherds she had met as a young woman— along with General Edward Beale. Neither a snob nor a sycophant, she lived her life on the edge of society but with a wide range of friends. She sat at the table in Coppa's restaurant as she dined with the Hoovers or cooked at Mabel Dodge Luhan's in Taos. Austin's was a representative Western, or maybe American story of self-transformation and grit. She understood herself to be, as she tells in her autobiography, someone who wrote what she lived, what she had observed and understood, and notwithstanding the struggles in her own life she believed that the ills of the world were remediable. Living with courage, she remained to the last hopeful and defiant, or as she put it, "unconvinced of death."[18]

NOTES

PREFACE

1. Ansel Adams, "A Note on the Land and on the Photographs," in *The Land of Little Rain,* by Mary Austin, photographs by Ansel Adams, introduction by Carl Van Doren (Boston: Houghton Mifflin, 1950), 109.

2. Mary Austin to Mabel Dodge Luhan, [c. 1925], Mabel Dodge Luhan Papers, Yale Collection of American Literature, Beinecke Rare Book and Manuscript Library.

3. Mary Austin, Box 11, AU140, Huntington Library, San Marino, CA.

I. DESERT PLACES

1. Mary Austin, notes for her autobiography, Box 122, folder 1, Austin Papers, Huntington Library, San Marino, CA.

2. There is some confusion about Susanna's name since Susanna frequently signed herself Savilla S. Hunter on official documents. See, for example, her marriage certificate, homesteader's deed (27 November 1888) and affidavits, and claim for George Hunter's pension (11 August 1891), Huntington Library. Only one census report lists her names reversed. Austin, however, refers to her mother as Susanna Savilla (Graham) Hunter.

3. Mary Austin, *Earth Horizon,* ed. Melody Graulich (Albuquerque: University of New Mexico Press, 1991), 187.

4. Austin, *Earth Horizon,* 190. For a description of Austin, see Elizabeth Shepley Sergeant, "Mary Austin: A Portrait," *The Saturday Review of Literature* 11 (8 September 1934): 96.

5. Mary Austin, "One Hundred Miles on Horseback," in *A Mary Austin Reader,* ed. Esther F. Lanigan (Tucson: University of Arizona Press, 1996), 28.

6. Carey McWilliams, *Southern California Country, an Island on the Land,* ed. Erskine Caldwell (New York: Duell, Sloan & Pearce, 1946), 167.

7. Charles Nordhoff, *California for Health, Pleasure, and Residence* (New York: Harper & Brothers, 1875), 121.

8. Charles Dudley Warner, "Our Italy," *Harper's Magazine* 81 (November 1890): 820.

9. Austin, *Earth Horizon,* 188–89.

10. Austin, explanation of the circumstances surrounding the writing of four poems, Box 14, AU182, Huntington Library.

11. Austin, "Woman Alone," in *Mary Austin Reader,* 169.

12. Austin claimed Louis Daguerre, inventor of the daguerreotype, as a relative.

13. Austin, *Earth Horizon,* 87.

14. T. M. Pearce, *The Beloved House* (Caldwell, ID: Caxton Printers, 1940), 79.

15. Mary Austin, *A Woman of Genius* (Old Westbury, NY: The Feminist Press, 1985), 126.

16. Effie Graham Curtis to Austin, 1 April 1931, Box 72, AU2071, Huntington Library.

17. Austin, *Earth Horizon,* 116.

18. Austin, *Earth Horizon,* 139, 142.

19. Austin, *Earth Horizon,* 144, 145.

20. Box 122, folder 3, Austin Papers, Huntington Library. They named themselves after a male member of the group.

21. Nordhoff, *California: For Health, Pleasure, and Residence,* 229. For information about Beale, see Gerald Thompson's useful biography, *Edward F. Beale and the American West* (Albuquerque: University of New Mexico Press, 1983).

22. Thompson, *Edward F. Beale and the American West,* 240.

23. Mary Austin, *The Flock* (Reno: University of Nevada Press, 2001), 219.

24. Quoted in Thompson, *Edward F. Beale and the American West,* x.

25. Austin, *Earth Horizon,* 159.

26. Austin, Tejon journal, Box 17, AU267, Huntington Library.

27. Austin, *Earth Horizon,* 191.

28. Mary Austin, *The Land of Little Rain,* introduction by T. M. Pearce (Albuquerque: University of New Mexico Press, 1974), 32–33.

29. Austin, *Land of Little Rain,* 33.

30. See the manuscript for *Earth Horizon,* Box 51, AU775, Huntington Library. Austin attributes her college breakdown to her "beginning resistance to

whatever in her environment was intelligently felt to be the best in herself. Or I should say, it was the beginning of intelligently feeling that there was something in herself that justified resistance."

31. Austin, *Earth Horizon*, 193.

32. Austin, *Earth Horizon*, 195.

33. Austin, *Earth Horizon*, 195.

34. Norman Angell, *After All: Autobiography* (London: H. Hamilton, 1951), 47.

35. Austin, Tejon journal, Box 17, AU267, Huntington Library.

36. Mark T. Hoyer, *Dancing Ghosts: Native American and Christian Syncretism in Mary Austin's Work* (Reno: University of Nevada Press, 1998), 6.

37. Austin, *The Flock*, 224, 227.

38. Austin, *The Flock*, 11.

39. Austin, Tejon journal, Box 17, AU267, Huntington Library.

40. Susanna Hunter to Brother Kep[linger], 3 June 1899, Box 89, AU3200, Huntington Library.

41. Austin, *Woman of Genius*, 44.

42. Austin, *Earth Horizon*, 130.

43. Austin, *Earth Horizon*, 128–29.

44. Norris Hundley Jr., *The Great Thirst: Californians and Water, A History* (Berkeley: University of California Press, 2001), 94.

45. Austin, Box 14, AU182, Huntington Library.

46. Austin, *Earth Horizon*, 209.

47. See Hundley, *Great Thirst*, 93–99.

48. John Muir, *San Francisco Bulletin*, 29 October 1874, quoted in David Igler, *Industrial Cowboys: Miller and Lux and the Transformation of the Far West, 1840–1920* (Berkeley: University of California Press, 2001), 96.

49. Austin, Tejon journal, Box 17, AU267, Huntington Library,.

50. Austin, *Earth Horizon*, 171.

51. Mary Austin, *The Basket Woman*, foreword by Mark Schlenz (Reno: University of Nevada Press, 1999), 68–69.

52. Mary Austin, "Frustrate," in *Western Trails: A Collection of Short Stories by Mary Austin*, ed. Melody Graulich (Reno: University of Nevada Press, 1987), 229.

53. Donald P. Ringler, "Mary Austin: Kern County Days, 1888–1892," *Southern California Quarterly* 45 (March 1963): 157.

54. Austin, discarded pages of *Earth Horizon*, Box 51, AU776, p. 358, Huntington Library.

55. Typed, undated manuscript notes for *Earth Horizon*, titled "Addenda," Box 51 AU776, p. 3, Huntington Library. See obituary, *Carlinville Democrat*, 30 October 1878. Also see Rae Galbraith Bullard, "Earth Horizon: The Imperfect Circle" (PhD diss., Claremont Graduate School, 1977), Huntington Library.

56. Austin, "Frustrate," in *Western Trails*, 230.

57. Helen M. Doyle, *Mary Austin: Woman of Genius* (New York: Gotham House, 1939), 132.

58. Ringler, "Mary Austin: Kern County Days, 1888–1892," 160.

59. The *Overland Monthly* also published Austin's "The Wooing of the Senorita" (March 1897).

60. See John J. McCusker, "How Much Is That in Real Money? A Historical Price Index for Use as a Deflator of Money Values in the Economy of the U.S.," *Proceedings of the American Antiquarian Society* 101, part 2 (Worcester, MA: American Antiquarian Society, 1992), 332.

61. Austin, *Earth Horizon,* 228.

62. Austin, *Earth Horizon,* 230.

63. Austin, "The Mother of Felipe," in *Mary Austin Reader,* 74.

64. Quoted in Josephine DeWitt Rhodehamel and Raymund Francis Wood, *Ina Coolbrith, Librarian and Laureate of California* (Salt Lake City: Brigham Young University Press, 1973), 77.

65. Quoted in Kevin Starr, *Americans and the California Dream, 1850–1915* (New York: Oxford University Press, 1973), 240.

66. Louis Untermeyer, *Modern American Poetry* (New York: Harcourt, Brace and Co., 1930), 11.

67. Bayard Taylor to Edward Beale, 27 August 1871, quoted in O. W. Frost, *Joaquin Miller* (New York: Twayne, 1967), 113.

68. See Rhodehamel and Wood, *Ina Coolbrith,* 150–151.

69. Austin, *Earth Horizon,* 231.

70. Frances Laurence, *Maverick Women: Nineteenth Century Women Who Kicked Over the Traces* (Carpentaria, CA: Manifest Publications, 1998), 119–20.

71. Ringler, "Mary Austin: Kern County Days, 1888–1892," 53.

72. Austin, *Earth Horizon,* 232.

2. OWENS VALLEY

1. Mary Austin, *Earth Horizon,* ed. Melody Graulich (Albuquerque: University of New Mexico Press, 1991), 260.

2. Austin, *Earth Horizon,* 262.

3. Lucius Beebe and Charles Clegg, eds., *The American West: The Pictorial Epic of a Continent* (New York: Dutton, 1966), 278.

4. Austin, *Earth Horizon,* 262.

5. Austin, *Earth Horizon,* 250.

6. Austin, *Earth Horizon,* 81.

7. Mary Austin, "Early Verse," Box 11, AU125, Huntington Library, San Marino, CA.

8. Austin, *Earth Horizon,* 234–35. Also see Jane Wehrey, ed., *Voices from This Long Brown Land: Oral Recollections of Owens Valley Lives and Manzanar Pasts,* Palgrave Studies in Oral History (New York: Palgrave Macmillan, 2006).

9. Julian Steward, "Myths of the Owens Valley Paiutes," *University of California Publications in American Archaeology and Ethnology* 34 (1934–36): 368.

10. Austin, *Earth Horizon,* 236.

11. Austin, *Earth Horizon,* 242.

12. Mary Austin, *A Woman of Genius* (Old Westbury, NY: The Feminist Press, 1985), 78.

13. Austin, *Earth Horizon,* 242–43.

14. Mary Austin, "Frustrate," in *Western Trails: A Collection of Short Stories by Mary Austin,* ed. Melody Graulich (Reno: University of Nevada Press, 1987), 228.

15. Mary Austin, "Woman Alone," in *A Mary Austin Reader,* ed. Esther F. Lanigan (Tucson: University of Arizona Press, 1996), 167.

16. Austin, *Earth Horizon,* 239.

17. Austin, *Earth Horizon,* 245.

18. Austin, *Earth Horizon,* 246.

19. Sir Francis Galton, "Hereditary Character and Talent," *MacMillan's Magazine* 11 (November 1864): 165–66.

20. Austin, *Earth Horizon,* 255.

21. Austin, *Earth Horizon,* 256.

22. Austin, *Earth Horizon,* 257.

23. Mary Austin, "The Readjustment," in *Lost Borders* (New York: Harper & Brothers, 1909), 155, 156.

24. Charlotte Perkins Gilman, *The Living of Charlotte Perkins Gilman: An Autobiography* (New York: D. Appleton-Century Co., 1935), 163–64.

25. Mary Austin to Charles F. Lummis, 28 December 1918, in *Literary America, 1900–1936: The Mary Austin Letters,* ed. T. M. Pearce (Westport, CT: Greenwood Press, 1979), 26.

26. Austin, *Earth Horizon,* 265.

27. Austin, "A Case of Conscience," in *Lost Borders,* 36, 37, reprinted in *Western Trails,* 50.

28. Judy Trejo, "Coyote Tales: A Paiute Commentary," *The Journal of American Folklore* 87 (January-March 1974): 66.

29. Mark T. Hoyer, *Dancing Ghosts: Native American and Christian Syncretism in Mary Austin's Work* (Reno: University of Nevada Press, 1998), 8–9.

30. Austin, *Earth Horizon,* 267.

31. For biographical information on Doyle, see Helen MacKnight Doyle, *A Child Went Forth: The Autobiography of Dr. Helen MacKnight Doyle,* foreword by Mary Austin (New York: The Junior Literary Guild and Gotham House, 1934).

32. Helen M. Doyle, *Mary Austin: Woman of Genius* (New York: Gotham House, 1939), 201–3. The book is curious in the sense that Doyle clearly admires Austin, yet repeats much of the gossip that has made her a caricature.

33. Austin, *Earth Horizon,* 270–71.

34. Austin, *Earth Horizon,* 273.

35. Austin, "Woman Alone," in *Mary Austin Reader,* 169.

36. Austin, "The Kitchen Complex," Box 19, AU274, Huntington Library, published in *The Suffragist* (October 1920): 237–40.

37. *Mary Austin on the Art of Writing: A Letter to Henry James Forman,* [17 September 1918], introduction by James E. Philips (Los Angeles: Friends of the UCLA Library, 1961), 1.

38. Austin, *Earth Horizon,* 276.

39. Austin, *Earth Horizon,* 33.

40. Austin, *Earth Horizon,* 126.

41. Mary Austin, *Experiences Facing Death* (Indianapolis: Bobbs-Merrill, 1931), 25.

42. Austin, "The Garden Book," 30 September [1913–16], Box 14, AU198, Huntington Library.

43. Austin to Mr. Schroeder, 12 November [1919], Box 60, AU1222, Huntington Library.

44. Edward R. Bingham, *Charles F. Lummis: Editor of the Southwest* (San Marino, CA: Huntington Library, 1955), 20–22.

45. Eve Lummis to Austin, 10 April 1905, Box 73, AU2138, Huntington Library. See "The Strange Romance of a New Hampshire Schoolma'm," *Boston Herald* Sunday magazine, 28 January 1906, an account of Charles Lummis meeting a daughter he never knew he had.

46. Austin, *Earth Horizon,* 293.

47. Franklin Walker, *A Literary History of Southern California* (Berkeley: University of California Press, 1950), 137.

48. Spud Johnson Collection, 17 November 1963, 4.8, Harry Ransom Center, University of Texas, Austin.

49. Quoted in Bingham, *Charles F Lummis,* 31.

50. Charles F. Lummis, *Mesa, Cañon and Pueblo: Our Wonderland of the Southwest—Its Marvels of Nature—Its Pageant of the Earth Building—Its Strange Peoples—Its Centuried Romance* (New York: The Century Co., 1925), vii.

51. Walker, *Literary History of Southern California,* 138.

52. Bingham, *Charles F. Lummis,* 74.

53. Charles F. Lummis to Austin, 24 November 1904, in *Literary America, 1900–1936,* 19–20.

54. Austin to Spud Johnson, 17 December 1928, 4.8, Harry Ransom Center.

55. Austin, *Earth Horizon,* 292.

56. Austin to Eve Lummis, 14 August 1929, Box 58, AU 1093, Huntington Library.

57. Austin to Daniel T. MacDougal, 2 January [1922], Box 59, AU1144, Huntington Library.

58. Austin, Tejon journal, Box 17, AU267, Huntington Library.

59. Austin, *Earth Horizon,* 294.

60. Austin, "The Fakir," in *Lost Borders,* 115–16, reprinted in *Western Trails,* 67.

3. INDEPENDENCE

1. See John Walton, *Western Times and Water Wars: State, Culture, and Rebellion in California* (Berkeley: University of California Press, 1992), 154–82. Although there are conflicting reports about these events, we have drawn on Walton's account for much of this section.

2. Walton, *Western Times and Water Wars,* 164.

3. Helen Gunn to Mary Austin, 6 April 1931, Box 80, AU2603, Huntington Library, San Marino, CA.

4. Willie Arthur Chalfant to Austin, 8 November 1932, Box 71, AU1984. Huntington Library.

5. Wallace Stegner, *The Sound of Mountain Water: The Changing of the American West* (New York: Dutton, 1980), 15.

6. Helen M. Doyle, *Mary Austin: Woman of Genius* (New York: Gotham House, 1939), 135.

7. Mary Austin, "How I Learned to Read and Write," in *A Mary Austin Reader,* ed. Esther F. Lanigan (Tucson: University of Arizona Press, 1996), 150.

8. Doyle, *Mary Austin: Woman of Genius,* 180.

9. *Inyo Register,* 25 March 1886, quoted in Walton, *Western Times and Water Wars,* 124.

10. Doyle, *Mary Austin: Woman of Genius,* 203.

11. See Pete Giraud to Stafford Wallace Austin, 8 May 1904, Box 79, AU2534, Huntington Library.

12. [Stafford] Wallace Austin to A. R. Orr, 4 February 1904, RG No. 115, Box 18, Entry 3, U.S. National Archives and Records Administration (NARA), College Park, MD.

13. Austin, "Song," Box 26, AU381, Huntington Library.

14. Quoted in Walton, *Western Times and Water Wars,* 145. See also William L. Kahrl, *Water and Power: The Conflict over Los Angeles' Water Supply in the Owens Valley* (Berkeley: University of California Press, 1982), 45–79; and Abraham Hoffman, *Vision or Villainy: Origins of the Owens Valley–Los Angeles Water Controversy* (College Station: Texas A&M University Press, 1981), 99–135.

15. S. W. Austin to Theodore Roosevelt, 4 August 1904, RG No. 115, Box 18, Entry 3, NARA.

16. S. W. Austin to Theodore Roosevelt, 4 August 1904, RG No. 115, Box 18, Entry 3, NARA. Austin may have written her own letter to Roosevelt. See Stewart Edward White to Mary Austin, 29 September 1905, in *Literary America, 1903–1934: The Mary Hunter Austin Letters,* ed. T. M. Pearce (Westport, CT: Greenwood Press, 1979), 14.

17. See Kevin Starr, *Material Dreams: Southern California through the 1920s* (New York: Oxford University Press, 1990), 52–55.

18. See W. A. Chalfant, *The Story of Inyo* (1922; Chicago: The Author, 1933).

19. Austin to Miss Williams, 27 October [1904], Box 60, AU1290, Huntington Library.

20. *Los Angeles Times,* 21 October 1905, p. 7.

21. Mary Austin, *The Ford,* foreword by John Walton (Berkeley: University of California Press, 1996), 95.

22. Austin, *The Ford,* 67.

23. C. A. Moody to Austin, 15 August 1905, in *Literary America, 1903–1934,* 12.

24. Mary Austin, "The Owens River Water Project," *San Francisco Chronicle,* 3 September 1905, p. 19.

25. Elsie Watterson to Austin, 4 April 1928, Box 118, AU5166, Huntington Library.

26. Mary Austin, *Earth Horizon,* ed. Melody Graulich (Albuquerque: University of New Mexico Press, 1991), 154.

27. Bliss Perry to Austin, 31 July 1902, Box 54, AU1055, Huntington Library.

28. Originally published by Houghton Mifflin as a holiday book, *The Land of Little Rain* sold for two dollars. Houghton Mifflin printed fifty-five hundred copies in all. See Karen S. Langlois, "Mary Austin and the Houghton Mifflin Company: A Case Study in the Marketing of a Western Writer," *Western American Literature* 23, no. 1 (May 1988): 31–42.

29. Mary Austin, *The Land of Little Rain,* ed. T. M. Pearce (Albuquerque: University of New Mexico Press, 1974), 12–13.

30. Mary Austin, "The Folk Story in America," *The South Atlantic Quarterly* 33 (January 1934): 10. Austin's father owned an early edition of the *Poems* and *Representative Men,* and a childhood friend gave her Emerson's two-volume correspondence with Thomas Carlyle. She quotes Emerson in *The Land of Little Rain* as the poet who "named all the birds without a gun" (9).

31. Austin, *Land of Little Rain,* xvi. Also see Walter J. Scheick, "Mary Austin's Disfigurement of the Southwest in *The Land of Little Rain,*" *Western Literature* 27 (Spring 1992): 37–46; Mark Schlenz, "Waters of Paradise: Utopia and Hydrology in *The Land of Little Rain,*" in *Exploring Lost Borders: Critical Essays on Mary Austin,* ed. Melody Graulich and Elizabeth Klimasmith (Reno: University of Nevada Press, 1999), 133–202; and Michelle Campbell Toohney, "Mary

Austin's *The Land of Little Rain:* Remembering the Coyote," in *Exploring Lost Borders,* 203–20.

32. John C. Van Dyke, *The Desert: Further Studies in Natural Appearances* (New York: Charles Scribner's Sons, 1911), 27. See Peter Wild, "Sentimentalism in the American Southwest: John C. Van Dyke, Mary Austin, and Edward Abbey," in *Reading the West: New Essays on the Literature of the American West,* ed. Michael Kowalewski (Cambridge: Cambridge University Press, 1996), 127–43; and Peter Wild, *The Opal Desert: Explorations of Fantasy and Reality in the American Southwest* (Austin: University of Texas Press, 1999), 76, 78, 81–82.

33. Raymond Williams, *Problems in Materialism and Culture: Selected Essays* (London: Verso, 1980), 83.

34. Austin, *Land of Little Rain,* xvi.

35. Mary Austin, *Lost Borders* (New York: Harper & Brothers, 1909), 3.

36. Austin, *Land of Little Rain,* 59.

37. Austin, *Land of Little Rain,* 9, 7.

38. Isabel Watterson to Austin, 2 June 1907, Box 118, AU5171, Huntington Library. See Penny L. Richards, "Bad Blood and Lost Borders: Eugenic Ambivalence in Mary Austin's Short Fiction," in *Evolution and Eugenics in American Literature and Culture, 1880–1940: Essays on Ideological Conflict and Complexity,* ed. Lois A. Cuddy and Claire M. Roche (Lewisburg, PA: Bucknell University Press, 2003), 160n7. Richards sees it as a family story.

39. Austin, *Earth Horizon,* 362.

40. Austin, *Land of Little Rain,* 49.

41. Austin, *Land of Little Rain,* 40.

42. See Amy Kaplan, "Romancing the Empire: The Embodiment of American Masculinity in the Popular Historical Novel of the 1890s," *American Literary History* 40 (Winter 1990): 666.

43. Austin, *Earth Horizon,* 187.

44. Mary Austin, "Hoover and Johnson: West is West," *The Nation,* 15 May 1920, 642–44.

45. Austin, "Essay on Regional Literature," Box 11, AU140, Huntington Library.

46. Mary Hallock Foote to Austin, 12 October 1902, Box 77, AU214, Huntington Library.

47. Wallace Austin to A. R. Orr, 4 February 1904, RG No. 115, Box 18, Entry 3, NARA.

48. Quoted in Doyle, *Mary Austin: Woman of Genius,* 198.

49. Van Wyck Brooks, "Reviewer's Note-Book," *The Freeman* 1 (9 June 1920): 311.

50. Austin to Charles F. Lummis, 28 December 1918, in *Literary America, 1900–1936,* 25–26.

51. Austin to Eve Lummis, [1903], Box 58:, AU1091, Huntington Library.

52. Helen Gunn to Austin, 6 April 1931, Box 80, AU2603, Huntington Library.

53. Mary Austin, *The Basket Woman: A Book of Indian Tales,* foreword by Mark Schlenz (Reno: University of Nevada Press, 1999), 42, 55.

54. Alice C. Fletcher, "The Indian Messiah," *Journal of American Folk-Lore* 4 (1891): 60. See Ronald E. Martin, *The Languages of Difference: American Writers and Anthropologists Reconfigure the Primitive, 1878–1940* (Newark: University of Delaware Press, 2005), 43.

55. Sir James George Frazer, *The Golden Bough: A Study in Magic and Religion* (repr., New York: St. Martin's Press, 1976), vii.

56. Frank Hamilton Cushing, *Zuni Folk Tales,* ed. Mary Austin (New York: G. P. Putman's Sons, 1931), 2.

57. Austin to Alfred Vincent Kidder, [1929], Box,58, AU1124, Huntington Library.

58. Mary Austin, "Regionalism in American Fiction," in *Beyond Borders: The Selected Essays of Mary Austin,* edited and with an introduction by Reuben J. Ellis (Carbondale: University of Southern Illinois Press, 1996), 130.

59. Mary Austin, "American Indian Dance Drama," *Yale Review* 19 (June 1930), 737.

60. See Julian Steward, "Myths of the Owens Valley Paiutes," *University of California Publications in American Archaeology and Ethnology* 34 (1934–36), 357; and Austin, *Land of Little Rain,* 110.

61. Quoted in Doyle, *Mary Austin: Woman of Genius,* 215–16.

62. Doyle, *Mary Austin: Woman of Genius,* 203–4.

4. CARMEL

1. Mary Austin, *Earth Horizon,* ed. Melody Graulich (Albuquerque: University of Nevada Press, 1991), 297.

2. Upton Sinclair, *American Outpost: A Book of Reminiscences* (Pasadena, CA: Privately printed, 1932), 210.

3. See Warren Unna, *The Coppa Murals: A Pageant of Bohemian Life in San Francisco at the Turn of the Century* ([San Francisco]: The Book Club of California, 1952).

4. Michael Orth, "Identity to Reality: The Founding of Carmel," *The California Historical Society Quarterly* 48 (September 1969): 200.

5. Austin, *Earth Horizon,* 284.

6. Austin, *Earth Horizon,* 295.

7. Austin, *Earth Horizon,* 295.

8. See, for example, Austin's letters to Grace Ellery Channing, Schlesinger Library, Harvard University.

9. Quoted in Franklin Walker, *The Seacoast of Bohemia* (1966; Santa Barbara: Peregrine Smith, 1973), 1.

10. See Augusta Fink, "Carmel-by-the-Sea," in *Monterey: The Presence of the Past* (San Francisco: Chronicle Books, 1972), 219.

11. Quoted in Fink, "Carmel-by-the-Sea," in *Monterey: The Presence of the Past,* 220.

12. Gertrude Atherton, *Patience Sparhawk and Her Times* (New York: John Lane, 1897), 8.

13. For a fuller background of the Carmel colony, see Franklin Walker, Augusta Fink, and Sydney Temple, *Carmel-by-the-Sea: From Aborigines to Coastal Community* (Monterey, CA: Angel Press, 1987*)*.

14. Gertrude Atherton, "A Native on the California Missions," *The Critic* 9 (1888): 271.

15. Harold Gilliam and Ann Gilliam, *Creating Carmel* (Salt Lake City: Gibbs Smith, 1992), 82.

16. Mary Austin, "George Sterling at Carmel," *The American Mercury* 11 (May 1927): 65.

17. Carey McWilliams, "A Letter from Carmel," *The Saturday Review of Literature* 6 (4 January 1930): 622.

18. Mary Austin, "Three at Carmel," *The Saturday Review of Literature* 5 (29 September 1928): 165.

19. Richard O'Connor, *Jack London* (Boston: Little, Brown, 1963), 259.

20. Austin, "George Sterling at Carmel," 66.

21. Quoted in Gilliam and Gilliam, *Creating Carmel,* 79.

22. Thomas E. Benediktsson, *George Sterling* (Boston: Twayne, 1980), 34.

23. Quoted in Walker, *Seacoast of Bohemia,* 33.

24. Quoted in Unna, *Coppa Murals,* 28.

25. Austin, "George Sterling at Carmel," 67.

26. Austin, "George Sterling at Carmel," 69.

27. Austin, "George Sterling at Carmel," 65.

28. Van Wyck Brooks, *An Autobiography* (New York: E. P. Dutton, 1965), 196.

29. Arnold Genthe, *As I Remember* (New York: Reynal & Hitchcock, 1936), 75.

30. Mary Austin to Blanche Partington, [1906], Bancroft Library, University of California, Berkeley.

31. Austin to Charles F. Lummis, 28 December 1918, Box 19, AU1139, Huntington Library.

32. Elsie Martinez, "San Francisco Area Writers and Artists," an interview conducted by Franklin D. Walker and Willa Klug Baum, with an introduction by Franklin D. Walker (Regional Oral History Office, Bancroft Library, University of California, Berkeley, 1969), 220.

33. Mary Austin, "The Walking Woman," in *Western Trails: A Collection of Short Stories by Mary Austin,* ed. Melody Graulich (Reno: University of Nevada Press, 1987), 94.

34. Edith Wharton, *The Touchstone,* in *Madame de Treymes and Others: Four Novelettes* (New York: Charles Scribner's Sons, 1970), 11.

35. Jack London, *The Valley of the Moon,* foreword by Kevin Starr (Berkeley: University of California Press, 1999), 314–15.

36. Austin, "George Sterling at Carmel," 66.

37. George Sterling, *Beyond the Breakers and Other Poems* (San Francisco: A. M. Robertson, 1914), 64.

38. Van Wyck Brooks, *Scenes and Portraits: Memories of Childhood and Youth* (New York: E. P. Dutton, 1954), 190.

39. Quoted in Walker, *Seacoast of Bohemia,* 94.

40. Austin, *Earth Horizon,* 290.

41. Benediktsson, *George Sterling,* 34.

42. Benediktsson, *George Sterling,* 38–39.

43. Austin, *Earth Horizon,* 349.

44. Benediktsson, *George Sterling,* 34.

45. See Martin Green, *Mountain of Truth: The Counterculture Begins; Ascona, 1900–1920* (Hanover, NH: University Press of New England, 1986), especially 234–35. Green's is the definitive work on Ascona and related communities.

46. See Linda Leigh Paul and Radek Kruzai, *Cottages by the Sea: The Handmade Home of Carmel, America's First Artist Community* (New York: Universe, 2000).

47. Austin, "The Garden Book [notebook] Carmel-by-the-Sea, 1913–1916," entry for 12 May 1913, Box 14, AU198, Huntington Library.

48. Henry David Thoreau, *Journal,* ed. Bradford Torrey and Frances H. Allen, foreword by Walter Harding (repr., New York: Dover, 1962), 10:89–90.

49. Quoted in Walker, *Seacoast of Bohemia,* 125.

50. Quoted in John Castillo Kennedy, *The Great Earthquake and Fire* (New York: William Morrow, 1963), 20.

51. Josephine DeWitt Rhodehamel and Raymund Francis Wood, *Ina Coolbrith, Librarian and Laureate of California* (Salt Lake City: Brigham Young University Press, 1973), 255.

52. Ina Coolbrith to Lorenzo Sosso, n.d., Society of California Pioneers, San Francisco, quoted in Rhodehamel and Wood, *Ina Coolbrith,* 257–58.

53. Austin to Ina Coolbrith, 29 May and 14 June 1906, Bancroft Library.

54. The project embarrassed Coolbrith, who did not want to be seen as a charity case, and generated little income. Gertrude Atherton organized a much more successful benefit reading. See Emily Wortis Leider, *California's Daughter: Gertrude Atherton and Her Times* (Stanford: Stanford University Press, 1991), 219–23.

55. Austin, "The Tremblor: A Personal Narrative," in *The California Earthquake of 1906,* ed. David Starr Jordan (San Francisco: A. M. Robertson, 1907), 343, 344.

56. Austin, "The Tremblor," 346.

57. Austin, "The Tremblor," 350, 351, 346.

58. Austin, "The Tremblor," 351–52.

59. Mary Austin, *Isidro,* illustrated by Eric Pape (Boston: Houghton, Mifflin, 1905), 43.

60. Austin, *Isidro,* 79.

61. Austin, *Isidro,* 412.

62. Austin, *Isidro,* 180.

63. Austin, *Earth Horizon,* 188.

64. See David Wyatt, *The Fall into Eden: Landscape and Imagination in California* (Cambridge: Cambridge University Press, 1986), 33.

65. This discussion of *The Flock* draws partly on the work of Barney Nelson. See Nelson's afterword to Mary Austin, *The Flock,* 267–311; and Nelson, "*The Flock:* An Ecocritical Look at Mary Austin's Sheep and John Muir's Hoofed Locusts," in *Exploring Lost Borders: Critical Essays on Mary Austin,* ed. Melody Graulich and Elizabeth Klimasmith (Reno: University of Nevada Press, 1999), 221–43.

66. Austin, *Earth Horizon,* 188.

67. Austin to Houghton Mifflin, 11 June 1907, Box 58, AU1109, Huntington Library.

68. Houghton Mifflin to Austin, 30 September 1907, Box 58, AU1112, Huntington Library.

69. Elizabeth Shepley Sergeant, "Mary Austin: A Portrait," *The Saturday Review of Literature* 11 (8 September 1934): 36.

5. IN ITALY AND ENGLAND

1. Mary Austin, *Earth Horizon,* ed. Melody Graulich (Albuquerque: University of New Mexico Press, 1991), 309.

2. Augusta Fink, *I-Mary: A Biography of Mary Austin* (Tucson: University of Arizona Press, 1983), 139.

3. Mary Austin to Vernon Kellogg, 4 December 1907, quoted in Fink, *I-Mary,* 139.

4. See Austin, *Earth Horizon,* 308.

5. Mary Austin, *Christ in Italy: Being the Adventures of a Maverick among the Masterpieces* (New York: Duffield & Co., 1912), xiv.

6. Austin, *Christ in Italy,* 28–31.

7. Austin, *Christ in Italy,* 87.

8. See for example, Patricia Meilman, ed., *The Cambridge Companion to Titian* (Cambridge: Cambridge University Press, 2004), 11–13.

9. Austin, *Christ in Italy,* 93.

10. Austin, *Christ in Italy,* 101, 105.

11. Mary Austin, *Experiences Facing Death* (Indianapolis: Bobbs-Merrill, 1931), 300.

12. Mary Austin to Eve Lummis, 7 September 1908, Charles Fletcher Lummis Papers, courtesy of Braun Research Library, Autry National Center, Los Angeles.

13. Austin, *Earth Horizon,* 310.

14. Austin, *Earth Horizon,* 310.

15. See Laudia Calen, ed., *The Papal Encyclicals, 1903–39,* especially the injunction against Modernism, "Pascendi Dominici Gregis," 8 September 1907, 71–98. By 1910, Pius X demanded that priests take an oath against Modernism.

16. See Bernetta Quinn, *Give Me Souls: A Life of Raphael Cardinal Merry del Val* (Westminster, MD: Newman Press, 1958).

17. See *Records of the American Catholic Society of Philadelphia* 65 (March–December 1954): 201, 210.

18. Peter Kurth, *Isadora: A Sensational Life* (Boston: Little, Brown, 2001), 105.

19. Edward Gordon Craig, *Index to the Story of My Days* (New York: Viking, 1957), 262.

20. Austin, *Earth Horizon,* 309.

21. Austin, *Earth Horizon,* 309.

22. See Mary Austin, Box 123, which contains notes she took from Craig's *Art of the Theatre,* Huntington Library, San Marino, CA.

23. See Austin, *Earth Horizon,* 310.

24. Austin, *Earth Horizon,* 310–11.

25. James Wilkinson to Austin, n.d., Box 119, AU5253, Huntington Library.

26. Mary Austin to Grace Ellery Channing, 12 March [1909], Schlesinger Library, Harvard.

27. Austin to Channing, January 12 [1909 or 1910], Schlesinger Library.

28. Austin to Channing, August 12 [1908], Schlesinger Library.

29. Austin to Channing, January 12 [1909 or 1910], Schlesinger Library.

30. Austin to Channing, January 12 [1909 or 1910], Schlesinger Library.

31. Austin to Channing, [1909?], Schlesinger Library.

32. Mary Austin, *Outland* (New York: Boni and Liveright, 1929), 37.

33. Austin, *Outland,* 306.

34. Mary Austin, *Santa Lucia* (New York: Harper & Brothers, 1908), 346.

35. Austin, *Santa Lucia,* 74.

36. William Dean Howells to Aurelia H. Howells, 8 April 1906, in William Dean Howells, *Selected Letters,* edited and annotated by George Arms et al.,

textual eds., Don L. Cook, Christoph K. Lohmann, and David J. Nordloh (Boston: Twayne, 1879–1983), 5:170.

37. Reginald Bliss [H. G. Wells], *The Mind of the Race* (New York: George H. Doran, 1915), 146.

38. Mary Austin, "An Appreciation of H G. Wells," *American Magazine* 72 (October 1911): 735.

39. See Warren Wagar, *H. G. Wells: Traversing Time* (Middletown, CT: Wesleyan University Press, 2004), 17–18, 47; and Anthony West, *H. G. Wells: Aspects of a Life* (London: Hutchinson, 1984), 314–15.

40. Mary Austin, "My Fabian Summer," *The Bookman* 4 (December 1921): 351.

41. Austin, *Earth Horizon,* 311. The first edition contains the offending passage; others do not.

42. Austin, *Earth Horizon,* 312.

43. Mary Austin, introduction to *Typhoon,* by Joseph Conrad (1928), manuscript, Box 17, AU258, p. 4, Huntington Library.

44. Austin, introduction to *Typhoon,* 2–5. See also Mary Austin, "Joseph Conrad Tells What Women Don't Know about Men," *Pictorial Review* 102 (September 1923): 4.

45. Mary Austin, *Lost Borders* (New York: Harper & Brothers, 1909), 54.

46. Austin, introduction to *Typhoon,* 5.

47. Austin, introduction to *Typhoon,* 1, 4.

48. Quoted in Austin, *Earth Horizon,* 313.

49. Austin, *Earth Horizon,* 313.

50. Austin, *Earth Horizon,* 313.

51. Austin to Channing, 25 November [1909], Schlesinger Library.

52. Austin, *Earth Horizon,* 314.

53. Herbert Hoover, *The Memoirs of Herbert Hoover: Years of Adventure, 1874–1920* (New York: Macmillan, 1951), 121–22.

54. Austin, *Earth Horizon,* 314.

55. Austin to Channing, 25 November [1909], Schlesinger Library.

56. Austin to Channing, 14 August 1909, Schlesinger Library.

57. Austin to Channing, 28 December 1909, Schlesinger Library.

58. George Sterling to Austin, 1 September 1910, Box 112, AU4758, Huntington Library.

59. Gertrude Atherton, *My San Francisco: A Wayward Biography* (Indianapolis: Bobbs-Merrill, 1946), 99.

60. Austin, "My Fabian Summer," 351.

61. Austin, "My Fabian Summer," 354.

62. Austin, "My Fabian Summer," 355.

63. Austin, *Lost Borders,* 1.

64. Austin, *Lost Borders,* 8, 10–11.

65. Mary Austin, "The Walking Woman," in *Western Trails: A Collection of Short Stories by Mary Austin,* ed. Melody Graulich (Reno: University of Nevada Press, 1987), 97.

66. Austin, "The Walking Woman," in *Western Trails,* 96.

67. Austin, *Earth Horizon,* 316.

68. Austin, *Earth Horizon,* 35.

69. See Duncan James McMillan to Austin, 10 April 1929, Box 99, AU3820, Huntington Library.

70. Austin, *Earth Horizon,* 316.

71. Austin, *Earth Horizon,* 316.

72. Austin, *Earth Horizon,* 316–17.

73. Austin to Channing, [1909?], Schlesinger Library.

74. Henry James, *The American Scene,* introduction and notes by Leon Edel (Bloomington: Indiana University Press, 1969), 366.

6. NEW YORK

1. At this time, Austin had Paul Revere Reynolds, one of the most successful agents, marketing her work.

2. Mary Austin, *Earth Horizon,* ed. Melody Graulich (Albuquerque: University of New Mexico Press, 1991), 320.

3. James Trager, *The New York Chronology* (New York: Harper Resource, 2003), 323–25.

4. Mary Austin, journal, impressions of New York, Box 18, AU268, p. 31, Huntington Library, San Marino, CA.

5. Austin, *Earth Horizon,* 347.

6. See Mary Austin to Lou Hoover, 12 May 1912, Herbert Hoover Presidential Library, West Branch, IA.

7. Austin to Dear Sirs, 6 May 1921, Box 58, AU1089, Huntington Library.

8. Austin to Dear Sirs, 6 May 1921, Box 58, AU1089, Huntington Library. Austin, who saw *Joan of Arc* as a sex film, predicted that films would be censored. She also argued the need to understand the psychology of audience and commercial pressures.

9. T. M. Pearce, "Mary Austin and the Pattern of New Mexico," *Southwest Review* 22 (1937): 140.

10. Austin to Charles F. Lummis, 8 March 1924, Box 58, AU1134, Huntington Library.

11. Austin to Daniel T. MacDougal, 8 March [1922], Box 59, AU1156, Huntington Library.

12. Austin to Mabel Dodge Luhan, 26 August 1929, Mabel Dodge Luhan Papers, Yale Collection of American Literature, Beinecke Rare Book and Manuscript Library.

13. Lincoln Steffens to Laura Steffens, 25 December 1910, in Lincoln Steffens, *The Letters of Lincoln Steffens,* ed. Ella Winter and Granville Hicks, with a memorandum by Carl Sandburg (New York: Harcourt, Brace and Co., 1938), 1:255.

14. See Karen S. Langlois, "Mary Austin and Lincoln Steffens," *Huntington Library Quarterly: A Journal for the History and Interpretation of English and American Civilization* 49, no. 4 (Autumn 1986): 327–53. We are indebted to Langlois for her research on the Austin-Steffens relationship.

15. Lincoln Steffens to Austin, 8 May 1911, in *Literary America, 1900–1936: The Mary Austin Letters,* ed. T. M. Pearce (Westport, CT: Greenwood Press, 1979), 43.

16. Lincoln Steffens to his mother, Mrs. Frank Steffens, 4 February 1892, in Steffens, *The Letters of Lincoln Steffens,* 1:70.

17. Mary Austin, *No. 26 Jayne Street* (Boston: Houghton Mifflin, 1920), 250.

18. Justin Kaplan, *Lincoln Steffens: A Biography* (New York: Simon and Schuster, 1974), 93.

19. Mary Austin to Lincoln Steffens, 9 March [1911], Steffens Papers, Columbia University.

20. Austin, "The Interview," Box 17, AU251, p. 7, Huntington Library.

21. Austin to Daniel T. MacDougal, 18 May [1922], Box 59, AU1164, Huntington Library.

22. Austin, journal, impressions of New York, 28 March 1911, Box 18, AU268, Huntington Library.

23. Austin, journal, impressions of New York, 29 March 1911, Box 18, AU268, Huntington Library.

24. Austin to unnamed correspondent ("Dear"), n.d., AU1088, Huntington Library.

25. Quoted in Warren Unna, *The Coppa Murals: A Pageant of Bohemian Life in San Francisco at the Turn of the Century* ([San Francisco]: The Book Club of California, 1952), 51.

26. Elsie Martinez, "San Francisco Area Writers and Artists," an interview conducted by Franklin D. Walker and Willa Klug Baum, with an introduction by Walker (Regional Oral History Office, Bancroft Library, University of California, Berkeley, 1969), 219–20.

27. Austin, *No. 26 Jayne Street,* 169.

28. Martinez, "San Francisco Area Writers and Artists," 219–20. See Mary Austin, *The Ford* (Berkeley: University Press of California, 1997), 263: "You think that's all a woman needs," one of the heroines exclaims, "to be liked and respected, and to wait . . . wait . . . until some man gets done fussing about and finding what *he* likes, what *he* wants to do and can make of his life . . . and then comes and invites her into it! And she isn't supposed to have any feelings while she waits, nor to make anything of *her* life . . . nor to change nor to think . . . and all she gets out of it is to be liked and respected!"

29. Lincoln Steffens, "Mary Austin," *American Magazine* 72 (June 1911): 181.

30. Austin to Lou Hoover, 15 June [1911], Herbert Hoover Presidential Library.

31. Austin to Lou Hoover, 14 July [1911], Herbert Hoover Presidential Library.

32. Mabel Dodge Luhan, *Movers and Shakers* (Albuquerque : University of New Mexico Press, 1985), 67–68.

33. Austin to Steffens, n.d., Steffens Papers, Columbia University.

34. Austin to Steffens, n.d., Steffens Papers, Columbia University.

35. Austin to Steffens, n.d., Steffens Papers, Columbia University.

36. Austin to Steffens, n.d., Steffens Papers, Columbia University.

37. Austin to Steffens, n.d., Steffens Papers, Columbia University.

38. Austin to Steffens, n.d., Steffens Papers, Columbia University.

39. Austin to Lou Hoover, 15 June [1911], Herbert Hoover Presidential Library.

40. Austin to Lou Hoover, 16 October [1911], Herbert Hoover Presidential Library.

41. Austin to Steffens, n.d., Steffens Papers, Columbia University.

42. Gussie Burgess Nobbes to Laura Suggett, 10 July 1924, quoted in Kaplan, *Lincoln Steffens,* 278.

43. Mary Austin, *A Woman of Genius* (Old Westbury, NY: The Feminist Press, 1985), 143.

44. Mabel Dodge Luhan to Austin, [July 1929], Box, 95 AU3603, Huntington Library.

45. Austin to Mabel Dodge Luhan, 26 August 1929, Mabel Dodge Luhan Papers, Yale Collection of American Literature, Beinecke Rare Book and Manuscript Library.

46. Mary Austin, *Love and the Soul Maker* (New York: D. Appleton and Co., 1914), 286.

47. Austin saved a newspaper clipping in which Sickels denied that his estranged wife pawned her jewels to acquit his debt. She used the incident in *No. 26 Jayne Street,* where Sickels and his wife appear as General and Mrs. Rittenhouse.

48. Neith Hapgood to Mabel Dodge, December 1915, Mabel Dodge Luhan Papers, Yale Collection of American Literature, Beinecke Rare Book and Manuscript Library, quoted in Ellen Kay Trimberger, "The New Woman and the New Sexuality," in *1915, the Cultural Moment: The New Politics, the New Woman, the New Psychology, the New Art and the New Theater in America,* ed. Adele Heller and Lois Rudnick (New Brunswick, NJ: Rutgers University Press, 1991), 113.

49. Hutchins Hapgood, *A Victorian in the Modern World* (New York: Harcourt, Brace and Co., 1939), 320.

50. Quoted in Mabel Dodge Luhan, *Movers and Shakers* (Albuquerque: University of New Mexico Press, [1985], c1936), 241.

51. Mabel Dodge Luhan, *Movers and Shakers,* 45.

52. See Mary Austin to Mr. Watson, 8 May [1918], Berg Collection, New York Public Library.

53. Austin, *Earth Horizon*, 329.

54. Austin to Henry Chester Tracy, 1 January 1929, Box 60, AU 1253, Huntington Library.

55. Austin to Mabel Dodge, 5 December 1922, Mabel Dodge Luhan Papers, Yale Collection of American Literature, Beinecke Rare Book and Manuscript Library.

56. Henry David Thoreau to Harrison Gray Otis Balke, 27 March 1848, in Henry David Thoreau, *Familiar Letters,* ed. F. B. Sanborn (Boston: Houghton Mifflin, 1906), 160–64.

57. Jimmy Hopper to Austin, September 1911, in *Literary America, 1903–1934,* 57.

58. Austin, *Woman of Genius,* 289.

59. Austin, *Woman of Genius,* 87.

60. Elizabeth Barrett Browning, *Aurora Leigh,* ed. Margaret Reynolds (Athens: Ohio University Press, 1992), 419.

61. Mary Austin, "Woman Alone," *A Mary Austin Reader,* ed. Esther F. Lanigan (Tucson: University of Arizona Press, 1996), 169.

62. Austin, *Woman of Genius,* 167.

63. Austin, *Woman of Genius,* 275.

64. Austin, *Woman of Genius,* 62.

65. Mary Austin, "The Woman at the Eighteen-Mile," in *Western Trails: A Collection of Short Stories by Mary Austin,* ed. Melody Graulich (Reno: University of Nevada Press, 1987), 63.

66. Austin, *Earth Horizon,* 351.

67. James A. Hearne, "Art for Truth's Sake in the Drama," *The Arena* 17 (February 1897): 361–70; and Alan S. Downer, ed., *American Drama and Its Critics* (Chicago: University of Chicago Press, 1965), 3–9.

68. The 1911 scenario centers on a novelist named Sterling who, having gone west to study primitive women, brings home an Indian girl, who had stabbed her lover, to be his maid. She is of course in love with Sterling, but he, engaged to a woman of his class, does not know it. Learning about his engagement and furious that he has been studying her, the girl stabs him, thus completing his realistic acquaintance with primitive women. See Austin, "The Realist," Box 31, AU474, Huntington Library.

69. See Austin, "Island of Desire," Box 17, AU263, Huntington Library.

70. See Walter Prichard Eaton, *Washington Square Plays* (Garden City, NY: Doubleday, Page, and Co., 1917); Arthur Frank Wertheim, "The Little Theater Movement," in *The New York Little Renaissance: Iconoclasm, Modernism, and Nationalism in American Culture, 1908–1917,* ed. Arthur Frank Wertheim (New York: New York University Press, 1976), 149–63; Constance D'Arcy Mackay, *The Little*

Theatre in the U.S. (New York: Holt, 1917); Sheldon Cheney, *The New Movement in the Theatre* (1914; repr., Westport, CT: Greenwood Press, 1971); Brenda Murphy, *American Realism and American Drama* (London: Cambridge University Press, 1987); and Patricia D. Denison, "The Legacy of James A. Hearne: American Realities and Realisms," in *Realism and the American Dramatic Tradition,* ed. William W. Demastes (Tuscaloosa: University of Alabama Press, 1996).

71. For a definition of "folk drama," see David Krasner, *A Beautiful Pageant: African American Theater, Drama, and Performance in the Harlem Renaissance, 1910–1927* (New York: Palgrave, 2002), 130.

72. Austin to Lou Hoover, 3 December [1910], Herbert Hoover Presidential Library.

73. Cheney, *New Movement in the Theatre,* 279.

74. Austin, *Woman of Genius,* 94.

75. Mary Austin, "The Reorganization of the New Theatre," *American Magazine,* November 1911, p. 102.

76. Mary Austin, *The Arrow Maker: A Drama in Three Acts* (New York: Duffield and Co., 1911), 128.

77. Clayton Hamilton, "The Personality of the Playwright," *The Bookman* 33 (April 1911): 140–41; and Clayton Hamilton, "The New Play," *Theatre Magazine* (April 1911): 106–7.

78. " 'The Arrow Maker' A Pictorial Play," *New York Times,* 28 February 1911, p. 8.

79. Austin, "The Reorganization of The New Theatre," *American Magazine,* November 1911, p. 102.

80. Austin had also had a falling out with Elmer Harris about their collaboration on *The Coyote Doctor.* Apparently she did not think he was representing her interests or doing his share of the work.

81. For one of the few discussions of this play, see Mark Hoyer, "Ritual Drama / Dramatic Ritual: Austin's 'Indian Plays,' " in *Exploring Lost Borders: Critical Essays on Mary Austin,* ed. Melody Graulich and Elizabeth Klimasmith (Reno: University of Nevada Press, 1999), 39–63.

82. The Goodman Memorial Theater of the Chicago Art Institute staged this play as *Christmas Island, or How Christmas Came to the Colonies,* on 12 November 1917.

83. Mary Austin, "New York Dictator of American Criticism," *The Nation,* 31 July 1920, 129–30.

84. See Alan Trachtenberg, *Shades of Hiawatha: Staging Indians, Making Americans, 1880–1930* (New York: Hill and Wang, 2004), 164–67.

85. Jean Toomer, "Americans and Mary Austin," *The New York Call,* 10 October 1920, p. 2. For a discussion of Austin's anti-Semitism, see Charles Scruggs, "My Chosen World: Jean Toomer's Articles in *The New York Call,*" *Arizona Quarterly* 51 (Summer 1995): 103–26, especially 109–12.

86. Austin, *Earth Horizon,* 351.

87. Austin to Mabel Dodge, 9 November [c. 1920], Mabel Dodge Luhan Papers, Yale Collection of American Literature, Beinecke Rare Book and Manuscript Library.

88. Austin to Daniel T. MacDougal, 18 May [1922], Box 59, AU1164, Huntington Library.

89. Austin to Lou Hoover, 18 June [1914], Herbert Hoover Presidential Library.

90. Mary Austin, *The Man Jesus: Being a Brief Account of the Life and Teaching of The Prophet of Nazareth* (New York: Harper & Brothers,1915), 20–21.

91. Van Wyck Brooks, "A Reviewer's Notebook," *Freeman* 9 (June 1920): 310–11.

92. Mary Austin to Houghton Mifflin, October 1915, Bancroft Library, University of California, Berkeley.

93. Austin to Houghton Mifflin, 16 October 1915, Bancroft Library.

94. Ferris Greenslet to Austin, 15 December 1915, Bancroft Library.

95. Austin to Lou Hoover, 18 June [1914], Herbert Hoover Presidential Library.

96. See Janis P. Stout, "Mary Austin's Feminism: A Reassessment," *Studies in the Novel* 30 (1998): 77–101. Also see Elizabeth Klimasmith, "A Taste for Center Stage: Consumption and Consumerism in *A Woman of Genius,*" in *Exploring Lost Borders,* 129–59.

7. THE VILLAGE

1. James Boardman Jr., undated report to Mary Austin, [c. 1913], Box 42, AU660, Huntington Library, San Marino, CA.

2. See Judith Schwarz, *Radical Feminists of Heterodoxy: Greenwich Village, 1912–1940* (Lebanon, NH: New Victoria Publishers, 1982). Austin had brief connections with the Heterodoxy Club, founded to bring together distinguished women who prided themselves on being different. The club met twice a month to hear and discuss addresses from prominent women, among them Helen Keller and Grace Mayo Johnson.

3. Mary Austin, "A Forward Turn," *The Nation,* July 1927, 57.

4. Mary Austin, "Joseph Conrad Tells What Women Don't Know about Men," *Pictorial Review* 102 (September 1923): 4.

5. Austin to Mabel Dodge Luhan, [1925], Mabel Dodge Luhan Papers, Yale Collection of American Literature, Beinecke Rare Book and Manuscript Library.

6. Willa Cather, *A Lost Lady* (New York: Vintage Books, 1990), 147.

7. See Willa Cather, "Katherine Mansfield," in *Willa Cather on Writing* (Lincoln: University of Nebraska Press, 1988), 109.

8. T. M. Pearce, *The Beloved House* (Caldwell, ID: Caxton Printers, 1940), 17.

9. Lincoln Steffens, "Mary Austin," *American Magazine* 72 (June 1911): 181.

10. Carl Van Doren, *Contemporary American Novelists, 1900–1920* (1922; New York: Macmillan, 1931), 141.

11. Floyd Dell, *Homecoming: An Autobiography* (New York: Farrar & Rinehart, 1933), 272. See Kenneth S. Lynn, "The Rebels of Greenwich Village," in *Perspectives in American History*, ed. Donald Fleming and Bernard Bailyn (Cambridge, MA: Charles Warren Center for Studies in American History, Harvard University, 1974), 8:335–80.

12. Mabel Dodge Luhan, *Movers and Shakers* (Albuquerque: University of New Mexico Press, 1985), 88.

13. Van Wyck Brooks, *The Confident Years* (New York: E. P. Dutton, 1952), 482.

14. Mary Austin, *Earth Horizon,* ed. Melody Graulich (Albuquerque: University of New Mexico Press, 1991), 326.

15. Austin to Mabel Dodge Luhan, [1925], Mabel Dodge Luhan Papers, Yale Collection of American Literature, Beinecke Rare Book and Manuscript Library.

16. Dell, *Homecoming,* 247.

17. June Sochen, *The New Woman: Feminism in Greenwich Village 1910–1920* (New York: Quadrangle Books, 1972), 51.

18. Amelia Fry, "Along the Suffrage Trail: From West to East for Freedom Now!" in *History of Women of the United States,* ed. Nancy F. Cott (Munich: K. G. Saur, 1994), 681.

19. Anne Martin, "A Tribute to Mary Austin," *The Nation,* 10 October 1934, 409.

20. Inez Haynes Irwin to Austin, 3 May 1923, Box 89, AU3231, Huntington Library.

21. Shubael Cottle, "Owed to Mary," Box 42, AU665, Huntington Library. Also see, "National Arts Bulletin Carries Amusing Story on Mary Austin," *Santa Fe New Mexican,* 10 April 1935, p. 2.

22. Austin, *Earth Horizon,* 330.

23. "William Dean Howells," *North American Review* 212 (July 1920): 9.

24. William Allen White, *The Autobiography of William Allen White* (New York: Macmillan, 1946), 370.

25. Mary Austin to Hutchins Hapgood, 4 April 1919, in Hutchins Hapgood, *A Victorian in the Modern World* (New York: Harcourt, Brace and Co., 1939), 439–40.

26. Austin to Mabel Dodge Luhan, [1925], Mabel Dodge Luhan Papers, Yale Collection of American Literature, Beinecke Rare Book and Manuscript Library.

27. Mary Austin, "Art Influence in the West," *The Century* 67 (1915): 829–33.

28. See Mary Austin to Albert Bender, 4 September 1929, Special Collections, F. W. Olin Library, Mills College.

29. Mary Austin, *California, the Land of the Sun* (London: Adam and Charles Black, 1914), 129, 134, 135, 136, 139.

30. Austin, *California, the Land of the Sun*, 20.

31. Austin, *California, the Land of the Sun*, 7, 20.

32. Mary Austin to Katherine Leckie, 1 December 1915, in *Literary America, 1903–1934: The Mary Austin Letters*, ed. T. M. Pearce (Westport, CT: Greenwood Press, 1979), 82.

33. Austin to Hoovers, 23 August 1916, Herbert Hoover Presidential Library, West Branch, IA.

34. Herbert Hoover to Austin, 23 June 1917, Box 84, AU2884, Huntington Library.

35. Austin to Herbert Hoover, 4 June 1918, in *Literary America, 1900–1936*, 94.

36. Herbert Hoover to Austin, 14 March 1918 and 11 April 1918, in *Literary America, 1903–1934*, 90, 91.

37. Austin to Herbert Hoover, 18 July 1918, quoted in *Literary America, 1903–1934*, 92.

38. Austin to Lou Hoover, [29?] September [1918], Herbert Hoover Presidential Library.

39. Austin to Lou Hoover, [29?] September [1918], Herbert Hoover Presidential Library. See Janis P. Stout, "Mary Austin's Feminism: A Reassessment," *Studies in the Novel* 30 (1998): 77–101.

40. Lou Hoover to Austin, 12 April 1918, Box 84, AU2898, Huntington Library.

41. Herbert Hoover to Austin, 3 May 1920, Box 84, AU 2889, Huntington Library.

42. Austin, "American Literature as an Expression of American Experience," [1921–22], Box 1, AU8, Huntington Library.

43. R. W. B. Lewis, *Edith Wharton: A Biography* (New York: Charles Scribner's Sons, 1985), 423–24.

44. Mary Austin, *The Ford* (Berkeley: University Press of California, 1997), 95, 437.

45. Mary Austin, *The Young Woman Citizen* (1918; New York: The Woman's Press, 1920), 124–25.

46. Austin, *The Ford*, 403, 384.

47. Mary Austin, "Germany's Mexican Intrigue—What It Means," *New York Times*, 11 March 1917, p. SM2.

48. Also see Mary Austin, "What the Mexican Conference Really Means," *New York Times*, 29 October 1916, p. SM7–8,

49. Mary Austin, "Wanted: A New Method in Mexico," *The Nation*, 21 February 1920, 228.

50. Austin to H. G. Wells, 24 January 1917, in *Literary America, 1903–1934*, 106.

51. Austin, *Young Woman Citizen,* 159, 163, 154. Concerned that the publisher was not bringing out the book on schedule, Austin consulted a lawyer.

52. Austin, *No. 26 Jayne Street* (New York: Houghton Mifflin, 1920), 303.

53. Austin, *No. 26 Jayne* Street, 152.

54. Mabel Dodge Luhan, *Mary Austin: A Memorial* (Santa Fe: Laboratory of Anthropology, 1944), 21; Austin, *No. 26 Jayne Street,* 353. Austin revisits the themes of *No. 26 Jayne* Street in a posthumously published novella, *Cactus Thorn* (Reno: University of Nevada Press, 1988). The heroine, Dulcie Adelaid, kills her straying lover, Grant Arliss, an up-and-coming politician.

55. Carl Van Doren, *Contemporary American Novelists* (New York: Macmillan, 1922), 142–43.

56. Austin to Sonya Levien, 1 September 1917, in *Literary America, 1903–1934,* 111.

57. Deborah Blum, *Ghost Hunters: William James and the Search for Scientific Proof of Life after Death* (New York: Penguin, 2006), 104.

58. Austin to Levien, 1 September 1917, in *Literary America, 1903–1934,* 111.

59. See George Hunter to Austin, 4 August [1917], Box 89, AU3184, Huntington Library.

60. Austin, "It needs not that the dead should walk," 10 May 1915, Box 17, AU264, Huntington Library.

61. Austin, "The Lame Little Lad," Box 19, AU289, Huntington Library.

62. Austin to Daniel T. MacDougal, 10 November [1922], Box 59, AU1174, Huntington Library.

63. Anzia Yezierska to Austin, 12 April [1920], Box 121, AU5430, Huntington Library.

64. Elizabeth Sergeant, *Willa Cather: A Memoir* (Philadelphia: J. B. Lippincott, 1953), 33–34.

65. Sergeant, *Willa Cather,* 51.

66. Van Wyck Brooks, *An Autobiography* (New York: E. P. Dutton, 1965), 259.

67. Austin to Ferris Greenslet, 28 January 1919, quoted in Janis P. Stout, "Willa Cather and Mary Austin: Intersections and Influence," *Southwest American Literature* 21 (1996): 42. We acknowledge our debt to Stout in our discussion of Austin and Cather. For a description of Greenslet, see Sergeant, *Willa Cather,* 129.

68. Austin to Greenslet, 7 August 1920, quoted in Stout, "Willa Cather and Mary Austin," 42.

69. Austin to the editor of *Youth Companion,* 12 March 1909, Alderman Library, University of Virginia.

70. Austin, "Willa Cather," *El Palacio* 9 (March–April 1920): 91.

71. Henry James, "The Art of Fiction," in *Henry James: Literary Criticism,* ed. Leon Edel (New York: Library of America, 1984), 53.

72. Austin, "Indian Detour," *The Bookman* 66 (February 1928): 657; and Cather, *On Writing,* 37.

73. Committee of rangers (W. B. Taylor, E. L. Springer, H. J. Brown), 18 April 1906, Box 110, AU4608, Huntington Library.

74. Marjorie Kinnan Rawlings, "Regional Literature of the South," *The English Journal* 29 (February 1940): 93.

75. Willa Cather, *O Pioneers!* (1913; Boston: Houghton Mifflin, 1988), 38.

76. Quoted in E. K. Brown, "Willa Cather," in *Willa Cather and Her Critics,* ed. James Schroeter (Ithaca, NY: Cornell University Press, 1967), 82.

77. Cather, "The Demands of Art" (1895), in *The Kingdom of Art: Cather's First Principles and Critical Statements 1843–1896,* ed. Bernice Slote (Lincoln: University of Nebraska Press, 1967).

78. Mary Austin to Ida Hilliard, 5 December 1916, quoted in Augusta Fink, *I-Mary: A Biography of Mary Austin* (Tucson: University of Arizona Press, 1983), 178.

8. THE CALL OF THE WEST

1. "Speech at Dinner to Mary Austin, January 8, 1922," Box 42, AU670, Huntington Library, San Marino, CA.

2. Mary Austin to Daniel T. MacDougal, 9 January 1922, Box 59, AU1145, Huntington Library.

3. Austin to Daniel T. MacDougal, 9 January 1922, Box 59, AU1145, Huntington Library.

4. David Edström to Austin, 10 August 1930, Box 75, AU2285, Huntington Library.

5. Austin to Daniel T. MacDougal, 9 January 1922, Box 59, AU1145, Huntington Library.

6. Mary Austin, *Experiences Facing Death* (Indianapolis: Bobbs-Merrill, 1931), 241.

7. Mary Austin, "The Woman at the Eighteen-Mile," in *Western Trails: A Collection of Short Stories by Mary Austin,* ed. Melody Graulich (Reno: University of Nevada Press, 1987), 61.

8. Austin to Daniel T. MacDougal, 4 May 1923, Box 59, AU1181, Huntington Library.

9. Austin to [Theodore] Schroeder, 8 April [1919], Box 60, AU1218, Huntington Library.

10. Austin to Schroeder, 23 January 1919, Box 60, AU1216, Huntington Library.

11. Augusta Fink, *I-Mary: A Biography of Mary Austin* (Tucson: University of Arizona Press, 1983), 209.

12. Mary Austin, "Love Coming Late," quoted in Fink, *I-Mary,* 206–7. For a different version, see *The Nation,* 11 July 1928; and Esther F. Lanigan, *A Mary Austin Reader* (Tucson: University of Arizona Press, 1996), 226.

13. Mary Austin to Lou Hoover, 9 May 1916, Herbert Hoover Presidential Library, West Branch, IA.

14. Austin to Mabel Dodge, 5 March 1920, Mabel Dodge Luhan Papers, Yale Collection of American Literature, Beinecke Rare Book and Manuscript Library.

15. Mary Austin, "On Receiving a Book of Erotic Verse," Box 29, AU421, Huntington Library.

16. Austin to Daniel T. MacDougal, 15 August 1920, Box 59, AU1191, Huntington Library.

17. Mary Austin, "Woman as Audience," *The Bookman* 55 (March 1922): 82.

18. H. Croly to Austin, 23 July 1925, Box 104, AU4165, Huntington Library.

19. Daniel T. MacDougal to Austin, 10 November 1923, Box 98, AU3768, Huntington Library.

20. Austin to Daniel T. MacDougal, 2 January 1921, Box 59, AU1144, Huntington Library.

21. Daniel T. MacDougal to Austin, 5 April 1920, Box 96, AU3665, Huntington Library.

22. Daniel T. MacDougal to Austin, 8 November 1923, Box 98, AU3767, Huntington Library.

23. Jane Baumann, "Remembering Mary Austin," in *Mary Austin: A Memorial,* ed. Willard Hougland (Santa Fe: Laboratory of Anthropology, 1944), 8–9.

24. Daniel T. MacDougal to Austin, 26 May 1920, Box 96, AU3666, Huntington Library.

25. Daniel T. MacDougal to Austin, 16 March 1918, Box 96, AU3655, Huntington Library.

26. Harold Stearns to Louise MacDougal, 6 March 1922, Box 98 AU3690, Huntington Library.

27. Austin to Daniel T. MacDougal, 31 December 1921, Box 59, AU1143, Huntington Library.

28. Austin to Daniel T. MacDougal, 31 December 1921, Box 59, AU1143, Huntington Library.

29. Austin to Daniel T. MacDougal, 2 January [1922], Box 59, AU1144, Huntington Library.

30. Daniel T. MacDougal to Austin, 2 January 1922, Box 97, AU3680, Huntington Library.

31. Daniel T. MacDougal to Austin, 3 January 1922, Box 97, AU3681, Huntington Library.

32. Austin to Daniel T. MacDougal, 28 October [1922], Box 59, AU1172, Huntington Library.

33. Daniel T. MacDougal to Austin, 4 January 1922, Box 97, AU3682, Huntington Library.

34. Daniel T. MacDougal to Austin, 12 January 1922, Box 97, AU3683, Huntington Library.

35. Austin to Daniel T. MacDougal, 14 January 1922, Box 59, AU1147, Huntington Library.

36. Carl Van Doren, "The American Rhythm: Mary Austin," in *Many Minds* (New York: Alfred A. Knopf, 1924), 10–11.

37. William Dean Howells to James B. Pond, 10 November 1899, in William Dean Howells, *Selected Letters,* edited and annotated by George Arms et al., textual eds., Don L. Cook, Christoph K. Lohmann, and David J. Nordloh (Boston: Twayne, 1979–1983), 4:225.

38. Mary Austin, "Zuni Folk Tales," review of Frank Hamilton Cushing's *Zuni Folk Tales* and *Outlines of the Zuni Creation Myth, The Dial* 71 (July 1921): 112.

39. Austin, "Zuni Folk Tales," 112–13.

40. Daniel T. MacDougal to Mary Austin, 16 March 1919, Desert Laboratory Collection, Special Collections, University of Arizona Library.

41. Mary Austin to Daniel T. MacDougal, 5 July 1920, quoted in Larry Evers, introduction to *The Land of Journeys' Ending,* by Mary Austin (1924; Tucson: University of Arizona Press, 1983), xvi.

42. Austin to Daniel T. MacDougal, 11 October 1922, Box 59, AU1171, Huntington Library.

43. Ina Sizer Cassidy, "I-Mary and Me: The Chronicle of a Friendship," *New Mexican Quarterly Review* 9 (November 1939): 203, 205.

44. Mary Austin, *The American Rhythm* (New York: Harcourt, Brace and Co., 1923), 4–5.

45. Austin, *American Rhythm,* 4.

46. Mary Austin, *The Green Bough: A Tale of Resurrection* (Garden City, NY: Doubleday, 1913), 2–3.

47. Austin, *American Rhythm,* 64–65.

48. Austin to Daniel T. MacDougal, 22 October [1923], Box 59, AU1193, Huntington Library.

49. See Austin to Daniel T. MacDougal, 27 October [1923], Box 59, AU1194, Huntington Library.

50. Mary Austin, *The Land of Journeys' Ending* (New York: The Century Co., 1924), 391–92.

51. Larry Evers, introduction to *Land of Journeys' Ending,* xxi.

52. Austin, *Land of Journeys' Ending,* 223.

53. Austin, *Land of Journeys' Ending,* 264–65.

54. Austin, *Land of Journeys' Ending,* 231.

55. See Charles Lummis to Fanny Bandelier, 4 July 1918, Charles Fletcher Lummis Papers, courtesy of Braun Research Library, Autry National Center, Los Angeles. He refers to her as "Governor Mary."

56. Reproduced in Ray Galbraith Ballard, "Mary Austin's *Earth Horizon:* The Imperfect Circle" (PhD diss., Claremont Graduate School, 1977), 687.

57. Mabel Dodge to Austin, n.d., Box 95, AU3572, Huntington Library. Dodge drew a hand with the index finger pointing to "you."

58. Mabel Dodge Luhan, *Edge of the Desert* (New York: Harcourt, Brace and Co., 1937), 19, 20.

59. Hutchins Hapgood, *A Victorian in the Modern World* (New York: Harcourt, Brace and Co., 1939), 349.

60. Mabel Dodge Luhan quoting Lawrence, "Taos—A Eulogy," *Creative Arts* 9 (1931): 289–95, quoted in Elmo Baca, *Mabel's Santa Fe and Taos* (Salt Lake City: Gibbs Smith, 2000), 10.

61. Arrell Morgan Gibson, *The Santa Fe and Taos Colonies: Age of the Muses, 1900–1942* (Norman: University of Oklahoma Press, 1983), 28.

62. Mary Austin, "Indian Detour," *The Bookman* 68 (February 1929): 653–58, quotation p. 656.

63. Mabel Dodge Luhan, *Edge of the Desert,* 62.

64. Mabel Dodge Luhan, *Taos and Its Artists* (New York: Duell, Sloan & Pearce, 1947), 27.

65. Elisa Sims, *New York Times Book Review,* 25 December 1921, quoted in *Mabel Dodge Luhan: New Woman, New Worlds,* by Lois Rudnick (Albuquerque: University of New Mexico Press, 1984), 179.

66. Joseph Foster, *D. H. Lawrence in Taos* (Albuquerque: University of New Mexico Press, 1972), 10–11.

67. Quoted in Gibson, *Santa Fe and Taos Colonies,* 11.

68. Austin to Eve Lummis, 14 August 1929, Box 58, AU1093, Huntington Library.

69. Daniel T. MacDougal to Austin, 28 February 1923, Box 97, AU3745, Huntington Library.

70. Austin to Daniel T. MacDougal, 27 October [1923], Box 59, AU1194, Huntington Library.

9. SANTA FE

1. Chris Wilson, *The Myth of Santa Fe: Creating a Modern Regional Tradition* (Albuquerque: University of New Mexico Press, 1997), 242–45. See Mary Austin to Mabel Dodge Luhan, 23 June n.y., Mabel Dodge Luhan Papers, Yale Collection of American Literature, Beinecke Rare Book and Manuscript Library.

2. Alice Corbin Henderson to Mary Austin, 20 November 1920, Box 82, AU2733, Huntington Library, San Marino, CA.

3. Austin to the *Chicago Daily News,* 8 June 1922, Box 57, AU1078, Huntington Library.

4. Unpublished page from Austin's *Earth Horizon,* in "Mary Austin's Earth Horizon: The Imperfect Circle," by Rae Galbraith Ballard (PhD diss., Claremont Graduate School, 1979), 689.

5. George Hunter to Austin, 17 August 1922, Box 89, AU3188, Huntington Library.

6. Austin to Hunter, 15 April 1927, Box 58, AU1119–1122, Huntington Library.

7. Austin to Mabel Dodge Luhan, 30 April n.y., Mabel Dodge Luhan Papers, Yale Collection of American Literature, Beinecke Rare Book and Manuscript Library.

8. Austin, "In Hospital," n.d., Box 16, AU234, Huntington Library.

9. Anna de Mille to Austin, 20 September 1928, Box 73, AU2163, Huntington Library.

10. Fanny Bandelier to Charles Lummis, 28 April 1920, MS 1.1207 O, Charles Fletcher Lummis Papers, courtesy of Braun Research Library, Autry National Center, Los Angeles.

11. Hutchins Hapgood, *A Victorian in the Modern World* (New York: Harcourt, Brace and Co., 1939), 349.

12. See Esther Lanigan Stineman, *Mary Austin: Song of a Maverick* (New Haven, CT: Yale University Press, 1989), 165.

13. Austin to Mabel Dodge Luhan, n.d., Mabel Dodge Luhan Papers, Yale Collection of American Literature, Beinecke Rare Book and Manuscript Library.

14. For a discussion of the various circles in Santa Fe, see Molly H. Mullin's informative book, *Culture in the Marketplace: Gender, Art, and Value in the American Southwest* (Durham, NC: Duke University Press, 2001).

15. Alice Corbin Henderson, comp., *The Turquoise Trail: An Anthology of New Mexico Poetry* (Boston: Houghton Mifflin, 1928), vii.

16. Mary Austin to Carey McWilliams, 2 January 1931, Center for Southwest Research, University of New Mexico.

17. Witter Bynner to Austin, 5 December 1929, Box 67, AU1755, Huntington Library.

18. Richard Wilbur, ed., *Works of Witter Bynner: Selected Poems* (New York: Farrar, Straus, Giroux, 1978), lix, quoted in Daria Labinsky and Stan Hieronymus, *Frank Applegate of Santa Fe: Artist and Preservationist* (Albuquerque, NM: LPD Press, 2001), 101.

19. Witter Bynner to Waldo Frank, 3 November 1930, Lilly Library, Indiana University.

20. See Witter Bynner to Mary Austin, 26 May 1930, in *Literary America, 1903–1934: The Mary Austin Letters,* ed. T. M. Pearce (Westport, CT: Greenwood Press, 1979), 231–32.

21. Anne Knish and Emanuel Morgan [Arthur Davison Ficke and Witter Bynner], "The Spectra School of Poetry," *Forum* 55, no. 1 (June 1916): 675–78.

22. Mary Austin, "Rural Education in New Mexico," *The University of New Mexico Bulletin* 2 (1 December 1931): 30.

23. Edna Ferber to Austin, 17 November 1931, Box 76, AU2372, Huntington Library.

24. See Marie Drennan to Austin, 5 February 1933, Box 75, AU2263, Huntington Library.

25. Amy Lowell to Austin, 28 April 1922, Box 94, AU3560, Huntington Library.

26. Austin to Daniel T. MacDougal, 28 January [1922], Box 59, AU1148, Huntington Library.

27. Willa Cather to Austin, 9 May 1928, Box 70, AU1940, Huntington Library.

28. Mary Austin, "Willa Sibert Cather," *El Palacio* 8 (March-April 1920): 89.

29. Quoted in *Literary America, 1903–1934,* 205.

30. Austin to Ferris Greenslet, 6 December 1930, Box 58, AU115, Huntington Library.

31. Mary Austin, *Earth Horizon,* ed. Melody Graulich (Albuquerque: University of New Mexico Press, 1991), 359.

32. Austin, method of locating writing talent, Box 20, AU306, Huntington Library.

33. Mary Austin, *Everyman's Genius* (Indianapolis: Bobbs-Merrill, 1925), 46.

34. Austin, *Everyman's Genius,* 347.

35. Mary Austin, "Papago Wedding," in *Western Trails: A Collection of Short Stories by Mary Austin,* ed. Melody Graulich (Reno: University of Nevada Press, 1987), 200–1.

36. O'Henry Memorial Society of Arts and Sciences, Box 104, AU4226, Huntington Library.

37. D. H. Lawrence, "Altitude: The First Scene of an Unfinished Play," *Laughing Horse* 20 (1938): 11–35.

38. Mary Austin, *Can Prayer Be Answered?* (New York: Farrar & Rinehart, 1934), 12.

39. Louis Adamic, *My America, 1928–1938* (New York: Harper & Brothers, 1938), 479.

40. Austin, *Earth Horizon,* 363, 308.

41. John Gunther, *Inside USA* (New York: Harper & Brothers, 1947), 214–15, 150.

42. "The Colorado River Controversy," *The Nation,* 9 November 1927, 510–12.

43. "The Colorado River Controversy," 510–12.

44. Gary D. Weatherfold and F. Lee Brown, eds., *New Courses for the Colorado River: Major Issues for the Next Century,* foreword by Governor Bruce Babbitt (Albuquerque: University of New Mexico Press, 1986), xi, 18, 39–40.

45. Adamic, *My America, 1928–1938,* 56–57.

46. Ferris Greenslet to Austin 19 May 1926, Box 85, AU2954, Huntington Library.

47. Sinclair Lewis to Austin, 15 December [1920], Box 93, AU3475, Huntington Library, quoted in *Literary America, 1903–1934,* 134–35.

48. Austin to Sinclair Lewis, 28 February 1931, Box 58, AU1131, Huntington Library.

49. Effie Graham Curtis to Austin, 18 December 1932, Box 72, AU2076, Huntington Library.

10. INDIAN DETOURS AND SPANISH ARTS

1. See *Spanish New Mexico,* vol. 2, *Hispanic Arts in the Twentieth Century,* ed. Donna Pierce and Marta Weigle (Santa Fe: Museum of New Mexico Press, 1996), 10–13.

2. Austin, "Indian Detour," *The Bookman* 68 (February 1929): 653–58.

3. Mary Austin, "The Wonders of the Pueblo," speech before the National Popular Government League on the Burson [sic] Bill, Washington, D.C., 17 January 1923, Box 41, AU51, Huntington Library, San Marino, CA.

4. John C. Van Dyke, *The Desert: Further Studies in Natural Appearances* (New York: Charles Scribner's Sons, 1911), 59.

5. The most intensive expedition to date, it lasted from 1917 to 1923.

6. Eudora Welty, *One Writer's Beginnings* (Cambridge, MA: Harvard University Press, 1984), 68–69.

7. Charles Lummis journals, 1928 April 16–22, MS 1.2.838, Charles Fletcher Lummis Papers, courtesy of Braun Research Library, Autry National Center, Los Angeles.

8. Because this chapter looks backward and forward, we simplify by using "Mabel Dodge Luhan" and "Mabel."

9. Mabel Dodge Luhan, *Movers and Shakers* (Albuquerque: University of New Mexico Press, 1985), 323.

10. See Mary Austin to Mabel Dodge Luhan, 4 April n.y., Mabel Dodge Luhan Papers, Yale Collection of American Literature, Beinecke Rare Book and Manuscript Library.

11. Austin, "The Wonders of the Pueblo," Box 3, AU51, Huntington Library.

12. Lou Hoover to Austin, 17 December 1922, Box 84, AU2906, Huntington Library.

13. Lou Hoover to Austin, 14 June 1923, Box 84 AU2908, Huntington Library.

14. Quoted in Daria Labinsky and Stan Hieronymus, *Frank Applegate of Santa Fe: Artist and Preservationist* (Albuquerque: LPD Press, 2001), 267.

15. Mabel Dodge [Luhan] to Mary Austin, [December 1922], in *Literary America, 1903–1934: The Mary Austin Letters,* ed. T. M. Pearce (Westport, CT: Greenwood Press, 1979), 172.

16. Mary Austin "The Indivisible Unity," *Survey Graphic* (15 December 1925): 327.

17. Oliver La Farge, with the assistance of Arthur N. Morgan and foreword by Paul Horgan, *Santa Fe: The Autobiography of a Southwestern Town* (Norman: University of Oklahoma Press, 1959), 281–82.

18. Mary Austin, "Why Americanize the Indian?" *The Forum,* September 1929, p. 171.

19. Luhan, *Movers and Shakers,* 533–34.

20. W. E. B. Du Bois, review of Carl Van Vechten's *Nigger Heaven,* in *Nigger Heaven* (New York: Harper Colophon, 1971), vii–x. See Elizabeth Jane Harrison, "Zora Neale Hurston and Mary Hunter Austin's Ethnographic Fiction: New Modernist Narratives," in *Unmanning Modernism: Gendered Re-Readings,* ed. Harrison Peterson and Shirley Peterson (Knoxville: University of Tennessee Press, 1997), 44–58.

21. Mary Austin, "Zuni Folk Tales," *The Dial* 71 (July 1921): 113–14.

22. Du Bois, review of Carl Van Vechten's *Nigger Heaven,* vii.

23. Austin to Mr. Rhoads, Bureau of Indian Affairs, 4 April 1926, Box 60, AU1268, Huntington Library. See Alfred Vincent Kidder to Austin, [1929], Box 58, AU1124, Huntington Library.

24. Austin, "Indian Arts and Crafts," Box 16, AU238, Huntington Library.

25. Mabel Dodge [Luhan] to Austin, [December 1922], in *Literary America, 1903–1934,* 172.

26. Leslie Marmon Silko, *Conversations with Leslie Marmon Silko,* ed. Ellen L. Arnold (Jackson: University Press of Mississippi, 2000), 8–9.

27. Luther Standing Bear, preface to *My People, the Sioux* (Boston: Houghton Mifflin Company, 1927).

28. Theodore Roosevelt, *The Winning of the West* (New York, 1889–1896), 1:334–35, quoted in *Race: The History of an Idea in America,* by Thomas F. Gossett (Dallas: Southern Methodist University Press, 1963), 238. Austin claimed familiarity with the Yokuts, Paiutes, Washos, Utes, Shoshones, Gabrielenos, Mojaves, Pimas, Papagos, Mescalero Apaches, Tewas, Taos, and "an occasional Plainsman. Better than I knew any Indian, I knew the land they lived on." See Mary Austin, *The American Rhythm: Studies and Reexpressions of Amerindian Songs,* new and enlarged edition (Boston: Houghton Mifflin, 1930), 38.

29. Austin, response to Dr. Franz Boas' criticisms of her review of Dr. Ruth Leah Bunzel's *The Pueblo Potter,* Box 2, AU16, Huntington Library.

30. James Clifford, *The Predicament of Culture: Twentieth-Century Ethnography, Literature and Art* (Cambridge, MA: Harvard University Press, 1988), 10.

31. Quoted in Molly H. Mullin, *Culture in the Marketplace: Gender, Art, and Value in the American Southwest* (Durham, NC: Duke University Press, 2001), 91.

32. Sinclair Lewis, *Main Street* (New York: Signet, 1980), 232.

33. Unidentified newspaper clipping, 31 October 1933, Bancroft Library, University of California, Berkeley.

34. Carl Van Vechten, *Spider Boy* (New York: Alfred A. Knopf, 1928), 168.

35. Sotero Ortiz to Austin, 29 December 1929, Box 105, AU4247, Huntington Library.

36. Chief Standing Bear to Austin, 8 September 1930, AU4740, Huntington Library.

37. For discussions on this topic, see Karen S. Langlois, "Marketing the American Indian: Mary Austin and the Business of Writing," in *Living of Words: American Women in Print Culture,* ed. Susan Albertine (Knoxville: University of Tennessee Press, 1995), 151–61; Noreen Groover, " 'There Was a Part for Her in the Indian Life': Mary Austin, Regionalism, and the Problems of Appropriation," in *Breaking Boundaries: New Perspectives on Women's Regional Writing,* ed. Sherrie A. Inness and Diana Royer (Iowa City: University of Iowa Press, 1997), 124–39; Heike Schaefer, *Mary Austin's Regionalism* (Charlottesville: University of Virginia Press, 2004); and Peter Wild, "Sentimentalism in the American Southwest: John C. Van Dyke, Mary Austin, and Edward Abbey," in *Reading the West: New Essays on the Literature of the American West,* ed. Michael Kowalewski (New York: Cambridge University Press, 1996), 127–43.

38. Mary Austin, *Everyman's Genius* (Indianapolis: Bobbs-Merrill, 1925), 37.

39. See, for example, Alain Locke, "The Concept of Race as Applied to Social Culture," *Howard Review* 1 (1924): 290–99, quoted in *The Philosophy of Alain Locke,* ed. Leonard Harris (Philadelphia: Temple University Press, 1989), 195; and Austin, lecture on *Green Pastures,* Box 15, AU216, Huntington Library.

40. Austin, "Educating Our Ancestors," Box 11, AU128, Huntington Library.

41. Mary Austin, *Indian Poetry* (New York: Exposition of Indian Tribal Arts, 1931), 3. See Austin's romanticized description of the Pueblos before the Spanish arrived in *The Land of Journeys' Ending* (New York: The Century Co., 1924), 244: they "had no rich, no poor, no paupers, no prisons, no red-light district, no criminal classes, no institutionalized orphans, no mothers of dependent children penalized by their widowhood, no one pining for a mate, who wished to be married."

42. Editor of *The Atlantic Monthly* to Austin, 27 December 1920, Box 56, AU1060, Huntington Library. Ellery Sedgwick edited the magazine in 1920.

43. Carl Jung, and after his death M.-L. von Franz, *Man and His Symbols* (New York: Doubleday & Co., 1964), 89.

44. Mabel Dodge [Luhan] to Austin, 28 November [1922], Box 95, AU3581, Huntington Library.

45. D. H. Lawrence, *Studies in Classic American Literature* (New York: Thomas Seltzer, 1923), 4.

46. D. H. Lawrence, "The Red Wolf," in *The Turquoise Trail: An Anthology of New Mexico Poetry,* comp. Alice Corbin Henderson (Boston: Houghton Mifflin, 1928), 79.

47. Dorothy Shipman to Austin, 8 January 1933, Box 110, AU4596, Huntington Library.

48. See Austin to Mabel Dodge [Luhan], 14 May [1921], Mabel Dodge Luhan Papers, Yale Collection of American Literature, Beinecke Rare Book and Manuscript Library.

49. Stuart Chase, *Mexico: A Study of the Two Americas* (New York: Macmillan, 1931).

50. John Gunther, *Inside USA* (New York: Harper & Brothers, 1947), 895.

51. Albert Campa to Austin, 6 November 1929,Box 68, AU1781, Huntington Library.

52. Mary Austin to Bronson M. Cutting, 30 October 1930, Library of Congress.

53. Campa to Austin, 1 April 1931, Box 68, AU1792, Huntington Library.

54. Campa to Austin, 27 April 1931, Box 68, AU1793, Huntington Library.

55. See Mary Austin, "Frank Applegate," *The New Mexico Quarterly* 2 (August 1932): 213–18. Austin recalls the problematic naming of the organization. Also see Mary Austin to Mrs. Fields, 15 November 1933, Center for Southwest Research, University of New Mexico. The name itself is misleading since many of the pieces in the collection were postcolonial or made after 1821. As Campa, who shared her labors, pointed out, Spanish influences had undergone changes along the way, in Mexico first and in the United States. See Albert Campa, "Spanish Religious Folktheatre in the Southwest," *The University of New Mexico Bulletin* 5 (June 1932): 6–7.

56. Donna Pierce and Marta Weigle, eds., *Spanish New Mexico* (Santa Fe: Museum of New Mexico Press, 1996), 2:12–17; Mary Austin, "Spanish-American Theater," *Theatre Arts* 12 (1929): 564–65, quoted in Arrell Morgan Gibson, *The Santa Fe and Taos Colonies: Age of the Muses, 1900–1942* (Norman: University of Oklahoma Press, 1983), 211–12.

57. Philip Stevenson to Austin, 16 February 1931, Box 113, AU4786, Huntington Library. For our portrait of Applegate, we are indebted to Daria Labinsky and Stan Hieronymus and their *Frank Applegate of Santa Fe.*

58. See Mollie H. Mullin's anthropological study, *Culture in the Marketplace: Gender, Art, and Value in the American Southwest* (Durham, NC: Duke University Press, 2001), to whom we are indebted for part of this section.

59. Mary Austin, "Blue Roses," in *Western Trails: A Collection of Short Stories by Mary Austin,* ed. Melody Graulich (Reno: University of Nevada Press, 1987), 293.

60. Austin to Daniel T. MacDougal, 2 January 1922, Box 59, AU1144, Huntington Library.

II. LAST YEARS

1. Albert Bender to Mary Austin, 23 March 1929, Box 62, AU1432, Huntington Library, San Marino, CA.

2. Morley Baer, *Room and Time Enough: The Land of Mary Austin,* photographs by Morley Baer, introduction by Augusta Fink, lines by Mary Austin (Flagstaff, AZ: Northland Press, 1979), 12–13. See Mary Street Alinder, *Ansel Adams: A Biography* (New York: Henry Holt, 1996), 68–71.

3. See Augusta Fink, *I-Mary: A Biography of Mary Austin* (Tucson: University of Arizona Press, 1983), 243.

4. The term *santos* can include *bultos,* hand-carved wooden statues of saints; *crucifijos,* images of Christ on the cross; and *retablos,* religious paintings on wood and on hide.

5. See Austin to Ansel Adams, 24 August 1929, Box 57, AU1125, Huntington Library.

6. Austin to Adams, 23 February 1929, Box 57, AU1121, Huntington Library.

7. Austin to Adams, 30 August 1929, Box 57, AU1126, Huntington Library.

8. Austin to Adams, 3 September 1929, Box 57, AU1127, Huntington Library.

9. Austin to Adams, 18 September 1929, Box 57, AU1130, Huntington Library.

10. Austin to Adams, 9 April 1930, Box 57, AU1134, Huntington Library.

11. Austin to Adams, 2 January 1931, Box 57, AU1144, Huntington Library.

12. Alinder, *Ansel Adams: A Biography,* 71.

13. Austin to Adams, 5 July 1928, Box 57, AU1116, Huntington Library.

14. *Taos Pueblo,* photographed by Ansel Easton Adams and described by Mary Austin (San Francisco: Grabhorn Press, 1930), 1.

15. *Taos Pueblo,* 6.

16. *Taos Pueblo,* 14.

17. Mary Austin, "Frank Applegate," *The New Mexico Quarterly* 2 (August 1932): 216–17.

18. Austin to Adams, 14 February 1931, Box 57, AU1147, Huntington Library.

19. Jane [Baumann] to Witter Bynner, 9 January 1932, Center for Southwest Research, University of New Mexico.

20. Mary Austin to Betty Applegate, 22 February 1931, Center for Southwest Research, University of New Mexico.

21. Austin, manuscript for *Earth Horizon,* Box 51, AU777, Huntington Library.

22. Quoted from interviews with Gretchen Beale by Daria Labinsky and Stan Hieronymus in *Frank Applegate of Santa Fe: Artist and Preservationist* (Albuquerque, NM: LPD Press, 2001), 100.

23. Philip Stevenson to Austin, 16 February 1931, Box 113, AU4786, Huntington Library, quoted in Labinsky and Hieronymus, *Frank Applegate of Santa Fe,* 269.

24. Mary Austin, *The Land of Journeys' Ending* (New York: The Century Co., 1924), 247.

25. Austin to Arthur Davison Ficke, 6 November 1929, Center for Southwest Research, University of New Mexico, quoted in Labinsky and Hieronymus, *Frank Applegate of Santa Fe,* 245.

26. See Labinsky and Hieronymus, *Frank Applegate of Santa Fe,* 255–61.

27. See Labinsky and Hieronymus, *Frank Applegate of Santa Fe,* 183–87. See Henry Holt to Austin, 5 May 1919, Box 83, AU2844, Huntington Library. Austin explained to Holt that she had conducted experiments on the advice of William James seeking access to the minds of the dead.

28. Quoted in Labinsky and Hieronymus, *Frank Applegate of Santa Fe,* 169.

29. Mary Antin to Austin, 11 March 1925, Box 56, AU986, Huntington Library.

30. Austin to Bynner, 8 August [1934], Center for Southwest Research, University of New Mexico. Jane Baumann asked Bynner to try and rouse Austin after Applegate's death.

31. Austin, *Land of Journeys' Ending,* 247.

32. Mary Austin, *Experiences Facing Death* (Indianapolis: Bobbs-Merrill, 1931), 19, 173.

33. Austin to Mr. Shively, Bobbs-Merrill, 16 February 1931, Box 57, AU1071, Huntington Library.

34. Austin, *Experiences Facing Death,* 24.

35. Ellen Glasgow, *The Woman Within* (New York: Harcourt, Brace and Co., 1954) 165–67.

36. Zora Neale Hurston, *Their Eyes Were Watching God* (New York: Perennial Classics, 1998), 11.

37. Austin to Bynner 26 September 1932, Center for Southwest Research, University of New Mexico.

38. Austin, *Experiences Facing Death,* 259.

39. Mary Austin, "Do We Need a New Religion?" *Century Magazine* 106 (September 1923): 756.

40. Austin, *Experiences Facing Death,* 292.

41. Mary Austin, "What Religion Means to Me," *Religion Today* (1933), Box 39, AU628, Huntington Library.

42. Austin to Mr. Schroeder, n.d., Box 60, AU1239, Huntington Library.

43. Antin to Austin, 11 March 1925, Box 56, AU986, Huntington Library.

44. Elizabeth Conner Lindsay to Mary Austin, 17 February 1932, in *Literary America, 1903–1934: The Mary Austin Letters,* ed. T. M. Pearce (Westport, CT: Greenwood Press, 1979), 211.

45. Frank Gelett Burgess to Austin, 15 September 1922, Box 67, AU1725, Huntington Library.

46. Ezra Pound to Austin, 13 April 1930, in *Literary America, 1903–1934,* 235.

47. Henriette Harris to Hal [Bynner], 2 November 1932, Center for Southwest Research, University of New Mexico.

48. Mary Austin, *Starry Adventure* (Boston: Houghton Mifflin, 1931), 4.

49. Austin, *Starry Adventure,* 95.

50. Adams to Austin, 10 August 1931, Box 54, AU894, Huntington Library.

51. Austin to Carey McWilliams, 12 July [1932], Center for Southwest Research, University of New Mexico.

52. Austin to Ficke, 4 May 1929, Center for Southwest Research, University of New Mexico.

53. Austin to Ficke, 8 August 1929, Center for Southwest Research, University of New Mexico.

54. Austin to Mabel Dodge Luhan, 10 August [1929], Mabel Dodge Luhan Papers, Yale Collection of American Literature, Beinecke Rare Book and Manuscript Library.

55. See Austin to Carey McWilliams, 15 November 1929, Center for Southwest Research, University of New Mexico.

56. See, for example, Abraham Hofffman, *Vision of Villainy: Origins of the Owens Valley–Los Angeles Water Controversy* (College Station: Texas A&M University Press, 1981).

57. Mary Austin, *Earth Horizon,* ed. Melody Graulich (Albuquerque: University of New Mexico Press, 1991), 85–86.

58. Harrison Leussler to Austin, 6 December 1932, Box 93, AU3468, Huntington Library.

59. H. G. Wells to Houghton Mifflin Company, 14 November 1932, Box 118, AU5181, Huntington Library. And see Austin, *Earth Horizon,* 343.

60. Austin to Wells, 4 November 1932, Box 60, AU1282, Huntington Library.

61. See Austin to Virginia Adams, 29 April 1932, Box 57, AU1161, Huntington Library.

62. Anne Henrietta Martin to Austin, 4 December 1932, Box 100, AU3912, Huntington Library.

63. Austin, *Earth Horizon,* 314.

64. Martin to Austin, 4 December 1932, Box 100, AU3912, Huntington Library.

65. Anne Martin, "A Tribute to Mary Austin," *The Nation,* 10 October 1934, 409.

66. Austin to Carey McWilliams, 12 February 1929, Center for Southwest Research, University of New Mexico.

67. See Austin to Carey McWilliams, 16 December 1929, Center for Southwest Research, University of New Mexico.

68. Austin, *Earth Horizon,* 368.

69. Mary Bucknam to Austin, 6 March 1933, Box 66, AU1712, Huntington Library.

70. Robinson Jeffers, "George Sterling's Death," in *Cawdor and Other Poems*

(New York: Horace Liveright, 1928), 152. Also published in the *Overland Monthly* (March 1927) as "Winter Sundown."

71. Austin to Robinson Jeffers, 29 October 1929, Huntington Library.

72. Robinson Jeffers, "Hungerfield," in *Hungerfield and Other Poems* (New York: Random House, 1951), 23.

73. Fannie Hurst to Harriet V. Noble, 28 June 1932, Box 89, AU3213, Huntington Library.

74. Edwin Ibbetson to Austin, 14 February 1934, and "Woman Slayer Ruled Insane," *Los Angeles Times,* Box 89, AU3216, Huntington Library.

75. Austin, "Bequest of Brain," Austin Papers, Box 122, Huntington Library.

76. Austin, "Bequest of Brain," Austin Papers, Box 122, Huntington Library.

77. James Papez to Austin, 4 January 1928, Box 105, AU4270, Huntington Library.

78. Carl Van Doren, "Mary Hunter Austin: 1868–1934," *New York Herald Tribune,* Books section, 26 August 1934; also *Scholastic* 25 (29 September 1934): 2, 23.

79. See T. M. Pearce, *The Beloved House* (Caldwell, ID: Caxton Printers, 1940), 190–91.

80. H. G. Baca, New Mexico Office of the U.S. Property and Disbursing Officer, 27 October 1932, Box 103, AU4139, Huntington Library.

81. Andrew Dasburg to Austin, 10 May 1933, Box 73, AU2120, Huntington Library. See *Literary America, 1903–1934,* 260–63.

82. Adams to Austin, 29 June 1931, Box 54, AU829, Huntington Library.

83. Mary Austin, *One-Smoke Stories* (Boston: Houghton Mifflin, 1934), xv.

84. Ficke to Austin, 21 December 1933, Box 77, AU2390, Huntington Library.

85. Austin to Adams, 10 March 1934, Box 57, AU1158, Huntington Library.

86. Francis Wilson to Mary Hunter, 23 July 1934, Box 119, AU5284, Huntington Library.

87. Ferris Greenslet to Mary Hunter, 6 August 1934, Box 120, AU5338, Huntington Library.

88. Austin, "When I Am Dead," quoted in Pearce, *Beloved House,* 211–12.

89. Mary Austin, *No. 26 Jayne Street* (New York: Houghton Mifflin, 1920), 13.

90. Oliver D. Hogue to Mary Hunter, 15 August 1934, Box 83, AU2804, Huntington Library.

91. Hogue to Austin, 12 March [1932], Box 83, AU2803, Huntington Library.

92. Pearce, *Beloved House,* 219.

12. THE ACCOUNTING

1. "William Dean Howells," *North American Review* 212 (July 1920): 9.

2. All else was to be equally divided between the Indian and Spanish Arts funds. See Mary Austin to Francis C. Wilson, 13 May 1933, Box 119, AU5282, Huntington Library, San Marino, CA.

3. Henry S. Canby, "A Letter," in *Mary Austin: A Memorial* (Santa Fe: Laboratory of Anthropology, 1944), 11–12.

4. Ina Sizer Cassidy, "In Defense of Solitude," in *Mary Austin: A Memorial,* 48.

5. Elizabeth Willis DeHuff, "For the Sake of Ten," in *Mary Austin: A Memorial,* 32.

6. Mabel Dodge Luhan, "Mary Austin: A Woman," in *Mary Austin: A Memorial,* 19, 22.

7. Carl Van Doren, "Mary Austin," in *Mary Austin: A Memorial,* 14.

8. Edward Abbey, introduction to *The Land of Little Rain* (New York: Penguin, 1988), xi–xii.

9. Carey McWilliams, "Mary Austin," *Los Angeles Times,* 14 September 1934, p. A4.

10. Ansel Adams, "Notes on Mary Austin," in *Mary Hunter Austin: A Centennial Booklet Published by the Mary Austin Home* (Independence, CA: Mary Austin Home, 1968), 7.

11. Ansel Adams, "A Note on the Land and on the Photographs," in *The Land of Little Rain*, by Mary Austin, photographs by Ansel Adams, introduction by Carl Van Doren (Boston: Houghton Mifflin, 1950), 109, 111.

12. Morley Baer, *Room and Time Enough: The Land of Mary Austin,* photographs by Morley Baer, introduction by Augusta Fink, lines by Mary Austin (Flagstaff, AZ: Northland Press, 1979), vii–viii.

13. Austin planned to write a book to be called "The Shape of Society," with chapters titled "The School, The Herd and the Flock," as well as "The Pack" and "The Gang."

14. See, for example, John Opie, "Frontier Perspective in Environmental History: New Perspectives, New Dimensions," in *The American West, New Perspectives, New Dimensions,* ed. Jerome O. Steffen (Norman: University of Oklahoma Press, 1979), 9–34.

15. Mary Austin to Huebsch, 12 December [1920], Newberry Library, Chicago.

16. Wallace Stegner, *The American West as Living Space* (Ann Arbor: University of Michigan Press, 1987), 22. Also see Nicolas Witschi, " 'The Culture of the Northwest': A Rediscovered Essay by Mary Austin," *North Dakota Quarterly* 65 (1998): 80–90.

17. William Carlos Williams, "Kenneth Burke," in *Imaginations,* ed. Webster Schott (New York: New Directions, 1970), 356.

18. Austin, "Credo," Box 18, AU268, Huntington Library.

INDEX

Abbey, Edward Wallace, 58, 190, 268, 271
Acoma pueblo, 223
Adamic, Louis, 213, 215, 252, 253
Adams, Ansel, ix, 90, 178, 197, 199, 245,
254, 256, 260, 261, 270; collaboration
with Austin, 239–43; edition of *The
Land of Little Rain,* ix, 269–70; *Taos
Pueblo,* 240, 241–43, 269
Adams, Henry, 254, 271
Adams, Virginia, 239–40, 256
Addams, Jane, 43, 256
Alden, Henry Mills, 93–94
All-Pueblo Council, 223
Alma-Tadema, Lawrence, 77
American Indian Defense Fund, 66, 220
Ames, Winthrop, 138–39, 140
Anderson, Sherwood, 14, 123, 134; *Poor
White,* 271
Angell, Norman, 10
Anthony, Susan B., 38
Antin, Mary, 246–47, 249; *The Promised
Land,* 246
Applegate, Alta, 235, 244–45, 247, 256, 263
Applegate, Betty, 243–45
Applegate, Frank, 178, 197, 199, 235–38,

240, 251, 256, 265, 266; death of,
243–46, 250, 258; *Indian Stories from
the Pueblos,* 236; *Native Tales of New
Mexico,* 236
Atherton, Gertrude, 72, 75, 92, 113, 133,
156, 284n54; *Before the Gringo Came
(The Splendid Idle Forties),* 72
Atlantic Monthly, 19, 45, 56–57, 93–94
Austin, Mary Hunter: on African Americans, 121, 225–26, 230; and the American West, ix-x, 2, 3–4, 24, 26, 37, 50,
58–59, 61, 86, 104, 192, 208–10,
269–72; and anthropology, 66–68,
237–38; and Bakersfield, CA, 19, 21,
88; birth of daughter Ruth, 30;
Bishop, CA, 26, 33–36, 49, 60; breast
cancer, 92, 93, 95, 97–99, 101, 102;
Carmel, 60–70, 72–84, 103; Casa
Querida, 198–99, 201, 209, 262, 263;
and Catholic church, 87; and Chinese
immigrants, 51; death, 259–60,
261–63; descriptions of: x-xi, 3, 5,
36–37, 39, 50, 71, 77–78, 92, 146–48,
154, 244, 250–51; development as a
writer: 3, 6–7, 10–13, 19–22, 32, 33,

Seton, Ernest Thompson, 228, 246
Seven States Conference, 213–16
Sharp, Joseph Henry, 195
Shaw, George Bernard, 106–7, 109, 100, 113–14
Shoshone (tribe), 27, 32, 65, 156, 304n38
Shuster, Will, 199
Silko, Leslie, 190, 227
Sinclair, May, 110, 113, 160
Sinclair, Upton, 82; *A Journal of Impressions in Belgium,* 160
Sloan, John, 149, 194, 195, 229
Smith, Sylvester C., 54
Smith, E. Boyd, 62
Smith, Joseph, 22
Snyder, Mary Patchen. *See* Patchen, Mary
Society for the Revival of Spanish Colonial Arts (Spanish Colonial Arts Society), 210, 227, 235, 236–37, 245, 265, 306n55
Spanish-American War, 60
Spencer, Herbert, 14, 182
St. Nicholas, 56
Standing Bear, 227, 230; *My People, the Sioux,* 227
Stearns, Harold, 179
Stedman, Edmund, 135
Steffens, Josephine Bontecou, 124–25, 128, 131
Steffens, Lincoln, 75, 83, 12, 133, 134, 145, 148, 149, 164, 168, 175, 177; relationship with Austin, 123–31, 159, 174, 178, 252; *The Shame of the Cities,* 123–24; *The Struggle for Self-Government,* 124
Stegner, Wallace, 50, 271; *The American West as Living Space,* 214; *Angle of Repose,* 62; *The Big Rock Candy Mountain,* 272; *The Sound of Mountain Water,* 50
Stein, Gertrude, 156
Sterling, Caroline ("Carrie"), 74–75, 85
Sterling, George, 73–77, 78, 95, 100, 104, 112, 123, 131, 148, 178, 205, 253; as Bohemian, 69–71, 74–75; death of, 81; and Robinson Jeffers, 257; and Jack London, 75–76, 80–81; and Panama-Pacific Exposition, 113; and *Outland,* 85, 103; "The Rack," 79; *The Testi-*

mony of the Suns, 76; *The Triumphs of Bohemia,* 80; "Wine of Wizardry," 80
Sterne, Maurice, 193, 225
Stetson, Charles Walter, 34, 98
Stevenson, Philip, 245
Stevenson, Robert Louis, 71, 72, 87; *Treasure Island,* 87
Stoddard, Charles Warren, 21, 22, 63, 70, 75
Stowe, Harriet Beecher, 183
Stowe, Lyman Beecher, 183
Summer, John S., 250
Sykes, Godfrey, 173

Taos pueblo, 222–23, 225, 242–43, 304n28
Tarbell, Ida, 122, 124, 153, 264–65
Taylor, Bayard, 22
Terry, Ellen, 25, 100
Texan Santa Fe Expedition of 1841
Thoreau, Henry David, 83, 90, 133, 268
Tilden, Samuel, 152
Tinnemaha, 40
Titian, 96; *Sacred and Profane Love,* 96–97, 117
Tiwa (tribe), 193, 304n28
Tolstoy, Leo, 62, 110
Toomer, Jean, 141–42, 226
Turner, Frederick Jackson, x
Twain, Mark, 4, 19, 21, 22, 25, 36, 43; 70, 125, 184, 205, 264, 269; *Adventures of Huckleberry Finn,* 61; "The Bad Man from Bodie," 25; *The Gilded Age,* 4; *Roughing It,* 43
Tyrrell, George, 99

Ute (tribe), 304n28

Van Doren, Carl, 62, 148, 164, 173, 183, 267, 269; *Contemporary American Novelists,* 148; *Many Minds,* 183
Van Dyke, John, 50, 57–59, 186, 190, 220; *The Desert,* 57–58, 268; *The "New" New York,* 126
Van Vechten, Carl, 225–26; *Nigger Heaven,* 225; *Spider Boy,* 229–30
Veronica, Mother (nun), 99, 248
Vierra, Carlos, 195

Text: Adobe Garamond
Display: Perpetua and Adobe Garamond
Compositor: Binghamton Valley Composition, LLC
Printer and binder: Sheridan